W9-BTQ-969

{The Concise Guide to}

XFREE86 FOR LINUX

Aron Hsiao

A Division of Macmillan USA
201 West 103rd Street, Indianapolis, Indiana 46290

Aron Hsiao

The Concise Guide to XFree86 for Linux

Aron Hsiao

International Standard Book Number: 0-7897-2182-1

Library of Congress Catalog Card Number: 99-65622

Printed in the United States of America

First Printing: *November, 1999*

01 00   4 3 2

Trademarks

Warning and Disclaimer

Associate Publisher
Dean Miller

Executive Editor
Jeff Koch

Development Editor
Maureen A. McDaniel

Managing Editor
Lisa Wilson

Project Editor
Tonya Simpson

Copy Editor
Kate Givens

Indexer
Kevin Fulcher

Proofreader
Louise Martin,
BooksCraft, Inc.

Technical Editor
David Dawes

Team Coordinator
Cindy Teeters

Interior Designer
Trina Wurst

Cover Designer
Radar Design

Copy Writer
Eric Borgert

Production
Dan Harris
Ayanna Lacey
Heather Miller
Mark Walchle

About the Author

Aron Hsiao is a computing entrepreneur and freelance network consultant with a background in UNIX-like operating systems stretching back to the mid-1980s. Aron has spent time as both an independent contractor and as a proprietor working in computer hardware and software retail, real-time software development, network deployment, Internet development, and Internet marketing. He has also worked as a volunteer in several different computing-related and educational capacities in his local area. Aron has collaborated in the past with Sams Publishing and Que Corporation on several Linux- and UNIX-oriented texts as a technical editor. He has served as the About.com guide to Linux since 1997.

Dedication

To Jennie, who keeps me awake and alert enough to proceed with the work of life, and Quincy, who always manages to spill every single drink in sight on the nearest computer, usually while I'm typing on it.

Acknowledgements

Thanks go first and foremost to my parents, who once upon a time provided me with my first personal exposure to computing by purchasing one of the (at that time) newly released Apple Macintosh computers with 128k RAM, on which I did all my homework and on which I also wrote my first few computer programs in BASIC. Thanks also to the University of Utah computer science and engineering departments, which showed me the light by giving me my first access to UNIX on a variety of hardware platforms, all of them faster and shinier than anything I'd seen before. Fast forwarding to the present, thanks also go to my fiancée, who has put up with my after-hours work for several months and has continually brought me snack foods as this book was being written. Finally, thanks go to Jeff Koch, who brought me into the publishing fold and suggested that I write a book in the first place.

Contents

INTRODUCTION

The face of Linux has changed a great deal since I first encountered it, and nowhere more than on the Linux desktop, where twm and fvwm have gradually been replaced by KDE and GNOME as the state-of-the-art in Linux point-and-click. Such changes are necessary and welcome as Linux begins to come of age in the wider market; the KDE and GNOME contributors and project leaders are among the best friends Linux could ever have.

Still, it sometimes seems that, in many cases, a deeper understanding of the mechanisms that lie behind the Linux desktop has been lost for many new Linux users, and that, along with such a loss, the ability to utilize Linux to its fullest goes as well. Many users are unaware of the power and network-readiness of X, now hidden behind an easy-to-use graphical user interface. Other users have some idea of X's capabilities, but lack the knowledge and documentation necessary to make use of the features in question. XFree86 and Linux make an unbeatable pair, but only if the best features of both can be exploited.

This book is intended as a basic reference for the underlying X system on Linux machines that allows the Linux desktop, as well as the KDE and the GNOME, to be what they are today. The information presented here gets at the features of X and XFree86 that were once considered user-level, but have recently been relegated to the status of system-level or even esoteric in classification.

With the basic tools documented here and a little intuition, network users will hopefully be able to more easily bring to fruition goals such as network-centric computing, remote network and system administration, thin client computing, and multiplatform interoperability. Consumer Linux users, on the other hand, can use these tools to help in personalizing X and Linux in terms of both hardware and desktop software, for the greatest possible comfort and throughput in everyday tasks.

## PART I

X11R6, XFREE86, AND LINUX

1

X11R6 AND THE XFREE86 PROJECT

X Structure

X11R6 is a modular, network-transparent windowing system that uses a client/server architecture to operate. The two most important parts of the X Window System are the *clients*, or application and utility programs that run under X, and the *server*, a large program that interacts with the clients, the user, and with a workstation's graphics hardware. The relationship between the X clients and the X server requires some explanation.

X Is Network-Transparent

Before discussing client and server issues more fully, it's important to note that at the most fundamental level, X is a method for representing graphics operations as a stream of data, suitable for use as a network protocol. X is designed to operate over a network in a transparent fashion. Generally speaking, anything that will be displayed, or any input that will be accepted by X on a Linux computer system, must pass through a network interface, whether such an interface is Ethernet, a modem PPP line, or a local loopback interface. Of course, there are exceptions to this rule. For example, certain extensions allow X to render some graphics directly to the display, but for Linux computers in the general case, this rule certainly holds—at least for now.

Because all X display and input/output information can be transmitted over a network, there is no reason why a program designed to run under the X Window System should not be able to execute on one machine but interact with the user and display graphics primitives on a separate machine. Indeed, this is often the case. Because of this distributed model, X is often used in environments where one or relatively few very large computers run applications and complete calculations, all while users interact with these applications on separate, smaller machines whose only roles are to display the graphics and accept input. Under X, the specifications of the displaying system don't even need to match those of the system on which an application runs. A computer system with a monochrome display or no graphics display at all can easily run X applications and display them on another machine on the network that has a color display. The only requirement is that both machines be able to "speak" X.

X Uses a Client/Server Architecture

As is the case with most network protocols, the X protocol uses a client/server model to communicate. Most users familiar with the World Wide Web, telnet, FTP, email, or any number of other protocols are accustomed to thinking of their desktop workstation as a *client* machine, which then initiates connections to *server* machines somewhere on the network for data exchange. X is often confusing in this regard because, in the case of X, the desktop workstation at which the user sits runs the program called the *server*, while the displayed applications, which often run on other, larger computers on the network, are called the *clients* (see Figure 1.1). Whenever or wherever an X application runs, such a client/server relationship exists.

When an X application (client) is launched, it makes a request over the network to connect to either the specified or the default X server—the program that will display the application and accept input from the user. The X server program will use the display and input hardware of the computer on which it runs to interact with the connecting client (see Figure 1.2). The X server program is responsible not only for input/output and graphics display, but for other issues as well, such as basic font management and connection security. All this interaction takes place over the network.

On single-user personal computers such as those common in the Linux community, both the applications and the X server often run on the same machine, with the local X server configured as the default X server. In such cases, the X server is present to interact with the user at the keyboard and mouse and to display graphics on the video hardware through the monitor; at the same time, all the X clients are running on the same host, connecting to and interacting with the server using UNIX-domain sockets, or, if they aren't included in the running kernel, the local loopback interface (see Figure 1.3).

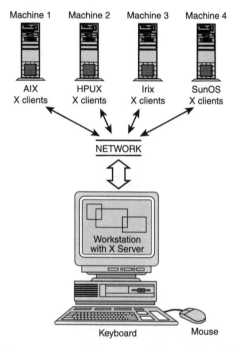

Figure 1.1   Clients running on several large machines without displays all interact on a single workstation display. All X data moves over the network.

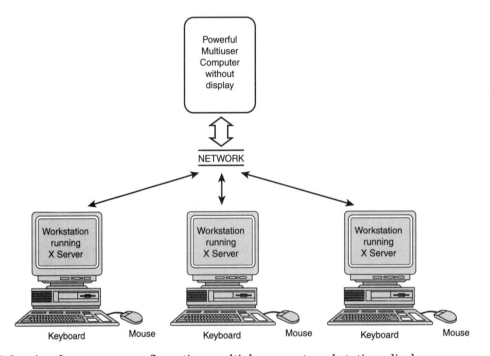

Figure 1.2 Another common configuration: multiple users at workstations display processor-intensive X applications from a single, larger machine. The large machine runs the computation-intensive clients, while the workstations run the X servers.

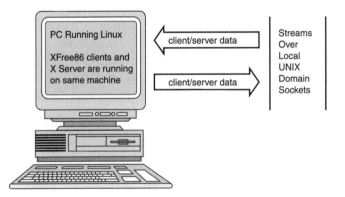

Figure 1.3 In the Linux desktop world, the X clients and server often run on the same machine. Local X data is transferred over the most efficient interface present.

To see evidence of these connections on a Linux machine running X, try issuing the following command:

```
netstat ¦ grep X11
```

This command provides a list of the open X connections on the machine in question. Whether the X clients and server run on the same or different machines, the underlying functionality of X remains unchanged. Clients contact the server over a network interface, and the server responds to the client's requests in the same way, creating on the display what appears to be a seamless desktop.

This network-centric separation between client and server, while seemingly unnecessary on a single computer, is the reason for the dominance of X in network-distributed computing. Because all connections in X are network connections, and because all applications display across the network, distributed computing and remote management become mundane tasks accomplished in the normal course of use. Indeed, the "thin client" craze of the mid 1990s was nothing new to X users, who have been running graphical applications across the network for over a decade.

X Is Modular

The network-transparent, client/server model also serves to keep X quite modular. Because the easiest way for clients to speak X across the network is to use the C-language interface, the X library is paradoxically separate from the X server, which will display X library primitives. In situations in which an X client and server are running on separate machines, both are using their own, independent X libraries as well!

To keep code portable across a large number of systems, and to keep the network-transparent hardware-neutrality of the X protocol intact, X is built more as a series of extensible, replaceable components rather than as a single, monolithic GUI unit. This is the case in some common graphical operating systems. Furthermore, to promote "mechanism rather than policy," the X protocol and X servers include no official high-level GUI library of their own. Instead, high-level GUI libraries are linked to clients, which can then generate widgets and other graphics that can be sent across the network using the X protocol.

To illustrate: A given Linux computer's X installation contains an X11 server, clients, and library, as well as the GTK high-level GUI library and the Mesa3D library for 3D graphics acceleration. An SGI computer across the hallway, on the other hand, contains an X11 server, clients, and library, but instead of the GTK GUI toolkit, the SGI contains the OSF/Motif high-level GUI toolkit and the OpenGL library for high-end 3D graphics acceleration.

Because of the differences between their libraries and hardware, it might seem unlikely that the two X installations are interoperable. Thanks, however, to the modular magic of X, a Motif application (client) running on the SGI machine can successfully display and interact with the user on the Linux machine correctly, even though no Motif library is present on the Linux system. Likewise, a GTK-based 3D application running on the X11R6 Linux machine can connect to the SGI machine and function correctly, even though the SGI machine contains no GTK library and uses OpenGL rather than Mesa3D. Furthermore, if the Linux user decides to upgrade his local library and applications from the older GTK 1.0 toolkit to the newer GTK+ 1.3 toolkit without telling anyone, nothing will break. No changes to the SGI machine across the hallway must be made for new GTK+ 1.3 applications on the Linux box to display correctly on the SGI box. Similarly, the Motif 1.2 applications on the SGI box can be replaced with Motif 2.0 applications without affecting the performance or functionality of X itself, whether displaying locally or to the Linux machine on the other side of the hallway.

Because of the modular, extensible nature of X and the separation between client and server over the network, X has survived as a viable and innovative user interface for more than 15 years in spite of the rapid pace of change within the computer industry.

Why Is XFree86 Different from X11R6?

XFree86 is one of the most important components of nearly every Linux distribution, and yet it is rarely mentioned by name, either by the distribution maintainers' literature or by end users. Just what is XFree86? The following is from the XFree86 Web page at `http://www.xfree86.org`:

> "The XFree86 Project, Inc is a non-profit organization that produces XFree86. XFree86 is a freely redistributable implementation of the X Window System that runs on UNIX(R) and UNIX-like operating systems (and OS/2). The XFree86 Project has traditionally focused on Intel x86-based platforms (which is where the '86' in our name comes from), but our current release also supports other platforms."

The common term *X11R6* stands for *X Window System version 11, release 6*. The second-most-recent release of the X Window System code by X.Org is known as X11R6.3, and it is the release with which the current version of XFree86 was built. So what's the difference between XFree86 and X11R6.3?

X11R6.3 includes a great deal of code—code defining things like basic graphics primitives, window behavior and properties, and the implementation of the X network protocol. What X11R6.3 does not include is code to talk to specific types of PC-style graphics and input/output hardware. This means that devices like ISA, VLB, or PCI graphics adapters, graphics chipsets, mice, trackballs, scroll wheels, and so on aren't directly supported by the code officially known as X11R6.3. This is done by design, so that individual vendors of such hardware can add support for their own devices in their own releases of the X Window System. In the PC world, however, where UNIX isn't the mainstream, most vendors of graphics or input hardware don't release "X drivers" or X servers complete with drivers for their products.

This is the reason for the existence of the XFree86 Project. In essence, the XFree86 Project writes what can loosely be thought of as X drivers for a wide variety of PC hardware and operating systems; then it combines such "drivers" with the official X11 code, releasing the result as the XFree86 software distribution.

Thus, a given XFree86 release is based on an X.Org release of the core X Window System code with extra code added to support PC-style graphics and input/output hardware, as well as a number of PC operating systems such as Linux and OS/2.

The XFree86 Distribution

The official XFree86 distribution consists of several distinct component archives, which are in turn released for several different supported hardware and software platforms. Choosing and obtaining an XFree86 distribution is therefore the process of first identifying the hardware and underlying operating system in question, and then installing each component of the XFree86 distribution specific to that platform.

Supported Platforms

XFree86 is supported for the following hardware and operating system platforms. Note that some platforms (such as x86 machines running Linux or a BSD variant) are more likely to be well supported and hardware-current than others.

It's no accident that Linux is so well supported by XFree86. XFree86 is the single most common distribution of the X Window System included with Linux operating systems, on all architectures.

Linux, Digital Alpha/AXP Architecture

This binary distribution supports a wide variety of graphics hardware on Digital Alpha/AXP machines running the Linux operating system. This is the X Window System distribution included in all AXP Linux operating systems.

Linux, x86 Architecture, glibc 2.x (aka libc6)

This binary distribution supports a wide variety of PC-type graphics and input/output hardware running versions of the Linux operating system that are based on the GNU C library 2.x release, such as Red Hat 5.x and later, Debian 2.x and later, and Caldera OpenLinux 2.2. This is the X Window System distribution included in most x86/libc6 Linux operating systems. This is perhaps the most widely used of all XFree86 platforms, accounting for much of the current Linux community.

Linux, x86 Architecture, glibc 1.x (aka libc5)

This binary distribution supports a wide variety of PC-type graphics and input/output hardware running versions of the Linux operating system, which are based on the GNU C library 1.x release or derivatives—such as Slackware Linux, Red Hat 4.x and earlier, and Caldera OpenLinux 1.x. This is the X Window System distribution included in most late x86/libc5 Linux operating systems, though many earlier x86/libc5 Linux operating systems also included competing products such as Metro-X from MetroLink, Inc. This is likely the second most widely used of all XFree86 platforms, accounting for much of the remainder of the Linux community.

Linux, Motorola m68k Architecture

This binary distribution operates on m68k-based machines such as those by Amiga, Atari, or Apple (Macintosh), which are also running the Linux operating system for m68k machines. Note that only the virtual framebuffer X server is included, meaning that a working Linux framebuffer console on the machine in question is required for this XFree86 distribution to work. This is the X Window System distribution included in all m68k Linux operating systems.

Linux, PowerPC Architecture, libc 1.99 or pre-2.1

This binary distribution operates on PowerPC-based machines such as IBM RS6k or Power Macintosh machines, which are also running the Linux operating system for PowerPC machines. Note that only virtual framebuffer X server is included, meaning that a working Linux framebuffer console on the machine in question is required for this XFree86 distribution to work. Note also that there are two versions of this binary XFree86 distribution, one for PowerPC Linux systems using GNU libc 1.99 and one for PowerPC Linux systems using GNU libc pre-2.1. This is the X Window System distribution included in all PowerPC Linux operating systems.

Other (Non-Linux) Supported Platforms

XFree86 also supports several non-Linux platforms. Some of these, like the BSD-based operating systems, are quite popular in their own right, while others (such as the DG/UX platform) are more esoteric and market-specific. A complete list can be found in Table 2.1.

Table 2.1   Other Supported XFree86 Platforms

Architecture	Operating System Platform
x86 (Pentium+)	DG/UX 4.20 Aviion
x86 (386+)	FreeBSD 2.2.x (a.out binary format)
x86 (386+)	FreeBSD 3.0 (ELF binary format)
x86 (386+)	GNU HURD
x86 (386+)	LynxOS (16MB memory required)

Architecture	Operating System Platform
x86 (386+)	NetBSD 1.2 and 1.3
x86 (386+)	OS/2 Warp 3, Warp 4, Warp Connect, Warp Server, and Warp Server SMP (16MB memory required)
x86 (386+)	OpenBSD
x86 (386+)	UNIX SVR4.0 and SVR4.2
x86 (386+)	Solaris
x86 (386+)	UnixWare

Major Files and Components

The specific list of files included with an XFree86 release (especially the list of included X servers) varies from platform to platform. Because this text is primarily about Linux versions of XFree86, this chapter will give details with respect to Linux systems in this section.

Because the X server and the X clients are such important parts of XFree86, accounting for nearly all the "direct contact" a user will make with X, it is tempting to split the XFree86 distribution into two major pieces: the server and the X clients. In truth, there's much more to an X distribution than just the server and the applications that will run on it. Even so, the X server is probably the most important part of the XFree86 distribution (it certainly requires the largest amount of configuration), so this chapter covers servers first before moving on to the rest of the XFree86 components.

Note that any of the files included with an XFree86 distribution for Linux can appear in one of several formats. The `.tgz` format refers to a gzipped, tarred file, commonly considered to be a generic Linux packaging format. The information in the rest of this section applies to the "canonical" binary XFree86 distribution maintained in `.tgz` format at the `ftp.xfree86.org` FTP site.

Many Linux operating systems include XFree86 in other formats (such as `.rpm` or `.deb`) and may break the components down into smaller packages or merge two or more packages into a single larger package. Thus, the following guidelines might not exactly match all Linux computer systems, but they do match the XFree86 distribution from the XFree86 Project.

XFree86 Servers

The list of separate XFree86 servers is actually quite short, given the wide range and variety apparent in the PC graphics hardware market today. Fortunately, the XFree86 project manages to support a long list of graphics hardware with this short list of X servers. The list in Table 2.2 is complete, but general. For a specific list of supported graphics hardware under Linux, please refer to Appendix B, "XFree86 3.3.5 Details."

Note that *color depth* refers to the amount of memory used to store each pixel on the X display. A larger color depth indicates better color display capability. For example, an 8-bit color depth is generally a 256-color display, while a 24-bit color depth is capable of displaying over 16 million colors simultaneously. For a complete discussion of XFree86 and color management, please refer to Chapter 7, "Runtime Server Configuration."

A normal XFree86 installation will contain two servers: the XVG16.tgz server and another server that more specifically supports the graphics hardware of the machine on which XFree86 will operate. These servers are kept in the Servers/ directory off of each architecture's main tree on the XFree86 FTP site.

Table 2.2 XFree86 Servers and Supported Graphics Hardware

Server	Color Depths	Supported Hardware
X3DL.tgz	8,15,16,32	Accelerated server for high-end chipsets from 3Dlabs. Hardware-based 3D acceleration isn't supported.
X68FB.tgz	framebuffer-dependent	Console framebuffer server for m68k Linux systems including 68k Macintosh machines, Amiga, and some Atari systems.
X8514.tgz	8	Accelerated server for the relatively uncommon IBM 8514/a SVGA chipset.
XAGX.tgz	8,15,16	Accelerated server for the IBM XGA chipsets often found on older IBM Microchannel graphics adapters.
XFB.tgz	framebuffer-dependent	Console framebuffer server for x86 Linux systems. Commonly used in conjunction with the Linux VESA framebuffer console to support hardware that is VESA-compliant, but otherwise incompatible with XFree86.
XI128.tgz	8,15,16,24	Accelerated server supporting the Number Nine Imagine 128 graphics accelerator and compatible chipsets.
XMa32.tgz	8,15,16	Accelerated server supporting the Mach32 chipsets commonly found on late-model ISA and nearly all ATI VLB graphics adapters.
XMa64.tgz	8,15,16,32	Accelerated server for ATI Mach64 and later chipsets commonly found on PCI and AGP 2D and 3D graphics adapters manufactured by ATI. Hardware-based 3D acceleration isn't supported.
XMa8.tgz	8	Accelerated server for early ATI ISA VGA and SVGA graphics cards.
XMono.tgz	Monochrome	Unaccelerated server for older single-plane (monochrome) ISA graphics adapters.

Server	Color Depths	Supported Hardware
XP9K.tgz	8,15,16,32	Accelerated server for cards using the Weitek Power 9000 graphics chipset. Note that this server doesn't support the Power 9100 chipset.
XS3.tgz	8,15,16,24	Accelerated server supporting most of the ubiquitous 2D S3 graphics chipsets found on ISA, VLB, and early PCI video cards. An alternate implementation for identical hardware can be found in the XSVGA.tgz server.
XS3V.tgz	8,15,16,24	Accelerated server supporting the S3 ViRGE 3D chipsets. This server doesn't support the older S3 chipsets; for older S3 chipsets, see XS3 (above) or the XSVGA server (below). Hardware 3D acceleration is not supported by this server.
XSVGA.tgz	8,15,16,24,32	This accelerated server supports by far the widest variety of graphics hardware supported by any of the XFree86 X servers. This server employs the new XAA, or *X Acceleration Architecture*, internally. Among the graphics chipsets supported by this server are those by 3Dfx Interactive, Tseng Labs, Weitek, NeoMagic, nVidia, Rendition, Trident, Paradise, Western Digital, and others. Hardware 3D acceleration isn't supported by this server.
XTGA.tgz	8	This unaccelerated server supports the Digital 21030 graphics chipset commonly found on older Alpha/AXP machines.
XVG16.tgz	4 (16 colors)	This unaccelerated server supports the "generic" 16-color VGA hardware that can be found on nearly any modern PC. This server should work just about anywhere, and because of this, it is used by XF86Setup to configure more complex XFree86 servers.
XW32.tgz	8	This accelerated server supports the Tseng Labs ET4000/W32 series of graphics chipsets and the similar ET6000 series from the same manufacturer. This server has been replaced by the alternate implementation in the XSVGA.tgz server (above) and is thus rarely used any longer.

Users should note that several extra XFree86 servers can be found in the PC98-Servers/ subdirectory, each of which supports graphics hardware found only on Japanese "PC98" architecture machines. Most users won't need to use the servers from the PC98-Servers/ directory, but will instead be served by one of the servers listed previously. Users needing PC98 support should consult the RELNOTES file in the platform distribution directory for details on the servers in the PC98-Servers/ directory.

XFree86 Clients and Libraries

Aside from the X server, the next most visible and used parts of the X Window System are the standard X clients (applications and utilities) and the X shared libraries, which hold a great deal of the X client and server functionality. The standard X clients include a large number of utilities, tools, and things like a basic window manager (twm) and graphical terminal (xterm). The clients and libraries are contained in the following two packages, which overlap:

Xbin.tgz	Contains most of the standard X clients and libraries. Examples from this package include Imake, xclock, twm, xdm, xman, xmag, and libraries like the Athena widgets (libXaw) and the X11 library (libX11).
	Install Subtrees: bin/, lib/
	Install Priority: Required
Xshlib.tgz	Contains the same libraries included in Xbin.tgz, without all of the clients.
	Install Subtree: lib/
	Install Priority: When needed

XFree86 Fonts

After the X server, which controls the display hardware, and the X clients, which interact directly with the user, the next most visible XFree86 components are the fonts. XFree86 includes a complete set of bitmapped fonts, including proportional serif and sans serif fonts as well as a Courier font and several other fixed-width fonts. XFree86 fonts are found in the following XFree86 packages:

Xf100.tgz	The 100 dpi (dots per inch) bitmapped fonts are contained in this package. These fonts aren't designed to be scalable; instead, they come in predefined sizes and typefaces and are sized for users who specify that they have a 100 dpi display.
	Install Subtree: lib/X11/fonts/100dpi/
	Install Priority: Recommended
Xfcyr.tgz	These are the Cyrillic fonts for XFree86. They are of interest to users in eastern Europe but will not be of interest to other users around the world.
	Install Subtree: lib/X11/fonts/cyrillic/
	Install Priority: When needed
Xfnon.tgz	Other non-English fonts can be found here, including some fonts for Big5 and GB (Chinese) displays and some Japanese and Hebrew fonts as well.
	Install Subtree: lib/X11/fonts/misc/
	Install Priority: When needed
Xfnts.tgz	The 75 dpi bitmapped fonts are contained in this package. These fonts, like the fonts in Xf100.tgz aren't designed to be scalable and come in pre-rendered

sizes and typefaces. The fonts in this package are sized for the default user, who is assumed to have a 75 dpi display. This package is normally installed even if Xf100.tgz is also used because Xfnts.tgz also contains the main miscellaneous series of fonts, which are often used as defaults or baseline fonts.

Install Subtrees: `lib/X11/fonts/75dpi/`, `lib/X11/fonts/misc/`

Install Priority: Required

Xfscl.tgz — The scalable fonts are contained in this package. They are PostScript Type I fonts, which are the type most commonly used with XFree86 when scalable fonts are needed.

Install Subtrees: `lib/X11/fonts/Speedo/`, `lib/X11/fonts/Type1/`

Install Priority: Recommended

Other XFree86 Servers or Extensions

Another class of server components are part of XFree86 but are separate and different from the X servers listed previously. These servers provide other sorts of functionality for XFree86 that aren't easily implemented by other means. Most of these are listed here:

Xfsrv.tgz — This package contains the X font server, which allows X clients to display fonts that aren't hosted on their own machine. The X font server therefore serves fonts to clients across the network, which in turn display these fonts on X servers.

Install Subtrees: `bin/, lib/, man/`

Install Priority: When needed

Xnest.tgz — This package contains the nested X server, which is an X server that runs as a client on another X server. This allows a virtual X display within an X display; the physical X display has its clients, among them the nested server, and the nested server, as a full-fledged X server, also has its own clients, independent of those connected to the host server.

Install Subtree: `bin/`

Install Priority: When needed

Xprt.tgz — This package contains the X print server, which is an X server that supports output to printer devices using the core X drawing requests. The server adds requests for job control and page control to the X protocol and also adds extensions for communicating the attributes and capabilities of the printing device in question.

Install Subtree: `bin/`

Install Priority: When needed

Xvfb.tgz   This is the XFree86 virtual framebuffer package. It emulates a framebuffer device, but normally displays nowhere and accepts input from nowhere. It is normally used only for test and debugging purposes.

Install Subtree: `bin/`

Install Priority: When needed

XFree86 Configuration Tools

The three primary configuration tools for XFree86 are all incarnations of the same tool, known as XF86Setup (more on this in the next section). They are included in three separate packages to serve three distinct classes of users. All three incarnations depend on the XVG16 server to work properly:

X9set.tgz   This package is the XF86Setup tool for computers based on the PC98 x86 architecture. Most users will not use this XF86Setup incarnation.

Install Subtrees: `bin/`, `lib/X11/XF86Setup/`, `man/`

Install Priority: When needed

Xjset.tgz   This package is the XF86Setup tool configured to use Japanese fonts and input rather than English fonts and input.

Install Subtrees: `bin/`, `lib/X11/XF86Setup/`, `man/`

Install Priority: When needed

Xset.tgz   This package is the XF86Setup tool that most users will use. It works with standard Linux PC machines and displays and accepts input in English.

Install Subtrees: `bin/`, `lib/X11/XF86Setup/`, `man/`

Install Priority: Recommended

XFree86 Documentation

XFree86 ships with several different documentation packages in several formats. The documentation generally duplicates itself across each format, so users need only pick a preferred format and install that package to get all documentation.

Xdoc.tgz   The XFree86 README documentation in plain text format, readable just about anywhere.

Install Subtree: `lib/X11/doc/`

Install Priority: Recommended

Xhtml.tgz   The XFree86 README documentation in HTML format, viewable with a Web browser such as Netscape Communicator or Lynx.

Install Subtree: `lib/X11/doc/html/`

Install Priority: Recommended

Xjdoc.tgz	The XFree86 README documentation in plain text format for Japanese users.
	Install Subtree: lib/X11/doc/Japanese/
	Install Priority: When needed
Xps.tgz	The XFree86 README documentation in PostScript format, suitable for pretty printing to a PostScript-compatible printer or through an interpreter such as GhostScript.
	Install Subtree: lib/X11/doc/PostScript/
	Install Priority: When needed

Other Components

Without wanting to place the remaining packages into a miscellaneous category, let's go over them one by one. Most of the remaining packages have to do with XFree86 development, but others have to do with documentation or configuration.

Xcfg.tgz	This package contains the default configuration information for the X Display Manager (XDM) binary installed as part of Xbin.tgz. Although it's possible to generate a configuration from scratch, it's highly recommended that users interested in using xdm install Xcfg.tgz.
	Install Subtrees: lib/X11/xdm/, lib/X11/xinit/, lib/X11/proxymngr/
	Install Priority: Recommended
Xlib.tgz	This package is a sort of catchall for the remaining configuration information XFree86 needs to properly operate. This package includes locale data, keyboard mapping data, bitmap images, the default twm configuration, and other miscellaneous configuration and data files.
	Install Subtree: lib/X11/
	Install Priority: Required
Xlk98.tgz	This package is the PC98 x86 version of the XFree86 link kit, which enables users to build and link their own X servers. Most users will not use this package, but will instead use the package for normal PC-type computers.
	Install Subtree: lib/Server/
	Install Priority: When needed
Xlkit.tgz	This package is the normal version of the XFree86 link kit, in case the user must rebuild and link an X server. This is rarely necessary.
	Install Subtree: lib/Server/
	Install Priority: When needed

Xman.tgz   This package contains the library of manual pages (used by the man command) for the X Window System, X servers, and X clients included with XFree86.

Install Subtree: man/

Install Priority: Recommended

Xprog.tgz   This package contains the X11 includes needed to create clients (applications) that can run under the X Window System. Static versions of the X libraries and Imake configuration information are also in this package. This will be useful to anyone who plans to compile some of his or her own applications or applications downloaded from the Internet.

Install Subtrees: lib/, include/

Install Priority: Recommended

Navigating the XFree86 FTP Site

The main XFree86 FTP site can be found at ftp.xfree86.org. The site permits anonymous logins, so anyone can log in and download XFree86. The base directory for the binary XFree86 3.3.5 distribution on the ftp.xfree86.org site is /pub/XFree86/3.3.5/binaries/. As this text is being written, XFree86 3.3.5 is the most recent release available for Alpha or x86 Linux users, but other Linux users will find that XFree86 3.3.3.1 or 3.3.4 are the most recent releases for their platform. If you are an m68k or PowerPC user, you should instead visit the 3.3.3.1/binaries/ subtree at the XFree86 ftp site. In an XFree86 binaries directory are a combination of several platform-specific subdirectories. Subdirectories relevant to Linux users are summarized in Table 2.3.

Table 2.3   Important Trees in /pub/XFree86/3.3.x/binaries/

Directory	What's Contained There
Linux-axp/	XFree86 (3.3.5) binary distribution for Digital Alpha/AXP systems running Linux.
Linux-ix86-glibc/	XFree86 (3.3.5) binary distribution for x86 PC-style systems running libc6/glibc2.x Linux platforms.
Linux-ix86-libc5/	XFree86 (3.3.5) binary distribution for x86 PC-style systems running libc5/glibc1.x Linux platforms.
Linux-m68k/	XFree86 (3.3.3.1) binary distribution for Motorola 68k systems running the Linux operating system.
Linux-ppc-glibc-1.99/	XFree86 (3.3.3.1) binary distribution for PowerPC systems running Linux versions based on glibc 1.99.
Linux-ppc-glibc-pre2.1/	XFree86 (3.3.3.1) binary distribution for PowerPC systems running Linux versions based on glibc pre-2.1 releases.

Each of these subtrees is a complete binary distribution of XFree86 for the platform in question. Each of these subtrees also contains a directory called Servers/ that houses the X servers supported by that platform, though the m68k and PPC platforms support only one server, X68FB.tgz.

Downloading XFree86 3.3.5 or 3.3.3.1 for your Linux platform is simply a matter of downloading a server or servers to match your hardware from the Servers/ directory, choosing the packages you'll need by consulting the information earlier in the chapter, and then downloading the packages in question to your own system via FTP. Note that you should also take care to download the preinst.sh, postinst.sh, and extract scripts for your platform from the same directory.

2

INSTALLING AND
CONFIGURING XFREE86

Checking for an Existing Installation

Most Linux users install XFree86 by default as a part of their Linux installation. If your Linux configuration includes a graphical user interface, chances are that XFree86 is already installed and running on your machine.

Users still unsure who is using RPM-based Linux operating systems can check for the presence of XFree86 packages by issuing the following command:

```
rpm -qa ¦ grep XFree86
```

If XFree86 is installed, this command should turn up a list of several packages whose names begin with *XFree86* and end with some of the components listed earlier. If your Linux system is RPM-based but this command produces no results, XFree86 is probably not yet installed on your system.

For other users, such as those without an rpm package manager, checking for the existence of a /usr/X11R6 directory tree on the system is another surefire way to detect the presence of X. If there is no /usr/X11R6 directory tree on your system, XFree86 is probably not installed.

Installing XFree86

Most Linux users will never need to install XFree86 by hand because every distribution under the sun will include XFree86 as part of a standard workstation install. Sometimes, however, it can be convenient to choose a so-called "server install" that doesn't typically include XFree86, even though you'd like to have XFree86 installed afterward. Sometimes it also becomes necessary to upgrade an XFree86 distribution, even if upgrade packages haven't yet become available from your distribution maintainer. In such cases, it is important to understand how to install XFree86.

Installing from the CD-ROM

Most users who discover that XFree86 isn't installed on their systems will want to install it from the CD-ROM on which their Linux operating system is packaged because there is every chance that XFree86 will indeed be present on the CD-ROM.

The process of locating XFree86 packages on a CD-ROM isn't a complicated one. First, the CD-ROM must be mounted. On most current distributions, this is accomplished by inserting the CD-ROM and then typing the following:

```
mount /mnt/cdrom
```

Note that a more complex command might at times be required if the relevant information hasn't been inserted into /etc/fstab:

```
Mount -t iso9660 /dev/cdrom /mnt/cdrom
```

Note also that you might need to be using the root account for the command to work. After the CD-ROM is located, the XFree86 packages can usually be found by issuing a find command similar to this one:

```
find /mnt/cdrom -name 'XFree86*' -print
```

After the packages have been located, installing XFree86 is simply a matter of visiting the directory containing the packages and installing them. Refer to the list of components in Chapter 1, "X11R6 and the XFree86 Project," if you need help in deciding which parts of XFree86 to install. If the component files on the CD-ROM don't exactly match those listed there, rpm users can query each package for details on what it contains like this:

```
rpm -qpi package
```

Replace *package* with the name of the package file to query. Some users might find it useful to print the information about what each of the XFree86 packages contains before making decisions about which packages to install. This can be accomplished with

```
rpm -qpi XFree86* ¦ lpr
```

Note that if your CD-ROM doesn't appear to contain XFree86 packages, it might be time to upgrade to a newer or more mainstream version of Linux!

Installing the Official Distribution

Users who are installing XFree86 from the CD will naturally be using the package tools that came with their Linux operating systems to install the individual XFree86 packages. Users who downloaded the XFree86 distribution from ftp.XFree86.org will need to use an alternative method of installing because the official XFree86 binary packages are provided only in .tgz format.

Three scripts, preinst.sh, postinst.sh, and extract from the platform-specific binary directory on the FTP site, are used to automate the installation of the many XFree86 .tgz packages. To use them, follow these steps. We'll assume here for the sake of clarity that the X*.tgz files, the preinst.sh, postinst.sh, and extract scripts all reside in /tmp after being downloaded. If your files were downloaded to another location, substitute it in place of /tmp. Note that you should normally log in as or become the root user before proceeding with the installation.

First, make a directory for the XFree86 distribution on your file system. This should almost always be /usr/X11R6; don't put XFree86 somewhere else unless you're really sure about what you're doing. Then, run the pre-installation script by issuing these commands:

```
cd /usr/X11R6
sh /tmp/preinst.sh
```

The pre-installation script "checks out" the system to make sure that the rest of the installation will go smoothly. You might be presented with warnings or further instructions that you should follow before continuing with the XFree86 installation. If the pre-installation script finishes without problems, you can proceed to extract the X*.tgz files using the following commands:

```
cd /usr/X11R6
chmod 755 /tmp/extract
/tmp/extract /tmp/X*.tgz
```

These commands first mark the extract binary as executable and then proceed to use it to unpack all the download packages to their correct locations inside the /usr/X11R6 directory. After the files have been successfully extracted, call the post-installation script.

```
cd /usr/X11R6
sh /tmp/postinst.sh
```

The most important operation performed by the post-installation script is the addition of the /usr/X11R6/lib/ directory to the /etc/ld.so.conf file and the subsequent execution of the ldconfig command. This sequence of steps tells Linux where the newly installed XFree86 libraries reside and will allow Linux to use them when appropriate. For the paranoid, these steps can be verified or repeated by hand. First, check to make sure that the /usr/X11R6/lib/ directory has been added to the /etc/ld.so.conf file by displaying the file onscreen:

```
cat /etc/ld.so.conf
```

Then, after you have verified that the /usr/X11R6/lib/ directory appears in the file, call ldconfig to update the cache:

```
/sbin/ldconfig
```

Assuming everything has gone as planned, XFree86 should now be installed on your system.

If Everything Didn't Go as Planned

In rare cases where everything didn't go as planned, there is a second, more kludgy method for installing the official XFree86 distribution. This is an unsupported method, meaning that you shouldn't complain to the XFree86 maintainers if it fails to work. It does often work, however, when one or more of the three scripts has produced an unidentifiable or unresolvable error.

To use the kludgy installation method, follow these steps carefully. First, make the directory to hold XFree86:

```
mkdir /usr/X11R6
```

Then, extract all the downloaded packages directly using the tar command. Be sure to visit the directory first.

```
cd /usr/X11R6
for package in /tmp/X*.tgz; do tar -xzvf $package; done
```

These two commands should complete without error. If either one of them fails, be sure that you have disk space available using the df command and perhaps even re-download the packages. Assuming that they did unpack without problems, you can proceed to add the /usr/X11R6/lib directory to the library cache by hand with the following two commands:

```
echo '/usr/X11R6/lib'>> /etc/ld.so.conf
/sbin/ldconfig
```

Note the use of two greater-than symbols (>). Do not use a single greater-than symbol because it will render parts of your Linux system inoperable! Now you must update your font directories by hand. To do so, first visit /usr/X11R6/lib/X11/fonts:

```
cd /usr/X11R6/lib/X11/fonts
```

Once there, visit each of its subdirectories, issuing the command mkfontdir in each directory. A for loop to simplify the process is shown here:

```
cd /usr/X11R6/lib/X11/fonts
for dir in *; do
cd $dir
/usr/X11R6/bin/mkfontdir
cd ..
done
```

After you've completed this step, the "kludgy" install should be complete. Be aware that there might be subtle problems with this install method in any given release of XFree86. Unfortunately, sometimes this method is necessary anyway.

Tying Up Loose Ends

XFree86 is now mostly installed on your system. However, there might still be one or two loose ends to clean up. The first of them applies no matter which of the two installation methods you chose, or even if you installed XFree86 from your Linux CD-ROM. You must check to make sure that the symbolic link at /usr/X11R6/bin/X points to the X server you want to use. To find out, type this command at a shell prompt:

```
ls -l /usr/X11R6/bin/X
```

If this symbolic link doesn't exist, or if it points to the wrong server, you'll want to remove it and link it to the correct server. The name of the correct server will be similar to the name of the server package you chose to install, but will start with XF86_ instead of X and will not end with .tgz. For example, if you want to use the server contained in XSVGA.tgz as your default server, you'll need to create a symbolic link to /usr/X11R6/bin/XF86_SVGA. If you want to use the server contained in XAGX.tgz as your default, create your symbolic link to /usr/X11R6/bin/XF86_AGX. Here's an example, first using rm to remove the old link if it is incorrect, and then ln to create the new one:

```
rm /usr/X11R6/bin/X
ln -s /usr/X11R6/bin/XF86_SVGA /usr/X11R6/bin/X
```

Assuming that one of the normal (script files, CD-ROM packages) or abnormal (kludgy) install methods worked, and that you've verified the correctness of the symbolic link at /usr/X11R6/bin/X, you can now safely assume that XFree86 is installed on your system and proceed to configuration.

Configuring XFree86

Now XFree86 is installed on your computer. Unfortunately, if you're running an x86 architecture PC system, XFree86 still doesn't know enough to do any work for you. Before you can use XFree86, you must tell it all about your system. You'll need to provide information about your graphics hardware, what type of mouse you have, what resolutions your monitor can support, and so on. This information is stored in a large, segmented text file that XFree86 reads each time the server starts. Luckily, this configuration file can normally be built automatically by one of two programs that will ask you about your hardware, and then output a configuration to match. Although it is possible to configure an XFree86 installation entirely by hand from within a text editor such as Emacs, most users prefer to use either XF86Setup or xf86config.

XF86Setup is the nicer of the two because it uses the 16-color VGA server to operate and is therefore point-and-click driven. Most aspects of XFree86 can be easily configured using XF86Setup, and because of this, XF86Setup has become the configuration tool of choice for most Linux operating systems, often running automatically at install time.

xf86config isn't as visually pleasing or as intuitive to use as XF86Setup, but it has certain advantages. The most important advantage is that it runs in a text-based console, enabling it to work on systems lacking 16-color VGA hardware, which XF86Setup won't support.

Note that if you're using a non-PC architecture that takes advantage of the X68FB.tgz frame-buffer server and only allows for one kind of mouse device (like, for example, a 68K Macintosh machine), some of the information about configuring a wide variety of hardware throughout the rest of this chapter might not apply to you. For help on configuring such non-PC hardware for XFree86, it is best to visit the homepage of your distribution on the Web or to contact the distribution maintainer for current instructions and details on whether your particular system's console driver is even supported by the server in X68FB.tgz.

Learning About Your Hardware

Before you can supply a configuration program with details about your display hardware and input hardware, you must know a thing or two about it yourself. Important facts to know about your video card are the graphics chipset it uses, the amount of video memory installed, the ramdac and clock chip used, and the name of the card's manufacturer. On newer PCs, much of this information isn't essential because XFree86 servers can often autodetect some of it and because all these functions are often integrated into a single chip, but it's still a good idea to know the details in case they're needed. Important facts to know about your mouse or input device are the protocol it uses (usually this will be Microsoft or PS/2, but there are some others) and how it is physically connected to your system.

You'll also probably want to know something about your monitor, especially if it is an older monitor. It is actually possible, though very rare, to blow out a monitor by configuring it incorrectly for X. Usually, instead of a blowout with a bad configuration, you'll just get an unreadable display. Most of the time, it is possible to stick to a few known safe settings, but you'll get much more out of XFree86 if you have your monitor manual handy.

Video Card Detective Work

Finding out about your video card is sometimes a difficult task because a computer system's video hardware details are often considered over the heads of end users. Still, the information is usually there to be found somewhere or other, and the following three methods can help you ferret it out.

First, the easiest way to find out about your video adapter or the video hardware in your computer system is to check the spec-sheet that came with it. Most PCs these days ship with a separate video card that plugs into a slot on the motherboard. Often, the manual that came with the card, or even the box in which the card came, will give information such as the amount of video memory installed and the graphics chipset installed. Sometimes even a ramdac is mentioned. Sometimes this information alone is enough; other times it isn't.

The second easy, but slightly less reliable, way to find out about your video card is to use the SuperProbe program to find out. SuperProbe simply probes your graphics hardware and dumps what it finds out to the display. It sounds convenient, but it has several drawbacks. Most importantly, it can lock up your system before it prints anything at all, forcing a reboot. This is because SuperProbe finds out about your hardware simply by trying to talk to it. If a piece of hardware that SuperProbe isn't looking for answers back, bad things happen, leading to a crash. The second problem with SuperProbe is that it is often inaccurate, especially on older hardware or esoteric hardware that can behave in unexpected ways. Still, SuperProbe is useful and accurate about 80 percent of the time, so it is an important utility, especially for those who don't want to try finding out about their hardware using method number three. To use SuperProbe, call it like this:

```
/usr/X11R6/bin/SuperProbe
```

When called like this, SuperProbe will pause for five seconds to give you time to abort if you chicken out, and will then proceed to probe your hardware. The process should take a maximum of about 10 seconds before it prints the information you want. If more time than this elapses, your system might have locked up, meaning that it could be time for method number three.

The third way to find out about your graphics hardware is also known as the hard way in most circles. Take the case top off of your computer (taking care to inform yourself about things like warranty issues) and look at your video card. Be sure to do this only in a relatively clean and static-free environment. Before touching any computer internals, touch the metal frame to ground yourself and dissipate any static. Repeat this process often as you work inside the box. Carefully unbolt the card (if the video adapter is on a card) and slide it out of the slot. Copy down exactly the identification marks of any chips on the board that have such marks. Also take care to read any silkscreen printing on the board about the amount of memory installed or the name of the manufacturer. When you're finished, slide the card back into the slot, tighten the screw, and replace the case on your computer.

If your monitor plugs directly into your motherboard, rather than into an expansion card, you're probably better off sticking with SuperProbe or letting the X server try to autodetect your hardware.

Mouse or Input Device Detective Work

The two facts you'll want to know about your input device (mouse, trackball, or otherwise) before configuring XFree86 are the protocol it uses to communicate and the port to which it is physically connected.

Luckily for most users, the PC input device market has really calmed down in recent years. Although a wide variety of devices can still be purchased for PCs, nearly all current devices use one of two protocols to communicate. For most users, this means that if your mouse is connected to a serial port, it uses the Microsoft protocol, and if it is connected to a little round PS/2 port on your motherboard, it uses the PS/2 protocol.

If you are using a serial mouse, but you know for a fact that it isn't a Microsoft protocol mouse, or if your mouse isn't a serial mouse at all, you'll need to consult the documentation for the mouse to find out what protocol it does use. Many older Logitech serial mice use the Logitech protocol, and there are a few others out there as well. Using the Auto protocol can allow some mice to communicate without a specific protocol specification, but there is no reliable way to autodetect protocols for older mice, so it's up to you if you own such a mouse to do some detective work.

The next thing you'll need to know about your mouse or input device is where it is connected. Most of the time, your Linux distribution has already done this for you and has linked your mouse device to the /dev/mouse device node. To see if this is the case, try issuing the following command:

```
ls -l /dev/mouse
```

If /dev/mouse exists, chances are that your mouse port has already been configured for you as being /dev/mouse and that you won't have to remember any other device name. If there is no /dev/mouse device on the other hand, you'll need to check Table 2.1 for some common mouse devices in Linux. An overwhelming percentage of users will find that their mouse is served well by one of the first three entries in the table—either /dev/ttyS0, /dev/ttyS1, or /dev/psaux.

Table 2.1 Common Mouse Devices in Linux

Device	Mouse Type and Related Port
/dev/ttyS0	Microsoft, Logitech, MouseMan, Mouse Systems, or IntelliMouse devices connected to COM1
/dev/ttyS1	Microsoft, Logitech, MouseMan, Mouse Systems, or IntelliMouse devices connected to COM2
/dev/psaux	Any type of input device connected through a built-in PS/2 type mouse port
/dev/logibm	Mice connected through a Logitech bus mouse port or Logitech bus mouse card
/dev/atibm	Mice connected to an ATI XL bus mouse port
/dev/inportbm	Mice connected to a Microsoft bus mouse port or Microsoft bus mouse card

If you can't identify your pointing device's protocol or port, you might have to do some experimenting through trial and error when configuring XFree86 until you can get the device to work.

Monitor Detective Work

The two most important things you'll want to learn about your monitor are its horizontal and vertical scan rate ranges. Most good monitors will give such ranges somewhere in the manual or on a spec sheet. If you can find them, keep them handy or copy them down somewhere.

If you can't find them, be sure you can at least find a text description or resolution description of your monitor, something like one of these examples, which will usually give enough information to safely configure a monitor with conservative settings:

14-inch Super VGA

15-inch XGA

17-inch 1280×1024

If you can't find any information at all about your monitor, you can also try checking your Windows configuration to see what resolution you're using in Windows. This will often enable you to figure out the basic capabilities of your monitor and conservatively match it to one of the known monitor types later.

Configuring with XF86Setup

The preferred configuration tool for configuring XFree86 that should be used whenever possible is called XF86Setup. XF86Setup is a graphical configuration tool that will try to autodetect your mouse and will allow you to adjust the display size and position for your monitor. To start XF86Setup, give its absolute path on a command line:

```
/usr/X11R6/bin/XF86Setup
```

If you type the command and the system responds by saying that it isn't installed, please get and install Xset.tgz or another of the XF86Setup packages listed in Chapter 1.

Use Existing XF86Config File for Defaults

If you are upgrading from an existing installation of XFree86, you will be asked whether you want to use the existing XF86Config file for defaults. If you choose yes, XF86Setup will load the information in your existing configuration file and use those values as the default values.

Switching to Graphics Mode

XF86Setup will notify you that it is going to attempt to switch to graphics mode. After you press Enter, XF86Setup will try to start the 16-color VGA X server (XF86_VGA16) in order to display graphically.

This process normally proceeds without errors. It should take between 5 and 30 seconds to switch to graphics mode, depending on the speed of your hardware, the amount of memory present, and the number of other processes currently running on the system in question. If after such a period of time you see nothing happen, or if you encounter an error of some sort while switching to graphics mode, you might want to kill all processes or reboot into single-user mode and try to launch XF86Setup again.

If you are still unable to successfully launch XF86Setup, your only remaining option for automated configuration is the xf86config program discussed in the next section.

Navigating Inside XF86Setup

After XF86Setup has successfully started, the title screen shown in Figure 2.1 will be displayed. Most users at this point will find that their mouse or pointing device has been automatically enabled, and that they can move the pointer around and navigate without problems.

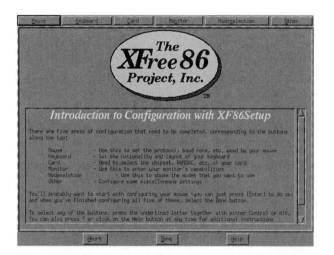

Figure 2.1　The XF86Setup title screen gives some general instructions for using XF86Setup. Note the five configuration sections listed across the top.

If your mouse wasn't detected, don't despair—the first step in the process is configuring your mouse, and it can be done using your keyboard. Using the keyboard is easy. Note that the labels on most buttons have an underlined character. Pressing the corresponding key on your keyboard will have the effect of pressing the button in question. Also notice that there is a dark outline around one button or widget on the screen. When you press the Enter key, the widget with the dark outline will act as though it had been clicked by the mouse. You can move the dark outline to different widgets around the screen using the Tab key.

Across the top of the display, notice that there are six buttons labeled Mouse, Keyboard, Card, Monitor, Modeselection, and Other. These are the six major configuration sections of XFree86. Clicking any of these buttons or pressing the related key will cause the configuration options for that section to appear on the display.

Mouse Configuration

The Mouse configuration section, shown in Figure 2.2, contains options related to the operation of a mouse or other pointing device inside XFree86.

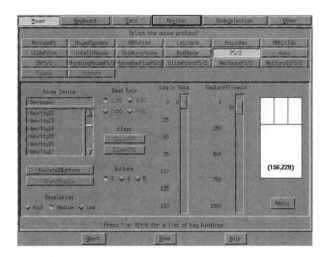

Figure 2.2   If your mouse isn't working when XF86Setup starts, you'll likely need to spend time in the Mouse configuration section.

When you first switch to the Mouse configuration section, a window will appear that gives general instructions on configuring your mouse using XF86Setup as well as specific instructions on how to navigate the Mouse section using only your keyboard as a pointing device. Most of the specific actions for keyboard users are given in Table 2.2.

Table 2.2   Mouse Configuration Keys

Key	Action
a	Apply most recent changes
b	Switch to next higher baud rate
c	Toggle ChordMiddle option
d	Toggle ClearDTR option
e	Toggle Emulate3Buttons option
l	Switch to next higher resolution
n	Set the name of the device node
p	Switch to the next protocol listed
r	Toggle ClearRTS option
s	Increase the mouse sample rate
t	Increase the three-button emulation timeout
3	Specify that your pointer has three buttons
4	Specify that your pointer has four buttons
5	Specify that your pointer has five buttons

If your mouse already works with XF86Setup, you might not need to do anything at all, though you should pay attention to the Emulate3Buttons option. If you're not sure whether your mouse is working, try moving it around. The pointer should move as you expect it to and should not suffer from movement glitches or suddenly get stuck in a single location. When you click your mouse buttons, the corresponding buttons in the mouse image on the screen should light up in response.

If your mouse isn't already working with XF86Setup, you're going to need to use the keyboard to navigate this section. The first step is to select a protocol that matches your mouse. There is a long list of protocols represented in the buttons across the top of the section. Nearly all users will find that they are well served by the Microsoft or PS/2 protocols. Users whose PS/2 mice have extended capabilities (such as scroll wheels) might need to choose an extended protocol from the third row whose name matches the name of their pointing device.

The next step is to enter your device node into the device box or to choose your device node from the list below the device box. For most users, the /dev/mouse device will yield best results. If /dev/mouse isn't available, serial mice users will find that their mouse resides either at /dev/ttyS0 (COM1) or /dev/ttyS1 (COM2). Users of PS/2 mice will most often need to select /dev/psaux. For a list of other Linux mouse types, refer to Table 2.1.

If you're not sure about your protocol or mouse port, XF86Setup makes it easy to try several different combinations. Each time you've selected a new combination using your keyboard, press the A key to apply your changes, and XF86Setup will try to activate your mouse. If the mouse still fails to work, you probably need to try still another combination.

A few extra options help to further refine mouse operations inside XFree86. You might need to use one or all of them.

The Emulate3Buttons toggle will be the most common. If your mouse has only two buttons, toggling this option is advisable because it will give you third-button capability. To use the third button on a mouse with this option set, simply click both buttons at the same time.

The ChordMiddle toggle is also common among users of three-button serial mice. If you find that your left and right buttons appear to work, but your middle button doesn't light up the middle mouse button on the display, you should try setting ChordMiddle to see if it will activate your middle button.

If you are unable to get your serial mouse to work properly, you might need to adjust the baud rate or the ClearDTR or ClearRTS flags, which affect the serial port to which your mouse is connected. In most cases, the baud rate should be set to 1200 and both ClearDTR and ClearRTS should not be set, but some mice require these options to be changed.

Users of extended pointing devices, such as those with scroll wheels, should be sure to configure XFree86 to listen for all five buttons in addition to choosing an extended protocol because most such pointing devices send upward and downward scroll motion as clicks on the fourth and fifth buttons, respectively.

Other options such as resolution and sample rate should be adjusted for personal taste. When you have your mouse working just as you want it to, you can proceed to the next section.

Keyboard Configuration

The Keyboard configuration section (see Figure 2.3) presents a fairly self-explanatory set of options. For most users, the keyboard model will be Generic 101 key PC and the language will be US English. If you have an extended keyboard that appears in the list of models or if you will be using a keyboard with a non-English layout while using XFree86, feel free to set the related options accordingly.

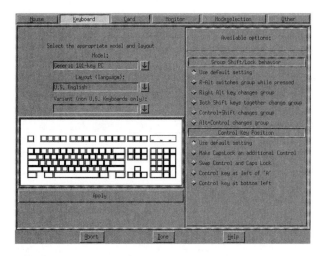

Figure 2.3 Keyboard configuration is fairly straightforward.

The group shift/lock behavior and the control key positioning should probably be left on their default settings unless you know for sure that you want to change them or you discover later that you're uncomfortable with the defaults. For most users, these options won't need to be changed, and choosing options other than the default can lead to confusing keyboard behavior while using XFree86.

Card Configuration

The Card configuration section initially presents an extensive list of supported video cards to choose from, as shown in Figure 2.4.

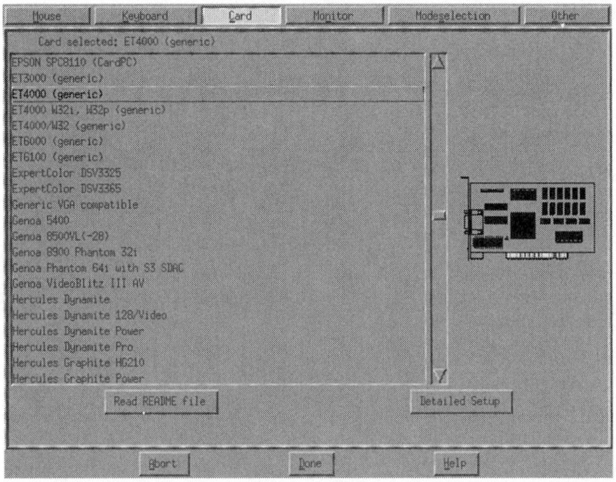

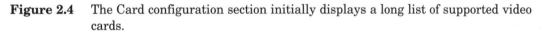

Figure 2.4   The Card configuration section initially displays a long list of supported video cards.

Scroll down the list alphabetically to see if your card is explicitly listed. If it is, you have it easy—just select your card from the list and proceed to the next step. If your card isn't listed, you'll have to pull out some of that research data you compiled about your computer. Specifically, you're looking for your chipset to be listed, either by manufacturer, or by model number. For example, if your chipset was labeled Tseng Labs ET4000AX, you should first look toward the end of the list for Tseng Labs. If you can't find your chipset by manufacturer, just search for the model alone. Entries that have the word generic in parenthesis after them refer to graphics chipsets, so these are the entries you're looking for.

In our example, the ET4000AX chipset isn't listed but the ET4000 is, so we'll choose that one because it seems to be the most similar. Often, there will be several similar matches but no exact match, and you might need to try each of them before finding the one that works for your hardware.

After you've chosen either a video card or a generic video chipset from the list, click the Detailed Setup button to visit the detailed graphics hardware setup screen, shown in Figure 2.5. Before doing anything else, click the Read README File button to get any specific additional instructions that have to do with your graphics chipset or card choice.

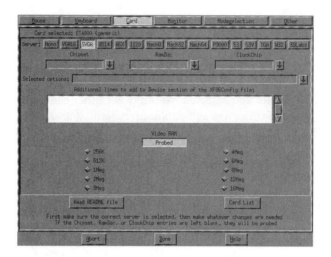
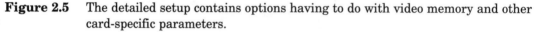

Figure 2.5   The detailed setup contains options having to do with video memory and other
card-specific parameters.

On the second line of the display, in the upper left, is the card or chipset you chose. If you
made a mistake, you can return to the card list at any time by clicking the Card List button
on the lower right.

The third line of the display contains buttons that refer to each of the X servers included with
XFree86. The default server for the card or chipset you specified will already be selected, and
it is normally not a good idea to change this unless you know what you are doing. Below this
line are Chipset, Ramdac, and ClockChip options. Leaving them blank means that XFree86
will autoprobe for them when it starts. For recent graphics chipsets or cards, this is the preferable configuration. However, if your graphics adapter is very old, or if you have trouble starting XFree86, you might need to adjust these values to specifically refer to the chipset, ramdac,
and clock chip on your card.

The Selected Options drop-down list contains a list of options that can be enabled on the X
server selected at the top of the display. Options you select from this list will appear in the
next box immediately below it and will be added to the XFree86 configuration when it is written to disk. Normally, you will not need to enable options, but you might be forced to do so if
you have trouble later on. For specific information about which options you might want to
enable, refer again to the README file for your chipset or card by clicking the Read
README File button.

The lower half of the Detailed Setup screen is dedicated to video memory. Normally, a box labeled Probed is checked, meaning that you haven't specified a value and that XFree86 will attempt to determine how much video memory your card contains each time it starts. In rare cases, this probing will fail, and you will need to re-enter XF86Setup and choose a memory value.

Depending on the card or chipset you selected, you may see other configuration options in the detailed setup as well. Some of these are self-explanatory, others aren't. Generally, if you're unsure, consult the README file. If you're still unsure, leave the options set at their defaults.

Monitor Configuration

The XF86Setup Monitor configuration section is shown in Figure 2.6. Notice that there are no monitors listed by make and model, but only a small list of archetypal monitor groups. Believe it or not, nearly all monitors in existence will be supported well by one of the monitor types in the list.

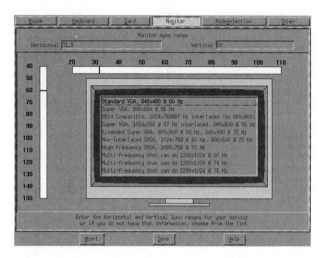

Figure 2.6   The Monitor configuration section lists only a small number of standard monitor types rather than a large list by make and model.

Here you will again need to refer to the research you conducted earlier about the hardware details of your monitor. Try to choose a monitor that closely matches the capabilities of your own monitor without exceeding your own monitor's numbers.

If you're not sure about your monitor's exact capabilities, try to choose based on the most conservative refresh value for the resolution you know your monitor can support. For example, if you know that your monitor can support 800×600 operation, but you don't know what the maximum refresh rate is, choose the monitor in the list that supports 800×600 at the lowest refresh rate.

If you're absolutely unsure about the capabilities of your monitor, just choose the Standard VGA option at 640×480. This is a safe choice because in order to have launched XF86Setup in the first place, your monitor must support at least this mode. Be warned that you should never choose a monitor specification in XF86Setup that you know exceeds the capabilities of your own monitor; doing so could result in an early death for the monitor in question!

Modeselection Configuration

After you have chosen a monitor, you can proceed to the Modeselection configuration, shown in Figure 2.7.

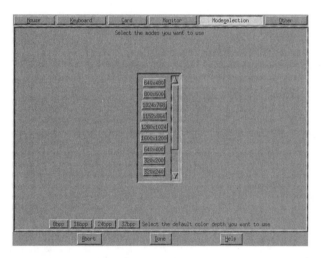

Figure 2.7   The Modeselection configuration enables you to choose modes for XFree86 and a default color depth.

A list of valid display modes (resolutions) will be listed in the main widget in the center of the display. The number of entries in this list will depend on the specifications of the monitor you selected. The better the capabilities of your monitor, the more modes will be available for you to choose from. To enable a mode, click the corresponding button. Click it again to disable it.

The list of modes you select here will all be available to you after you start XFree86, and you'll be able to switch between them on-the-fly while XFree86 is running.

At the bottom of this screen is a list of supported color depths. Choose the one you want to be the default color depth. Beware that some modes might not be available in some color depths, so if you find that your favorite mode isn't available when you first launch XFree86, it probably means that you've selected either too deep a default color depth or that your favorite mode is too high-res!

Other Configurations

The Other configuration screen, shown in Figure 2.8, is the final configuration section in
XF86Setup. This screen lists five toggle options for you to enable or disable.

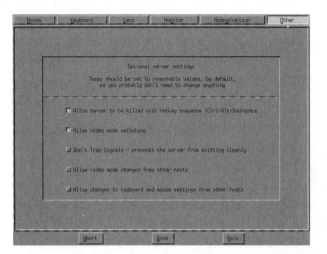
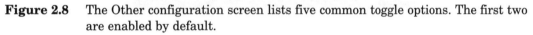

Figure 2.8   The Other configuration screen lists five common toggle options. The first two
are enabled by default.

The first option, Allow Server To Be Killed With Hotkey Sequence decides whether you'll be
able to instantly kill XFree86 at any time by pressing the Ctrl+Alt+Backspace key combination. This is often useful when debugging programs or playing overly resource-intensive games
but can be a problem in a multiuser environment. For most Linux home PCs, this option
should be left checked, just in case.

The next option, Allow Video Mode Switching, decides whether you'll be allowed to switch
between resolutions on-the-fly while XFree86 is running by pressing Ctrl+Alt+<Plus> or
Ctrl+Alt+<Minus>. In most cases, you'll want to leave this option enabled. If you selected only
one video mode in the Modeselection configuration screen, this option will have no effect.

The last three options, Don't Trap Signals, Allow Video Mode Changes From Other Hosts, and
Allow Changes To Keyboard and Mouse Settings From Other Hosts are all rarely useful to the
average user and should probably be left unchecked. The first of the three is useful mainly for
debugging purposes, when server crashes are expected. The second and third options permit
other computers on the network to change aspects of the X desktop on your computer
remotely—rarely something that users want to make possible.

Saving XF86Setup Configuration

After you've gone through each of the six configuration sections and you're ready to write the configuration to disk, click the Done button at the bottom of the display. The screen shown in Figure 2.9 appears, instructing you to click the Okay button if you're really done.

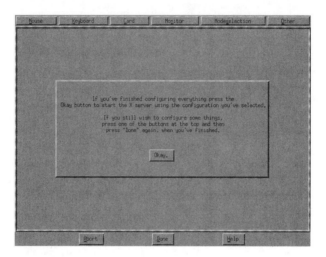

Figure 2.9   After you've clicked Done, click the Okay button to finish XF86Setup or one of the sections across the top to keep configuring.

If you need to go back and make further changes before you're finished, simply click any of the six configuration section buttons across the top of the screen. If you really are finished, click the Okay button, and XFree86 will attempt to start the X server with the configuration options you've specified. If all goes well, the server will start and you'll be presented with a Congratulations screen and three choices: Save the configuration as-is, run xvidtune, or abort.

If the display looks good to you and is properly centered, save the configuration as-is. If the image is off-center, too short, too tall, too narrow, or too wide, choose to run xvidtune now.

Using xvidtune

After starting xvidtune, a rather ugly window will pop up giving a warning about improper use of xvidtune. This warning is absolutely correct and should be heeded. If you incorrectly speci-fied your monitor's capabilities in the XF86Setup monitor section, you'd better press Ctrl+Alt+Backspace now and start the configuration over again; using xvidtune in such circum-stances can definitely blow your monitor, though such occurrences are rare.

If you're confident you selected the correct monitor for you in XF86Setup, click the button labeled OK to remove the warning and continue with xvidtune, as shown in Figure 2.10.

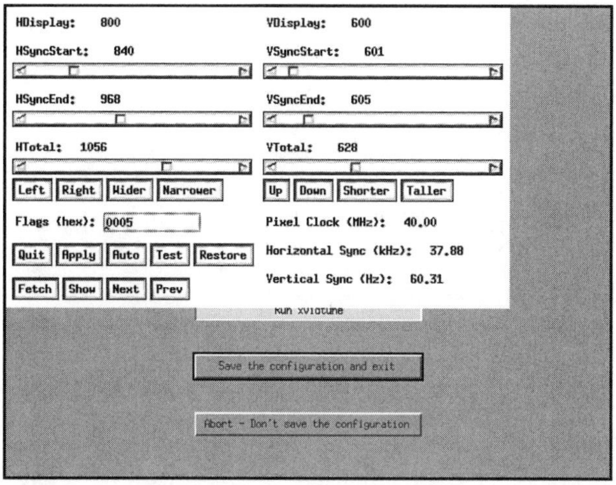

Figure 2.10   The xvidtune utility enables you to adjust your display in all sorts of interesting ways: up, down, left, right, shorter, taller, narrower, or wider.

Use of xvidtune is fairly straightforward. If the image you see on your screen needs to be shifted left or right, made wider or narrower, shifted up or down, or made shorter or taller, simply click the corresponding button. Each time you make a change, clicking the Apply button will cause the changes to take effect. Assuming you correctly configured your monitor in XF86Setup, xvidtune will not allow the display to move in any way that is beyond the monitor's capabilities. If at some point you need to revert to the display's original state and start over again, click the Restore button and then the Apply button in sequence.

After your display is properly sized and centered, choose Quit to close the xvidtune window, and then click the Save the Configuration and Exit button to make your changes permanent and write a final version of the configuration file to /etc/XF86Config.

It is interesting to note that the xvidtune application is obsolete to some degree; many users can bypass xvidtune altogether, making the changes using their multisync monitor's adjustments instead. If you have such a monitor, feel free to make adjustments as needed using monitor controls rather than bothering with xvidtune.

Configuring with xf86config

The xf86config utility is most useful for Linux users whose hardware doesn't support 16-color VGA operation. This includes most users of non-x86 platforms, such as the Motorola m68k or PowerPC users. Even though the xf86config interface isn't as nice as the graphical interface of XF86Setup, xf86config was the only XFree86 configuration tool for years, and it should therefore be perfectly adequate for XFree86 configuration in most cases.

The xf86config utility should be called on a text-based console while logged in as the superuser (in order to be able to write to the systemwide /etc/XF86Config file). It is called like this:

```
/usr/X11R6/bin/xf86config
```

After launching xf86config, you'll be presented with a screenful of information about the utility, telling you what it does and giving a few pointers on what you should have ready before proceeding—things like knowing which graphics chipset your video adapter uses and how much video memory is installed on it. When you're ready to begin configuration, press the Enter key. If you decide for some reason that you're not ready to proceed with the configuration, press Ctrl+C to abort and try again later.

Mouse or Pointer Configuration

After pressing Enter to proceed with the configuration, you'll be presented with the first question screen that asks you to specify the protocol used by your mouse with a list like the following:

```
 1.  Microsoft compatible (2 button protocol)
 2.  Mouse Systems (3 button protocol)
 3.  Bus Mouse
 4.  PS/2 Mouse
 5.  Logitech Mouse (serial, old type, Logitech protocol)
 6.  Logitech MouseMan (Microsoft compatible)
 7.  MM Series
 8.  MM HitTablet
 9.  Microsoft IntelliMouse
10.  Acecad tablet
```

Specify the protocol you decided upon earlier. Again, for most users of serial mice, the Microsoft Compatible option will work. PS/2 mouse users should select the corresponding PS/2 option. Other users will need to consult their mouse's documentation.

After choosing a mouse protocol, many users will be asked whether three-button emulation is desired. If your mouse has only two buttons, it is a good idea to enable three-button emulation, which will allow you to send the middle button click event to applications by pressing both buttons at once. Yes, many Linux programs *do* expect a third, middle button.

The next question asked by xf86config will be about the device name of your mouse. Most of the time, an answer of /dev/mouse will suffice because your Linux distribution will have configured the mouse device for you during install. If you have no such device, enter the device node you chose from Table 2.1. If you have no idea what kind of port your mouse is connected to, perhaps it's time to go out and get a nice, new serial or PS/2 mouse; they are extraordinarily cheap these days.

Old Versus New Keyboard Layout

Next you'll be asked by xf86config whether you want to use the old or the new-style keyboard layout. Unless you know what you're doing and specifically want the old keyboard layout, there's no real reason not to choose the newer method by choosing Y and pressing Enter.

You'll see a screen of text that contains some information about the new keyboard layout method. Read it and then press Enter again to proceed to the next screen, where you'll see a list of predefined keyboards from which you can choose:

```
 1  Standard 101 key, US encoding
 2  Microsoft Natural, US encoding
 3  KeyTronic FlexPro, US encoding
 4  Standard 101 key, US encoding with ISO9995 3 extensions
 5  Standard 101 key, German encoding
 6  Standard 101 key, French encoding
 7  Standard 101 key, Thai encoding
 8  Standard 101 key, Swiss/German encoding
 9  Standard 101 key, Swiss/French encoding
10  None of the above
```

Select the one that most closely matches your keyboard and your needs. For most users, the first choice for a standard 101 key PC-style keyboard will be adequate.

Monitor Configuration

Now you should see a half screen of text explaining that xf86config is about to try to configure settings and resolutions for your monitor. Read the page, and then press Enter to continue. You'll be presented with what looks like a complicated list of horizontal refresh rates to choose from:

```
     hsync in kHz; monitor type with characteristic modes
 1  31.5; Standard VGA, 640x480 @ 60 Hz
 2  31.5 - 35.1; Super VGA, 800x600 @ 56 Hz
 3  31.5, 35.5; 8514 Compatible, 1024x768 @ 87 Hz interlaced (no 800x600)
 4  31.5, 35.15, 35.5; Super VGA, 1024x768 @ 87 Hz interlaced, 800x600 @ 56 Hz
 5  31.5 - 37.9; Extended Super VGA, 800x600 @ 60 Hz, 640x480 @ 72 Hz
 6  31.5 - 48.5; Non Interlaced SVGA, 1024x768 @ 60 Hz, 800x600 @ 72 Hz
 7  31.5 - 57.0; High Frequency SVGA, 1024x768 @ 70 Hz
 8  31.5 - 64.3; Monitor that can do 1280x1024 @ 60 Hz
 9  31.5 - 79.0; Monitor that can do 1280x1024 @ 74 Hz
10  31.5 - 82.0; Monitor that can do 1280x1024 @ 76 Hz
11  Enter your own horizontal sync range
```

If you have a good monitor with good documentation, the job is easy. Just look at the horizontal scan rate before the semicolon and choose the line that matches best. If none of the lines match closely, choose the last option and enter the documented range yourself. Don't attempt to fabricate your own numbers and enter them here! You'll blow your monitor!

If you don't have specific information available about your monitor, it is best to try to match your monitor's English description to one of the English descriptions in the table. If you're still unsure, try consulting the list of common monitor terms in Table 2.3.

Table 2.3   Common Monitor Terms and Matching Capabilities

Term	Capability
VGA (Standard VGA)	640×480 at 60Hz
EVGA (Ergonomic VGA)	640×480 at 67Hz
SVGA (Super VGA)	800×600 at 56Hz
ESVGA	800×600 at 60Hz
Interlaced Super VGA	1024×768 Interlace at 87Hz
XGA	1024×768 at 60Hz
VESA-compliant XGA	1024×768 at 72Hz

If you're still completely unsure about your monitor, the safest thing to do is to choose basic VGA at a resolution of 640×480 and a refresh rate of 60 Hz. Unfortunately, this will give you very little screen real estate to work with.

After you answer the horizontal sync question, you'll be presented with a list of vertical refresh rates to choose from:

```
1  50-70
2  50-90
3  50-100
4  40-150
5  Enter your own vertical sync range
```

Again, if none of these closely match your monitor's documented range, feel free to select the last option and enter the numbers yourself. And it also deserves repeating that you should not attempt to make up your own numbers and enter them. If you are unsure about your monitor's capabilities, choose the first (most conservative) option and go on from there.

After entering the horizontal and vertical sync and refresh rates for your monitor, you'll be asked to input an identifier, a vendor, and a model name for your monitor. This part is easy; enter something memorable, descriptive, and short as an identifier, and then answer the following two questions with the make and model of your monitor. Note that your answers are for your benefit only; they appear in the configuration file xf86config generates so that if you have to edit the configuration file directly, you'll know which sections of the configuration file apply to the monitor in question.

Choosing Your Video Card or Chipset

Now we've come to the most difficult question you'll encounter in xf86config and the one most Linux users have most trouble with. Read the information on the screen, and then type a Y and press Enter to look at the video card database. When the card database begins to display, notice that it is basically a list of video cards, identified by their model name on the left and the video chipset they use on the right. The following is a section of this list:

```
 6  ASUS PCI AV264CT                    ATI Mach64
 7  ASUS PCI V264CT                     ATI Mach64
 8  ASUS Video Magic PCI V864           S3 864
 9  ASUS Video Magic PCI VT64           S3 Trio64
10  AT25                                Alliance AT3D
11  AT3D                                Alliance AT3D
12  ATI 3D Pro Turbo                    ATI Mach64
13  ATI 3D Pro Turbo PC2TV              ATI Mach64
14  ATI 3D Xpression                    ATI Mach64
```

As you can see, the database lists cards in alphabetical order by manufacturer. To proceed to the next page of the database, press Enter all by itself.

If you're lucky enough to find an exact match for your video card's make and model in the list, simply enter the corresponding number and proceed with the rest of the xf86config process. If you proceed all the way to the end of the list without finding your card there by manufacturer, press Enter again to go back to the beginning of the list, and this time watch for the video chipset you found on your video card. For example, if the largest chip on your card is labeled with the painted S3 logo and has the label Vision864 86c864 on it, you'd choose this entry:

```
435  S3 86C864 (generic)                 S3 864
```

If you can't find your card listed by chipset either, you're probably in trouble. You can try similar chipsets to begin with. For example, a Western Digital WD90C26 chip will sometimes work with a WD90C24 driver. An ET4000AX chip will work with the generic ET4000 driver. Still, you're really trying your luck at this point, and it might be time just to go out and get a new video card if at all possible.

Choosing an X Server

After you've selected either a video card or a video chipset for XFree86 to use, it's time to select an X server. The server you want to select the most often, when present, is the last one:

```
 5  Choose the server from the card definition
```

This choice is usually the best because it is based on what XFree86 knows about your graphics hardware. The name of an X server will be listed at the end of this option; if you haven't installed that server, you should select this option and remember to install the matching server after you are finished with xf86config. For installation help, see the section called "Installing XFree86," earlier in this chapter.

If you're sure you need to choose another server, you should do so. Usually when you disagree with XFree86's choice, the only other server you should consider using is the XF86_SVGA server contained in xsvga.tgz, which often contains alternative drivers for certain types of video hardware. The other server choices, XF86_VGA16 and XF86_Mono, are either very limited in capability or work only on special older hardware that is rarely used any longer.

After you've selected a server, xf86config might ask you if you want to create a symbolic link to the new server at /usr/X11R6/bin/X. In almost all cases, this is necessary, and you should choose Y here unless you are absolutely sure that you don't want the new server to operate yet.

Video Card Memory and Identifier

After you've selected the server you want to use, you'll be asked to enter some more information about your video card. The first question you'll be asked has to do with the amount of memory installed on your video card. Choose the amount of memory that matches your card's configuration or select the last option, Other, and input your own number in kilobytes.

The next screen will ask you again for an identifier, a vendor, and a model name, only this time for your video card instead of your monitor. Again, the answers you give here are primarily for your information only should you choose at some point to edit the configuration file by hand. Choose an identifier that is short and easy to remember, and input the vendor and model name at the following two prompts.

Selecting a Ramdac

On the next screen, you'll be given a two-page list of ramdac chips to choose from. It begins like this:

```
1  AT&T 20C490 (S3 and AGX servers, ARK driver)       att20c490
2  AT&T 20C498/21C498/22C498 (S3, autodetected)       att20c498
3  AT&T 20C409/20C499 (S3, autodetected)              att20c409
4  AT&T 20C505 (S3)                                   att20c505
5  BrookTree BT481 (AGX)                              bt481
6  BrookTree BT482 (AGX)                              bt482
```

To see the second page of choices, press Enter all by itself.

Only users of the S3, AGX, W32, and SVGA servers need to pay attention to this question. Other users should enter Q to have XFree86 autodetect their ramdac each time X is launched. Users who do need to answer this question should check the list to see whether it contains the ramdac given by SuperProbe or whether any of the entries in the list match any of the chip names they copied down while looking at their video card physically. If your ramdac isn't listed exactly, the best thing to do is choose Q and attempt to have XFree86 autodetect your DAC each time it starts. Most of the time, XFree86 will get it right if your DAC is supported.

Selecting a Clock Chip

After you've selected your ramdac or elected to have XFree86 try to detect it at launch time, you're asked to select a clock chip for your video card from a similar list:

```
 1  Chrontel 8391                                    ch8391
 2  ICD2061A and compatibles (ICS9161A, DCS2824)     icd2061a
 3  ICS2595                                           ics2595
 4  ICS5342 (similar to SDAC)                         ics5342
 5  ICS5341                                           ics5341
 6  S3 GenDAC (86C708) and ICS5300 (autodetected)    s3gendac
 7  S3 SDAC (86C716)                                  s3_sdac
 8  STG 1703 (autodetected)                           stg1703
 9  Sierra SC11412                                    sc11412
10  TI 3025 (autodetected)                            ti3025
11  TI 3026 (autodetected)                            ti3026
12  IBM RGB 51x/52x (autodetected)                    ibm_rgb5xx
```

The same instructions apply: If an entry in the list matches exactly your clock chip or the markings you copied from looking at your video card, select that entry. If none of them match exactly, or if you're not sure which clock chip to choose, just press Enter to let XFree86 try to autodetect your clock chip when the server starts.

Deciding Whether to Probe Clocks

After you've chosen a clock chip or elected to have XFree86 autodetect yours, xf86config asks if you'd like to have your card probed for valid clocks automatically. This technique is for older video cards that had a limited number of clock generator settings with which to display information.

Virtually no video cards manufactured in the last five years still use old, fixed-clock settings. As a rule of thumb, if your card is an older, unaccelerated VGA or Super VGA ISA-type card with less than a full megabyte of memory, probing for fixed clock rates is a good idea. Otherwise, it shouldn't be done.

If you're unsure, choose N and go on. Even if your card does happen to use fixed clock rates, choosing not to probe for them now just means that XFree86 will end up realizing this about your card and probing for them when you start X.

Choosing Your Resolutions and Color Depths

After deciding whether to have your card's clocks probed, you're finally approaching the end of the xf86config run. You're shown a list of color depths that XFree86 thinks are supported by your card, along with a list of resolutions that your card should be able to display at each depth. The list will look something like this, though the specific numbers and the depths will depend on the capabilities you entered for your video card and your monitor:

```
"640x480" "800x600" "1024x768" "1280x1024" for 8bpp
"640x480" "800x600" "1024x768" for 16bpp
```

```
"640x480" "800x600" for 24bpp
"640x480" "800x600" for 32bpp
```

After this list, you're given the choice to either change the resolutions available for a given color depth or accept the list as-is and use it. For almost all situations, the automatically generated list is correct and should be used.

If you're sure that your monitor supports modes that aren't listed, or that your monitor doesn't support modes that are, you can choose to edit the list of modes for each color depth. Otherwise, choose the last option, These Modes Are OK, to move to the last step of the configuration process.

Writing the Configuration

After finishing with the modes and color depths, you'll be asked if you want to write the configuration to /etc/XF86Config. Normally, you'll answer Y here, unless there is an obvious reason why you shouldn't. Note that if you don't choose to output the configuration to /etc/XF86Config, all the work you've just done won't become active as the new configuration.

If you choose not to write the configuration just generated to /etc/XF86Config, you'll be asked successively about writing it to other locations. If you continue to choose No, you'll eventually be asked where you want to write the configuration you just generated. Again, understand that if you choose not to write the configuration to /etc/XF86Config, it won't become the active configuration until you copy the output to that location.

After you've saved the configuration somewhere, you're finished with xf86config! Whew!

Configuration Troubleshooting

The most common problem encountered while trying to use XF86Setup and xf86config is the failure of the X server to properly start after the initial configuration is saved. There are several possible causes for this problem, but the solution is always the same: Start over with the configuration program in question and try, try again, this time using different settings. Here are some pointers.

At times, you might have to try several different similar chipset settings before you find the chipset that matches yours properly. For example, the Trident chipsets are notorious for being inconsistent in their labeling. Sometimes a TVGA8900 chip really only wants to work with the TVGA9000 driver or vice-versa. If you chose your settings by video card make and model, this won't be a problem nearly as often.

Take time to study the README file for your chipset thoroughly. Those little options might seem innocuous, but they can mean the difference between a properly functioning video card and one that displays nothing at all.

If you've allowed XFree86 to try autodetecting a large number of settings, it may be time to start filling in the blanks. Try explicitly configuring your ramdac, clock chip, and the amount of video memory present on your card. Sometimes the XFree86 probe goes wrong, and a card will work properly only if these settings are explicitly configured.

Make sure that the correct X server has been specified. Did you change the default X server suggested by XF86Setup? Did you forget to create the symbolic link to the X server in xf86config? If so, this is likely the cause of your problems.

Last but not least, simply go over every setting again to make sure that you didn't misclick or mistype anywhere. Just as typos commonly cause problems, so do clicks that missed their mark ever so slightly. A quick double-check can often eliminate hours of hair pulling.

If in the end you are simply unable to get your video card to function properly after hours of work, you have four choices:

■ The first option is to visit newsgroups on Usenet and post your question to a newsgroup such as comp.os.linux.hardware, lt.linux, or comp.os.linux.x. List specifically the make and model of the video card you are trying to use, as well as the version of Linux and the version of XFree86 involved. Perhaps someone else has already had the same problems as you, solved them, and will be willing to share the answer.

■ The second option is to purchase an alternative X11R6 implementation that will support your card explicitly. There are two major alternative X11R6 implementations for Linux users: Accelerated-X, available from Xi Graphics at http://www.xig.com, and Metro-X, available from Metro Link at http://www.metrolink.com.

■ The third option, and probably the easiest in most cases, is to go out and buy a new video card. Computer hardware is ridiculously cheap these days, and you might be surprised to find that you can purchase a video card that is much faster than your current one and is supported by XFree86 for less than it would cost to purchase an alternative X11R6 implementation.

■ The fourth option is to proceed to the next section, "Advanced Configuration," and pound on the configuration text files for a few more hours in an attempt to get your current hardware to work.

Advanced Configuration

Even under the best of circumstances, the automated configuration tools are sometimes inadequate for the job at hand. Most users will find themselves heading for Emacs and the /etc/XF86Config file at one time or another while using Linux. Because it's extremely rare to find anyone willing to build an /etc/XF86Config file by hand anymore, this section makes the assumption that direct editing will be done only on a file that has already been generated using another method, either XF86Setup or xf86config.

/etc/XF86Config Section by Section

The /etc/XF86Config file, sometimes found at /etc/X11/XF86Config and also found every now and then at /usr/X11R6/lib/X11/XF86Config, is a plain text file broken into several sections in a regular format, represented here:

```
Section "ThisSection'sName"
    ConfigEntry [parameters if needed]
    ConfigEntry [parameters if needed]
    ...
    SubSection "ThisSubsection'sName"
       ConfigEntry [parameters if needed]
       ...
    EndSubSection
EndSection
```

Not all sections will have subsections, and not all configuration entries will have parameters. Still, the file manages to look quite regular and is fairly easy to follow when printed out. Sections and configuration entries don't need to follow any particular order, but a convention is generally followed, and the following sections use the same ordering convention. Lines that begin with the hash (#) symbol are comments and are ignored.

This chapter was intended as a section-by-section read along to tweak an existing XF86Config file generated either by XF86Setup or xf86config. Extra details on supporting specific devices or special configuration are included where appropriate. There is so much to configure that a great deal of card-specific and server-specific information has been omitted. Especially when reading about the Device section, please be sure to visit the manual page for your X server and the chipset-specific README files installed by the XFree86 packages in /usr/X11R6/lib/X11/doc.

The Files Section

The Files section of the /etc/XF86Config file is generally found first, and contains configuration options that tell the X server where to find specific files that it needs to operate.

The Files section will almost always look exactly like this after having been generated by programs such as XF86Setup or xf86config:

```
Section "Files"
    RgbPath     "/usr/X11R6/lib/X11/rgb"
    FontPath    "/usr/X11R6/lib/X11/fonts/misc:unscaled"
    FontPath    "/usr/X11R6/lib/X11/fonts/75dpi:unscaled"
    FontPath    "/usr/X11R6/lib/X11/fonts/100dpi:unscaled"
    FontPath    "/usr/X11R6/lib/X11/fonts/Type1"
    FontPath    "/usr/X11R6/lib/X11/fonts/Speedo"
    FontPath    "/usr/X11R6/lib/X11/fonts/misc"
    FontPath    "/usr/X11R6/lib/X11/fonts/75dpi"
    FontPath    "/usr/X11R6/lib/X11/fonts/100dpi"
```

```
    FontPath    "/usr/X11R6/lib/X11/fonts/Symbol"
EndSection
```

Table 2.4 details the configuration options that can be used within the `Files` section of the `XF86Config` file. Each of these options takes a parameter or list of parameters that should be enclosed in a single pair of quotation marks.

Table 2.4 Valid `Files` Section Options

Option	Parameters	Description
FontPath	*pathname*	Sets the search path for fonts that will be available to the X server. The parameter is a comma-separated list of directories or font servers where fonts can be found.
		Adding `:unscaled` to the end of a directory will tell XFree86 not to allow the fonts in that directory to be scaled.
		A server is specified using the format *packet*/*host*:*port* where *packet* is the packet type (usually `tcp`), *host* is the host name of the font server, and *port* is the port that should be queried (usually 7100).
		This option can be used multiple times and each entry will be added to the font path.
RGBPath	*pathname*	Refers to the file containing the RGB color database for the X server. It should not normally need to be changed.
ModulePath	*pathname*	Sets the search path for modules that will be available to the X server. The parameter is a comma-separated list of directories. This option can be used multiple times, and each entry will be added to the module path.
Load	*pathname*	Name of a module to be loaded by the X server at start time. If a full path isn't given, all the directories in the module path will be searched. A complete list of available modules can be found by visiting the `/usr/X11R6/lib/modules` directory.

The `ServerFlags` Section

This section is reserved for several flags or toggles that modify the way in which the X server will behave. It is generally empty in files that have been automatically generated, but the available options are listed in Table 2.5. Most of the time, there is no reason to add any of these options, so it is best to leave them out, unless you are sure that a given option is needed.

Table 2.5 Valid ServerFlags Section Options

Option	Description
NoTrapSignals	This flag allows the X server to core dump on certain errors instead of attempting to trap them. This is generally not desirable behavior unless you are trying to debug an X server before compiling and linking it.
DontZap	This flag doesn't allow the X server to be killed with the Ctrl+Alt+Backspace key combination. Useful in some multiuser situations, but generally bad in a single-user context because it removes the most common method of emergency exit from the X server.
DontZoom	This flag doesn't allow the X server to switch video modes with the Ctrl+Alt+[Plus] and Ctrl+Alt+[Minus] key sequences. Normally there isn't reason to disable these key sequences unless you need to use an X client that is expecting such key sequences.
AllowNonLocalXvidtune	This flag allows connections to this X server from xvidtune clients that aren't running on the local host. There is normally little reason to change this unless the XF86Config file for a given display is residing on another host.
DisableVidMode	This flag disables certain parts of xvidtune that allow the changing of video modes.
AllowNonLocalModInDev	This flag allows clients on other hosts to modify the keyboard and mouse settings of the local server.
DisableModInDev	This flag disables certain parts of the Misc extension that can be used for modifying input device configuration.
AllowMouseOpenFail	This flag starts the server even if the mouse doesn't work, can't be initialized, or seems not to be present. Normally if your mouse isn't working, you don't want the server to start anyway because there is little you can do without a pointing device. Note that enabling both AllowMouseOpenFail and DontZap on machines with only a single virtual console is a recipe for a potential lockout should the mouse go bad.

The Keyboard Section

The Keyboard section configures the X server's keyboard handling, including the protocol that will be used to process keypresses and the keyboard mapping that will be used to interpret them. Table 2.6 shows the valid Keyboard section configuration options.

Table 2.6 Valid Keyboard Section Options

Option	Parameters	Description
Protocol	*protocol*	The name of the keyboard protocol, either Standard or Xqueue, enclosed in a single pair of quotation marks. Xqueue is normally used only in conjunction with the event queue driver on SVR3 and SVR4 systems, and thus, Standard should be specified on Linux systems.
AutoRepeat	*num num*	Two parameters separated by spaces are expected following this keyword. The first is the wait in hundredths of a second before key repeat will begin when a key is held down. The second is the rate of the key repeat. This option works only on keyboards that can accept such input. Most AT and PS/2 class enhanced keyboards can accept such input, but some cannot. Many non-PC Linux platforms will also find this option useless.
ServerNumLock		This flag tells the X server to handle the keyboard NumLock key internally. Might be required if you find that applications don't utilize your 10-key number pad and NumLock keys correctly. Not recommended because it can cause problems with other types of keyboard management.
LeftAlt	*function*	Map the left Alt key to one of the following functions, given as a parameter: Meta (normal Alt behavior), Compose, ModeShift (normal Shift behavior), Mode Lock (normal Caps Lock behavior), Scroll Lock, and Control. The default mapping for the LeftAlt key is Meta.
RightAlt	*function*	Same as LeftAlt but applies to the right Alt key. The default mapping for the RightAlt key is Meta.
ScrollLock	*function*	Same as LeftAlt but applies to the Scroll Lock key. The default mapping for the Scroll Lock key is Compose.
RightCtl	*function*	Same as LeftAlt but applies to the right Ctrl key. The default mapping for RightCtl is Control.
XLeds	*num ...*	Makes the keyboard LEDs available to X clients who are written to take advantage of them. Include a space-separated list of LEDs, numbered 1 to 3, as parameters.

continues

Table 2.6 Continued

Option	Parameters	Description
VTSysReq		This flag enables the alternative method of switching virtual consoles. Instead of using Ctrl+Alt+F*n*, where *n* is the number of the console desired, X will listen for Alt+SYSRQ (the Print Screen key on most PCs) followed by F*n*, where *n* is the number of the console desired. This is normally needed only if you need to use a client that expects the Ctrl+Alt+F*n* sequence.
VTInit	*command*	Runs a command, given as a parameter enclosed in quotes, in a fresh virtual console before the X server is started there. Used when some sort of virtual console initialization is required. Not normally useful for Linux users.
XkbDisable		This flag disables the XKEYBOARD extension.

Further keyboard options have to do with the XKEYBOARD (Xkb) extensions to XFree86 and assume that the XkbDisable flag has not been given. There are two basic ways to use Xkb: the first is by specifying a keyboard model and layout (preferred), and the second is by specifying keyboard parameters directly from the Xkb files, most commonly a keymap file.

The Xkb-related options are given in Table 2.7. For complete details on what each of these options mean, which ones to use and in what order, how to supply them parameters, and how to manage XFree86 keyboard mapping using XKEYBOARD, please see Chapter 7, "Runtime Server Configuration."

Table 2.7 Xkb Configuration Options

Option	Description
XkbRules	Specify a rules file for the XKEYBOARD extension as a single parameter enclosed in quotes. The default is XFree86 and should not normally be changed. Other choices can be found in the rules/ directory.
XkbModel	Specify an alternative keyboard model to use as a single parameter enclosed in quotes. The default is pc101 and should work for just about everybody.
XkbLayout	Specify a keyboard layout to use as a single parameter enclosed in quotes. Most users will be using the default us layout.
XkbVariant	Specify a keyboard variant. The default is no variant, which can be specified with an empty pair of quotes.
XkbOptions	Specify keyboard options. The default is no additional options, which can be specified with an empty pair of quotes.

Option	Description
XkbKeymap	Specify a keymap file to use, enclosed in quotation marks. A common value for US users will be XFree86(us). Other choices can be found in the keymap/ directory.
XkbKeycodes	Specify a set of keycodes to use, enclosed in quotation marks. Choices can be found in the keycodes/ directory.
XkbTypes	Specify keyboard types, enclosed in quotation marks. Choices can be found in the types/ directory.
XkbCompat	Specify the compatibility adaptations file, enclosed in quotation marks. Choices can be found in the compat/ directory.
XkbSymbols	Specify the key-to-symbol mapping file, enclosed in quotation marks. Choices can be found in the symbols/ directory.
XkbGeometry	Specify the geometry (architecture) of your keyboard enclosed in quotes. Choices can be found in the geometry/ directory.

The Pointer Section

The Pointer section contains options that have to do with mice or other pointing devices. This is where the protocol, device node, and other parameters are given. A simplified Pointer section looks like this:

```
Section "Pointer"
    Protocol       "Microsoft"
    Device         "/dev/mouse"
    BaudRate       1200
    Emulate3Buttons
EndSection
```

The first option in the Pointer section is the Protocol option, which deserves a table all its own. In Table 2.8, you'll find a list of all the valid protocols, along with the devices or port types with which they are associated.

Table 2.8   Valid Protocols and Devices/Ports

Protocol	Device or Port
Auto	Attempt to autodetect the mouse type and connection. Not always reliable, and not available on all systems. Note that even when using the Auto protocol, you must still supply the correct Device option.
BusMouse	Use with most bus mice, including those by Logitech, Microsoft, and ATI.
GlidePoint	Use with the serial version of the Alps GlidePoint touchpad pointing device and compatible devices.

continues

Table 2.8 Continued

Protocol	Device or Port
GlidePointPS/2	Use with the PS/2 version of the Alps GlidePoint touchpad pointing device and compatible devices.
IntelliMouse	Use with the serial version of the Microsoft IntelliMouse and compatible devices.
IMPS/2	Use with the PS/2 version of the Microsoft IntelliMouse and compatible devices.
Logitech	Use with older Logitech serial mice. Later Logitech serial mice use the Microsoft protocol.
Microsoft	Use with almost any standard serial mouse produced over the past 5 to 8 years. By far the most common serial mouse protocol in use.
MMHitTab	Use with older Logitech HitTablet series serial port devices.
MMSeries	Use with older Logitech MouseMan series serial port devices.
Mouseman	Use with later Logitech MouseMan series serial port devices.
MouseManPlusPS/2	Use with the PS/2 Logitech MouseMan Plus and compatible devices.
MouseSystems	Use with serial mice that use the Mouse Systems protocol, including many older optical-only mice.
NetMousePS/2	Use with the PS/2 Genius NetMouse and compatible devices.
NetScrollPS/2	Use with the PS/2 Genius NetScroll Mouse and compatible devices.
OSMouse	Use with operating systems that provide their own mouse and click event queue, such as SCO's SVR3 and OS/2.
PS/2	Use with almost any standard PS/2 mouse produced over the past 5 to 8 years. This is easily the second most common protocol choice for Linux and XFree86 users.
SysMouse	Use the FreeBSD system mouse device located at node /dev/sysmouse.
ThinkingMouse	Use with the Kensington Thinking Mouse series serial port devices.
ThinkingMousePS/2	Use with the PS/2 Kensington Thinking Mouse and compatible devices.
Xqueue	Must be specified as the mouse protocol if it was also specified as the keyboard protocol in the Keyboard section.

Aside from the Protocol option, several other options can be specified in the Pointer section. The rest of these options are shown in Table 2.9.

Table 2.9 Other Valid `Pointer` Section Options

Option	Parameters	Description
Device	*pathname*	Specify the pointer device's system device node here enclosed in quotation marks. For most users, this should be /dev/mouse because Linux should have already configured a mouse. If not, use /dev/ttySn for serial devices where *n* is a number from 0–4, or /dev/psaux for PS/2 devices. If you have a bus mouse of some sort, refer to Table 2.1 earlier in this chapter.
Port	*pathname*	Same as the Device option and rarely used.
BaudRate	*num*	Specify the baud rate to use to communicate with the serial pointing device in question. In almost all cases, this should be set to 1200, though some early Logitech mice could communicate at higher rates.
Buttons	*num*	Specify a number here that represents the number of buttons X expects to be able to use with the mouse. Normally set to 3, but can be set higher for scrolling mice who will use the ZaxisMapping option.
Emulate3Buttons		This flag emulates a middle mouse button on a two-button mouse. The user can press the third button by simultaneously pressing the two physical buttons on the device.
ChordMiddle		This flag is for mice whose physical middle button indicates a click event by sending simultaneous left and right click events to the server.
SampleRate	*num*	The given parameter sets the number of events the mouse will send per second. Not supported by most mice.
Resolution	*num*	Specify an alternative number here that sets the resolution in counts-per-inch of the pointing device being used. Some mice don't support this functionality.
ClearDTR		This flag clears the DTR line on the serial port when the X server starts. In conjunction with ClearRTS, allows certain mice to operate in MouseSystems mode.
ClearRTS		This flag clears the RTS line on the serial port when the X server starts. In conjunction with ClearDTR, it allows certain mice to operate in Mouse Systems mode.
ZAxisMapping	X, Y, or *n n*	Accepts one or two space-separated parameters that specify how the imaginary Z axis of motion is mapped inside XFree86. In practice, this is most often used with scrolling mice, where the numbers supplied are 4 and 5 to map scrolling motion inside X applications to the 4th and 5th buttons, or scroll wheel up and down, respectively. Z axis motion can also be mapped to X (horizontal movement) or Y (vertical movement) motion.

The `Xinput` Section

The `Xinput` section is for configuring devices other than the primary mouse to be used by the X server and X clients. Such devices can include graphics tablets, joysticks for playing games, or even a second mouse. Most users will never use the `Xinput` section, and the entire thing is commented out by default, but it exists, just in case.

Many of the devices supported by `Xinput` require extensions in the form of a module to be loaded by the X server in order to function properly. Some devices (such as the joystick) also require kernel-based support.

The `Xinput` section consists of several subsections, one for each device that is to be added to the X server's input capability. Note that only a finite set of devices are supported; if a workable subsection doesn't exist, you can't include it in the `Xinput` section of the `XF86Config` file. The valid subsections are shown in Table 2.10.

Table 2.10   Valid `Xinput` Subsections

Subsection	Extension Driver	Related Device
Joystick	xf86Jstk.so	Joystick device, normally for playing games.
WacomStylus	xf86Wacom.so	Stylus for a Wacom input tablet.
WacomEraser	xf86Wacom.so	Eraser for a Wacom input tablet.
WacomCursor	xf86Wacom.so	Cursor for a Wacom input tablet.
Elographics	xf86Elo.so	Elographics touchscreen display.
SummaSketch	xf86Summa.so	SummaSketch tablet.
Mouse		Extra mice in addition to the primary mouse or pointing device defined in the `Pointer` section earlier.

As can be seen in Table 2.10, most `Xinput` subsections require that a corresponding extension driver module be loaded by the X server, which can be done with the `Load` option in the `Files` section discussed earlier.

Any of the completed subsections, when seen within the `Xinput` section of the `XF86Config` file, will be formed like this:

```
BeginSubSection "subsection"
   Option ["parameters if needed"]
   ...
EndSubSection
```

There can be as many subsections in `Xinput` as are needed to support existing devices. The most common use of `Xinput` for Linux users is for joystick input, so before discussing any of the other input devices, it's a good idea to discuss joystick support.

Before adding a joystick subsection to the XF86Config file, supporting a joystick in Linux first requires that you compile support for a joystick into the kernel, a task beyond the scope of this text. A device node for the joystick must also be in the /dev directory. Because such a node usually doesn't exist by default on most Linux systems, you must create one following Table 2.11.

Table 2.11   Linux Joystick Device Nodes

Device	Command to Make the Device Node
1st analog joystick	mknod /dev/jsa0 c 15 0
2nd analog joystick	mknod /dev/jsa1 c 15 1
1st digital joystick	mknod /dev/jsd0 c 15 128
2nd digital joystick	mknod /dev/jsd1 c 15 129

After the joystick device has been created and joystick support has been compiled into the kernel, the related Joystick subsection can be added to the Xinput section of the XF86Config file using the options in Table 2.12.

Table 2.12   Joystick Subsection Options

Option	Parameters	Description
Port	path	Path to the related joystick device node.
DeviceName	text	Set the name of this device.
TimeOut	num	Set the delay in milliseconds between polls of the driver for new data.
MaximumXPosition	num	Set the maximum x-coordinate position to be reported.
MinimumXPosition	num	Set the minimum x-coordinate position to be reported.
MaximumYPosition	num	Set the maximum y-coordinate position to be reported.
MinimumYPosition	num	Set the minimum y-coordinate position to be reported.
CenterX	num	Set the x-coordinate position to be reported when the device is free-floating (centered).
CenterY	num	Set the y-coordinate position to be reported when the device is free-floating (centered).
Delta	num	Set the maximum movement value to be reported to the X server. When this value is set high, sensitivity will be high. When this value is set low, sensitivity will be low.
AlwaysCore		Assume that the device in question will generate movement and button events for the core X pointer.

Several other less common devices are also supported by XFree86, and some by Linux, most notably the Wacom graphics tablets. Options supported by each of the related subsections are found in Tables 2.13–2.16.

Table 2.13   Subsection Options for All Wacom Subsections

Option	Parameters	Description
Port	*path*	Path to the related serial port device node.
DeviceName	*text*	Set the name of this device.
Suppress	*num*	Don't report movement if it would represent a shift of more than num position units. Useful for filtering out movement noise that shouldn't be processed.
Mode	*function*	Supply either Relative or Absolute in place of function to indicate how position will be interpreted.
TiltMode		This flag enables tilt reporting when supported. When enabled, only one Wacom device can report at a time.
HistorySize	*num*	Set the motion history size, normally zero (no history).
AlwaysCore		Assume all device pointers to be the core pointer, that is, share the core pointer among multiple normal and Xinput devices.
TopX	*num*	Specify the top x-coordinate of the active input zone.
TopY	*num*	Specify the top y-coordinate of the active input zone.
BottomX	*num*	Specify the bottom x-coordinate of the active input zone.
BottomY	*num*	Specify the bottom y-coordinate of the active input zone.
KeepShape		This flag uses the TopX and TopY values, but calculates the bottom values by maintaining the aspect ratio of the input area with respect to the display area.

Table 2.14   Elographics Subsection Options

Option	Parameters	Description
Port	*path*	Path to the device node where the touchscreen input is located.
DeviceName	*text*	Set the name of this device.
MaximumXPosition	*num*	Set the maximum x-coordinate position to be reported.
MinimumXPosition	*num*	Set the minimum x-coordinate position to be reported.
MaximumYPosition	*num*	Set the maximum y-coordinate position to be reported.
MinimumYPosition	*num*	Set the minimum y-coordinate position to be reported.
ScreenNo	*num*	The screen number of the touchscreen display.

Option	Parameters	Description
UntouchDelay	*num*	Specify the number of tens of milliseconds required for the device to assume that an untouch has occurred.
ReportDelay	*num*	Set the delay in milliseconds between polls of the driver for new data.
AlwaysCore		Assume that the device in question will generate movement and button events for the core X pointer.

Table 2.15   SummaSketch Subsection Options

Option	Parameters	Description
Port	*path*	Path to the related SummaSketch device node.
DeviceName	*text*	Set the name of this device.
Mode	*function*	Supply either Relative or Absolute in place of *function* to indicate how position will be interpreted.
Cursor	*function*	Supply either Stylus or Puck in place of *function* to specify how the input functions.
Increment	*num*	Set the maximum movement size before new movement is reported.
HistorySize	*num*	Set the motion history size, normally zero (no history).
AlwaysCore		Assume that the device in question will generate movement and button events for the core X pointer.

The Mouse subsection supports all the options listed earlier in the Pointer section, plus the options in Table 2.16.

Table 2.16   Mouse Subsection Options

Option	Parameters	Description
DeviceName	*text*	Set the name of this device.
AlwaysCore		Assume that the device in question will generate movement and button events for the core X pointer.

The Monitor Section

There can be multiple Monitor sections in the XF86Config file, each referring to a different monitor, but only one will be used on any given run because there is currently no support for multi-head display in XFree86. Each of these sections must begin with Section Monitor and end with EndSection.

This has traditionally been one of the stickiest areas of the XF86Config file because it is here where the XFree86 display modes are defined. *Display modes* are a series of numbers that specify the resolution and refresh rate at which a monitor can display.

Before we get into display modes, let's first go over the other options that can be configured in the Monitor section. These options are shown in Table 2.17.

Table 2.17   Valid Monitor Section Options

Option	Parameters	Description
Identifier	*text*	This is the text string by which this monitor will be identified throughout the rest of the XF86Config file. This text can be anything you like, but it must be reproduced exactly in the Screen section of the file when referring to this monitor.
VendorName	*text*	The name of the vendor that assembled or sold this monitor. This text is for your benefit only and can be anything you like.
ModelName	*text*	The name of the particular model of this monitor. This text is for your benefit only and can be anything you like.
HorizSync	*num-num*	The horizontal sync range supported by this monitor. For example, a typical 1280×1024 60Hz monitor might have a horizontal sync range of 31.5–64.3 kilohertz that should be provided in just this format as a parameter to HorizSync.
VertRefresh	*num-num*	The vertical refresh rate range supported by this monitor. For example, the same monitor mentioned earlier might have a vertical refresh rate range of 60–78Hz that should be provided in just this format as a parameter to VertRefresh.
Gamma	*num* or *n n n*	Either a single number or a composite set of three numbers (one each for Red, Green, and Blue) representing the gamma adjustment for the monitor in question. Not all X servers support this adjustment.

Now that we've covered the other options, it's time to discuss video modes. In many other operating systems, Windows included, several predefined modes are available for use by everyone, and any other modes aren't supported at all. These predefined modes are 640×480, 800×600, 1024×768, 1280×1024, and 1600×1200, usually at either 60Hz or 72Hz refresh rates.

Actually getting the video hardware to display at a specific resolution and refresh rate involves quite a bit of black magic because monitors by nature display information with a swinging electron gun, one line at a time. Traditionally, XFree86 has left such trickery up to the user, providing an interface by which the user can specify his or her own display modes. This interface is through the Mode subsection in the Monitor section of the XF86Config file.

Luckily this older build-your-own mode philosophy, which leaves nearly everyone confused, has been mitigated to some degree by XFree86's recent decision to include a standard set of modes, which means that the construction of display modes now falls soundly outside the scope of this text. Still, the basic format for specifying modes bears repeating. The Mode subsection follows this basic format:

```
Mode "modename"
    DotClock clock
    HTimings display start end total
    VTimings display start end total
    Flags "flag" "flag" "..."
    HSkew skewval
EndMode
```

The DotClock value is the video card clock rate, in megahertz, for this mode. Note that cards with fixed clocks values will have a limited number of dot clocks available. The display, start, end, and total values for the HTimings and VTimings options indicate the displayed number of pixels, scan start, end, and total length values for each scan line, respectively. One Mode subsection exists in the section for each display mode that will be available to the user of this monitor. Valid flags given to the Flags option in the Mode subsection are shown in Table 2.18.

Table 2.18 Valid Flags in the Mode Subsection

Flag	Description
Interlace	Indicates that this mode is interlaced.
DoubleScan	Indicates a mode where each scan line is doubled.
+HSync	Selects a positive horizontal sync polarity.
-HSync	Selects a negative horizontal sync polarity.
+VSync	Selects a positive vertical sync polarity.
-VSync	Selects a negative vertical sync polarity.
Composite	Sends horizontal and vertical sync together as composite sync. This option isn't supported on all video hardware.
+CSync	Selects a positive composite sync polarity.
-CSync	Selects a negative composite sync polarity.

An abbreviated form of the Mode subsection is the mode *line*, which follows this format and is simply inserted as an option into the Monitor section:

```
ModeLine "name" clk hdpy hst hend htot vdpy vhst vend vtot flags
```

There must be at least one valid ModeLine option or one Mode subsection within the Monitor section for XFree86 to be able to display on a monitor.

Here's where some degree of user-friendliness re-enters the picture. XF86Setup and xf86config both create a large number of modelines automatically that roughly match the standard modes most users know about. To illustrate, here is an excerpt from a newly generated XF86Config file's Monitor section:

```
# 640x480 @ 100 Hz, 53.01 kHz hsync
Modeline "640x480"      45.8    640  672  768  864    480  488
➥ 494  530  HSync Vsync
# 1152x864 @ 60 Hz, 53.5 kHz hsync
Modeline  "1152x864"    89.9   1152 1216 1472 1680    864  868
➥ 876  892  HSync -Vsync
# 800x600 @ 85 Hz, 55.84 kHz hsync
Modeline  "800x600"     60.75   800  864  928 1088    600  616
➥ 621  657  HSync -Vsync
# 1024x768 @ 70 Hz, 56.5 kHz hsync
Modeline  "1024x768"    75     1024 1048 1184 1328    768  771
➥ 777  806  hsync -vsync
# 1280x1024 @ 87 Hz interlaced, 51 kHz hsync
Modeline  "1280x1024"   80     1280 1296 1512 1568   1024 1025
➥ 1037 1165 Interlace
```

Dissecting the first mode line above, the mode is called 640×480 and uses a video card clock rate of 45.8 megahertz. The horizontal display, scan start, scan end, and total values are 640, 672, 768, and 864, respectively. The corresponding vertical values are 480, 488, 494, and 530. Both horizontal and vertical sync signals are set to negative polarity. Fortunately, because this mode line is also labeled clearly with a comment, we can see that it is a 640×480 resolution image at a 100Hz refresh rate.

Chances are that your monitor won't support all the modes generated by XF86Setup or xf86config, and XFree86 knows this. Provided you've correctly specified your monitor's horizontal sync and vertical refresh capabilities using the HorizSync and VertRefresh options detailed earlier in this section, XFree86 will automatically pick through the generated list of modes for you, disabling modes your monitor won't support, and enabling the highest refresh rate supported by your monitor for each available mode.

If you need to alter the list of available modes yourself, you can comment out the unwanted lines by inserting a hash (#) character at the beginning of each line. Inserting your own modes can be a rewarding process because it often allows a monitor to display a little more than it otherwise could, for example, at 850×650 rather than 800×600. On the other hand, you can easily blow your monitor trying to create your own modes. Because it is so dangerous and at the same time so difficult to construct a nonstandard mode, we're not going to discuss how to do it here. There is, however, a How-To file for those who are so inclined. "The XFree86 Video Timings How-To" by Eric S. Raymond can be found with the rest of the Linux Documentation Project How-To documents at http://metalab.unc.edu/LDP/HOWTO/.

The Device Section

The Device section is where all the graphics hardware on your video card gets configured. There can be multiple Device sections in the XF86Config file, each referring to a different graphics adapter, but only one will be used on any given run because there is currently no support for multihead display in XFree86.

Because the graphics hardware is the most easily detected aspect of an X console, many of the options in the Device section are optional, used only when autodetection fails. It is generally a good idea only to specify explicitly as many options as you must to get X to operate properly and to allow the rest of the settings to be autodetected.

Many of the Device section options listed in Table 2.19 are also chipset- or server-specific, so please check the README or manual page for the related server or chipset to see if a given option is supported in your case.

Table 2.19 Valid Device Section Options

Option	Parameters	Description
Identifier	text	This is the text string by which this video card will be identified throughout the rest of the XF86Config file. This text can be anything you like, but it must be reproduced exactly in the Screen section of the file when referring to this video card.
VendorName	text	The name of the vendor who assembled or sold this video card. This text is for your benefit only and can be anything you like.
ModelName	text	The name of the particular model of this video card. This text is for your benefit only and can be anything you like.
Chipset	text	Use this option to explicitly specify the graphics chipset that this video card uses. A complete list of supported chipsets in XFree86 and the related servers can be found in Appendix B, "XFree86 3.3.5 Details."
Ramdac	text	Use this option to explicitly specify the ramdac that this video card uses. For a list of ramdacs supported by your chipset, please see the chipset README in /usr/X11R6/lib/X11/doc or the manual page for your X server.
DacSpeed	num	Use this option to explicitly specify the ramdac speed, in megahertz.

continues

Table 2.19   Continued

Option	Parameters	Description
Clocks	*num num ...*	Use this option to explicitly provide a list of clock speeds supported by this video card. More than one Clocks option can be specified if necessary because the list of clocks will contain all listed clocks. Use this option only when you understand that it is necessary; most current video cards use a clock generator that can be programmed to any clock rate, making this option obsolete.
ClockChip	*text*	Use this option to explicitly specify the programmable clock chip present on this video card. For a list of clock chips supported by your chipset, please see the chipset README in /usr/X11R6/lib/X11/doc or the manual page for your X server.
ClockProg	*textnum*	Run the given command to set the clock generator's speed rather than using the internal XFree86 code. The command is passed two arguments, first the needed clock rate, second the index of the rate in the Clocks list. The command is run with the real users UID and GID, with stdin and stdout set to the graphics console. The optional numeric parameter indicates the clock rate that should be set on server exit or VT switch to restore proper text mode display.
Option	*text*	Set any number of card-related options. Many of these options are the easiest way to fix a broken display. Due to the sheer number of available options, they aren't listed here. Please see the README documentation for your graphics chipset.
VideoRam	*num*	Use this option to explicitly specify the amount of video memory present on your graphics card in kilobytes.
BIOSBase	*address*	Use this option to explicitly specify the video BIOS base address for your video card. This option is sometimes needed for esoteric or onboard graphics hardware that places the video BIOS at nonstandard locations. The BIOS address should be given in the 0xFFFFFF format.
MemBase	*address*	Use this option to explicitly specify the memory base address for your video card.
IOBase	*address*	Use this option to explicitly specify the input/output base address for your video card.
DACBase	*address*	Use this option to explicitly specify the ramdac base input/output address for your video card.

Option	Parameters	Description
POSBase	*address*	Use this option to explicitly specify the POS base input/output address for your video card. This option is used only by the AGX server.
COPBase	*address*	Use this option to explicitly specify the COP base input/output address for your video card. This option is used only by the AGX server.
VGABase	*address*	Use this option to explicitly specify the VGA memory base address for your video card.
Instance	*num*	This option specifies the Instance of the graphics chip in question. When multiple chips of the same type are present in the system, this option specifies which one should be used.
Speedup	*text*	This option enables a number of server "speedups" that are server- and chipset-dependent.
S3MNAdjust	*num num*	This option allows some S3 chipset memory timing parameters to be retuned from defaults. This option is rarely used.
S3MClk	*num*	This option allows the memory clock to be explicitly set on S3 805i, 864, and Trio chipset cards. This option should not normally be used with an S3 Gendac or a Trio64.
S3RefClk	*num*	This option allows the PLL reference clock in cards that use the IBM RGB5xx series ramdacs to be explicitly specified.

The Screen Section

The Screen section is generally the final section in the XF86Config file. The purpose of the Screen section is to establish a number of defaults, including the monitor and video cards specified in earlier sections that should be used, the color depths available, the resolutions legal for each color depth, and the virtual desktop size. A well-formed Screen section should be structured as follows:

```
Section "Screen"
   Driver "type"
   Device "card identifier"
   Monitor "monitor identifier"
   DefaultColorDepth bpp
   ...
   SubSection "Display"
      Depth bpp
      Modes "modename" "modename" "..."
      ...
   EndSubSection
   SubSection "Display"
      Depth bpp
```

```
    Modes "modename" "modename" "..."
    ...
EndSubSectionEndSection
```

The options supported by the Screen section are shown in Table 2.20. Note that there can be multiple Screen sections in an XF86Config file, but at this point, only one of them will be used.

Table 2.20   Valid Screen Section Options

Option	Parameters	Description
Driver	*text*	The driver should be one of FBDev, Accel, Mono, SVGA, VGA2, or VGA16. Screen sections that use the VGA2 or VGA16 driver will be used when the XF86Config file is read by the 16-color VGA server. Mono is for the monochrome server. Screen sections using SVGA as a driver will be used when starting the SVGA server. The FBDev driver will be used for the FBDev servers, found most commonly on 68K or PPC Linux machines. Sections that use the Accel driver will be used when any other server is started. At least one Screen section with a driver that matches your server must be present in the XF86Config file.
Device	*text*	Here you must specify the same text string you gave the Identifier option when configuring your video card in the Device section. If more than one Device section is present, this Screen section refers to the video card with the matching identifier.
Monitor	*text*	Here you must specify the same text string you gave the Identifier option when configuring your monitor in the Monitor section. If more than one Monitor section is present, this Screen section refers to the monitor with the matching identifier.
DefaultColorDepth	*num*	Specify the default color depth for this Screen section in bits per pixel. If no color depth is specified when X is launched, this is the color depth that will be used. Legal values are 1, 2, 4, 8, 15, 16, 24, and 32. Not all values are legal for all servers or video cards.
ScreenNo	*num*	Not currently very useful for Linux system, this option, when included in all Screen sections, overrides the default screen numbering in multiheaded configurations. Because multiheaded operation isn't currently supported by XFree86 in Linux, this option is relatively useless.

Option	Parameters	Description
BlankTime	*num*	Sets the inactivity screen-blanking timeout for this screen, in minutes.
StandbyTime	*num*	Sets the inactivity DPMS standby timeout, in minutes. Requires a DPMS-compatible monitor and the power_saver option to be set on supported servers.
SuspendTime	*num*	Sets the inactivity DPMS suspend timeout, in minutes. See StandbyTime for restrictions.
OffTime	*num*	Sets the inactivity DPMS power-off timeout, in minutes. See StandbyTime for restrictions.

Multiple Display subsections are normally included in a given Screen section, one subsection for each color depth supported by the video hardware to which the Screen section applies. The keywords that might appear in a Display subsection are shown in Table 2.21.

Table 2.21   Valid Display Subsection Options

Option	Parameters	Description
Depth	*num*	The depth, in bits-per-pixel, to which this particular Display subsection applies. At least one subsection with a Depth option matching runtime display depth must exist or the server will abort.
Weight	*num*	The color weighting to use when running in 16 bits-per-pixel mode. Values supported are 555 or 565, which is the default.
Virtual	*num num*	Specify the size of the virtual desktop, in pixels, x-coordinate by y-coordinate. This size must be larger than the largest display mode configured for this screen at this color depth. If this option isn't supplied, the largest resolution supported at this depth will be used as the virtual desktop size.
ViewPort	*num num*	Specify the initial upper-left corner of the viewable area of the display on a virtual desktop that is larger than the display. If this option isn't supplied, the viewable area will be centered on the virtual desktop.
Modes	*text ...*	Specify the valid display modes for this screen at the display depth specified in this subsection. The names of the modes are the same names given in the Monitor section that is associated with this Screen section.

continues

Table 2.21 Continued

Option	Parameters	Description
InvertVCLK	text num	Reverse the default VCLK state for the given mode, or switch it explicitly on and off by supplying either 0 or 1 as the second parameter. Applies only to the S3 Accel server.
EarlySC	text num	Reverse the default EarlySC setting for the given mode, or switch it explicitly on and off by supplying either 0 or 1 as the second parameter. Applies only to the S3 Accel server.
BlankDelay	text num num	Alter the default blank delay only for the mode given. Applies only to the S3 Accel server.
Visual	text	Explicitly set the root window visual type with one of StaticGray, GrayScale, StaticColor, PseudoColor, TrueColor, or DirectColor (for 1bpp, 4bpp, or 8bpp displays), or TrueColor (for 15bpp, 16bpp, 24bpp, and 32bpp displays). This option is normally not specified, and using the default value, which is chosen based on color depth, is advisable.
Option	text	Apply driver-specific options, as found in the Device section earlier, but apply them only on this screen, at the depth specified in this subsection.
Black	n n n	Specify the red, green, and blue values for the black color when using the monochrome server.
White	n n n	Specify the red, green, and blue values for the white color when using the monochrome server.

Using Framebuffer Consoles and Servers

Until recently, the only way to use XFree86 with a PC was with one of the card-specific drivers inside any of the Accel servers or the SVGA server. If your video card wasn't explicitly supported by XFree86, you were out of luck. With kernel version 2.2, however, Linux has implemented a kernel-based framebuffer device, not unlike the console framebuffer devices available on 68K Linux machines or PowerPC Linux machines.

Instead of using a card-specific driver within XFree86, the new Linux VESA framebuffer console enables the user to have the Linux kernel drive a VESA 2.0 compliant video card using generic VESA modes. The XFree86 framebuffer server can then be run on the graphics console provided by the Linux kernel, instantly supporting many cards that aren't yet supported by XFree86 directly, including cards like the 3DFX Voodoo Banshee cards and newer 3D trident cards. Most PCI video cards are VESA 2.0 compliant, and nearly all AGP video cards are.

Enabling the Framebuffer Console

Enabling the framebuffer console is a two-step process. The first step is a recompilation and reinstallation of the Linux kernel. Although recompilation of the Linux kernel in total is beyond the scope of this book, specific notes on where to find the consoles aren't.

When using the `make xconfig` method of compiling the kernel, the Console Drivers panel shown in Figure 2.11 can be displayed by clicking the Console Drivers button on the main `xconfig` panel.

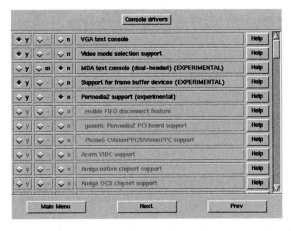

Figure 2.11   The Console Drivers panel is used to enable support for the VESA framebuffer device.

To enable the VESA framebuffer device, the option labeled Support for Frame Buffer Devices should be set to y. Then, scroll down approximately two windows until you can locate the option labeled VESA VGA Graphics Console, which should also be set to y. The Console Drivers panel can now be closed, and when the kernel is compiled, the VESA framebuffer will be ready to act.

When using the more mundane `make config` of compiling the Linux kernel, you must take care first to answer y to the very first question:

```
Prompt for development and/or incomplete code/drivers
➥(CONFIG_EXPERIMENTAL) [Y/n/?]
```

This is because the framebuffer consoles are still considered experimental code. Not to worry—in typical Linux fashion, they have proven stable and reliable in everyday use. After the first question, proceed with normal configuration until you reach the following point (preceding lines provided for context):

```
*
* Console drivers
*
VGA text console (CONFIG_VGA_CONSOLE) [Y/n/?] y
Video mode selection support (CONFIG_VIDEO_SELECT) [Y/n/?] y
MDA text console (dual headed) (EXPERIMENTAL) (CONFIG_MDA_CONSOLE) [N/y/m/?]
Support for frame buffer devices (EXPERIMENTAL) (CONFIG_FB) [N/y/?] y
```

To fully enable the console framebuffer, you must enable both Video Mode Selection Support and Support for Frame Buffer Devices. Two questions later, you should also answer Yes to

```
VESA VGA graphics console (CONFIG_FB_VESA) [N/y/?]
```

Again, proceed with configuration normally, and when you're finished and have recompiled, the VESA console driver will be included in the new kernel.

After the VESA console driver has been compiled into the Linux kernel, you must boot into a display of the resolution and color depth you want to use under X. This is done by first creating framebuffer console devices nodes with major 29, minor 0 at /dev/fb0 and /dev/fb0current:

```
mknod /dev/fb0 c 29 0
ln -s /dev/fb0 /dev/fb0current
```

Then, edit the /etc/lilo.conf file and either replace your current vga= line or add a vga= line using the table of VESA console resolution/depth identifiers shown in Table 2.22, taken from the Documentation/fb/vesafb.txt file off the Linux kernel source tree. Note that these numbers will not show up when booting with vga=ask even though they are valid.

Table 2.22   VESA Framebuffer VGA Modes

640×480 Modes	800×600 Modes	1024×768 Modes	1280×1024 Modes
769 (8bpp)	771 (8bpp)	773 (8bpp)	775 (8bpp)
784 (15bpp)	787 (15bpp)	790 (15bpp)	793 (15bpp)
785 (16bpp)	788 (16bpp)	791 (16bpp)	794 (16bpp)
786 (24bpp)	789 (24bpp)	792 (24bpp)	795 (24bpp)

If you prefer not to edit your /etc/lilo.conf file, you can generally specify the vga= option at boot time to the LILO boot: prompt like this:

```
LILO Boot: linux vga=792
```

This boot option, for example, would boot Linux into a 1024×768 graphics screen at 16.7 million colors (24 bits per pixel). It is a little clumsy to have to specify the graphics mode each time you boot, so it's recommended that you edit and update your LILO configuration. Note that you must boot into a VESA graphics mode in order to use the X framebuffer server with the VESA console.

Using the Framebuffer Console with XFree86

To start X on the framebuffer console, you must first have installed the framebuffer X server (see the list of XFree86 components in Chapter 1. After the framebuffer server from XFB.tgz is installed at /usr/X11R6/bin/XF86_FBDev, be sure to create the symbolic link to /usr/X11R6/bin/X:

```
rm /usr/X11R6/bin/X
ln -s /usr/X11R6/bin/XF86_FBDev /usr/X11R6/bin/X
```

Then, generate a basic XF86Config file using either XF86Setup or xf86config. Configure everything as you normally would, but don't spend any time on the graphics device section. Either select no graphics chipset or select any of them—it doesn't matter because the Device and Screen sections of the resultant XF86Config file will be replaced entirely. After the file has been generated, use a text editor such as Emacs or vi to remove all the Device and Screen sections from the file. After the existing Device and Screen sections have been removed, append the following framebuffer-friendly sections to the end of the file:

```
Section "Device"
    Identifier      "Console Framebuffer"
EndSection

Section "Screen"
    Driver          "FBDev"
    Device          "Console Framebuffer"
    Monitor         "(monitor identifier)"
    SubSection "Display"
        Modes       "default"
    EndSubSection
EndSection
```

Be sure to replace the parameter supplied to the (monitor identifier) with the identifier you chose for your monitor while configuring if you used xf86config, or with the text *Primary Monitor* if you used XF86Setup to generate the file.

After these changes have been made, your XFree86 installation should be ready to go, and you can proceed to the rest of the chapters in this book!

## PART II

STARTING AND USING XFREE86

3

LAUNCHING XFREE86

After XFree86 has been installed, the most fundamental way to launch X is to start the X server on the command line by itself. To start the X server alone, type the following command from a text console:

```
/usr/X11R6/bin/X
```

If you're not logged in as root, you'll need to start the server using the security wrapper, like this:

```
/usr/X11R6/bin/Xwrapper
```

When the X server is started in this way, it will read the XF86Config file either from /etc or /usr/X11R6/lib/X11 and start using the greatest possible resolution at the default color depth given in the file. The server displays a hatch pattern background and an X-shaped cursor, as shown in Figure 3.1. For a complete list of supported command-line options, see the manual page for X server.

Figure 3.1   The X server alone doesn't provide much functionality.

Several options are commonly supplied to the X server when starting it. The most common of these are shown in Table 3.1.

Table 3.1   Common X Server Command-Line Options

Option	Description
c *n*	Enable key-click using volume *n* (1–100). Enabling this will cause key presses to generate a clicking sound.
-bestRefresh	Choose the best refresh rate for the initial display mode rather than the highest resolution.
-bpp *n*	Launch at *n* bits per pixel rather than the default specified in the XF86Config file (or, if absent, 8 bits per pixel).
-bs	Disables backing store. This will reduce memory usage at the expense of redraw time.
-dpi *n*	Sets the monitor's dots-per-inch to *n*, normally 75. This option can be used to affect the font size; larger dots-per-inch settings will lead to larger default fonts.

3

LAUNCHING XFREE86

After XFree86 has been installed, the most fundamental way to launch X is to start the X server on the command line by itself. To start the X server alone, type the following command from a text console:

```
/usr/X11R6/bin/X
```

If you're not logged in as root, you'll need to start the server using the security wrapper, like this:

```
/usr/X11R6/bin/Xwrapper
```

When the X server is started in this way, it will read the XF86Config file either from /etc or /usr/X11R6/lib/X11 and start using the greatest possible resolution at the default color depth given in the file. The server displays a hatch pattern background and an X-shaped cursor, as shown in Figure 3.1. For a complete list of supported command-line options, see the manual page for X server.

Figure 3.1 The X server alone doesn't provide much functionality.

Several options are commonly supplied to the X server when starting it. The most common of these are shown in Table 3.1.

Table 3.1 Common X Server Command-Line Options

Option	Description
c n	Enable key-click using volume n (1–100). Enabling this will cause key presses to generate a clicking sound.
-bestRefresh	Choose the best refresh rate for the initial display mode rather than the highest resolution.
-bpp n	Launch at n bits per pixel rather than the default specified in the XF86Config file (or, if absent, 8 bits per pixel).
-bs	Disables backing store. This will reduce memory usage at the expense of redraw time.
-dpi n	Sets the monitor's dots-per-inch to n, normally 75. This option can be used to affect the font size; larger dots-per-inch settings will lead to larger default fonts.

Option	Description
`(-)dpms`	Depending on whether this option is prefixed with a dash (-) character, it will either enable or disable VESA DPMS monitor control.
`-query h`	Contacts host *h* for an XDMCP session. More on managing XDMCP sections can be found in Chapter 15, "Working on the Network."
`-su`	Disables save-unders support. This will reduce memory usage at the expense of redraw time.
`-weight nnn`	If launching at 16 bits per pixel, start with the specified color weight (replace *nnn* with either 555 or 565).

After experimenting for a moment in the X server, you'll notice that there doesn't really seem to be much user-oriented functionality built into it. Without clients, the X server alone is practically useless for most purposes.

Launching with xinit

So how does one start some clients? Normally, the first client that should be started is the *window manager*, a client that can be used to launch other clients and manipulate their appearance on the desktop.

By far the most common way to start the X sever along with at least a window manager client is to use the xinit scripts. The default xinit script is kept at /usr/X11R/lib/X11/xinit/xinitrc. To start using the xinitrc script, issue a different command from a text-based console. In general, the command used to launch XFree86 using xinit is startx and is called without options:

```
$ startx
```

If you have trouble using startx, you might need to add the path to XFree86 and try the command again:

```
$ export PATH=$PATH:/usr/X11R6/bin
$ startx
```

Calling startx in this way will start the X server at the default resolution and color depth and then call the xinitrc script to start X clients—usually at least one terminal window and a window manager—which can be used to manipulate the desktop or start other applications (see Figure 3.2). In the default XFree86 distribution, the window manager started will be twm, a minimal but fast window manager that remains the favorite of many veteran UNIX users. Other Linux distributions can be configured to start other window managers and applications when startx is called.

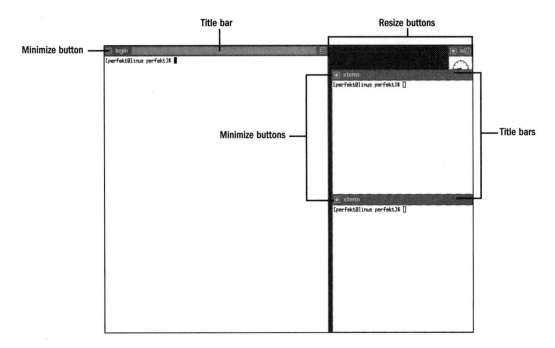

Figure 3.2   The default desktop as supplied by XFree86. Your default desktop can vary if
your XFree86 installation came as a part of a Linux operating system.

Note that startx normally starts the X server using the XF86Config and server defaults.
Occasionally, startx is called in such a way as to pass arguments to the X server, such as those
listed earlier. This is done by providing two dashes (--) as an argument to startx, followed by
any arguments that should be sent to the X server. The most common option used when starting this way is the -bpp option, which determines color depth:

```
$ startx -- -bpp 16
```

Note that not all servers or video hardware support all color depths. All the options given in
Table 3.1 can be used this way, as well as can the option given in the X server manual page. In
addition, several other server arguments can be valid for your specific server. For information
on server-specific arguments, consult the manual for your X server, for example:

```
$ man XF86_SVGA
$ man XF86_S3
$ man XF86_VGA16
```

X Desktop Components

It's now time to look at the basic components of the X desktop and who owns and controls what. You've already seen the X server running alone, and if you've started X using startx, you're now looking at the X desktop.

X Server and Root Window

In fact, whenever you're in XFree86, what you're really looking at, in the most basic sense, is the X server because everything that is displayed on the screen is displayed by the X server. A related concept, the *root window*, is the basic desktop area, which lies behind or under any applications or even the cursor. In the default XFree86 distribution, it is visible as a large area in a black-and-white hatch pattern by default. In other distributions included with Linux operating systems, the root window is a solid color by default.

The root window concept is important because, in X, the root window "owns" all other windows. In X, all windows (children) are owned by another window. Although there might be cases in which such ownership runs five or six levels deep (Window A owns Window B owns Window C owns Window D), ownership can always be traced back, in the end, to the root window, which is the most fundamental window in the tree. The root window cannot be closed without exiting XFree86, and conversely, stopping the X server closes the root window.

The root window is generally not "decorated" by the window manager or other utilities. That is to say that the root window never appears with a title, border, or any buttons with which to resize it. The root window is fundamentally the size of the virtual desktop (which is often also the size of the display resolution) in use and is also always "in back." It is possible, however, to decorate the root window in other ways—for example, by causing it to display an image (a process known as wallpapering by most users), a solid background color, or an animation. A few select applications can also take command of the root window and use it as a forum for interaction with the user.

Window Manager

The Window Manager can be visible at any given time. The window manager isn't an application in the typical sense of the word; instead, it is a program that is responsible for the creation and management of *child* (that is, nonroot) windows. Normally, whenever an XFree86 server is running, a window manager will also be running. Most users don't have the tenacity or the patience to try to run an X session and applications without an active window manager to aid in human interaction. You can most easily see that a window manager is active by checking the process list. When the default XFree86 desktop is running, this means issuing the following command:

```
$ ps ax ¦ grep twm
```

should return the process number of the window manager that is currently controlling the X desktop. In various Linux distributions' default X desktop, you might check for fvwm, fvwm2, kwm, or any number of other common window manager names. The XFree86 default twm window manager is an older window manager that is distributed with the X.Org X11R6 distribution. It is small and fast and still preferred by many hardcore UNIX users. It can at times, however, be less than friendly.

The best visual evidence that you'll see of the window manager's presence is the title bar across the tops (or, for some managers, the sides) of active windows. On the default XFree86 desktop, the xterm windows are decorated by the window manager with a sea-green title bar that contains the word *xterm* along with a couple of buttons (refer to Figure 3.2). On the left is a small square button with a circle in it. This is the *minimize* button. On the right is a small square button with some right angles in it. This is the *resize button*.

It is the window manager's job to decorate application windows with such a border, title bar, and buttons that are linked to certain functions. The functions linked to these buttons are such functions as window resizing, maximizing, killing, or minimizing—all necessary functions for a friendly desktop. It is the window manager's job to "listen" to these buttons for events and then cause such events to actually occur.

For example, a given X application might request that a window be created in which a graph can be displayed. The window manager responds by creating a set of decorations for the window, including a title, in this case something like "Graph," a border, and a button in the upper-right corner that can resize the window.

If the user clicks the resize button created by the window manager, the window manager will interact with the user, for example by drawing a "rubber band" as the mouse moves to indicate the updated size of the window. When the user selects a new size, usually by releasing the button, the window manager sends a request to the application indicating that the window's size has changed. The application responds by redrawing its content to fit the window's new size, and the window manager updates the title bar and border to match.

Window managers commonly create a few of their own windows as well in response to user events, most commonly in the form of menus that are displayed when a user clicks a certain area of the root or another window or decoration. For example, in the default twm window manager using the default configuration, right-clicking any part of the root window will cause twm to display a window containing several options from which you can select (see Figure 3.3).

Window managers also typically provide a means by which to "launch" certain X clients without having to explicitly run their binaries on the command line. Sometimes, such launch mechanisms are provided as menus, just as the menu seen in the default twm configuration when the mouse is right-clicked in the root window. Other window managers provide more explicit application launching functionality, such as the dock in the popular Window Maker window manager.

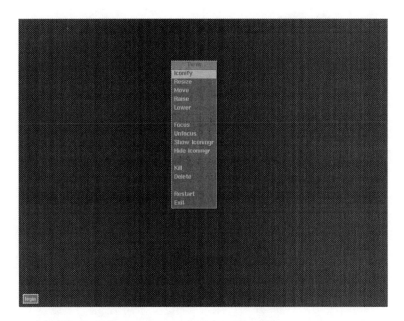

Figure 3.3   The default twm menu as supplied by XFree86.

Most X window managers are programmed with a certain clearly defined set of capabilities and behaviors that can then be enabled, disabled, or personalized by the user based on his or her own preferences. The most common forum for such configuration is a *dotfile*, a text-based configuration file that contains a configuration language known only to the window manager in question. This approach adds a great deal of complexity to the maintenance of a graphical user interface when compared to the fixed-functionality and fixed-appearance approaches of Windows or the Mac OSes, but it also adds a great deal of flexibility.

Applications

Most applications on an X desktop are easily identifiable; they appear as windows that usually contain some sort of information, data, or that allow some sort of user interaction. On the default XFree86 desktop, the applications can be thought of as any window areas that aren't the root window, mouse cursor, or window manager decorations.

The automatically launched login and xclock windows shown in Figure 3.4 are examples of just such application windows. Note that the window has been decorated by the window manager with a title bar, border, minimize, and resize buttons.

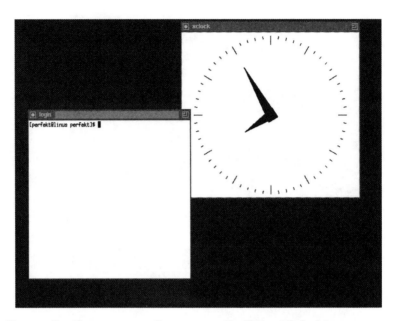

Figure 3.4   Two applications, login and xclock, on the XFree86 desktop.

Most applications will appear in the same way the xterm windows do—with a single, large, rectangular work area that is capable of accepting both keyboard input and mouse input in some way. Windows that aren't interactive in this way sometimes don't normally accept focus because there is no way to interact with them anyway.

Similarly, not all application windows must be decorated by the window manager. Indeed, it is sometimes desirable to leave application windows undecorated, and many window managers offer the capability to specify a set of windows that is to be left undecorated, most commonly meaning without a title bar or resize and minimize buttons. Some window managers also allow for decoration styles that can be applied to entire classes of applications.

The most common class of undecorated windows are known as *transient windows*, which are windows designed only to appear for a moment in order to interact with the user by accepting input or providing some sort of message. Common transient windows include some forms of drop-down menus, untitled dialog boxes asking for some sort of decision on the part of the user, and help windows. When an application is displaying a transient window, the application's main window will usually become inactive until the transient has been dismissed or dealt with. Note that though transients are generally undecorated, some window managers can be told to decorate them anyway, and they will do so happily.

Not all X applications even display inside a single large window. Some of them (such as the dock applications used by the Window Maker window manager) display information in their minimized state to an icon or similar window manager widget. Other applications open multiple active windows when they start; a common example of such an application is the WordPerfect 8 for Linux application, which starts both a document window and a program window when launched, both of which are active, neither of which is transient.

Widgets and More

The term *widget* has many historical meanings and additionally several meanings in the computing industry. In this text, however, the term refers to a visually distinct item or component on the screen with a well-defined set of properties.

Widget Basics

Examples of widgets include such things as the title bar, the minimize and resize buttons, pull-down menus, and even the large text-entry area in an xterm window.

Generally, the functionality of a widget is consistent across all instances of the widget. For example, the window resize button in twm will allow the user to resize the window no matter which window's resize button is being discussed. Furthermore, the resize button will always behave in a consistent manner regardless of which window's resize button the user is attempting to use.

Some widgets have variable functionality or appearance but still retain some measure of consistency across all instances of the widget. For example, a drop-down menu might have four choices or twelve; there can be any number of submenus, and one drop-down menu can contain options dealing with file access, whereas another contains choices related to buffer editing. Still, in an intuitive way, all drop-down menus behave in the same way: they drop down (appear) in response to a user click, present a list of single-line choices, and then take action based on the line selected.

It is also important to note for academic purposes that, in X, most widgets are windows of some type as well. The process for constructing a drop-down menu involves the creation of a child window and then the drawing the menu option text within that child window. The title bar drawn by the window manager is also a separate window that just happens to always be placed at the top of the application window in question (this attachment is kept current and aligned by the window manager).

Widget Kits, APIs, and X

Most graphical user interfaces for other operating systems include a predefined set of basic widget with which programmers can create applications with consistent appearances and behaviors. In this regard, X is somewhat different.

Although X does include one basic widget kit (the Athena toolkit, also commonly known as XAW, for X Athena Widgets), it's not a very complete or functional toolkit, even though it's the toolkit used by most of the basic X utilities. This is because the Athena toolkit was intended for use only in basic X utilities and, more importantly, as sample code for programmers who were to create more complex widget kits and more complex application programming interfaces (APIs).

Because of this, most users coming to X and Linux from other operating systems immediately notice the rather obvious diversity among X widget. Whereas in Windows or Mac systems all widgets are similar in appearance, look good together, and behave in rather the same way, in X, many different families of widgets are created by the many different toolkits used to create X applications. Some of these toolkits and their peculiarities are discussed in more detail in Chapter 5, "Linux/X Toolkit Particulars."

Interacting with X

To be able to use XFree86 effectively, it is important to understand how to use a few basic visual components and how to complete a few basic operations. Although some of these are similar to the components and operations commonly used in other graphical environments, certain items or keystrokes are unique to X or even to XFree86.

The Mouse Cursor

The mouse cursor in X behaves in much the same way that it does in other graphical operating systems such as Windows or Macintosh. There are, however, a few differences.

One of the most instantly recognizable for those using a window manager like twm is that the mouse cursor isn't in the shape of a pointer when it is over the root window. Instead, the mouse cursor appears as a rather oversized X that many users find quite annoying, in part because the cursor's hot spot is obscured in the middle of the X. In response to this problem, some newer window managers (such as Window Maker or AfterStep) specify an alternative, more typical pointer cursor.

Several users operating at 15, 16, 24, or 32 bits per pixel might have also experienced another initially shocking aspect of X behavior that is closely linked to the mouse cursor, that of panning across or up and down in the virtual desktop. You'll most likely see this behavior if there are one or more modes that your video card and monitor are capable of at 8bpp, but not capable of at higher depths. For example, if your video adapter and monitor can display 1024×768 at 8bpp, but only 800×600 at 16bpp, and you've started X at 16bpp, you'll find that X has configured a 1024×768 virtual desktop for you.

The virtual desktop looks and behaves just like a desktop would if it all fit onscreen—except it doesn't all fit onscreen. The net effect is that you can see only 800×600 pixels of the desktop at a time, and moving the cursor to any edge of the display will cause the visible window to scroll in that direction to the end of the virtual desktop.

Many users find this trick enlightening—the ability to use a larger desktop than the monitor can display is often considered to be a boon. On the other hand, many other users expect to be able to easily move their mouse cursors to the edge of the screen and stop, and such users often report "seasickness" or at least severe annoyance at the virtual desktop scrolling. If you find yourself in this camp, please refer to the "Advanced Configuration" section of Chapter 2, "Installing and Configuring XFree86," for XF86Config file options on limiting the size of the virtual desktop to the size of the visible display.

The final peculiarity about the mouse cursor, which isn't really an aspect of the cursor at all, but really an artifact of the Linux operating system and the way it interacts with X, is the lack of a "busy" cursor, such as the hourglass in Windows. Many new Linux users find themselves having difficulty adjusting to the lack of a busy cursor while a program is starting, leading some users to start a program twice or even three times, each time looking for the busy cursor to indicate that the program is loading.

Some applications do implement their own internal busy mouse cursor, which is displayed when an image is rendering or a file printing, for example. But in general, Linux and X are never too busy to accept your input—and therefore, no busy cursor will ever be displayed, even if a program such as Netscape or WordPerfect is in the process of loading.

Root or Start Menus

Although the individual appearances, behaviors, and configurations of the many different window managers vary greatly, one element is consistent across nearly all of them, with the exception of the environments like KDE and GNOME.

The root menu is a staple of UNIX desktops everywhere, though it sometimes masquerades as a Start menu (in the case of FVWM-95). The typical behavior of the root menu is to appear when the user clicks one of the mouse buttons (usually either the left or the right mouse button) while the mouse cursor is over the root window (not in any other window). When the user clicks the root window, a menu appears under the mouse cursor with several options. Typically, there will be options for window control, launching applications, or both, often listed in a series of cascading submenus. Some window manager configurations even implement more than one root menu. For example, a common configuration is to list applications when the user left-clicks the root window, window operations when the user right-clicks the root window, and running applications when the user middle-clicks the root window.

The default twm root menu from the XFree86 distribution was previously shown in Figure 3.3. This root menu is a window operations root menu, and the effects of the listed commands can be seen in Table 3.2.

Table 3.2 The Default twm Root Menu

Item	Use and/or Effect
Iconify	Minimizes a window so that it no longer uses up as much screen space. After being minimized, the window is represented by a small icon or block of title text. To restore the window, click the icon. To use, click in the window you'd like to iconify.
Resize	Performs the same action as the resize button on the twm title bar—resizes a window. To use, click in the window you'd like to resize. A rubber band outline appears. Move the mouse cursor around until the rubber band outline is the size you'd like the resultant window to be, and then click again.
Move	Performs the same action achieved by clicking a window's title bar and dragging it—the window is moved. To use, click in the window you'd like to move. A rubber band outline appears. Move the rubber band outline to the location where you'd like the window to be, and then click again.
Raise	Moves a window so that it appears to be on top of all other windows in the screen. Other windows that share the same physical space as the resized window will be partially obscured by it. To use, click in the window you'd like to raise.
Lower	Moves a window so that it appears to be underneath all other windows in the screen. Other windows that share the same physical space as the lowered window will partially obscure it. To use, click in the window you'd like to lower.
Focus	Gives a window focus (see the section "Focus and Other Window Manager Concepts" for details). To use, click in the window you'd like to have focus.
Unfocus	Removes a window's focus. To use, click in the window you'd like to take focus away from.
Show Iconmgr	Displays an icon manager to hold minimized window icons.
Hide Iconmgr	Removes the icon manager from view, allowing minimized icons to appear anywhere on the desktop.
Kill	Completely kills an X application. Note that you can loose whatever you're working on inside the application in question. To use, click in the window you'd like to destroy.
Delete	Remove a window owned by an X application. Much friendlier than Kill, Delete can theoretically be used to safely close windows owned by an application. To use, click in the window you'd like to delete.

Item	Use and/or Effect
Restart	Restart twm. This is not terribly useful to you yet, but will become useful later in Chapter 9, "Runtime Environment Configuration."
Exit	Exits twm. Note that the way the default XFree86 desktop is configured, this item will not exit XFree86—just the twm window manager. To exit XFree86, type exit in the login window or destroy the window because it is the controlling process. For more information on controlling the X session, see Chapter 6, "Runtime Session Defaults."

If you installed XFree86 as part of Linux, your window manager's root menu might be different or, in some cases, might be absent altogether. Several Linux configurations, most notably those of some Red Hat operating systems, use an FVWM variant as the default window manager, with a Windows 95-like Start menu in place of or in addition to a root menu.

Switching Consoles and Emergency Exits

Two of the more important functions to remember while inside XFree86 are console switching and the three-key exit.

You might already be familiar with the concept of virtual consoles inside Linux. If not, exit XFree86 now, and try this: Press Alt+F1, then Alt+F2, and so on, until you see a login prompt. Log in at this prompt, and then pick up where you left off, perhaps Alt+F3, and so on, until you see another login prompt. Log in there as well. Execute a command or two, and now press the first Alt+F*n* sequence where you logged in. Execute a command or two there, and then press the second Alt+F*n* sequence. What you're doing is switching between *virtual consoles*. These virtual consoles are like any number of separate displays that Linux knows about; each can host its own login and run its own programs.

When you start XFree86, you are displaying X on one of these virtual consoles. The rest of them, however, remain active, and you can switch to them and use them at any time. Unfortunately, the key sequence is a little different. When you're looking at the X display and need to switch to another virtual console, press Ctrl+Alt+F*n* to switch to the console in question. Afterward, you can press Alt+F*n* to switch back, though you might have to try a few virtual consoles to figure out which one X is running on. The easiest way to do this is simply to press Alt+F1 and count from there until you press F12. At some point, you'll find the X desktop you were looking for.

The other important keyboard trick when working with XFree86 is the three-key emergency exit. This exit is triggered when the Ctrl, Alt, and Backspace keys are all pressed at once. Unless you have explicitly disabled this action while configuring X, pressing this series of three keys together will force the X server to *punt*—to exit as quickly as possible, dropping you out of X, back at the command line, and leaving all running applications in the lurch, unable to continue.

Although this might seem like a drastic course of action, it is sometimes extremely useful, for example, when a rare rogue application has taken over normal aspects of the keyboard and mouse and you are unable to regain control. In other operating systems, a reboot would be required, but in Linux, thanks to the three-key emergency exit in XFree86, a reset can often be avoided. Instead, only X must be restarted.

It bears repeating here, though, that you should use Ctrl+Alt+Backspace only in the direst of emergencies. Using the emergency exit will in all likelihood cause all the data in running applications to be lost for good unless it has been saved to disk.

Focus and Other Window Manager Concepts

One or two more particulars about X window managers will be helpful to the average user before we move on to the next chapter and start using X clients.

Window Focus in X

First and foremost, it is the window manager's job to manage application window *focus*. At any given time, only one window or application on an X desktop can have focus. When a window has focus, all normal keystrokes entered by the user will belong to that window. Thus, the application that has focus is perceived by the user as the active application. It is the window manager's job to establish some policy by which focus is determined and some mechanism by which it is changed. Most window managers implement several possible focus methods and enable the user to choose.

When using a focus-follows-mouse policy, wherever the mouse goes, the focus follows. In such a scenario, the window that currently contains the mouse pointer will also receive all normal keystrokes. Changing the focus involves simply moving the mouse pointer over (or inside) another window. If the mouse pointer isn't contained within a window, keystrokes will not be sent to any application. This is the focus mode most commonly found on classic UNIX desktops.

When using a click-to-focus policy, a window is given focus when it is clicked upon by the mouse. After being clicked, all normal user keystrokes will go to the selected window until focus is explicitly changed (see Figure 3.5). Changing the focus involves clicking on (or sometimes inside) another window. The focus remains with the selected window regardless of where the mouse pointer actually resides onscreen. This is the focus mode most commonly seen in Windows and Mac OS systems.

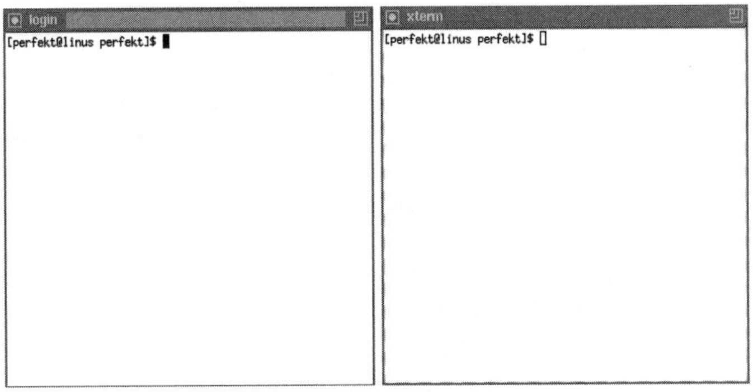

Figure 3.5 The window on the left has focus; the window on the right doesn't. Note that the title bar of the focused window is highlighted and that the window contains the mouse pointer.

When using a sloppy-focus policy, focus behaves much as it does under the focus-follows-mouse policy with one important exception: If no window (other than the root window) currently contains the mouse pointer, focus will remain with whichever window last held the mouse pointer. This focus mode is now commonly used by most former focus-follows-mouse advocates.

In the default XFree86 desktop (which uses the twm window manager), the focus policy is set to focus-follows-mouse.

Note that, in addition to establishing a focus policy and a mechanism by which focus is changed, a window manager will generally also need some mechanism by which the current focus is indicated. For example, setting a window's border and title to a different color is a common method for indicating that a window currently has focus.

Moving and Raising a Window

Although the twm root menu provides an item to aid the user in moving a window, not all readers are using the default XFree86 desktop that is so equipped. Furthermore, moving a window using the root menu Move item is perhaps not the easiest way to accomplish the task.

By far the easiest way to move a window, which is consistent across nearly all possible configurations of all X window managers, is the most intuitive way, shared by both the Windows and Mac operating systems—by clicking the window's title bar and dragging the window around the desktop.

Similarly, most standard X window manager configurations, the default XFree86 twm configuration included, will allow windows to be "raised" simply by clicking on the window's title bar. Although not everyone will find this to be the case, for those who do, it will definitely make the chapters ahead more bearable to be able to both move and raise windows easily.

Keyboard Shortcuts

Most X window managers are capable of implementing what are called *keyboard shortcuts.* Keyboard shortcuts are a set of keystrokes specified in the window manager configuration which, when entered by the user, will be intercepted by the window manager and not passed on to the application that has focus. These keystrokes are then interpreted by the window manager and used to perform various functions.

The keyboard shortcut configuration in X varies from window manger to window manager and from user to user, based on the configuration present on a given machine. Although none of these shortcuts is included in the standard twm configuration that is included with XFree86, the user can configure twm to accept keyboard shortcuts.

If you find that an application isn't behaving as expected—for example, it calls for you to press F1 to accomplish a certain task, but when you press F1, your window is minimized instead—it probably means that rather than passing the F1 key on to the window with focus, your window manager is using the F1 key as part of a keyboard shortcut. Generally speaking, the only way to fix such a problem is to edit your window manager's configuration directly and eliminate the keyboard shortcut in question.

For more information on keyboard shortcuts and the window manager you're using, please refer to Chapter 9.

Multiple Virtual Desktops

Although not a part of the behavior of the twm window manager included as standard with XFree86, many users might find that their window manager is capable of managing what are called *multiple virtual desktops,* often with the help of a *desktop manager* or *pager* window. In such configurations, the window manager maintains several virtual desktops simultaneously—usually allowing for a single desktop much larger than the screen but, in some cases (such as Window Maker desktop), simply allowing for multiple logical X desktop.

There is really no equivalent concept in either Windows operating systems or the Macintosh operating system; thus many users are initially stymied to some degree by the concept of multiple virtual desktops. It's best to think of them simply in the way that they are described—it is as though you had started XFree86 many times on many different monitors. Each multiple virtual desktop can hold application windows and icons. Each behaves as a mini X environment, in some cases with the added benefit that application windows can be moved between desktops or even made "sticky" so as to appear on them all. A small interface of some sort generally enables the user to switch between virtual desktops with the click of a mouse (see Figure 3.6).

Figure 3.6   The clip icon is Window Maker's interface for managing multiple virtual desktops. The number 1 in the upper-left corner indicates that the first desktop is currently visible.

If you find at some point that your application window has simply disappeared or that multiple application windows have done so, leaving you with a completely empty desktop, chances are that you have misplaced your application on another virtual desktop in the first case. It could also be that you have accidentally switched to another virtual desktop in the second if your window manager supports such functionality.

If you decide that virtual desktops aren't for you, don't despair: They can generally be disabled by changing the window manager's configuration. Please refer to Chapter 9 for details on how to work with your window manager's configuration.

Leaving X

In many XFree86 desktops that were installed as part of a Linux operating system, the process of leaving X is quite intuitive, accomplished with an Exit or Logout button somewhere on the display or in a menu. For those that have such a button available at this point, leaving X is easy.

Users of the official XFree86 distribution who are using the as-shipped twm desktop might be a little mystified, however, when they select the Exit option from the root menu only to leave them sitting at an undecorated login window with no window manager control or decoration whatsoever (see Figure 3.7). There are two ways to exit X in the standard distribution.

The first way is to exit or kill the controlling login window, either by typing `exit` at the command prompt, by using the `kill` command on the `xterm` process that represents the login window, or by using the Destroy or Delete operations from the root menu on the login window.

The second way is to use the Ctrl+Alt+Backspace emergency exit to leave the X server. The preferred method is the former, for obvious reasons.

The logic behind this configuration (that is, exiting window manager doesn't exit X) confuses many users, and indeed, it is the logic of an old UNIX hacker, not the logic of a desktop user. For those who want to be able to change this behavior or who want to understand more about the controlling process of an X session, these topics are covered in more detail in Chapter 6. For the moment, however, the default behavior should be adequate for basic XFree86 use.

Figure 3.7 The login window after the twm exit—no decorations, no more root menu. To exit X, type exit at the prompt.

4

STANDARD XFREE86
PROGRAMS AND UTILITIES

The Command Line in X

Aside from the server, which has occupied most of the text until now, several other important standard programs and utilities are included with XFree86. Many of them are essential aspects of a working Linux+X desktop.

The fundamental user interface in any UNIX or UNIX-like operating system is the command line. No matter how dressed up a UNIX system becomes thanks to the addition of X or aftermarket add-ons, it isn't yet possible to use UNIX-like systems to their fullest without access to a shell. Many X utilities must be launched from the command line, and many X configuration changes can be made only with shell commands.

But the concept of a keyboard and command-based user interface would seem to be at odds with the concept of a graphical user interface. The command line hearkens back to the days of the dumb terminal device, which displayed text only as purely a forum for shell and text-based application interaction. How did the designers of X merge the graphical desktop with the text-based, command-driven dumb terminal?

Terminal in a Window

Perhaps the most important X utility is xterm, the X terminal emulator, an X utility that creates a window that acts like a few specific dumb terminal makes and models to UNIX applications. The default XFree86 desktop starts three instances of the xterm program, two labeled as such, and one labeled *login*. All three of these windows look very much like dumb terminals to the shell and text-based applications run inside them.

You might have noticed that these three windows on the default desktop are endowed with a shell prompt, and that they accept any of the UNIX commands to which most users are accustomed. Nearly any command that can be run from a text console in Linux can also be run from an xterm window and will behave similarly. This includes text-based applications such as pine or vi, as well as output pagers such as more. Using xterm is rather like using the traditional dumb terminal, with one important difference: As the default desktop shows, multiple xterm windows can appear all at once on the same display, effectively multiplying your access to the shell.

There is one other important difference between the way in which xterm behaves and the way in which a text console displays. In truth, the difference isn't really an xterm phenomenon, but rather an effect of the presence of the X desktop itself. The xterm window can also be used to launch other X applications or utilities. When they are started this way, such X binaries won't display in the xterm window, but will (naturally) create a new window of their own in which to display. For example, you can open a new xterm window by typing the following command in an existing xterm window:

```
xterm
```

Depending on the window manager in use, a window might simply appear on its own or a rubber band outline of the window might appear for you to place. You *place* a window simply by moving the outline to the location where you'd like the window to appear and then clicking any mouse button. You'll find that the new xterm window behaves and acts just like any of the others, and just like a dumb terminal.

Several replacements for xterm have been written and released over the years. Some of them are parts of other applications or desktops, like the kvt and konsole from the KDE desktop and the cmdtool and shelltool applications from Sun's OpenWindows. All of them function more or less similarly to xterm in that they all provide a means by which users can interact with the shell from inside an X session. In spite of the successes of some of the xterm replacements, xterm itself remains the most widely used X terminal emulator to date.

Job Management

Most experienced UNIX shell users are familiar with the normal job management commands in UNIX. For those who need a refresher, Tables 4.1 and 4.2 provide a brief synopsis.

Table 4.1   Basic Job Management Commands for Shell Users

Command	Effect
jobs	Lists active jobs started as children of the current shell.
fg *jobid*	Brings the job with the specified *jobid* to the foreground.
bg *jobid*	Places the job with the specified *jobid* in the background.
kill *jobid*	Kills the job with the specified *jobid*.
nohup *cmd*	Starts the command *cmd*, ignoring any hang-up signal. Allows the command to remain active even if the parent shell has logged out.

Table 4.2   Basic Job Management Input Characters for Shell Users

Character	Effect
Command &	Appending the ampersand (&) character to the end of a command will start the command concurrently, in the background.
Ctrl+Z	The Ctrl+Z key sequence will suspend a foreground job. The job can be resumed either in the foreground or background with fg or bg or killed outright.
Ctrl+C	The Ctrl+C key sequence will cause most commands to quit immediately.

Users of the xterm utility in X will find that all these commands and key sequences work as expected from within an xterm window. You might have noticed that launching the new instance of xterm in the previous section left the shell in the original xterm window unavailable. This is because the child xterm process was launched in the foreground. To create a new xterm but leave the parent shell active, use the following command:

```
xterm &
```

Similarly, to place an existing xterm in the background and free up the parent shell, the user would focus the window containing the parent shell, use the Ctrl+Z key sequence, and then move the process to the background with bg.

The kill command can also be used from an xterm window, but when killing X applications, it is often easier to use the X counterpart to kill, xkill. To use xkill, simply type the command at an xterm shell prompt:

```
xkill
```

You'll find that the mouse cursor has changed to a skull and crossbones. Move this skull and crossbones over the application window you want to kill, and click to kill the application in question.

The nohup command can be used from an xterm window as well and is actually often more useful in X than at a text-based shell prompt. When using a shell outside X, the nohup command simply prevents a background application from being killed if the user logs out. Thus, the command takes effect only when the user leaves the work area. In X, however, where multiple xterm windows can be created and killed (or logged out) in sequence, nohup takes on a new measure of utility.

To illustrate, try starting an xclock from an open xterm window:

```
xclock &
```

After the clock has been successfully started, kill the xterm window, either with xkill or by using a kill option in your window manager's configuration (such as the one from the root-window menu in the default XFree86 desktop). Upon killing the xterm window, you'll notice that the xclock has been killed as well. The loss of a single xclock might not seem like a calamity. But if 20 separate applications have been started from a single xterm window that is then accidentally killed, or even killed on purpose to reduce clutter, the desktop could suddenly be completely cleared of applications, resulting in lost data and time. To prevent a window from being killed if the parent xterm shell process ends, use the nohup command:

```
nohup xclock &
```

Remember that nohup can save immense amounts of time and headache later on.

Commonly Used X Utilities

The number of utilities and applications that come with XFree86 is rather large, and we have time for only a few of them here. You can find the complete list of user binaries included with XFree86 by listing the files contained in the Xbin.tgz file. You can find official documentation for most of these binaries by consulting the installed manual page for each binary in question. Many of these utilities and clients also make available several X resource settings that can affect the client's behavior. For a listing of applicable resources for a given client, consult the manual page for the client in question. Details on using X resources can be found in Chapter 8, "Runtime Application Configuration."

All the utilities listed in the following sections are normally started in the same way, by supplying their name to the shell in an xterm window. For example, to start the xeyes client, the user would enter

```
xeyes &
```

All the client binaries can normally be found in the /usr/X11R6/bin/ directory, and their manual pages can be found in the /usr/X11R6/man/man1/ directory.

startx

The startx command launches the X server and starts the X session using the xinit scripts. To use startx after X has been configured, simply enter the command from any text console:

```
startx
```

The startx command isn't normally called with arguments of its own but is often called with two dashes as its first argument, allowing any other arguments that follow to be passed on to the X server.

xbiff

The xbiff utility monitors a user's mail spool file, changing color or optionally beeping when mail has arrived. Clicking in the xbiff window returns it to its original color. The most common command-line arguments accepted by xbiff are shown in Table 4.3.

Table 4.3   Most Common Arguments Accepted by xbiff

Argument	Description
-update *n*	Check for new mail and update the display every *n* seconds.
-file *name*	Check file *name* for mail activity, instead of the default user mail spool file.
-volume *n*	Set the new mail beep volume to *n* percent.

xcalc

The xcalc utility displays a graphical arithmetic calculator in a window that can be operated either by the mouse or by the numeric keypad. The xcalc utility can emulate either a TI-30 calculator or an HP-10C calculator. The most common command-line arguments accepted by xcalc are shown in Table 4.4.

Table 4.4   Most Common Arguments Accepted by xcalc

Argument	Description
-stipple	Draw calculator features using stippled areas instead of solid colors. Improves the appearance of the calculator on 1 and 2 bits-per-pixel (monochrome) displays.
-rpn	When supplied, this argument causes the calculator to emulate an HP-10C calculator and use reverse Polish notation for input. When omitted, xcalc will emulate a TI-30.

Use of the xcalc utility with the keyboard is straightforward with the numeric keypad except for one detail: Pressing Enter on the keypad doesn't have the same effect as pressing the equals (=) button on the calculator. To simulate pressing the equals button on the calculator, you must press the equals key on the keyboard (to the left of Backspace in most cases).

xclipboard

The xclipboard client enables the user to display, manipulate, and use text selections that have been sent to the X clipboard by well-behaved X applications. Not all applications are well-behaved, and thus, not all selected, cut, or copied text will appear in the xclipboard. The most common command-line arguments accepted by xclipboard are shown in Table 4.5.

Table 4.5   Most Common Arguments Accepted by xclipboard

Argument	Description
-w	Causes text displayed by xclipboard to automatically wrap or fill instead of extending past the end of the visible window.
-nw	Doesn't wrap lines that cannot be displayed in the width of the xclipboard window. This is the default behavior.

After a text item appears in the clipboard, it remains there until it is manually deleted using the xclipboard utility. To browse the current clipboard entries, use the Next and Prev buttons at the upper right of the window. In the absolute upper right, the number displayed indicates the number of the current clipboard entry in the queue. A new clipboard entry can be placed at the end of the queue by clicking New and then typing into the text widget. The text of a given clipboard entry can be saved to a file with the Save button.

To exit xclipboard, select the Quit button in the upper left of the window.

xclock and oclock

The xclock utility creates a graphical clock in a window that displays the current system time. The clock can be resized at will and can be set for either digital or analog operation. The most common command-line arguments accepted by xclock are shown in Table 4.6.

Table 4.6   Most Common Arguments Accepted by xclock

Argument	Description
-analog	Specifies that xclock should display a simulated analog clock, with hands and a face to indicate time. This is the default behavior.
-digital	Specifies that xclock should display the time digitally rather than with a simulated clock face.
-chime	Causes xclock to chime audibly, once on the half hour, twice on the hour.

Argument	Description
-hands *color*	Specifies the color of the analog clock's hands. The default color is black.
-highlight *color*	Specifies the color of the analog clock hand highlights (edges). The default color is black.
-update *n*	Instructs xclock to update the display to reflect the current time every n seconds. The default is to update every 60 seconds.
-padding *n*	Specifies the number of pixels of padding (empty space) that should appear between the edge of the window and the clock face or digital readout. The default values are 10 pixels for an analog clock and 8 pixels for a digital clock.

Users who prefer a more stylish desktop clock might want to use the oclock application, which will place a modern-shaped analog clock on the desktop instead of the more boxy clock generated by xclock. The most common command-line arguments accepted by oclock are shown in Table 4.7.

Table 4.7 Most Common Arguments Accepted by oclock

Argument	Description
-fg color	Specifies the color to use when displaying the hands of the clock and the jewel that appears at the 12 o'clock position.
-bg color	Specifies the color to use for the face of the clock.
-jewel color	Specifies the color to use when displaying the jewel that appears at the 12 o'clock position.
-minute color	Specifies the color to use when displaying the minute hand of the clock.
-hour color	Specifies the color to use when displaying the hour hand of the clock.
-transparent	When supplied, this argument causes the oclock to appear with a transparent face; only the hands, the outline of the face, and the jewel that appears at the 12 o'clock position will be visible.

Note that like xclock, oclock can be resized at will and adjusts to fit the size and shape of the window.

xedit

The xedit utility provides a simple, basic text editor for X not unlike the Notepad application found on many Windows systems. The xedit client includes basic features such as file saving and loading and should be started as follows:

```
xedit filename
```

The *filename* given is the name of the file the user wants to edit or create. The xedit window is built using basic Athena toolkit widgets, and as a result, the mouse cursor must physically enter any text area that is to accept keyboard input, including areas such as the filename entry box. For more information on the peculiarities of basic Athena widgets, see Chapter 5, "Linux/X Toolkit Particulars." A basic list of xedit keyboard commands can be found in Table 4.8.

Table 4.8 Basic xedit Keyboard Commands

Keys	Function
Ctrl+A	Moves to the beginning of the current line.
Ctrl+E	Moves to the end of the current line.
Ctrl+F or →	Moves forward one character.
Ctrl+B or ←	Moves backward one character.
Ctrl+N or ↓	Moves down one line.
Ctrl+P or ↑	Moves up one line.
Ctrl+V or PgDn	Moves down one page.
Alt+V or PgUp	Moves up one page.
Alt+< or Home	Moves to the beginning of the file.
Alt+> or End	Moves to the end of the file.
Alt+[	Moves to the beginning of the paragraph.
Alt+]	Moves to the end of the paragraph.
Alt+F	Moves to the beginning of the next word.
Alt+B	Moves to the beginning of the previous word.
Ctrl+D	Deletes the character following the cursor.
Ctrl+H or Backspace	Deletes the character before the cursor.
Alt+D	Deletes the next word.
Alt+H	Deletes the previous word.
Ctrl+W	Kills the selected block of text.
Ctrl+K	Kills the segment of the current line after the cursor. Doesn't remove the carriage return at the end of the line; to remove the carriage return, press Ctrl+K again.
Alt+K	Kills the portion of the current paragraph after the cursor.
Ctrl+Y	Inserts the last killed block of text. The last killed block of text is usually the text removed during the last Ctrl+W, Ctrl+K, or Alt+K keystroke.
Ctrl+I	Refreshes the window, positioning text so that the cursor appears in the center of the window.

Keys	Function
Ctrl+M or Enter	Inserts or moves to a new line.
Alt+Y	Inserts the last block of selected text here.
Ctrl+O	Splits the current line in two, moving the rest of the current line to a new line below.
Ctrl+T	Swaps the characters immediately before and after the cursor.
Ctrl+U	Repeats the next keystroke four times. For example, Ctrl+U followed by the Enter key will insert four blank lines.
Alt+I	Inserts a file into the text.
Ctrl+Z	Scrolls the text window up one line.
Alt+Z	Scrolls the text window down one line.

Users should note immediately that there is no undo function in xedit. Saving often and maintaining multiple backups are therefore prudent techniques for preserving one's data and sanity when using xedit.

xeyes

The xeyes client is more a toy than a useful utility, but it is nevertheless found on a great number of X desktops and remains a perennial favorite among new X users. Starting xeyes causes a pair of eyes to be displayed on the desktop that will continue to look at the cursor as the user works. The most common command-line arguments accepted by xeyes are shown in Table 4.9.

Table 4.9 Most Common Arguments Accepted by xeyes

Argument	Description
-fg color	Specifies a different color for the pupil of the eyes.
-bg color	Specifies a different background color for the xeyes window.
-outline color	Specifies a different color for the outline of the eyes.
-center color	Specifies a different color for the center (whites) of the eyes.
-shape	Uses the X shape extension to allow for floating eyes, as opposed to eyes in a window. This is the default behavior.
+shape	Disables the X shape extension, forcing the eyes to be drawn in a square window.

xfontsel

The xfontsel utility enables the user to browse and display fonts available to the currently running X server. As each font is displayed, the X Logical Font Description (XLFD) for the font is also displayed, making it easier to specify the font in question to applications. For more information on font names and font management in X, see Chapter 7, "Runtime Server Configuration." The most common command-line arguments accepted by xfontsel are shown in Table 4.10.

Table 4.10 Most Common Arguments Accepted by xfontsel

Argument	Description
-pattern *pattern*	Display only fonts that match the given pattern. Patterns are specified with a subset of standard regular expressions, most often using the asterisk character. For example, the pattern *courier* would select only the courier fonts for display. Take care to escape all wildcards so that they aren't interpreted by the shell.
-print	Causes the XLFD for the chosen font to be output to STDOUT when the client exits. This functionality can be useful in scripts, providing a mechanism by which the user can select a font and the script can obtain the chosen XLFD.
-sample *text*	Causes linearly indexed fonts to be displayed using the given text rather than the default sample text.
-sample16 *text*	Causes matrix-encoded fonts to be displayed using the given text rather than the default sample text.
-noscaled	Disables font scaling for bitmapped fonts in xfontsel.

Using xfontsel can be rather confusing to new users. A basic working knowledge of the X Logical Font Description format is required. The easiest way to select a font is to first select from the Fmly (family) drop-down menu. If a large number of fonts are available to the X server, however, it might be wiser to first select from the Fndry (foundry) drop-down menu. Afterward, selecting a size from the Pxlsz (pixel size) drop-down menu displays the font in what most users understand to be the point size of the font. Items in the Wght and Slant menus determine font thickness and slant (italic versus non-italic), respectively.

To quit xfontsel, select the Quit button at the upper-left of the window.

xkill

The xkill utility is used to graphically select a window that should be killed or to kill an X application by closing its connection to the X server. Note that in most cases, any unsaved data in the killed application will be lost. The most common command-line arguments accepted by xkill are shown in Table 4.11.

Table 4.11 Most Common Arguments Accepted by xkill

Argument	Description
-all	Instructs xkill to kill all current top-level clients owned by the active root window. When using this option, you will be asked to select the root window once with each button in order to confirm that this is what you really mean to do. This argument represents a "scorched earth" policy: every client will be closed.
-button *n*	Specifies that button *n* should be used as the Kill button. Specifying all in place of a button number will allow any button to be used in killing a client.
-id *resource*	Specifies the X client to be killed by supplying its resource identification. This number can be found using clients such as xwininfo or xprop.
-frame	Specifies that xkill should operate directly on children of the root window rather than attempting to detect top-level client windows in the normal manner. For example, this option will allow the user to kill the window manager by clicking a decoration (such as the title bar) that is owned by the window manager.

xload

The xload utility displays a running graph of the client system's load average in real time. If no horizontal bars appear in the graph, the load is less than 1.0. Each horizontal bar that appears in the graph represents a whole number increment. A graph that climbs above three horizontal lines therefore indicates a load average greater than 3.0. The most common command-line arguments accepted by xload are shown in Table 4.12.

Table 4.12 Most Common Arguments Accepted by xload

Argument	Description
-highlight *color*	Allows the user to specify the color of the highlight (horizontal scale) lines in the graph.
-jumpscroll *n*	Moves the graph *n* pixels to the left when the display reaches the right edge of the window. For smooth scrolling, set this value to 1.
-label *text*	Puts the given text above the graph as a label. The default configuration places the domain name of the client system above the graph.
-nolabel	Displays no label above the graph.
-lights	Specifies that xload should indicate the current system load using the keyboard LEDs. For example, a system load of 2.0 would be indicated when the first two keyboard LEDs are lit. No xload window will be displayed.

continues

Table 4.12 Continued

Argument	Description
-scale *n*	Specifies a minimum scale for the graph. When this option is given, the supplied number of horizontal bars will always be present. Under normal circumstances, the graph scale will be adjusted as necessary based on system load average activity, but this option causes at least the given number to always appear.
-update *n*	Updates the load average display every *n* seconds. The default is to update every 10 seconds.

xlogo

Completely useless for almost any practical purpose, the xlogo client nevertheless appears in almost all published X desktop screenshots and demos. The xlogo client simply causes the X Window System logo to be displayed in a window. This is done using the Athena toolkit's xlogo widget.

Only one command-line argument is accepted by xlogo. Supplying the -shape option will cause the X shape extension to be used in displaying the logo. When the option isn't supplied, the logo will be displayed in a square window instead.

xmag

The xmag client causes a section of the X display to be magnified and displayed in a window. Use of xmag is quite easy. After xmag is called, the mouse cursor will change; place the mouse cursor at the upper-left corner of the area to be magnified and click the left mouse button. This will cause a window to appear containing the magnified area of the display. The most common command-line arguments accepted by xmag are shown in Table 4.13.

Table 4.13 Most Common Arguments Accepted by xmag

Argument	Description
-mag *n*	Specifies the magnification factor to use. Each pixel in the magnified image will be blown up to a size of *n* by *n* pixels. The default factor is 5.
-source *geom*	Specifies the geometry of the source area to be magnified. For example, specifying an area of 250×250 will cause an area of the display 250 pixels high by 250 pixels wide to be displayed. Note that a magnified image window will be the source size multiplied by the magnification factor in both directions. For example, magnifying a 500×500 section of the window at a magnification factor of 3 will result in a 1500×1500 image, larger than most displays.

After a selected area of the display has been magnified, information about any of the magnified pixels can be displayed by clicking the pixel in question in the xmag window. When a pixel is clicked, a line of information will appear either at the top or bottom of the window providing the location of the selected pixel on the display and the color of the pixel in question using the RGB format.

When a new magnified section is desired, clicking the Replace button will cause the mouse cursor to again change to the magnification cursor. When a new position is clicked, the new section of the display is magnified and shown in the xmag window.

The Close button can be used to exit xmag at any time.

xman

The xman client is used for user-friendly graphical browsing, displaying, and scrolling of system manual pages. Manual pages can be searched for user-supplied text strings and can also be browsed by category. The most common command-line arguments accepted by xman are shown in Table 4.14.

Table 4.14 Most Common Arguments Accepted by xman

Argument	Description
-notopbox	Start the manual page browser directly, without the parent window containing Help, Quit, and Manual Page buttons.
-bothshown	Display both the current manual page and the manual page directory at the same time.

Using the Manual Page window inside xman involves first choosing a section from which manual pages are to be taken, and then choosing a specific manual page from the displayed list of pages in the selected section. After a specific page has been selected and displayed, the user can scroll forward and backward in the page or search it using the Search option in the Options menu.

To exit xman, select Quit from the Options menu in the Manual Page window, or click the Quit button in the xman window.

xmh

The xmh client provides a graphical interface to the commonly used mh mail user agent. The xmh client therefore requires that the mh program be installed and configured for use. The mh and xmh utilities are large and complex enough to deserve an entire book about them alone, and there are several. Perhaps the most widely known is *MH & xmh: E-mail for Users & Programmers* published by O'Reilly and Associates. The most common command-line arguments accepted by xmh are listed in Table 4.15.

Table 4.15 Most Common Arguments Accepted by xmh

Argument	Description
-path *path*	Specifies an alternate path to the directory containing MH-style mail folders. The default path is the Mail folder in the user's home directory.
-initial *name*	Specifies an alternate initial folder to receive new mail and which will be displayed each time xmh is started. The default initial folder is inbox.
-flag	Causes xmh to change its appearance when in an iconified state or the appearance of related folder buttons in the xmh window when new mail has arrived, rather than any time unread mail is present.

Using xmh can be a complex task; luckily, most of the concepts present in an xmh window are universal across a great number of other email clients as well. The first row of buttons across the top of the xmh window lead to several drop-down menus described in Tables 4.16–4.21.

Table 4.16 xmh Folder Drop-Down Menu

Item	Description
Open Folder	Opens the selected folder.
Open Folder in New Window	Clones the main xmh window and use the new window to display the selected folder.
Create Folder	Creates a new mail folder. Subfolders can also be created by specifying the parent folder's name, followed by a slash, followed by the name of the new folder.
Delete Folder	Deletes the selected folder and all its contents and subfolders.
Close Window	Closes the xmh window in question. If no other xmh windows exist, exits xmh.

Table 4.17 xmh Table of Contents Drop-Down Menu

Item	Description
Incorporate New Mail	Moves new messages to the displayed folder and displays the first of the new messages.
Commit Changes	Deletes messages in this folder marked for deletion, moves and copies all messages that are so marked, and commits the changes to disk.
Pack Folder	Renumbers all messages in the displayed folder. The first message will be message number 1.
Sort Folder	Sorts the messages in the folder so that they appear in order of the timestamp on each message.

Item	Description
Rescan Folder	Re-creates the list of messages in the current folder. This action is necessary whenever changes have been made to MH-style mail folders without telling xmh.

Table 4.18   xmh Message Drop-Down Menu

Item	Description
Compose Message	Begin a new message. An edit window will appear in which the message can be input. The edit window supports word-wrap and basic keyboard navigation. At the bottom of the edit window are basic message functions such as sending or canceling an email message.
View Next Message	View the selected message or the next message after the currently displayed message.
View Previous	View the last message selected or the previous message before the currently displayed message.
Delete	Mark selected messages for deletion. To actually delete the messages after they have been marked, select Commit Changes from the Table of Contents menu.
Move	Mark the selected messages to be move to the selected folder. To actually move messages after they have been marked for movement, select Commit Changes from the Table of Contents menu.
Copy as Link	Copy the selected messages to the selected folder. Note that the copy operation actually creates a symbolic link from the source message to the destination. Changes to the source will therefore also be reflected in the destination. To actually copy messages after they have been marked for copying, select Commit Changes from the Table of Contents menu.
Unmark	Remove Delete, Move, or Copy as Link flags from the selected messages.
View in New	View the selected or displayed message in a new window.
Reply	Create a new email message In Reply To the selected or displayed email message.
Forward	Create a new email message containing the body of the selected or displayed email message in encapsulated form.
Use as Composition	Create a new email message using the body of the displayed or selected message as the body of the new message.
Print	Print the selected or displayed messages.

Table 4.19 xmh Sequence Drop-Down Menu

Item	Description
Pick	Define a new sequence of messages. As sequences are defined, they will be listed at the bottom of the Sequence menu. The only sequence that exists by default is All.
Open Sequence	Use the selected sequence of messages. The currently open sequence will appear with a check mark next to it in the drop-down menu.
Add to Sequence	Add selected messages to the selected sequence of messages.
Remove from Sequence	Remove the selected messages from the selected sequence of messages.
Delete Sequence	Delete the selected sequence of messages (but not the messages themselves).

Table 4.20 xmh View Drop-Down Menu

Item	Description
Reply	Create a new email message in a separate window in reply to the currently displayed or selected message.
Forward	Create a new email message in a separate window containing the body of the displayed or selected message in an encapsulated form.
Use as Composition	Create a new email message in a separate window containing the body of the displayed or selected message for further editing.
Edit Message	Open the currently displayed or selected message in a new window for editing.
Save Message	Save changes made in an Edit Message view to the original message.
Print	Print the message in the active view.

Table 4.21 xmh Options Drop-Down Menu

Item	Description
Read in Reverse	Causes the current sequence of messages (or all messages if the default sequence is selected) to be reversed. When this option is enabled, a check mark will appear next to it in the drop-down menu.

The second line in the xmh window display indicates the currently selected folder. The third section in the xmh display contains the list of all known mail folders and their subfolders and so on. To select any one of them, simply click the corresponding button. The fourth section in the xmh window is the currently displayed folder.

When editing messages using the xmh composer, most of the same keyboard controls listed for the xedit command earlier work in the same ways.

You can exit the xmh application by selecting Close Window in the Folder menu of the last existing xmh window.

xsetroot

The xsetroot utility changes the appearance of the current display's root window, by changing either its color or its pattern or both. This utility can also be used to change certain aspects of the pointing device cursor when over the root window. The most common command-line arguments accepted by xsetroot are shown in Table 4.22.

Table 4.22   Most Common Arguments Accepted by xsetroot

Argument	Description
-def	Restores the default appearance for the root window as dictated by the X server. This is normally a black-and-white hatch pattern.
-cursor path *path*	Changes the cursor that will be used by the mouse whenever it is directly over the root window. The first file specified is the path to the cursor bitmap image, and the second file is the path to the image mask, normally completely black. X bitmap can be created using the bitmap command.
-cursor_name *name*	Changes the cursor that will be used by the mouse whenever it is directly over the root window. This option enables the use of any of the cursors from the standard cursor font. To choose a cursor and find its name, execute the command xfd -fn cursor and use it to find the number of the cursor you'd like to use. Then, search the cursor include file at /usr/X11R6/include/X11/cursorfont.h for the name that matches the cursor number you selected. Supply this name, omitting the XC_ at the beginning, as the *name* when using this argument. For example, cursor number 62, a heart, is listed as XC_heart in the include file. The corresponding *name* would therefore be heart.
-bitmap *path*	Fills the root window with tiles of the specified bitmap file.
-mod *x y*	Fills the root window with a grid of lines occurring every *x* pixels horizontally and every *y* pixels vertically.
-gray	Makes the root window a solid gray.
-grey	See -gray above.
-fg *color*	Uses *color* as the foreground color in conjunction with the -cursor, -bitmap, or -mod arguments.

continues

Table 4.22 Continued

Argument	Description
-bg *color*	Uses *color* as the background color in conjunction with the -cursor, -bitmap, or -mod arguments if supplied.
-rv	Reverses the foreground and background colors.
-solid *color*	Sets the background color of the root window to *color*.

The xsetroot command is often called from a user's xinit script to configure the cursor and root window based on the user's preferences during login. For more information on xinit and the X boot process, refer to Chapter 6, "Runtime Session Defaults."

xterm

The xterm application emulates any number of different dumb terminals in an X window so that text-based applications can be executed inside the window. Most commonly, xterm windows are used to run instances of the UNIX shell, or in the case of Linux, the bash shell. The user's default login shell is the default application started inside an xterm window if no other application is specified. The most common command-line arguments accepted by xterm are shown in Table 4.23. Please note that many, many more are available, most of them having to do with terminal emulation behavior. For a complete list, consult the xterm manual page.

Table 4.23 Most Common Arguments Accepted by xterm

Argument	Description
-ah	Doesn't display the cursor as a hollow box when the xterm window doesn't have focus; instead, always displays a solid box cursor.
+ah	Displays the cursor as a hollow box when the xterm window doesn't have focus.
-aw	Enables auto-wrap, causing text that extends to the rightmost margin to wrap to the beginning of the next line.
+aw	Disables auto-wrap, causing text that extends past the rightmost margin to be truncated.
-b *n*	Uses *n* pixels as empty padding space between the window border and the text that appears inside the xterm window.
-cm	Enables ANSI color escape sequences to be displayed.
+cm	Disables the displaying of ANSI color escape sequences. Note that when disabled, the sequences will still be displayed—as garbage text instead of color.
-cr *color*	Specifies the color to use for the text cursor.

Argument	Description
-e command args...	Starts the specified command instead of the user's login shell in the new xterm window, and passes all remaining arguments given to the command started, rather than interpreting them as arguments to xterm.
-fb font	Uses the specified font when displaying bold text.
-hc color	Uses the specified color as the background color for selected text.
-j	Enables jump scrolling for display speed. This option allows xterm to jump ahead in the display stream when text is being displayed rather than having to display each line.
+j	Disables jump scrolling.
-leftbar	Displays the scrollbar (when present) on the left side of the xterm window.
-ls	Starts a login shell in the xterm window rather than a child shell. When this option is specified, the shell will be started as if the user had just logged in.
+ls	Doesn't start the shell as a login shell.
-ms color	Uses color as the color for the mouse pointer cursor inside the xterm window.
-rightbar	Displays the scrollbar (when present) on the right side of the xterm window.
-sb	Displays a scrollbar and saves lines that scroll past the top of the window in a memory buffer so that the user can scroll up and down through the xterm shell session.
-sl n	Specifies the number of lines to save when the scrollbar is enabled.
-title name	Specifies the title of the xterm window.
-rv	Starts xterm in reverse video, with the foreground and background colors switched.
-bg color	Specifies the background color of the xterm window text.
-fg color	Specifies the foreground color of the xterm window text.
-fn font	Specifies the font to use for displaying xterm window text.
-name name	Specifies a new resource name for this instance of xterm. Name should contain alphanumeric text or underscore characters.

The xterm utility is the fundamental method of accessing the power of the Linux shell on X-enabled systems. It can also be used to X-enable normally text-based applications when started using certain options. For example, to start vi as an X application, the following command could be used:

```
xterm -title vi -name vi -e vi &
```

This would result in a window containing the vi application, with a title of vi, which obtained its resources under the application name vi. In window managers such as Window Maker, this can be used to give text-based applications their own application icon.

A small utility called resize can be used to account for the potential geometry changes in the dumb terminal as an xterm window is resized on the X desktop. If, after an xterm window resize, text-based applications are found to behave badly or display incorrectly, issuing the resize command can often fix the problem. The use of the -u or -c arguments when calling resize cause resize to use bourne shell (bash) or C-shell (tcsh) commands to effect the resize, respectively.

X Runtime Status Utilities

In addition to the utilities already covered—which are generally designed to accomplish some specific task on behalf of the user or to allow the user to interact with the system in some way—there are many X utilities whose primary function is to relay information about the X runtime to the user. Some of these aren't installed by default with certain Linux distributions, but they can usually be found on the CD-ROM as part of one of the XFree86 packages. All the following utilities are installed by default when using the canonical XFree86 binary distribution.

xdpyinfo

The xdpyinfo utility enables the user to obtain copious amounts of information about a running X display server. The utility provides information about server configuration, capabilities, available color depths and visuals, screen display size in pixels-wide by pixels-high, resolution in dots-per-inch, and more. The utility is normally called alone on an xterm command line:

```
xdpyinfo
```

If necessary, xdpyinfo can also be called to query a specific display for information. The -display argument is used as follows:

```
xdpyinfo -display [host]:server[.screen]
```

When called this way, xdpyinfo will display information about the specified display rather than about the local display. For more information on specifying a display, see Chapter 15, "Working on the Network."

xfd

The xfd utility is used to display all the characters in an available X font in an easy-to-see format. The utility creates a large window containing the X Logical Font Descriptor (XLFD) across the top of the display, a range of valid characters, and then a grid containing a single character glyph in each square. For more information on constructing and using XLFDs, please refer to Chapter 7. The most common command-line arguments accepted by xfd are shown in Table 4.24.

Table 4.24   Most Common Arguments Accepted by xfd

Argument	Description
-fn *font*	Specifies the font that should be displayed in the xfd window. This argument is required for xfd to start.
-box	Causes xfd to display a box around each character indicating the background area for that character.
-center	Causes xfd to center each displayed character glyph in the middle of the grid square.
-start *n*	Causes xfd to start displaying with character *n* in the upper-left corner of the grid.
-bc *color*	Specifies the color that will be used by xfd to draw the boxes around each character when the -box argument has been supplied.
-rows *n*	Specifies the number of rows that should be present in the grid xfd uses to display character glyphs.
-columns *n*	Specifies the number of columns that should be present in the grid xfd uses to display character glyphs.

The xfd utility is commonly used as a quick-and-dirty way of examining a font, especially if the user needs to examine certain characters within the font. One common use is in displaying the list of X cursors:

```
xfd -fn cursor
```

These cursors can then be used from applications or in conjunction with a command like xsetroot to set the root window cursor. The xfd utility can also be used to quickly find the XLFD of an aliased font. For example:

```
xfd -fn fixed
```

This command quickly displays the fixed font and provides the information that the proper XLFD for the fixed font is

```
-Misc-Fixed-Medium-R-SemiCondensed--13-120-75-75-C-60-ISO8859-1
```

The xfd window can be exited by clicking the **Quit** button in the upper left of the window.

xlsatoms

The xlsatoms utility is used to list the atoms currently defined in the running X server. In X, an *atom* can be thought of as a basic unit of anything. The X protocol uses these atoms to communicate across the network; an atom can represent a font, a cursor, a behavior, or even a property. Most users will never need to use the list generated by xlsatoms, but it can at times be useful for debugging purposes, especially when writing X-centric code like window managers. The most common command-line options accepted by xlsatoms are shown in Table 4.25.

Table 4.25   Most Common Arguments Accepted by xlsatoms

Argument	Description
-display *hss*	Specifies a host, server, and screen from which to extract a list of atoms in the format [*host*]:*server*[.*screen*]. For more information on specifying a display, see Chapter 15.
-format printf_str	Specifies an output format for each pair of values. The format specifier follows the format of the printf command in C. The default format is %ld\t%s, displaying a decimal atom number, followed by a tab, followed by the atom name.
-name *text*	Specifies the name of the atom to list.
-range *n-n*	Specifies a range of atoms to list, from low bound to high bound. If the low bound is omitted, the list will begin with atom number 1. If the high bound is omitted, the list will stop at the first undefined atom.

xlsclients

The xlsclients utility lists all the clients running on a given display or server. It is most useful in generating session management scripts. The most common command-line arguments accepted by xlsclients are shown in Table 4.26.

Table 4.26   Most Common Arguments Accepted by xlsclients

Argument	Description
-display *hss*	Specifies a host, server, and screen from which to extract a list of atoms in the format [*host*]:*server*[.*screen*]. For more information on specifying a display, see Chapter 15.
-a	Lists all clients connected on all screens, instead of just on the current screen. Most Linux users will not use this option because XFree86 doesn't yet support multihead display.
-l	Generates a long format listing, providing details about the window name, icon name, command line, and machine.
-m	Specifies the maximum length of the displayed command string. The default limit is 10,000 characters.

xlsfonts

The xlsfonts utility enables the user to search the list of fonts that are explicitly known about by the running X server and to search the list for a given pattern. When run with no arguments, the xlsfonts utility simply lists all known fonts. The most common command-line options accepted by xlsfonts are shown in Table 4.27.

Table 4.27   Most Common Arguments Accepted by xlsfonts

Argument	Description
-display *hss*	Specifies a host, server, and screen from which to extract a list of atoms in the format [*host*]:*server*[.*screen*]. For more information on specifying a display, see Chapter 15.
-l[ll]	Specifies the long listing format to include font attributes in addition to font name. Specifying a second l adds a listing of font properties. The third l adds a listing of font character metrics.
-m	Specifies that long listings should also give minimum and maximum bounds for each font.
-w	Specifies the width of the listing in character columns. The default is 79 columns.
-n *n*	Generates the listing in *n* columns. Specifying 0 for the number of columns tells xlsfonts to try to use as many columns as it can fit into the display width. This is the default behavior.
-o	Specifies that xlsfonts should try to open and/or query fonts to generate the list of available fonts, instead of simply listing them. This can help to generate more accurate listings when scaled fonts are found to be missing from the list.
-fn *pattern*	Lists only fonts that match the supplied pattern. The pattern can use wildcard characters. For example, *bold* would list all font names that contain the word *bold*. Remember to escape wildcard characters when appropriate so that they aren't interpreted by the shell.

xprop

The xprop utility enables the user to list the properties that are associated with a given window or font. The window or font whose properties will be listed can be specified on the command line, or, if none is specified on the command line, xprop will ask the user to click a window whose properties will be listed. The most common command-line arguments accepted by xprop are shown in Table 4.28.

Table 4.28 Most Common Arguments Accepted by xprop

Argument	Description
-grammar	Prints out a grammar list for the xprop utility. The grammar display explains the argument structure to use for accomplishing various tasks with xprop, but is rather cryptic.
-id *id*	Causes xprop to use the supplied window ID to determine the window whose properties will be displayed.
-name *name*	Causes xprop to use the supplied window name to determine the window whose properties will be displayed.
-font *font*	Causes xpropt to use the supplied font name to determine the font whose properties will be displayed.
-root	Specifies that xprop should display the root window's properties.
-len *n*	Tells xpropt to limit the display of any single property to *n* bytes.
-notype	Causes xprop not to display property types, instead of the default behavior of displaying them.
-frame	Specifies that the window manager frame should be seen instead of ignored when selecting a client by hand.
-remove *name*	Causes xprop to attempt to remove the property referred to by *name* from the selected or specified window.
-spy	When supplied, causes xprop to continue to execute indefinitely, displaying changes to client properties as they occur.

The most common way to use xprop is simply to start it without arguments, as follows:

```
xprop
```

After Enter has been pressed, the pointer cursor's appearance will change, indicating that xprop is waiting for the user to select a window whose properties will be displayed. Clicking a window or on the root window will cause xprop to output the list of properties for the chosen window.

xwininfo

The xwininfo utility is used to obtain information about an application window on the X display. Various kinds of information can be displayed. The most common command-line arguments accepted by xwininfo can be found in Table 4.29. Many other command-line arguments are also supported and can be used to obtain various other kinds of information. For a complete list of accepted arguments, please consult the xwininfo manual page.

Table 4.29   Most Common Arguments Accepted by xwininfo

Argument	Description
-id *id*	Causes xwininfo to display information about the window specified by the supplied *id* string.
-name *name*	Causes xwininfo to display information about the window whose name matches the supplied *name* string.
-root	Causes xwininfo to display information about the root window.
-int	Causes xwininfo to display window ID numbers as integer (decimal) values rather than in the default hexadecimal format.
-children	Causes xwininfo to display the names of the selected window's root, parent, and children windows.
-tree	Similar to the -children argument listed above, but causes xwininfo to display the information in a recursive, indented, tree-like format.
-frame	Specifies that the window manager frame should be seen instead of ignored when selecting a client by hand.
-stats	Causes xwininfo to display various physical attributes related to the selected window, including geometry (width, height, and offsets from the edge of the display), color depth, border width, class, positions of the corners, and several hints. This is the default xwininfo behavior.
-all	When supplied, this argument will cause xwininfo to display all information it can obtain about the selected window.
-metric	When supplied, this argument will cause offsets and distances in pixels to be displayed in metric units (millimeters and centimeters) based on the X server's assumptions about the display size.
-english	When supplied, this argument will cause offsets and distances in pixels to be displayed in English measurement units (inches and feet) based on the X server's assumptions about the display size.

By far the most common use of the xwininfo command is in obtaining information about a window's location and geometry settings. This information is given as an X-axis size (width), a Y-axis size (height), and offsets in pixels from two edges of the display. For more information on geometry specification, please refer to Chapter 8.

When xwininfo is called without arguments, it will ask the user to select a window to display information:

```
xwininfo: Please select the window about which you
          would like information by clicking the
          mouse in that window.
```

After clicking the mouse either in an application window or in the root window, the requested information will be displayed to standard output, which generally means the xterm window from which xwininfo was called.

x11perf and x11perfcomp

The x11perf and x11perfcomp utilities are designed to help users determine the relative speed of an X server on specific hardware and compare the determined speed with the speed results obtained on other test runs, presumably using a slightly different configuration. The x11perf and x11perfcomp utilities are intended to be used mainly as optimization tools, though they are also commonly used as benchmark for the latest-and-greatest PC graphics hardware.

The x11perf utility is a rather exhaustive X performance testing tool that tests most of the available X functions, from the drawing of lines, polygons, bitmaps, and fonts to functions like mapping and moving windows, displaying refreshes, and copying planes of data. Test runs are normally executed on a fresh system with a low system load, a newly launched X server, and a local display connection. Normally, each of the numerous tests is run five times. The mouse cursor should not be passed over the x11perf test windows while tests are running because such activity will affect the results. The most commonly supplied command-line arguments for x11perf are shown in Table 4.30.

Table 4.30   Most Common Arguments Accepted by x11perf

Argument	Description
-repeat *n*	Specifies that x11perf should run each of the numerous tests *n* times. The default number of runs for each test is 5.
-time *n*	Specifies that each of the x11perf tests should be run for *n* seconds. The default number of seconds for each test run is 5.
-all	Causes x11perf to run a full complement of tests—all that it knows about.

Most of the numerous arguments accepted by x11perf are to enable or disable specific tests. Many more tests exist than can be listed and explained here; users interested in a selecting a specific set of tests, instead of the -all option, should consult the x11perf manual page.

The x11perfcomp utility is designed to format the output from several x11perf runs into an easy-to-compare, tabular format for human analysis. The most basic way to use x11perfcomp is to supply it with a list of files containing x11perf output:

```
x11perfcomp testrun1.file testrun2.file testrun3.file
```

However, several additional arguments are accepted by x11perfcomp that modify its behavior slightly. These arguments are shown in Table 4.31.

Table 4.31   Arguments Accepted by x11perfcomp

Argument	Description
-r	When supplied, this option causes x11perfcomp to include relative server performance in the output. The baseline system will be the system from the first file supplied.
-ro	When supplied, this option causes x11perfcomp to include only relative server performance in the output.
-l *file*	Specifies the path to a label file generated by supplying the -label option during x11perf runs.

Most users will rarely need to use the x11perf and x11perfcomp pair because running the full complement of tests is a time-consuming process, and X server performance on modern hardware is nearly always adequate anyway. Even so, the tests are sometimes useful for diagnostic purposes, such as when switching between X server versions or enabling or disabling acceleration features.

5

LINUX/X TOOLKIT PARTICULARS

Any normal Linux user has run many different X applications in addition to those discussed in Chapter 4, "Standard XFree86 Programs and Utilities." You might have noticed that most X applications don't actually look all that much like those discussed in Chapter 4. This is because most X applications, including many of those covered in the last chapter, aren't written using a single, basic X API or the Xlib directly—they aren't designed for that. Instead, they are written using higher-level programming toolkits that include complete sets of widgets such as text boxes, drop-down menus, buttons, and scrollbars.

In X, any number of these widget toolkits can be used when creating an application. This is rather unlike some operating systems like Windows or the Mac, in which a single toolkit forms the basis for nearly all applications. Unfortunately, this also means that in X, as many new Linux users have discovered, there can be a large amount of variation between the look and feel of each application. Worse, different applications' widgets might even behave very differently, so it is important to be familiar with each toolkit.

Free and Linux-Era Toolkits

Although some classic commercial UNIX toolkits have been in use on UNIX desktops for years, most of them aren't popular among Linux programmers, either because they're too old and unsupported or because they aren't open-source products.

Among Linux users, the most popular toolkits tend to be the Athena widget set, which forms the basis for most XFree86 utilities, and several other toolkits that were written after the advent of the Linux kernel, several of which are open-source products using similar (or identical) licenses to the GNU General Public License, which is used by Linux.

Xt/Xaw

The Xt library (X Toolkit intrinsics) and the Xaw library (X Athena Widgets) are the basic toolkits for X programming, and the only higher-level toolkits included with the standard XFree86 distribution. They are both written in C and are designed to help X programmers avoid the lower-level Xlib library.

The Xt library is the lowest level at which most X application programmers ever operate; few (other than those writing window managers) ever take the time to make direct Xlib calls or to learn the ins and outs of Xlib directly. Instead, most X programmers who work with the basic X libraries will either subclass objects from the Xt toolkit, modifying and extending them to suit the application's purposes, or write using the widgets in the Athena widget set, which includes several prebuilt widgets that are subclasses of Xt objects.

Most of the basic X utilities are based on the X Athena widget set, and that's where the Xaw creators intended the reach of Xaw to end. Instead, many programmers have used the rather bare, unfriendly, and ugly Athena widgets in their own applications as well. Programs that use the Athena widgets are easy to identify if they are dynamically linked through use of the ldd command:

```
$ ldd /usr/X11R6/bin/xmh
        libXaw.so.6 => /usr/X11R6/lib/libXaw.so.6 (0x4000a000)
        libXmu.so.6 => /usr/X11R6/lib/libXmu.so.6 (0x4005d000)
        libXt.so.6 => /usr/X11R6/lib/libXt.so.6 (0x4006f000)
        libSM.so.6 => /usr/X11R6/lib/libSM.so.6 (0x400b2000)
        libICE.so.6 => /usr/X11R6/lib/libICE.so.6 (0x400bb000)
        libXext.so.6 => /usr/X11R6/lib/libXext.so.6 (0x400d0000)
        libX11.so.6 => /usr/X11R6/lib/libX11.so.6 (0x400db000)
        libc.so.5 => /lib/libc.so.5 (0x4017b000)
```

The presence of the libXaw and libXt libraries indicates that this application is linked to the X Toolkit intrinsics and the X Athena widgets library. Even when an application is statically linked, the Athena widgets are easy to identify. The aXe editor, shown in Figure 5.1, is one such application. Table 5.1 lists some general information about the Athena widgets, and Table 5.2 lists some of the peculiarities.

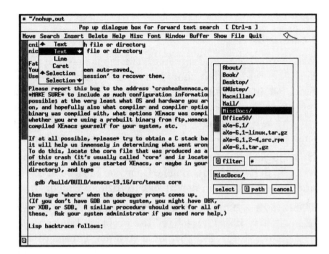

Figure 5.1 The aXe editor, with its spartan appearance, is based on the Xt intrinsic and Athena widgets.

Table 5.1 General Information About Athena Applications

Attribute	Details
Appearance	Extremely bare and undecorated, with a "flat" feel. Unless 3D-enhanced Athena library is in use, no shading or highlighting whatsoever. Applications look very primitive.
Examples	Standard XFree86 utilities.
Resources	Because Athena was developed early on, before the ultra-powerful, ultra-cheap computers of today, it boasts extremely low resource requirements. Will run in nearly no memory; microscopic CPU time requirements compared to other toolkits.

Table 5.2 Athena Peculiarities

Item	Peculiarity
Cursor	The Athena cursor doesn't blink and usually appears as a caret underneath the text rather than as a line between letters, which can make it extremely difficult both to locate within a body of text and to position within a line of text.
Drop-down Menu	The mouse button must be held down in order to operate Athena-based drop-down menus, similar to the operation of such menus in the Mac OS. Simply clicking a menu isn't enough; it will disappear after the mouse button has been released.

continues

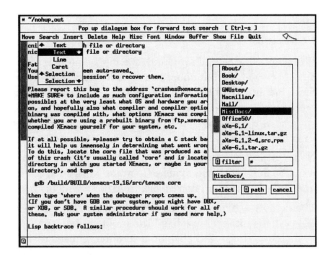

Figure 5.1   The aXe editor, with its spartan appearance, is based on the Xt intrinsic and Athena widgets.

Table 5.1   General Information About Athena Applications

Attribute	Details
Appearance	Extremely bare and undecorated, with a "flat" feel. Unless 3D-enhanced Athena library is in use, no shading or highlighting whatsoever. Applications look very primitive.
Examples	Standard XFree86 utilities.
Resources	Because Athena was developed early on, before the ultra-powerful, ultra-cheap computers of today, it boasts extremely low resource requirements. Will run in nearly no memory; microscopic CPU time requirements compared to other toolkits.

Table 5.2   Athena Peculiarities

Item	Peculiarity
Cursor	The Athena cursor doesn't blink and usually appears as a caret underneath the text rather than as a line between letters, which can make it extremely difficult both to locate within a body of text and to position within a line of text.
Drop-down Menu	The mouse button must be held down in order to operate Athena-based drop-down menus, similar to the operation of such menus in the Mac OS. Simply clicking a menu isn't enough; it will disappear after the mouse button has been released.

continues

Table 5.2   Continued

Item	Peculiarity
Text Entry	When entering text of any kind, the mouse pointer must be within the border of the widget that should receive the text. For example, when entering a filename into an entry box, the mouse pointer must appear inside the entry box as well, or typed text will not appear as intended. When using an editor such as aXe, the mouse pointer must appear inside the edit area; if it is on the menu bar, for example, all keystrokes will be lost.
Keyboard	No keyboard shortcuts exist to navigate widgets; all interaction with widgets must be done with the mouse. Common keys such as Home, End, Page Up, and Page Down often don't work in Athena widgets or text entry areas.
Scrollbar	The default Athena scrollbar mapping invariably drives new users nuts. Many distributions have fixed the problem, but as shipped, the scrollbars behave like this: A left click on a scrollbar causes text to scroll one page down. A right click on a scrollbar causes text to scroll one page up. The scrollbar can be dragged up and down only using the middle mouse button.

Because of the rather ugly appearance of the standard Athena widget set, a nonstandard Athena toolkit also exists, called the Xaw3D library. The three-dimensional Athena widgets are much prettier than the standard Athena widgets, giving a three-dimensional appearance using highlighting and shading. Several current Linux distributions ship with Xaw3D-enabled applications.

The behaviors of certain Athena widgets can also be modified by configuring X resources. It is thus common, for example, to see Athena scrollbars fixed to behave like users expect scrollbars to behave: with any of the three mouse buttons able to drag scroll the related area.

Gtk/Gtk+

The Gtk, or GIMP Toolkit, originally written to be used by the GNU Image Manipulation Program (GIMP), is a modern toolkit with a three-dimensional appearance written in ANSI C (see Figure 5.2). So-called wrappers also exist to allow Gtk, or the later Gtk+, to be used with other languages such as C++ or Python. The Gtk library is heavily object-oriented (as much so as one can get in C) and is licensed under the GNU General Public License.

The best-known application based on Gtk is the GIMP; the other well-known application of the Gtk library is as the basis for the GNOME desktop popular among Red Hat Linux users. Table 5.3 lists some general information about the Gtk widgets, and Table 5.4 lists some of the peculiarities.

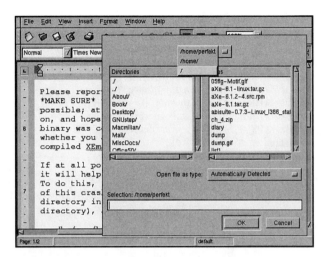

Figure 5.2 The appearance of Gtk applications is three-dimensional and similar to the appearance of Windows applications. Shown here is the AbiWord editor from AbiSource.

Table 5.3 General Information About Gtk Applications

Attribute	Details
Appearance	Decidedly similar to widgets seen in Windows 95/98 when not themed, complete with soft highlighting. Later, themed Gtk applications might look like almost anything at all.
Examples	The GIMP, AbiSource's AbiWord.
Resources	Older Gtk applications use minimal memory and CPU resources; newer Gtk+/GNOME applications are extremely memory- and CPU-hungry.

Table 5.4 Gtk Peculiarities

Item	Peculiarity
Cursor	The Gtk cursor doesn't blink, even when the widget that contains it is focused.
Phantom Buttons	For some reason, the designers of the Gtk originally gave nearly all widgets a raised, button-like look—even those widgets that don't normally interact with the user, such as labels and titles. Some Gtk applications (especially older ones) therefore appear to have many more buttons than are actually present. Don't get frustrated—if you've clicked on a button in a Gtk application several times and there has been no result, it probably isn't a button at all, but a label or other noninteractive widget instead.

The use of the Gtk library can generally be detected by its presence alongside the presence of its sibling Gdk library in an ldd call, as shown here:

```
$ ldd /usr/X11R6/bin/gimp
        libgtk.so.1 => /usr/X11R6/lib/libgtk.so.1 (0x4000a000)
        libgdk.so.1 => /usr/X11R6/lib/libgdk.so.1 (0x400b2000)
        libglib.so.1 => /usr/X11R6/lib/libglib.so.1 (0x400d1000)
        libXext.so.6 => /usr/X11R6/lib/libXext.so.6 (0x400dd000)
        libX11.so.6 => /usr/X11R6/lib/libX11.so.6 (0x400e8000)
        libm.so.5 => /lib/libm.so.5 (0x40188000)
        libc.so.5 => /lib/libc.so.5 (0x40191000)
```

Recent advances in the Gtk library have led to the highly themeable Gtk+ library, which is really a chameleon in toolkit's clothing. Themable Gtk+ applications can really take on almost any appearance at all.

The Gtk+ home page can be found at http://www.gtk.org.

Qt from Troll Tech

The Qt library from Troll Tech has been made popular by the KDE desktop, which uses Qt as the basis for the KDE libraries. Versions of the Qt library through the 1.x series were released under a free-for-noncommercial-use-only license, much to the chagrin of many Linux users who felt that software freedom was of paramount importance. Versions of the Qt library numbered 2.0 and later are released under the QPL, a free software license similar to the GPL, but with important differences.

The Qt library is a highly object-oriented C++ development platform. The Qt library is themable but, in the Linux world, is usually similar in appearance either to the Gtk library, seen earlier, or the Motif library, seen in the next section. The K Desktop Editor, or *kedit*, is shown in Figure 5.3. Table 5.5 lists some general information about the Qt widgets, and Table 5.6 lists some of the peculiarities.

Table 5.5   General Information About Qt Applications

Attribute	Details
Appearance	In the Linux world, Qt usually appears similar either to the Windows 95/98 widgets or the Motif widget set, depending on application and configuration. Later themed Qt applications might look like almost anything at all.
Examples	KDE applications, QT Nethack.
Resources	Older Qt applications use minimal memory and CPU resources; newer Qt 2.0 and KDE applications can be extremely memory- and CPU-hungry.

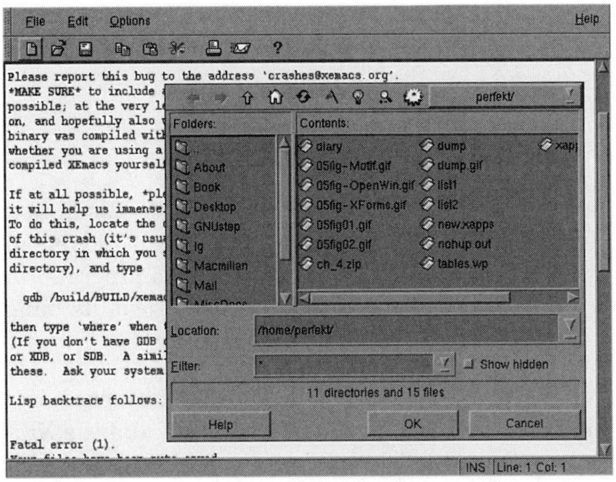

Figure 5.3   The Qt library usually appears as a part of the KDE, appearing similar either to the Gtk or (as shown here) the Motif widgets.

Table 5.6   Qt Peculiarities

Item	Peculiarity
Refresh	Qt widgets used in the K Desktop Environment seem to redraw themselves slowly, in part because each widget can refresh several times as a dialog is drawn. This can lead to a blinking effect or a built-as-you-watch effect when dialogs appear.
Identification	When using the KDE desktop, Qt applications often appear similar visually either to Gtk applications or to Motif applications. Qt and Gtk applications can be differentiated because Qt applications will have a blinking cursor. Qt and Motif applications can usually be differentiated by watching the application draw widgets—Motif widgets usually draw more quickly.

For Linux users, Qt almost always shows up alongside the KDE libraries when checked for using ldd, as shown here:

```
$ ldd /opt/kde/bin/kedit
        libkfile.so.1 => /opt/kde/lib/libkfile.so.1 (0x4000a000)
        libkfm.so.1 => /opt/kde/lib/libkfm.so.1 (0x40045000)
        libkdeui.so.1 => /opt/kde/lib/libkdeui.so.1 (0x40050000)
        libkdecore.so.1 => /opt/kde/lib/libkdecore.so.1 (0x400ed000)
        libqt.so.1 => /usr/lib/libqt.so.1 (0x4014c000)
        libXext.so.6 => /usr/X11R6/lib/libXext.so.6 (0x402a5000)
        libX11.so.6 => /usr/X11R6/lib/libX11.so.6 (0x402b0000)
        libg++.so.27 => /usr/lib/libg++.so.27 (0x40350000)
        libstdc++.so.27 => /usr/lib/libstdc++.so.27 (0x40388000)
```

```
libm.so.5 => /lib/libm.so.5 (0x403ba000)
libc.so.5 => /lib/libc.so.5 (0x403c3000)
```

The Qt home page can be found at `http://www.troll.no/qt/`.

XForms

The XForms library predates both the Gtk and Qt libraries for Linux users. When XForms initially emerged, some Linux users embraced it as a toolkit with widgets more attractive than the Athena widgets, yet an interface that was much easier to program than the interface of the Motif library. Other Linux users shunned XForms because of its binary-only distribution policy.

The two applications that brought the XForms library to prominence are the LyX editor by Mattais Ettrich, who went on to work with the KDE project, and the XFMail email user agent by Gennady Sorokopud. In spite of the fact that other toolkits (most notably Gtk and Qt) have come to dominate the Linux community's programming efforts in recent months, the popularity and importance of LyX and XFMail have kept XForms alive in the Linux community.

The LyX editor, one of the premier XForms applications for Linux users, can be seen in Figure 5.4. Table 5.7 lists some general information about the XForms widgets, and Table 5.8 lists some of the peculiarities.

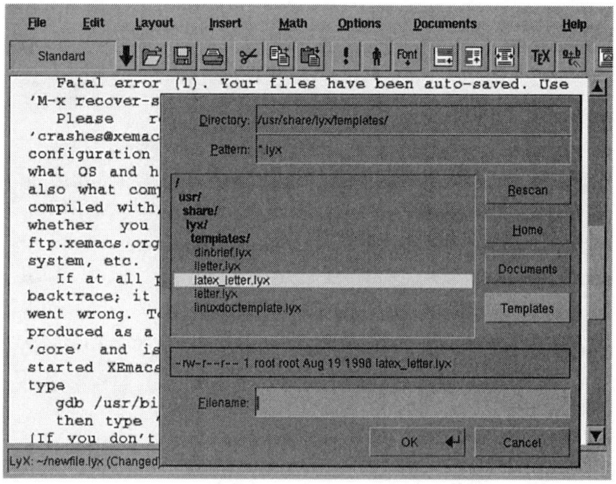

Figure 5.4   XForms applications have a distinctive look.

Table 5.7   General Information About XForms Applications

Attribute	Details
Appearance	XForms applications tend to have a homegrown feel to them. Widgets can seem unusually deep or shallow compared to applications written using other toolkits. Highlights are brighter and shadows darker than in other widget kits. Corners are hard rather than soft or rounded.
Examples	XFMail, LyX.
Resources	Minimal resources used. Shared library is small and relatively memory- and CPU-friendly.

Table 5.8   XForms Peculiarities

Item	Peculiarity
Cursor	The XForms cursor doesn't blink, even when the widget that contains it is focused.
Resizing	Resizing many XForms dialogs, especially those written with older versions of XForms, can "break" widgets, causing them to overlap or disappear altogether. It is therefore best not to try to resize XForms dialogs unless absolutely necessary.
Color	Don't adjust your display; default XForms widgets are a much darker gray than the widgets used by other libraries. Users are also often thrown by the yellow selection bar and blue cursor—these aren't indications of errors, but again simply default colors.

Linux XForms applications usually have a name that begins with xf and are usually dynamically linked, meaning that the library can be seen with a call to ldd:

```
$ ldd /usr/X11R6/bin/lyx
    libforms.so.0.86 => /usr/X11R6/lib/libforms.so.0.86 (0x4000a000)
    libXpm.so.4 => /usr/X11R6/lib/libXpm.so.4 (0x40076000)
    libSM.so.6 => /usr/X11R6/lib/libSM.so.6 (0x40084000)
    libICE.so.6 => /usr/X11R6/lib/libICE.so.6 (0x4008d000)
    libc.so.5 => /lib/libc.so.5 (0x400a2000)
    libm.so.5 => /lib/libm.so.5 (0x4015f000)
    libX11.so.6 => /usr/X11R6/lib/libX11.so.6 (0x40168000)
```

The XForms home page, from which the XForms library can be downloaded, is located at http://bragg.phys.uwm.edu.

Major UNIX Toolkits

Several different commercial X toolkits for UNIX have been developed over the years, but two of them stand out, largely because of the number of users each of them still boasts. As luck would have it, both are also available to Linux users.

Motif

The Open Software Foundation's Motif library represents a collaboration between many major UNIX vendors who years ago decided that a consistent UNIX desktop would be a good thing. Motif was a large, complex, and capable API that also functioned as the backbone for the Common Desktop Environment, or CDE, which today remains the reference desktop shipping with most UNIX workstation.

Unfortunately, Motif is a commercial, though "open," product, and its commercial nature shows—until very recently, there was no free implementation of Motif for Linux. Linux users interested in writing Motif applications had to purchase costly Motif development environments and then statically link the applications for distribution. Happily, a free Motif implementation known as LessTif is now available, but in the meantime, Motif has failed to catch on with the fastest growing segment of the UNIX-like population: Linux users.

Several large applications for Linux, notably, the commercial ones, use the Motif library as their basis. Among these are Netscape's Navigator and Communicator and Corel's WordPerfect for Linux (see Figure 5.5). Table 5.9 lists some general information about the Motif widgets, and Table 5.10 lists some of the peculiarities.

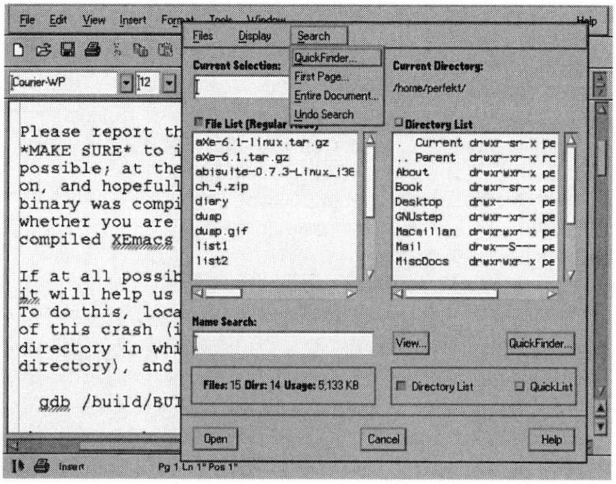

Figure 5.5   Corel's WordPerfect 8 for Linux is based on the classic Motif library, a mainstay in the UNIX world.

Table 5.9   General Information About Motif Applications

Attribute	Details
Appearance	Most applications have thick widgets with hard (unrounded) corners. Motif applications tend to be very consistent and professional, the choice of most commercial developers, but many still regard them as ugly widgets.
Examples	Corel's WordPerfect for Linux, Netscape Navigator and Communicator.
Resources	Dynamically linked Motif applications are relatively memory- and CPU-friendly. Unfortunately, most Motif applications are statically linked, increasing memory requirements when multiple Motif applications are run simultaneously.

Table 5.10   Motif Peculiarities

Item	Peculiarity
Check box	Motif check boxes can be difficult to use because they simply appear pushed in when checked or pushed out when not, forcing the user to rely on simulated lighting clues to determine the check box's status. If in doubt, operate the box a few times to determine its status. Remember, *in* for checked, *out* for unchecked.
Cursor	In some versions of Motif for Linux, the cursor can become stuck and refuse further keyboard input. The most common solution is to click the mouse cursor inside the border of another application's window, and then return to the problem application.
Shared Library	A recent advent in the Linux community is the emergence of a free Motif clone called LessTif, which can be found at `http://www.lesstif.org`. In order to maximize memory performance, users might want to try using the shared LessTif library along with dynamically linked Motif applications when available.

Because most Motif applications for Linux are statically linked, there is no simple technical way to prove or disprove that such an application uses Motif. In most cases, it must be visually identified.

It looks as though Motif's time in the Linux community is running short, ironically just as the free LessTif finally comes of age. Corel has indicated that it might be shifting its development efforts to the Wine API for Linux, which emulates the Windows API, and Netscape's next-generation Mozilla browser project has stopped using Motif as well.

OpenLook/XView

Just before Motif, there was OpenWindows, Sun Microsystems' own X distribution that was based on its OpenLook API. Most of the pre-Solaris versions of SunOS shipped with OpenWindows rather than the Open Software Foundation's Common Desktop Environment and Motif. Because of this, many of the scientific workstations in use around the world today are still based on the OpenLook API.

As Sun adopted Motif and the CDE, the code to OpenLook was released as free software as the Xview development platform. In the early days of Linux, years before KDE, GNOME, Gtk, or Qt, XView was a popular desktop environment because of its integration and good (though sometimes odd) looks. Many of the early Linux adoptees used OpenWindows on Sun workstation at work and Xview under Linux at home. Although Xview has been largely made obsolete by the development of the KDE and GNOME, the Xview desktop remains useful to those who need an integrated desktop that can run on a 386 with only 8 megabytes of memory—a low-memory, low-power feat of which KDE and GNOME can't even dream.

The Xview `textedit` application is shown in Figure 5.6. Table 5.11 lists some general information about the Xview widgets, and Table 5.12 lists some of the peculiarities.

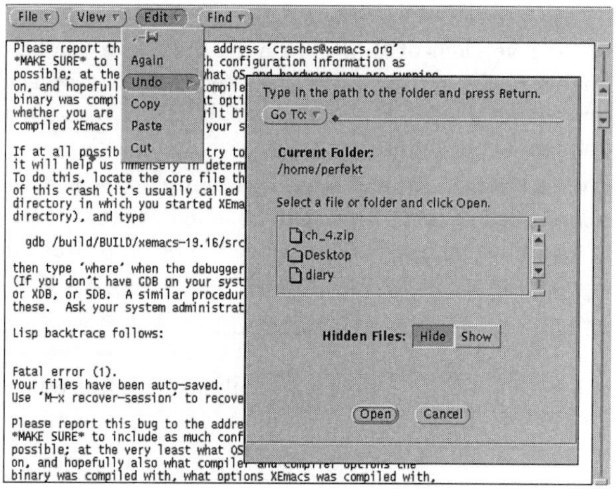

Figure 5.6 OpenLook/XView applications such as `textedit` have a very unusual appearance by today's standards and always turn a few heads.

Table 5.11   General Information About OpenLook/XView Applications

Attribute	Details
Appearance	The appearance of OpenLook/XView applications is unmistakable, from the odd cursor and pushpins to the circular buttons and drop-down menus. Many users feel that the appearance of OpenLook/XView applications is metallic or machine-like thanks to the single color and thin edges of OpenLook/XView widgets.
Examples	WorkMan, Perf.
Resources	Like the Athena widgets, OpenLook/XView was developed in an era when a 16MHz 32-bit workstation with 8MB memory was worth upward of $25,000. OpenLook is easy on memory and easy on the CPU as well.

Table 5.12   OpenLook/XView Peculiarities

Item	Peculiarity
Cursor	The OpenLook/XView cursor doesn't blink and can appear either as a small diamond or a small triangle below a line of text. Like the Athena cursor, the OpenLook/XView cursor can therefore be difficult to position.
Drop-Down Menu	In OpenLook/XView, each drop-down menu has a default action. When a drop-down menu is left-clicked, instead of the menu appearing, the default action is carried out. For example, users might find that a left click on the File menu instantly brings up the Save dialog rather than producing a menu of items from which to choose. To get the menu, use the *right* mouse button when clicking on a drop-down.
Scrollbar	The OpenLook/XView scrollbars place up and down arrows on the bar in the middle of the scroll area. The unexpected behavior occurs when these arrows are clicked; clicking them causes the mouse to move up or down the screen in the opposite direction of the text, often producing a dizzy sensation in new users.
Pushpin	Most users migrating to Linux from other operating systems will not be familiar with the pushpin that appears in OpenLook/XView applications. Clicking the pushpin allows a menu to be pinned to the screen indefinitely while other activity continues. To unpin a menu or dialog, click the pushpin again and pull it out of the pinhole.
Text Entry	In OpenLook/XView applications, the small text entry boxes with which most users are familiar appear only as otherwise undecorated horizontal lines. To enter text into the box, the user must click on or near the line. When the diamond-shaped cursor appears on the left side of the line, the user can enter text.

Most Linux users will have little or no trouble identifying an OpenLook/XView application without ever having to issue a command or perform a technical check. Still, for those users what want to identify an Xview application, ldd is again in most cases the ideal command:

```
$ ldd /usr/openwin/bin/textedit
        libxview.so.3 => /usr/openwin/lib/libxview.so.3 (0x4000a000)
        libolgx.so.3 => /usr/openwin/lib/libolgx.so.3 (0x4011d000)
        libXext.so.6 => /usr/X11R6/lib/libXext.so.6 (0x40129000)
        libX11.so.6 => /usr/X11R6/lib/libX11.so.6 (0x40134000)
        libc.so.5 => /lib/libc.so.5 (0x401d4000)
```

Many Linux users have Xview installed and don't even realize it. If you find a /usr/openwin directory on your disk, try this from a text console:

```
$ /usr/openwin/bin/openwin
```

When present, the openwin script works like the startx script in as much as it starts the X server and loads a few applications; but unlike the startx script, the openwin script will lead you to an OpenWindows desktop.

Little or no OpenLook/XView development occurs anymore; the Xview library is all but abandoned for new development, in large part because the library itself has experienced little or no development for the better part of a decade. Still, enough OpenLook/XView applications exist to keep the faithful computing for some time to come.

The best archive for the OpenLook/XView libraries, desktop, and related applications can be found on the Internet at http://step.polymtl.ca/~coyote/xview_main.html.

6

Runtime Session Defaults

Previous chapters have discussed the X server in quite a bit of detail. The X server's function is clear, and the repository for X server configuration, the XF86Config file, has been well documented. The standard XFree86 desktop and utilities have also been discussed at some length.

However, there is an important step between the moment the user types startx at the console prompt and the point at which the default desktop has finally been loaded. After the startx command has been loaded and the X server started, how does the system decide that the twm window manager and all the xterm windows should be started? On the default desktop, how is it decided that the login window should be the controlling process for the X session?

Clearly, some behavioral defaults are at work that decide which window manager to launch, which processes to start, and which process will be the controlling process. In fact, several other default actions are also performed at the start of an X session runtime in most XFree86 installations.

Global Defaults

Much of the default XFree86 behavior, and many properties of XFree86 clients and processes, are stored in subdirectories within the lib/X11/ directory off the main XFree86 tree. The files in these directories specify a global default set of behaviors for many X programs and processes, including the X session launch process.

Default xinit Behavior

The default xinitrc script is stored at /usr/X11R6/lib/X11/xinit/xinitrc. This is an executable shell script that is executed whenever the startx command is issued from the console, provided that the user doesn't have a replacement local file called .xinitrc in his or her home directory.

The default global xinitrc file, as shipped with XFree86 3.3.4, is shown in Listing 6.1. Note that line numbers have been added for clarity and aren't present in the actual file.

Listing 6.1 The /usr/X11R6/lib/X11/xinit/xinitrc Script

```
1  #!/bin/sh
2  # $XConsortium: xinitrc.cpp,v 1.4 91/08/22 11:41:34 rws Exp $
3
4  userresources=$HOME/.Xresources
5  usermodmap=$HOME/.Xmodmap
6  sysresources=/usr/X11R6/lib/X11/xinit/.Xresources
7  sysmodmap=/usr/X11R6/lib/X11/xinit/.Xmodmap
8
9  # merge in defaults and keymaps
10
11 if [ -f $sysresources ]; then
12     xrdb -merge $sysresources
13 fi
14
15 if [ -f $sysmodmap ]; then
16     xmodmap $sysmodmap
17 fi
18
19 if [ -f $userresources ]; then
20     xrdb -merge $userresources
21 fi
22
23 if [ -f $usermodmap ]; then
24     xmodmap $usermodmap
25 fi
26
27 # start some nice programs
28
29 twm &
30 xclock -geometry 50x50 1+1 &
```

```
31 xterm -geometry 80x50+494+51 &
32 xterm -geometry 80x20+494 0 &
33 exec xterm -geometry 80x66+0+0 -name login
```

Lines 1–2 of this file are comments indicating, first, that the file is a shell script which should be called via /bin/sh and, second, the author and creation date of the original file. As you can see from the date, August 22, 1991, the global xinitrc file has not changed in several years. All the tools and clients called from within the default xinitrc file are thus at least eight years old, meaning that these defaults should work equally well both on large, modern computers and on older machines lacking in CPU horsepower or memory by current standards.

Lines 4–7 of the file specify two pairs of files that are used to hold further default behavior. The first two files listed are the user-specific widget resources and keyboard mapping files. Note that they must exist in the user's home directory if they are to be used. The second two files correspond to the same functions respectively—that is, widget resources and keyboard mapping—but they are global default files, which will be used for everyone, regardless of a given user's own settings.

Lines 11–25 of the file check for the existence of each file specified in lines 4–7 in turn. If the file in question exists, the defaults contained therein will be used in starting and configuring the X session. The xrdb command is used to merge data into the X resource database. More information on using xrdb and X resources can be found in Chapter 8, "Runtime Application Configuration." The xmodmap command is used to alter default keyboard mapping. More information on managing keyboard settings can be found in Chapter 7, "Runtime Server Configuration."

Line 29 starts a window manager to manage the session. The manager called by default is twm, a lightweight, fast window manager that draws entirely in line art (no three-dimensional effects) and uses very few colors. It is nevertheless a rather handsome window manager and many users prefer it to this day. Note that twm is started in the background—that is, with an ampersand (&) after it. This means that after twm is launched, the script continues to execute, and the script doesn't depend on twm for its completion.

Lines 30–32 start several background X clients. First, an xclock is started, followed by two independent xterm clients. The -geometry argument supplied to the clients in lines 29–33 modifies one of the Athena widget resources in order to specify the location on the display at which the windows should appear and the size of each window. For more information on configuring the Athena widget resources, including the -geometry option, please refer to Chapter 8.

Finally, line 33 launches another xterm client. This command is a special one, however, because it is the controlling process for the X session. Notice two things about the structure of the command. First, exec is used to launch xterm. The exec command causes a shell, such as the one executing the script, to chain to the new process rather than fork to it. In plain terms, this means that the shell will exit, launching the new command *instead of* itself, rather than as a foreground or background process with respect to itself. Next, notice that this final xterm command isn't called in the background with the ampersand (&) character but rather, in the foreground, thus effectively halting processing of the script until it exits. The net effect of these details is that when the xterm process in line 33 exits, the entire script exits, closing the X session and all clients. The xterm command in line 33 is thus the controlling process of the X session.

Many users choose to launch the window manager as the controlling process for a session, starting it on the last line of the script in the foreground and all earlier clients in the background, so that when the window manager exits, the session also exits. To change one's session script in this way, the user's default script must generally be changed to reflect the new session. User defaults are covered later in this chapter.

Other Global Default Files

One or two other global default files can have an effect when running startx to start the X session from the console. Two of them have already been mentioned—the .Xmodmap and .Xdefaults files located in the /usr/X11R6/lib/X11/xinit/ directory. These files are used by the system administrator to create sitewide or networkwide default keyboard mapping and application widget resource settings. User-specific settings go in the related files in the user's home directory.

Also of importance is the global twm configuration file. Most window managers will keep a default configuration of some sort somewhere in the /usr/X11R6/lib/X11 directory tree. The default configuration for the twm window manager is stored at /usr/X11R6/lib/X11/twm/system.twmrc and should be changed by the system administrator if necessary to reflect sitewide or networkwide default settings for the twm desktop. Here again, the user can implement his or her own twm configuration by creating a file called .twmrc in his or her home directory. Details on configuring twm can be found in Chapter 9, "Runtime Environment Configuration."

Another less widely used file that can nevertheless be useful, especially in network situations with multiple potential login points, is the /usr/X11R6/lib/X11/xinit/xserverrc file. This file is used to launch the X server when present; it should be a shell script that contains code to check for platform and operating system information and then to start the X server with the proper arguments for the given environment. For a detailed look at multiplatform and networked operation, please see Chapter 17, "Heterogeneous Networks." Note that if no xserverrc file is present (as is normally the case), the X server will simply be called using the X binary, or in later XFree86 releases, the Xwrapper binary.

Changing Global Default Files

The global default files discussed in the /usr/X11R6/lib/X11 directory tree are very rough and very basic indeed. They can easily be changed to suit different needs, and should be by competent system administrators in multiple user situations to create the most effective default session and desktop for their users or for their company. Sitewide or networkwide keymaps can often be helpful when dealing with the company's esoteric PC pool buying habits. And it is often necessary to alter both the default list of launched clients and the default desktop presented to users, either with a different window manager altogether or by editing the twm manager's default behavior. In some cases, it might even be helpful to edit the script so that the user's own settings are ignored by commenting out those sections of the script that load files from the user's home directory.

On the other hand, in single-user (that is, Linux home desktop) installations, it is probably easier and more correct to maintain personal session preferences in the user's default files rather than by becoming root and editing the global defaults. In the home desktop environment, there is simply no need to spend time getting a sitewide or networkwide configuration right; it makes much more sense just to edit for your personal preferences as per the instructions in the next section.

User Defaults

Global settings are, of course, meant to be changed by the user whenever appropriate; the purpose of global settings is merely to provide for some baseline level and method of operation when no user preferences have been given.

The user-specified counterpart to the /usr/X11R6/lib/X11/xinit/xinitrc script is the .xinitrc script in the user's home directory. Note that the global script's name doesn't start with a period, while the user's script does, causing the file to be hidden in normal directory listings.

The startx Process

When the startx command is called, it first checks to see whether an .xserverrc file is present in the user's home directory. This file will be used as a special script to start the X server when present, but it is normally not needed. If no .xserverrc file is present in the user's home directory, and no global .xserverrc file can be found in /usr/X11R6/lib/X11/xinit, the X server will be started simply by forking to the X binary, or in later XFree86 releases, the Xwrapper binary.

After the server has been launched, startx will look for a file in the user's home directory called .xinitrc. If this file doesn't exist, startx will resort to the global default session script at /usr/X11R6/lib/X11/xinit/xinitrc. If an .xinitrc script does exist in the user's home directory and is executable, it will be called instead, and the global script won't be used.

Because most users still want the .Xmodmap and .Xdefaults files searched and used, both on a global and on a user level, the most common way to construct a personal .xinitrc script is to copy it to one's home directory from the global script, and then edit the last few lines (which call the clients, the window manager, and the controlling process) by hand:

```
$ cp /usr/X11R6/lib/X11/xinit/xinitrc ${HOME}/.xinitrc
$ vi .xinitrc
```

Important Differences

It is important to understand that the user's ${HOME}/.xinitrc and ${HOME}/.xserverrc files will be used instead of the global defaults for these files in /usr/X11R6/lib/X11/xinit, while the ${HOME}/.Xmodmap and ${HOME}/.Xdefaults files will be used in addition to the global defaults for these files in the same directory. It is also important to note that all four files appear in the user's home directory with the dot as their first character: .xserverrc, .xinitrc, .Xmodmap, .Xdefaults; in contrast, only the .Xmodmap and .Xdefaults files retain the dot in the global directory—the other two files appear as xserverrc and xinitrc (no dot) in the global directory.

7

RUNTIME SERVER
CONFIGURATION

A sizable percentage of the XFree86 configuration is accomplished through use of the XF86Config file documented in Chapter 2, "Installing and Configuring XFree86." However, many other configuration changes are normally made after XFree86 is started or during the XFree86 launch process in the xinitrc script discussed in the previous chapter. Several configuration changes also affect the way the user will interact with the X server at runtime, rather than just how the X server will interact with the system hardware.

This chapter is all about those server configuration options that are manipulated after the server has been started and also those configuration options that affect the way the user interacts with the server throughout the course of an X session.

Keyboard, Mouse, and Display Configuration

Several configuration options deal in a basic way with the interaction between the user and the keyboard, mouse, and display hardware at an X console. Among these are keyboard mapping, screen savers and screen blanking, mouse acceleration, and internationalization. Although many users never need to change any of these settings from their defaults, it is often necessary to tweak a configuration to get it just right for your own personal preferences, especially if you are a non-English speaker or you are running Linux on non-PC hardware.

Keyboard Mapping: Minor Changes or Tweaks

Usually when users ask about changing key mappings in XFree86, it is because their keyboard basically works okay, with one or two exceptions—such as a Backspace key that won't backspace, a Delete key that deletes to the left instead of to the right, or arrow keys that don't seem to cause the cursor to move when pressed. These sorts of minor problems are easily fixed using two commands, xev and xmodmap. The process is simple, so the detail level in this section is light. For the brave of heart, the next section goes into more detail about the way in which keyboard mapping works. For this section, however, it's best to think about keyboard mapping like this:

Each key on a keyboard looks like a number to the computer. XFree86 knows about lots of different kinds of keys. If a key isn't working, it's because the keyboard is sending a different number than X expects for the key in question. Fixing a broken key is then the process of telling XFree86 about the correct number for a given key.

Finding the Right Key with xev

The best way to find out what number a given key is sending is to use the xev command. The xev command is basically a window that sits on the desktop and listens for X events like keypresses, button clicks, or mouse movement, and then prints information about this activity on standard output. To start xev, simply supply its name on the command line, like this:

```
xev
```

Some distributions don't install xev by default; it might be part of an X development or extra package; if so, you'll have to install it before you can use it. Once started, xev appears simply as a window with a box in it, as shown in Figure 7.1.

The magic begins to happen when you do anything at all—move the mouse, press a key on the keyboard, or click a mouse button. Notice that, with each action of any kind, xev is printing copious amounts of information in the xterm window from which it was launched. This information is normally used for diagnostic work when writing X clients, but for keyboard work, we're interested in what it prints out when a key is pressed. Make sure the xev window has focus, and then press the key that is misbehaving. You should see output like this:

```
KeyPress event, serial 21, synthetic NO, window 0x3800001,
    root 0x26, subw 0x0, time 2146521803, (172,  11), root:(194,32),
    state 0x0, keycode 23 (keysym 0xff09, Tab), same_screen YES,
    XLookupString gives 1 characters: "        "

KeyRelease event, serial 21, synthetic NO, window 0x3800001,
    root 0x26, subw 0x0, time 2146521907, (172,  11), root:(194,32),
    state 0x0, keycode 23 (keysym 0xff09, Tab), same_screen YES,
    XLookupString gives 1 characters: "        "
```

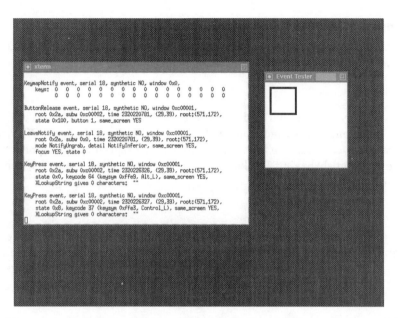

Figure 7.1   The xev tool—just a window with a box in it—and the xterm from which it was launched, full of information.

Be careful not to move the mouse too much after pressing the key or the information will scroll rapidly out of view. For our purposes, the important piece of information is the keycode supplied on the third line—in this example, the keycode is 23. Write this number down, close the xev window, and proceed.

Finding a Symbol in keysymdef.h

After you've learned the keycode for the key you'd like to modify, you must find the X keyboard function you'd like to match to the key in question. A list of these X keyboard functions can be found in the file include/X11/keysymdef.h off the main XFree86 directory tree.

Browsing this file reveals a long list of names beginning with XK_ and followed by a hexadecimal number. The names might seem cryptic at first but are usually easy to decipher. For example, XK_Return refers to the Enter symbol, XK_Backspace to the Backspace symbol, and XK_Page_Up and XK_Page_Down to the Page Up and Page Down symbols, respectively. Search through the list and find the symbol you'd like to attach to the key in question.

Using xmodmap to Make the Changes

After you've got the keycode for the key in question and the key symbol you'd like that key to be linked to, call the xmodmap command in the following manner:

```
xmodmap -e 'keycode n = Sym'
```

Replace *n* with the keycode number and Sym with the name of the symbol you'd like bound to the keycode in question, minus the XK_ at the beginning. For example, on a PC machine, the Tab key generates keycode 23. The tab function in X is referenced by the symbol XK_Tab. If a given machine had a misbehaving Tab key, it could be remapped to the X XK_Tab symbol using the following command:

```
xmodmap -e 'keycode 23 = Tab'
```

By far the two most common changes made to the default XFree86 keyboard mappings are for broken Backspace or Delete keys. On a standard PC keyboard, the Backspace and Delete keys have keycodes of 22 and 107, respectively. The XFree86 functions that most users expect to be bound to these keys are XK_Backspace and XK_Delete as given in the include/X11/keysymdef.h file. The commands to fix these keys on a PC keyboard are therefore these:

```
xmodmap -e 'keycode 22 = Backspace'
xmodmap -e 'keycode 107 = Delete'
```

Note that these keycodes apply only to the PC platform; users of other types of machines or of very nonstandard PC keyboards should use xev to find the correct keycodes when fixing broken Backspace or Delete keys.

Other Ways to Use xmodmap

There are several other ways to use xmodmap when reconfiguring a keyboard. The two most common are the add and remove expressions, which add a key symbol to a given modifier map or remove a key symbol from a given modifier map. A *modifier* is a keyboard state, such as being shifted (as normally happens when the shift keys are held down). A modifier *map* is the list of keys that will place the keyboard into that state. The most common modifiers for X users are shown in Table 7.1.

Table 7.1 The Four Most Common Modifier States

Modifier	Description
shift	Keys are shifted—letters appear in uppercase, numbers generate symbols.
lock	Some keys are locked in the shifted state—letters appear in uppercase permanently. More commonly known as Caps Lock.
control	Key behavior is altered, usually for keyboard shortcuts in applications.
mod1	Key behavior is altered, usually for keyboard shortcuts in applications. More commonly known to users as Alt.

The add and remove expressions tell xmodmap to add a key symbol to the list of key symbols that can generate a modified state. For example, assume that a user issued the following command:

```
xmodmap -e 'add shift = Tab'
```

After this command has been issued, any press and hold of the keys currently mapped to the XK_Tab symbol will cause the keyboard to be shifted—letters will appear in uppercase and symbols will appear instead of numbers. Usually, this means that the Tab key (which is generally mapped to the XK_Tab symbol) will act more or less like the user expects a Shift key to act. Luckily, this change can be undone:

```
xmodmap -e 'remove shift = Tab'
```

A list of current modifier mappings can be obtained simply by typing xmodmap alone at a command prompt. A more useful change than the preceding one involves reversal of the functionality of the Control and Caps Lock keys on a standard PC, a common change among computing veterans:

```
xmodmap -e 'add lock = Control_L'
xmodmap -e 'remove lock = Caps_Lock'
xmodmap -e 'add control = Caps_Lock'
xmodmap -e 'remove control = Control_L'
```

Note that calling xmodmap without arguments after making this change displays an updated map, where the Caps_Lock symbol appears on the control modifier map and the Control_L symbol appears on the lock modifier map.

Making xmodmap Changes Permanent

One of the problems with calling xmodmap on the command line as we've done is that the changes last only as long as the X session does; after the user logs out or the X server finishes its run, the new mappings will be lost. The remedy for this problem is xmodmap's capability to read its changes from a file. The file is normally just a series of expressions as shown previously, one per line. Often, these expressions are stored in the ${HOME}/.Xmodmap file, which most xinitrc scripts (including the default one) read each time X is launched. For example, the following .Xmodmap file would duplicate all the changes made earlier, fixing the Backspace and Delete keys and then reversing the Caps Lock and left Control keys (see Listing 7.1).

Listing 7.1   Sample ${HOME}/.Xmodmap File

```
keycode 22 = Backspace
keycode 107 = Delete
add lock = Control_L
remove lock = Caps_Lock
add control = Caps_Lock
remove control = Control_L
```

Note that you can store expressions for xmodmap in any file you like. To implement the changes, just call xmodmap with the name of the file containing the list of expressions as the only argument.

Keyboard Mapping: Radical Reconfiguration

For those who must make radical changes to their X keyboard layout, a complete keyboard remapping can be done before X is started using the XF86Config file described in Chapter 2. The relevant section of the file starts with this text:

```
Section "Keyboard"
```

Most of the settings in the XF86Config file were discussed in Chapter 2, but the settings that are related to keyboard mapping were postponed until now because they are quite involved.

Keyboard mapping refers to the process by which the X Window System and XFree86 translate the bit patterns generated by keypresses into meaningful actions. In effect, the literal, electronic action of each keypress is mapped to a logical XFree86 concept, like a newline or backspace or tab action.

It would, of course, be extremely painful to have to use xmodmap to map each key by hand, number to function, for an entire keyboard of over 100 keys. Because of this, XFree86 ships with several predefined keyboard mappings that are general enough to be useful across a wide variety of platforms and languages. Unfortunately, these prebuilt keyboard mappings are difficult to manage by hand; unless you absolutely need to change your X server's default keyboard mappings, avoid attempting to do so because the default settings are more than adequate for the vast majority of Linux users.

In the directory lib/X11/xkb off the main XFree86 tree are the files related to the predefined keyboard mappings. Several important subdirectories are located within the lib/X11/xkb directory, each of which contains files to perform a specific function. Instructing X to use a particular keymap requires some understanding of the formats of the files in these directories, their purposes, and the ways in which they are referenced.

The keycodes/ Subdirectory

Without the letters and numbers painted on them, all keys look the same. This seems like a silly and obvious statement, until one realizes that to a computer, which cannot actually see any of the painted symbols, the statement is very true. To a computer, each keypress is represented simply by a series of bits that in turn represent a number called a *keycode*. Unfortunately, these keycodes bear little resemblance to the key concepts humans are used to, such as the letters of the alphabet or Tab or Enter functionality—they're simply numbers representing the circuit that is bound to each key on a keyboard.

The files in the keycodes/ directory contain lists of these low-level keycodes for the keyboards of various hardware platforms and the key symbols that each code represents. For example, an Amiga computer generates a 77 when the Escape key is pressed, while a PC keyboard generates a 9 when the Escape key is pressed. Thus, the amiga file in the keycodes/ directory contains a line mapping the <ESC> symbol to the number 77, while the xfree86 (default PC) file in the keycodes/ directory contains a line mapping the <ESC> symbol to the number 9.

Each keycodes file is split into several sections delineated as follows:

```
[default] xkb_keycodes "set_name" {
    (...key code to symbol pairs...)
}
```

Each section can contain any number of keycode-to-symbol pairs between the beginning brace and the ending brace. The presence of the optional default keyword at the beginning of a section indicates that this section is the default section for the file in question and will be used if no specific section is given when referring to the file. Specific keycode sets are therefore referenced in one of the following two ways:

```
File
file(set_name)
```

The first representation is used when referring to the default section within the given file in the keycodes/ directory. The second representation is used when referring to one of the other (nondefault) sections within the given file in the keycodes/ directory.

The symbols/ Subdirectory

The files in this directory perform an additional layer of mapping, from the abstract symbols mapped in the keycodes/ files to X Keyboard Symbols as defined in the file include/X11/keysymdef.h off the main XFree86 directory tree.

This additional layer of abstraction is necessary because, as painted, a keyboard really isn't specific enough for the computer to understand. For example, the letter keys like A and B generate only one keycode each when pressed, and yet we expect them to be able to represent two separate entries each: an uppercase letter and a lowercase letter. The files in the symbols/ directory instruct X (for example) to watch the Shift key when a letter key is pressed and to decide which action was intended by the user—an uppercase letter or a lowercase letter.

International characters are also handled in the files in the symbols/ directory, allowing X to understand international keyboards and even to use some standard PC keyboards to generate international characters when directed to do so by the user.

The files in the symbols/ directory are structured similarly to the files in the keycodes/ directory. Each file contains several sections delineated as follows:

```
[default] xkb_symbols "name" {
    (...symbol mappings...)
}
```

Again, a specific set of symbol mappings is referenced based on the file in question and the section within the file. For example, consider the following reference:

```
us(pc101)
```

This string of text refers to the us file in the symbols/ directory, and then, more specifically, to the pc101 section within the file. The us symbol file alone contains 17 different sets of symbol mappings. There are approximately 140 sets in the default XFree86 distribution, when all the sections in all the symbol files are counted. To make matters more confusing, multiple symbol specifications are sometimes required, and are constructed by linking two symbol specifications together with a plus (+) sign:

```
us(pc101)+pl(basic)
```

Finding the correct symbol set for a given locale and piece of keyboard hardware can clearly be a daunting task.

The geometry/ Directory

The files in this directory provide a visual description for various types of keyboards, suitable for use by programs like xkbprint, which will generate a visual representation (in PostScript format) of a keyboard and the mappings of each of its keys. For example, the following lines show how to use the xkbprint command to generate a PostScript keyboard file, and then use gv to view it:

```
$ xkbprint :0.0 ~/MyKeyboard.ps
$ gv ~/MyKeyboard.ps &
```

The first argument to xkbprint is the display to open when obtaining the keyboard representation. The current display on a single-user Linux system is usually represented by :0.0. For more information on specifying displays other than the first display on a single-user machine, refer to Chapter 15, "Working on the Network." The second argument to xkbprint is the PostScript file to generate.

Although it's not necessarily as important to use an accurate geometry file as it is to use accurate keycodes and symbols files, it is nevertheless a bad idea to use an incorrect or nonexistent geometry file because the visual representation of your keyboard that X maintains will be inaccurate.

The files in the geometry/ directory are similar in structure to the files in the other two directories. Each section in a geometry file is constructed as follows:

```
[default] xkb_geometry "name" {
    (...geometry specification...)
}
```

Again, specific geometries are referenced by supplying both a file and a section within a file, like this:

```
pc(jp106)
```

The preceding reference would use the jp106 geometry from the pc geometry file in the geometry/ directory.

Other Directories

Two other directories, types/ and compat/, also have something to do with keyboard configuration. Both of these directories contain files that define additional keyboard states and compatibility kludges that are really too esoteric to explain in detail. They are similar in format to the other types of files discussed so far, and for most users the correct types file is the file called default in the types/ directory, and the correct compatibility file is the default file in the compat/ directory.

Specifying Keyboard Settings in XF86Config

After you've chosen a set of keycodes, a set of symbols, and a geometry to use, you must specify these settings to the X server via the XF86Config file. These settings can be explicitly specified using the XkbKeycodes, XkbSymbols, and XkbGeometry. The types and compatibility settings are set using XkbTypes and XkbCompat. A complete keyboard configuration in the Keyboard section of the XF86Config file would thus look like this for a run-of-the-mill PC user with a 101-key keyboard:

```
XkbKeycodes "xfree86"
XkbTypes    "default"
XkbCompat   "default"
XkbSymbols  "us(pc101)"
XkbGeometry "pc"
```

Unfortunately, not everyone is a run-of-the-mill PC user with a 101-key keyboard, and after you've spent a moment rummaging through all the subdirectories and files in the lib/X11/xkb/ directory, it will become clear that there are a dizzying number of possible configurations—so many that even if your own configuration is common, it might be difficult to figure out how to properly represent it in XF86Config.

Fortunately, there are two ways to shorten the amount of legwork you must do in configuring your keyboard in XF86Config. The first, and preferred method for PC users using English or Japanese, is the XkbRules and related keywords. The XkbRules keyword will allow the X server to construct a configuration for you based on one of the entries in a file in the rules/ directory. For example, the following set of entries configure a Microsoft Natural keyboard for an English-speaking Linux user:

```
XkbRules    "xfree86"
XkbModel    "microsoft"
XkbLayout   "us"
```

The first line instructs X to use keyboard rules from the xfree86 file in the rules/ directory. The second line selects the model within the rules file, and the third line selects the layout. A list of valid models and layouts for each rules file can be found by skimming the file with a pager like more.

For those users who don't see a workable configuration using the XkbRules method for configuring a keyboard, there is another even simpler method. Several predefined keyboard mappings have been constructed in the files in the keymap/ directory. These files contain sections similar to those in the other files we've discussed so far, and referencing a particular keymap is again a matter of specifying both a file and a section. Notice that each section in the keymap files contains five settings, one each for keycodes, types, compatibility, symbols, and geometry. Thus, a German user could simply specify the following line in the XF86Config Keyboard section to indicate a German keyboard layout:

```
XkbKeymap    "xfree86(de)"
```

This line simplifies matters quite a bit; by looking at the de section in the keymap/xfree86 file, we can see that this single line is equivalent to the following five lines:

```
XkbKeycodes "xfree86"
XkbTypes    "default"
XkbCompat   "default"
XkbSymbols  "en_US(pc105)+de"
XkbGeometry "pc(pc102)"
```

By using one of the predefined keymaps in the keymap/ directory, the user avoids having to specify all five lines in XF86Config, and even more importantly, avoids having to search through the keycodes, symbols, and geometry files by hand for the correct settings. On the other hand, this method isn't recommended by the XFree86 team; the more correct way should be used whenever possible to ensure that the keyboard layout is correctly defined:

```
XkbRules    "xfree86"
XkbModel    "microsoft"
XkbLayout   "de"
```

Unfortunately, there isn't any real documentation for the many sections in the many files that make up the lib/X11/xkb/ directory tree; if you require a nonstandard keyboard mapping, but cannot find a suitable one either in the rules/ or keymap/ files, it is up to you to search through the files in each of the keycodes/, types/, compat/, symbols/, and geometry/ directories for the correct settings for your situation. If you find yourself stumped, the best answer for international users might be to find a local Linux users' group who can supply the correct settings. Alternatively, a post to Usenet can often generate responses from other users who share your hardware or speak your language.

Mouse, Screen, and Non-Keymap Keyboard Configuration

Keyboard mapping is important, but other aspects of an X environment contribute to or detract from the overall experience. The two commands used most often to make changes to the X environment are xset and our friend xmodmap, which, as we are about to see, performs at least one important function beyond keyboard mapping.

The Other Use for xmodmap

For the left-handed user, the default XFree86 mouse button configuration is backward—clicks by the index finger result in the 2nd or 3rd mouse button being pressed, while a primary click event is generated by the ring finger. This is clearly an uncomfortable situation, and the xmodmap provides a way for lefties to fix it.

The pointer expression in xmodmap allows buttons to be reordered simply by supplying a list of mouse button numbers in relative positions. For example, to reverse the default button mappings for left-handed users, causing the right-most button to be button 1 and the left-most button to be button 2 or (for three-button mice) button 3 the following command is used:

```
xmodmap -e 'pointer = 3 2 1'
```

The number 3, representing the third physical button, is in the first position, making it the first logical button. The opposite holds true for the number 1, which was given last.

A similar trick can be used by users with scrolling mice that use buttons 4 and 5 to indicate scroll events. To reverse the direction of the scroll wheel, the following command could be issued:

```
xmodmap -e 'pointer = 1 2 3 5 4'
```

For the lefty with a scroll wheel, the following would generate a left-handed mouse with an inverted scroll sensitivity:

```
xmodmap -e 'pointer = 3 2 1 5 4'
```

As was the case with the keyboard mapping commands covered earlier, the xmodmap pointer expressions can easily be added to the ${HOME}/.Xmodmap file to make desired changes permanent.

Keyboard, Mouse, and Display Changes with xset

The xset command is the other most commonly used command for modifying the X server's keyboard, mouse, or display. The most common keyboard changes via xset are shown in Table 7.2. The most common mouse changes are shown in Table 7.3. The most common display and output options are shown in Table 7.4.

Table 7.2   Keyboard Configuration with xset

Command Line	Configuration Change
xset c on	Enables key click where supported; many different types of hardware don't support key click.
xset c off	Disables key click.
xset c n	Sets the keyclick volume to n, a number from 0 to 100.
xset led n	Turns on keyboard LED (light) numbered n; valid numbers are from 1–32.
xset -led n	Turns off keyboard LED numbered n.
xset r on	Enables keyboard repeat for all keys on the keyboard.
xset r off	Disables keyboard repeat for all keys on the keyboard.
xset r n	Enables key repeat for the key given by keycode n; doesn't affect other keys.
xset -r n	Disables key repeat for the key given by keycode n.
xset r rate n1 n2	On servers that support the XFree86-Misc extension, sets the keyboard-wide key repeat delay to n1 and repeat rate to n2.

Table 7.3   Mouse Configuration with xset

Command Line	Configuration Change
xset m n1 n2	Sets the mouse acceleration value to n1 and the acceleration threshold to n2. This causes the mouse to move n1 times faster when moved at least n2 units at once.
xset m default	Restores mouse settings to those that were active when the server started.

Table 7.4 Display and Output Configuration with xset

Command Line	Configuration Change
xset b on	Enables the terminal bell.
xset b off	Disables the terminal bell.
xset b *n*	Sets the terminal bell volume to *n*, a number from 0 to 100.
xset b *n1 n2 n3*	Sets the terminal bell volume to *n1*, a number from 0 to 100, the terminal bell pitch to *n2* in hertz, and the duration of the sound to *n3* in thousandths of a second.
xset +dpms	Enables display power management on systems with compatible hardware.
xset -dpms	Disables display power management.
xset dpms force standby	Forces the display into standby mode.
xset dpms force suspend	Forces the display into suspend mode.
xset dpms force off	Switches the display off.
xset dpms *n1 n2 n3*	Sets the delay, in minutes, before the display enters standby (*n1*) mode or suspend (*n2*) mode, or switches itself off (*n3*). Setting any of *n1*, *n2*, or *n3* to zero disables the related function.
xset p *n color*	Sets the color for colormap entry *n* to the color specification given by *color*. More information on colormaps and color specification can be found in "Fonts and Colors," later in this chapter.
xset s on	Enables the X server's built-in screen saver/blanker.
xset s off	Disables the X server's built-in screen saver/blanker.
xset s blank	Specifies that the X server should "blank" screens when screen saving occurs.
xset s noblank	Specifies that the X server should display a changing pattern when screen saving occurs.
xset s *n1 n2*	Specifies that the X server should begin screen saving after *n1* seconds without user activity and that the pattern on the display should be changed every *n2* seconds.

A complete list of the settings managed by xset and their current values can be obtained on stdout by supplying the q option alone to xset on the command line:

```
xset q
```

All configuration changes made by xset will be lost when the session ends or the X server exits. To make changes permanent, the user must add calls to xset to ${HOME}/.xinitrc or a similar session-start script.

Internationalization

The subject of internationalization is complex. Many X users would love to get X working in their own native language, at least enough to read and send email. The question of how to set up X for a given language is a common one. Unfortunately, things aren't always as simple as they seem, and in X, this is certainly the case.

Internationalization, as implemented now, is much more a function of the applications in question than of the X server or XFree86 system. Even the international keyboard mappings found in the lib/X11/xkb/ directory don't work with many applications, which, very simply, were designed to work in English and nothing else, completely ignoring foreign X key symbols. A number of international fonts aren't included with XFree86 and must be downloaded from around the Web.

The closest thing to a truly international desktop available for Linux at this point is the K Desktop Environment, which supports the great majority of Western European languages to one degree or another. Asian languages are a different matter (with the exception of Japanese katakana) because they require multibyte X server patches to allow for their large character sets.

Because of all these complications, a complete discussion of internationalization is well beyond the scope of this text; a different set of answers is correct for each language around the world. S.u.S.E. GMBH, which can be found at http://www.suse.de, sells a large number of European language-specific distributions that are preconfigured for European languages. TurboLinux, which can be found at http://www.turbolinux.com, serves the Pacific rim with Japanese and Chinese versions of Linux.

For those who need help getting X to run in their language, the best sources of information on the Web for international X are the language-specific HOWTO documents that can be found at http://metalab.unc.edu/LDP/HOWTO. Currently, HOWTO documents exist for the following languages: Chinese, Russian (Cyrillic), Danish, Esperanto, Finnish, French, German, Hebrew, Italian, Polish, Portuguese, Slovenian, Spanish, and Thai. Each of these HOWTOs contains information on configuring Linux and X for the language in question, as well as links to fonts, replacement X servers, or patched program binaries when necessary.

If the language you need isn't covered by a HOWTO, your best hope is to seek out a Linux users' group in your area or someone who speaks the language you need to use in XFree86.

Fonts and Colors

Beyond the purely utilitarian aspects of the X console, like screen blanking, keyboard use, and the console bell, the most interesting aspects of the X server runtime have to do with font management and color management. There isn't a user alive who doesn't love to add more fonts to his or her system, and on another tack, there are few 256-color X users who haven't wanted to smash their terminal at one time or another for lack of color cells.

X Color Management

Virtually all computer systems today are capable of displaying graphics images in fairly full color. The days of black-and-white monochrome displays are long past. Unfortunately, displaying colors and images on a computer isn't a simple task: clearly, there are an infinite number of colors in reality. Because of this, computer displays are always imperfect in their capability to reproduce the brilliance of real images; one responsibility of a graphical user interface such as XFree86 is to manage a computer's visual hardware in an attempt to allow multiple applications to display colors and images with the best possible quality.

There are two basic concepts to understand in X color management. They are the *visual*, or the way that color is represented and behaves in the computer's hardware, and the *colorspace*, a way of creating some sort of logical order for the infinite number of colors in reality.

PseudoColor and TrueColor (Choosing a Visual Class)

Although many different visual classes are available to XFree86 users, and still more are available to users of high-end graphics workstations, most Linux users will find only two visual classes useful: the PseudoColor visual (for 8 bits per pixel displays) and the TrueColor visual (for 15, 16, 24, and 32 bits per pixel displays).

The PseudoColor visual is so named because it represents not all color, but only a small, variable subset of the number of colors that are actually visible to the human eye. PseudoColor visuals are found when XFree86 runs on hardware capable of displaying only 256 colors onscreen at a time from a much larger set of colors (anywhere from 256,000 to 16.7 million). On PseudoColor hardware, each pixel on a screen is represented by one byte (8 bits) of information in memory. The 8 bits available to each pixel are enough to specify a color number for that pixel from 0–255 (a total of 256 colors possible). This color number maintained for each pixel then refers to a slot in a 256-slot color map. Each slot in this map contains one of the colors from the much larger colorspace the hardware is capable of displaying. When the color contained in one of these slots is changed, all the pixels on the display that take their color from that slot change color as well. Some applications take advantage of this property to create impressions of animation or swirling colors, a technique often called palette-switching or palette-cycling. Most older VGA hardware (such as 512k or 1MB ISA VGA cards) fall into this category.

TrueColor visuals, on the other hand, don't maintain a slot map of onscreen colors, chosen from a much larger list of potential colors. Instead, TrueColor visuals allow for a large, fixed set of colors to be onscreen all at the same time. 15-bit TrueColor displays represent each pixel on the screen with 15 bits of memory data, enough to count from 0–32,767, or enough to specify any one of nearly 33,000 colors for each pixel, far more colors than the 256 that can be displayed at once on an 8-bit PseudoColor display. The 16 bits used for each pixel on some displays are enough to allow a pixel to display any of nearly 66,000 colors. 24-bit TrueColor visuals allow for up to 16.7 million colors onscreen at once, and a 32-bit TrueColor visual theoretically contains enough information to allow for over 4 billion colors to be displayed onscreen at once, though most current video hardware doesn't exploit such potential.

The visual most Linux users decide to use when running XFree86 depends on the capabilities of their video hardware. Most users whose graphics cards can display at 15, 16, 24, or 32 bits-per-pixel choose to do so. For most intents and purposes, the TrueColor visual is infinitely superior to the PseudoColor visual. There are, however, some caveats. Because a PseudoColor visual uses only 8 bits for each pixel to be displayed, it can refresh a screenful of information twice as quickly as can a 16-bit display on identical hardware, which must move twice as much data to or from memory for each pixel. Also, though the number of onscreen colors is limited, PseudoColor visuals can typically fill the onscreen color slots from a much larger palette of 256,000 or 16.7 million colors, meaning that, paradoxically, a 256-color PseudoColor display can often display many colors that a nearly 66,000-color TrueColor display cannot. Finally, TrueColor displays don't allow for the palette-switching technique employed by many programs written for PseudoColor displays.

Choosing Your Visual Class at X Launch

The process of choosing a visual class for most users is really the process of choosing a color depth (8, 15, 16, 24, or 32 bits per pixel). The XFree86 server will normally configure an 8-bit display as a PseudoColor visual and a 15-, 16-, 24-, or 32-bit display with a TrueColor visual.

Choosing the display depth, in bits per pixel, can be done one of two ways. Both have been seen before, but it helps to summarize them now. The first is to include the DefaultColorDepth keyword in the Screen section of the XF86Config file, like this:

```
DefaultColorDepth 24
```

This example will cause X to start in 24-bits-per-pixel mode, and thus with a TrueColor visual by default, provided the graphics hardware is capable of displaying at that depth and relevant Display subsections are included in the XF86Config file. For more information on the XF86Config file, please refer to Chapter 2.

The other way to choose the color depth and thus the default visual class is at runtime, by supplying the -bpp option to the server or to the startx command following a pair of dashes:

```
startx -- -bpp 24
```

Most users choose to configure for the deepest visual their hardware supports, and then choose shallower color depths when necessary on the command line when starting XFree86.

The RGB Colorspace

The concept of a *colorspace* can be difficult to understand, but perhaps a simple question will help. How would you specify to series of individuals, without showing them any visual clues, an *exact* color from reality, or even just an exact shade of red so that each one of them could choose it correctly from the spectrum at some later date? The answer is that you couldn't; humans simply don't think about color in any way but visually.

This leads to a paradox when dealing with computers and color: computers don't have visual perception; they must obtain information about any color and decide which colors to display based purely on some written or mathematical form of data. This is where the concept of a colorspace comes in.

A *colorspace* is a logical space full of colors in a certain order or arrangement. Specifying a particular color in a nearly infinite spectrum then becomes the process of specifying a particular location in that colorspace. Although many colorspaces are available to X users, the one that is almost universally used by Linux users and the X community at large is the RGB colorspace. The RGB colorspace is quite simple; it is composed of three coordinates, one each for red, green, and blue. In the simpler RGB colorspace, each coordinate can be given a value from 0–255, with zero being the absence of light (black) and 255 being the brightest light displayable in that color. Table 7.5 lists some sample combinations to help illustrate.

Table 7.5   Sample R, G, and B Values and Resultant Colors

Red, Green, Blue	Resultant Color
0, 0, 0	Black (no light of any color)
255, 255, 255	White (all three at maximum light)
255, 0, 0	Brightest red
0, 255, 0	Brightest green
0, 0, 255	Brightest blue
100, 100, 100	A dark shade of gray
200, 200, 200	A lighter shade of gray
255, 255, 0	Brightest yellow
200, 200, 0	A dimmer yellow
255, 0, 255	Brightest purple
200, 0, 200	A dimmer purple

When specifying colors to XFree86 in the RGB colorspace, the values must be converted to Hexadecimal (base-16) numbers and preceded with a hash (#) mark. Table 7.6 shows the colors again, but this time using valid RGB colorspace references.

Table 7.6   The Same Colors as RGB Colorspace Items for X

RGB Color	Resultant Color
#000000	Black (no light of any color)
#ffffff	White (all three at maximum light)
#ff0000	Brightest red
#00ff00	Brightest green
#0000ff	Brightest blue
#646464	A dark shade of gray
#c8c8c8	A lighter shade of gray
#ffff00	Brightest yellow
#c8c800	A dimmer yellow
#ff00ff	Brightest purple
#c800c8	A dimmer purple

Most of the time, when you specify color to XFree86 or to XFree86 applications, you'll be using this RGB colorspace format, though some graphics-oriented applications (such as GIMP) will allow you to specify colors in any one of several other colorspaces as well. Many users have trouble converting from the decimal scale of 0–255 to the hexadecimal scale of 0–ff for each color. One way to do it is to use the awk command, like this:

```
echo n | awk '{ printf "%x\n", $1 }'
```

Replace n with the number, from 0–255, that you want to convert to hexadecimal, and awk will happily print the hexadecimal equivalent.

Note that there is an alternative format for navigating the RGB colorspace, which provides two bytes of information for each light color. This means that the user chooses a number from 0–65535 for each color, or 0–ffff in hexadecimal. RGB colorspace definitions done this way look like this:

```
#ffff0000c8c8
#c8dc9d01fceb
```

As you can see, this is a much longer format for specifying a location in the RGB colorspace, and a much more accurate one. Whereas the short format shown in Table 7.6 has only 16,777,216 (16.7 million) possible combinations, the long format shown above has hundreds of billions of possible combinations. On the other hand, consumer-class Linux hardware generally maxes out at 24 or 32 bits per pixel—enough to display 16.7 million colors, and enough to match the earlier, short format exactly. Because of this, most Linux users will never have the need for the longer RGB format, though it still works for specifying colors to X.

The Color Database

After you understand the RGB colorspace, it's really quite a simple concept—just add the correct amounts of red, green, and blue light and stir to get the color you want. On the other hand, if you just want something pinkish, it's a bore to have to play around with hexadecimal numbers for half an hour to come up with what should have been a simple result.

Because of this, XFree86 and most X implementations ship with a free X color database file, normally stored at lib/X11/rgb.txt off the main X directory tree. If you browse this file with a pager like more, you'll see that it's simply a list of red, green, and blue color values followed by a color name, one per line. This is the crayon box for X users—a series of premade colors, which you can specify by name in most cases when you don't want to have to come up with an RGB colorspace specification for Peach Puff or Midnight Blue.

Feel free to add colors to this list as needed, with one caveat that should be understood: Colors you add to your own system won't appear in the color database on other systems, so don't use any added color names in files that you'll need to carry from system to system.

8-Bit PseudoColor Displays

Readers with TrueColor visuals have it fairly easy: all the colors their card can display are available all the time, without interruption. This isn't the case for users of 8-bit displays with PseudoColor visuals. Remember that 8-bit displays employ a map of colors, a list of 256 active colors from a much larger palette. On high-end UNIX hardware, 8-bit PseudoColor displays aren't such a limiting factor because the hardware usually supports multiple colormaps, one for each application (meaning 256 colors per application), or *overlays*, areas of the screen that are at a different depth from the root window.

Unfortunately, XFree86 supports neither multiple colormaps (which is really a limitation of PC video hardware) or overlays (which can be complicated to use anyway). As a result, users of 8-bit displays are faced with the fact that all applications on a running desktop must share the same list of 256 chosen colors. What if one application wants one set of colors but another application wants another set of colors? Quite literally, they fight—and one application (and sometimes both) loses.

Colormap Management: A Difficult Game

The management of the 8-bit colormap is a complicated subject, but a simplified discussion of the basics is in order. Recall that there are exactly 256 color slots that can each contain a color that applications can use. If these slots were publicly modifiable by any application at any time, serious problems would result. For example, if you loaded a picture of the blue sky, it would likely allocate most, if not all, the 256 color slots for various shades of blue. If you then launched a picture of a rose on the other side of your display, and this second image viewer could modify the 256 color slots at will, you'd soon find a beautiful red rose on one side of your screen and a bright red sky on the other side. All those previously blue color slots have now been re-allocated for various shades of red.

Because of this problem, X lets some applications claim ownership of color slots while they run. Other applications that are launched afterward couldn't then simply reallocate the already used color slots for their own use. On the other hand, this means that if the first program you start, for example the image view of the blue sky, is a hog and demands ownership of all the color slots available, any applications you try to launch afterward will be denied ownership of any color slots. Some applications will take this in stride and attempt to fit themselves in to the colors already onscreen, while others will simply give up and quit with an error, saying that no colors were available. Even worse, many applications completely botch color management in one way or another, often leaving the user with black text on a black background, invisible buttons and pointers, or even a completely solid-color window where all widgets, text, outlines, and cursors are the same color.

There are two ways in which X tries to minimize this problem: private colormaps and color sharing.

Private colormaps are just that: colormaps that are private to a single application. This concept isn't to be confused with the multiple-colormaps concept mentioned earlier; private colormaps work somewhat differently. When many applications have allocated a private colormap, there is still only one real colormap for the display. When an application that maintains a private colormap gets window focus, it is given permission to use all the color slots for its own colors until focus is again lost—at which time the displayed colormap reverts back to the state it was in immediately before the application took focus. Applications with private colormaps will always appear with the correct colors when they have focus, but as a side effect, they may cause colormap flashing. Colormap flashing is an effect that causes all other applications on a desktop to suddenly lose their correct colors when a privately mapped application becomes active, then suddenly gain them back again when the privately mapped window loses focus. It is, to say the least, unpleasant to look at, and in some cases it can be downright disturbing, leading to headaches, eyestrain, and, in one rare reported case, epileptic seizures.

The other method XFree86 uses to try to mitigate the single colormap limitation is through the sharing of color slots. The rules for sharing are fairly complex, but they basically state that more than one application can own a color slot simultaneously if each is satisfied with the color it contains. In return, each application promises that it won't change the color in a slot as long as it is sharing that slot with other applications. Many applications support the sharing of some or all their color slots, and it appears to be a good system. Still, there are a couple of problems. No matter how friendly applications can be toward each other, 256 colors is still only 256 colors, and the more applications that appear on the desktop, the less likely it is that they will all be able to get all the colors that they need.

More importantly, many applications don't know how to approximate color—they fail to share color slots with other applications because the colors aren't an exact match. Rather than share the color #ff0000 (brightest red) with another application, most applications will simply allocate a new slot for themselves containing the color #fe0000, one indistinguishable shade darker, simply because the application hasn't been programmed to think in a fuzzy way—it doesn't see the exact shade it is searching for and doesn't see nonexact (but close) matches as candidates.

These problems together can lead to the 8-bit XFree86 blues: a perpetual shortage of colors, lots of colormap flashing due to private colormaps, and applications that refuse to start because they cannot allocate new colors of their own.

Tips for Misbehaving Colormaps

Although there aren't any major changes that can easily be made to fix the X colormap problem for 8-bit displays, a couple of simple tips can help reduce pain.

First, keep your applications' color needs low. Avoid keeping unnecessary images or icons on the screen that eat up valuable color slots. Many applications allow the user to tune the number of colors used when running. For example, the popular xv image viewer can be started like this:

```
xv -ncols n
```

The -ncols argument tells xv to use at most n colors while it is running, an important change because this program can otherwise eat up all available color slots in an instant.

Next, use private colormaps, when available, for applications that will be spending most of their time minimized at the bottom of the screen. For example, if you keep Netscape running all the time, but actually use it only to check your email once a day, consider launching it with the -install option so that it uses a private colormap. This will keep the slots that Netscape would normally have allocated free for other applications to use.

Finally, try to configure applications to use the exact same colors whenever possible. Many applications have configurable color resources, some in resource files (see the next chapter); configuring applications' colors so that multiple applications use identical colors can in some cases cause applications that otherwise wouldn't to share their color slots with each other, rather than allocating new ones. The same technique can apply to icons and graphics; if you are drawing a nice new icon set for use in your window manager, draw all your icons using the exact same set of colors, so that your window manager won't be forced to allocate a new set of color slots for each icon.

Perhaps the best tip of all, however, for most Linux users, is to upgrade if at all possible to newer hardware capable of supporting TrueColor operation under XFree86—effectively eliminating the colormap problem altogether.

Adding PostScript Fonts to X

Although X includes a basic set of fonts that are adequate for many uses, there are many instances in which it is desirable to add additional fonts to the X environment for tasks like Web design, desktop publishing, or just for beautifying the desktop.

The easiest types of fonts to add to an XFree86 environment are the PostScript Type 1 fonts popular among Macintosh and UNIX users. These fonts can be incorporated into an X environment with relatively little work following the instructions in this section.

Make a New Font Directory

Although not absolutely essential to the task, the addition of a new directory for server fonts will make the job of adding fonts much simpler. It will also provide an easy way to remove the new fonts if they become unsuitable at some point in the future, without having to search through all the original X fonts to find them.

The standard place for fonts in the X directory tree is in the lib/X11/fonts/ directory. For most users, then, creating the new directory is a two-step process:

```
cd /usr/X11R6/lib/X11/fonts
mkdir myfonts
```

Note that you can call the new directory whatever you like, but a name that identifies it as a set of optional or locally installed fonts will make things more clear in the future, should you ever have to understand the contents of the directory by sight.

Unpack the Fonts and Install Them

After a new directory has been created to hold them, the font files (which should have .pfa or .pfb extensions) can be placed directly in the new directory. Files that end in .afm are font metrics files (for printing and layout) and are (by convention) installed in a fontmetrics directory. Thus, if you find .afm files along side the .pfa or .pfb files in your font directory, make a new directory to hold them and move them there:

```
mkdir fontmetrics
mv *.afm fontmetrics
```

XFree86 depends on two other files in the font directory for information on the fonts that are present. These files are called fonts.scale and fonts.dir and contain font scaling information and a font directory, respectively. The fonts.dir file is automatically generated from the fonts.scale file using the mkfontdir program, but unfortunately, no command is included with XFree86 to build the fonts.scale file.

Luckily, there is such a program, called type1inst, included with many current Linux distributions. If you find that your particular distribution doesn't include it, you can download it from http://metalab.unc.edu/pub/Linux/X11/xutils as type1inst-0.6.1.tar.gz. The command is called without arguments inside the directory containing the font files. So, assuming that you have installed the type1inst utility in the /usr/local/bin directory, you would issue the following command:

```
/usr/local/bin/type1inst
```

You will see type1inst thinking as it tells you how many fonts it found and processes them. If there are any errors, one of the fonts doesn't agree with type1inst, and this is a bad thing because no other utility really exists to create a fonts.scale file for you. In such cases, it's better just to eliminate the offending font and try to do without it. After type1inst finishes, you should find a file called fonts.scale in the font directory that contains a number of lines that look more or less like those in Listing 7.2, taken from an XFree86 fonts.scale file.

Listing 7.2   The lib/X11/fonts/Type1/fonts.scale File

```
16
UTRG_____.pfa   adobe utopia medium r normal  0 0 0 0 p 0 iso8859 1
UTI_____.pfa   adobe utopia medium i normal  0 0 0 0 p 0 iso8859 1
UTB_____.pfa   adobe utopia bold r normal  0 0 0 0 p 0 iso8859 1
UTBI_____.pfa   adobe utopia bold i normal  0 0 0 0 p 0 iso8859 1
cour.pfa   adobe courier medium r normal  0 0 0 0 m 0 iso8859 1
couri.pfa   adobe courier medium i normal  0 0 0 0 m 0 iso8859 1
courb.pfa   adobe courier bold r normal  0 0 0 0 m 0 iso8859 1
courbi.pfa   adobe courier bold i normal  0 0 0 0 m 0 iso8859 1
c0648bt_.pfb   bitstream charter medium r normal  0 0 0 0 p 0 iso8859 1
c0649bt_.pfb   bitstream charter medium i normal  0 0 0 0 p 0 iso8859 1
```

continues

Listing 7.2 Continued

```
c0632bt_.pfb  bitstream charter bold r normal  0 0 0 0 p 0 iso8859 1
c0633bt_.pfb  bitstream charter bold I normal  0 0 0 0 p 0 iso8859 1
c0419bt_.pfb  bitstream courier medium r normal  0 0 0 0 m 0 iso8859 1
c0582bt_.pfb  bitstream courier medium i normal  0 0 0 0 m 0 iso8859 1
c0583bt_.pfb  bitstream courier bold r normal  0 0 0 0 m 0 iso8859 1
c0611bt_.pfb  bitstream courier bold i normal  0 0 0 0 m 0 iso8859 1
```

The first line of the file indicates how many fonts were found, and the remaining lines are the font filename, followed by the X Logical Font Descriptor that type1inst has generated for each font. After the fonts.scale file has been successfully generated, run mkfontdir in the directory to generate the fonts.dir file:

```
mkfontdir
```

This command, too, should finish without errors. When it does, the font directory has been prepared and your new fonts are ready for use.

Testing Them Out with xset

A few important features of the xset command covered earlier in the chapter were intentionally left out at that time so that we could cover them now. The features in question are those having to do with runtime font management. The xset command enables the user to change the X font path on-the-fly—meaning that you can use xset to make the fonts you just installed available.

To do so, the command you'll want to use is

```
xset fp+ fontpath
```

The fontpath in this case is the directory where you just installed your fonts. So, for example, if your *.pfa, *.pfb, fonts.scale, and fonts.dir files were installed in the /usr/X11R6/lib/X11/fonts/myfonts/ directory, you would issue this command:

```
xset fp+ /usr/X11R6/lib/X11/fonts/myfonts/
```

After issuing the command, you'll wait a moment while xset reads the fonts.dir file in the directory and collects information about the available fonts. They will then be added to the list of active fonts that can be displayed with the xlsfonts command:

```
xlsfonts
```

A complete list of the font-oriented operations supported by xset can be found in Table 7.7.

Table 7.7 The Font-Oriented xset Operations

Command Line	Configuration Change
xset fp+ *path*	Add the specified *path* to the end of the X font path and incorporate the fonts found there into the list of available fonts.
Xset +fp *path*	Add the specified *path* to the beginning of the X font path and incorporate the fonts found there into the list of available fonts.
xset fp- *path*	Remove the specified *path* and all associated fonts from the X font path and list of available fonts, respectively.
xset fp rehash	Rebuild the list of available fonts by rescanning the directories and servers included in the X font path.
xset fp=list	Set the complete X font path to the comma-separated list of directories and servers specified by list.
xset fp default	Restore the X font path to the original list of paths and servers at start time and rebuild the list of available fonts using the restored path.

Note that the font path can also include directions to font servers, which serve X fonts across a network. For more information on using font servers with XFree86, refer to Chapter 15.

After you've added the new directory to your font path, you should be able to view the new fonts you just installed, either in xfontsel or with xfd, supplying an X Logical Font Descriptor like the one generated by xfontsel. For more information on xfontsel and xfd, please see Chapter 4, "Standard XFree86 Programs and Utilities."

Add the New Fonts to XF86Config

After you're satisfied with your fonts, one last step usually remains in adding the new fonts to your X environment: The X server must be told in a permanent way that they exist. The font path editing done with xset will last only as long as the current X session lasts. Afterward, all changes will disappear unless they are made permanent. This is done by adding the directory containing the fonts to your XF86Config file.

Using an editor such as vi or emacs, edit the Files section to contain the path to your new fonts by adding a FontPath line after all the existing FontPath lines:

```
FontPath "/usr/X11R6/lib/X11/fonts/myfonts/"
```

Note that the order of the FontPath entries is important, so avoid placing the new FontPath entry at the top of the list unless you are sure that you want the new fonts to take precedence over all others.

After you save the edited file, your new PostScript fonts will appear in the list of available fonts whenever the X server is started.

Adding TrueType Fonts to X

Although there is an ample supply of PostScript fonts around on the Internet and on cheap department store bulk CD-ROMs, many of the more popular fonts available today are for the Windows platform and, as such, aren't PostScript fonts, but TrueType fonts instead, ending with the .ttf extension.

The XFree86 servers don't yet include native support for TrueType fonts, though built-in TrueType support is scheduled to appear with the upcoming XFree86 4.0 release. However, this lack doesn't have to stop current or future XFree86 3.x users from using TrueType fonts; the method for installing them is simply a little bit different.

xfstt: X Font Server for TrueType

The trick to using TrueType fonts with XFree86 3.x servers is the xfstt font server, a third-party font server that is designed to operate like the normal X font server, but to include support for TrueType fonts at the same time. The xfstt server can be downloaded from http://metalab.unc.edu/pub/Linux/X11/fonts as Xfstt-0.9.10.tgz. Before downloading xfstt, check to see whether your distribution CD includes a package by that name. If so, you're ready to proceed with the next step. If not, you'll have to install xfstt by hand.

After xfstt has been downloaded, installation is fairly straightforward and proceeds in the same way as any other package compiled and installed from source. The steps are to first use tar to extract the package, then to switch to the newly created directory and to make the binary:

```
tar -xzf Xfstt-0.9.10.tgz
cd xfstt0910
make && make install
```

After a great deal of compilation fanfare, you should find that everything completes normally and a new binary, xfstt, has appeared in /usr/X11R6/bin. If you need to change the install path, edit the makefile to reflect your own preferences. The xfstt.cpp file can also be edited if need be to alter some of the paths we'll discuss in a moment, but such changes aren't usually necessary and are thus generally ill-advised.

Installing the Fonts

After the xfstt binary has been installed, create a directory called /usr/ttfonts to hold the TrueType fonts and extract all your .ttf files there. The /usr/ttfonts directory is hard-coded into the xfstt source as a default, so if you want to change it, you'll have to use the --dir option when using xfstt.

It is common for Linux users to have multiboot systems containing Windows on the other partition. In such cases, it is often desirable to copy all the `.ttf` files from the `windows/` and `windows/system/` directories of the Windows partition into the `/usr/ttfonts` directory so that the traditional Windows fonts are also available from inside Linux and XFree86, a boon when browsing Web pages that specify Windows fonts explicitly.

After the `.ttf` files have been copied to `/usr/ttfonts`, it is necessary to synchronize the `xfstt` font cache, using the `--sync` option:

```
xfstt --sync
```

After working for a moment, `xfstt` should complete without errors, having updated its cache to reflect the locations of your newly installed fonts.

Starting the Font Server and Adding the Path

After all else has been done, start the new server from an `xterm` window or other command line to test it out:

```
xfstt &
```

This will start `xfstt` in the background and leave it running to answer font requests for the TrueType fonts it manages. Now that the server is active, it is necessary to edit the font path to reflect the changes. This is done via the following command:

```
xset fp+ unix/:7100
```

This command instructs `xset` to query the font server at port 7100 on the local UNIX domain for fonts. After the command has been run, the new TrueType fonts should appear when `xlsfonts` is run. Note that the X Logical Font Descriptor for TrueType fonts shows a foundry of `ttf` so that the new fonts can be gripped out of an `xlsfonts` listing like this:

```
xlsfonts | grep 'ttf-'
```

It is also interesting to note that the `xfstt` server adds several shorter font aliases to the list that look like garbage of some sort in the `xlsfonts` listing, but can be safely ignored.

In some cases, it might be necessary to start `xfstt` with an extra argument to avoid clashes with local configuration. A list of the command-line arguments understood by `xfstt` can be found in Table 7.8.

Table 7.8   Command-Line Arguments Accepted by xfstt

Argument	Description
--sync	Synchronize xfstt with the fonts installed in /usr/ttfonts. Note that this should not be done while xfstt is running.
--gslist	When supplied before the --sync option, causes xfstt to output a font list suitable for use with GhostScript printing as the fonts are synchronized.
--encoding	Remap the fonts to an encoding other than iso8859-1. Normally, this should be done only by non-US users in special circumstances.
--port n	Start the server on port n rather than the default of 7100, usually because another font server is already running.
--dir path	Operate on the directory given by path rather than on the default of /usr/ttfonts.
--res n	Force the fonts to a specific resolution in dots-per-inch. The default is 72.
--unstrap	Allow multibyte Unicode characters. This option should not be used on standard X servers, but only on those patched for international multibyte operation.
--once	Exit after the first font client disconnects.
--inetd	Necessary when xfstt will be used as a service by inetd rather than in standalone fashion.

Note that this list can be duplicated by supplying the standard --help option on the command line when calling xfstt.

Making TrueType Fonts Permanent

It is definitely difficult to have to start xfstt each time you start X and then to have to add its path manually using xset. Luckily, it is quite easy to add the TrueType font path to your X server's XF86Config configuration. Edit the XF86Config file with an editor such as vi or emacs, adding a FontPath line to the Files section of the file:

```
FontPath "unix/:7100"
```

Take care to add the FontPath entry after all the others unless you are sure that you want these fonts to take precedence because the list of FontPath entries is order-important.

Making sure that the xfstt server itself gets started each time X is run is a little more complicated; a call to xfstt could theoretically be added to a user's login or perhaps even to xinitrc (though this could require that xset be used each time to set a font path), but this leads to the undesirable consequence on multiuser systems of multiple instances of xfstt running anytime multiple X sessions are being hosted.

Because of this, the majority of users who use X regularly will want to start xfstt from inside one of the init scripts, preferably /etc/rc.d/rc.local (or whichever script their distribution uses for local init processes). The following script segment is one possible example of such an addition to /etc/rc.d/rc.local:

```
/bin/echo -n "Looking for TrueType font server: "
if [ -x /usr/X11R6/bin/xfstt ]; then
    /usr/X11R6/bin/xfstt &
    XFSTT_PID=$!
    echo "found, started PID $XFSTT_PID"
else
    echo "not found"
fi
```

Note that the xfstt font server can also be used to serve fonts across the network. For more information on using X font servers across a network, see Chapter 15.

For more information on using xfstt and beautifying fonts under XFree86, please see the XFree86 Font De-Uglification HOWTO document at http://www.frii.com/~meldroc/Font Deuglification.html.

8

RUNTIME APPLICATION
CONFIGURATION

In Windows and Mac OS systems, most applications that are configurable to any degree include a configuration panel on which such configuration changes are made. Although this is sometimes the case in Linux systems with larger applications (especially commercial ones), there exists in Linux a large class of applications that don't enjoy such obvious methods for configuration.

For these applications, most of which are based on the Xt Intrinsics or the Athena widgets toolkit, configuration is accomplished through largely nonobvious means, modifying information in a compilation of widget and application properties known as the X Resource Database, also sometimes simply referred to as X resources.

The X Resource Database

It isn't necessary to understand the underlying mechanism behind the X Resource Database to be able to use it effectively; it is easiest to think of the resource database as a list of matching keys and values. Each key refers to some property of an application or a widget. For example, one application might contain resources (keys) for whether a given widget is clickable, what color the background window for the application will be, and how many times the user must click an icon to obtain a desired result. For each of these resource keys, there is a value. For example: Yes, the widget is clickable, the background window should be blue, and the icon must be clicked three times for an action to occur.

Although the database of properties is maintained behind the scenes, as it were, there are several ways for the user to modify the values of various resources to alter or control the way in which a program behaves, similar to preferences or control panels in applications that support interactive configuration. Before you can change the values of an application's resources, however, you must know which aspects of the application can be altered, or, to put it another way, which resources exist that can be changed.

Widget Hierarchies

Before we learn to find these configuration resources, it is important to know what they look like. Most graphical applications are built in what can loosely be described as an object-oriented manner. That is to say, a window is really a series of objects that appear to interact with and contain one another. Each of these objects has several properties, including visual properties like size and color, as well as behavioral properties that are often less obvious.

For example, an xman application is an object that contains a window which is displayed to the user. The window is in turn an object, inside which you might find a button. Inside the button, you find a label, the text that appears in the button. In X, the hierarchy just described is commonly denoted beginning with the top object and moving downward in the list, separating each object with a period. For example, the following list logically illustrates the principle:

```
application.window.button.label
```

This list is a quick way to refer to a label that is inside a button which is inside a window that belongs to an application. If we wanted to refer to the button rather than to the button's label, we could logically say

```
application.window.button
```

In the real world, applications have names, windows have titles, and there can be more than one button in a given window. Thus, real-world lists of this type more often look like this:

```
xman.topBox.form.helpButton.label
```

This list refers to a label on a specific button (the help button) in a form (an assembly of buttons and other widgets) in a window known as topBox that is owned by an application called xman. Such a list as the preceding one is useful because it refers to a specific aspect of the xman program—the label on the help button in the topBox window. This list of xman components is an X resource. With it, the user can refer accurately and unambiguously to a specific object inside the xman program, in order to tell X to alter the object's properties.

Of course, it is difficult to understand just by reading theory and looking at xman what all this really means, where this list of widgets came from, or how to use a resource like the preceding. That is where the editres utility becomes useful.

Resources and `editres`

Discovering which aspects of an application are subject to configuration isn't a simple task. The basic method for discovering a list of resource keys is through use of the `editres` command. The `editres` command is like a universal, albeit cryptic, control panel for programs that are configured via X resources, instead of through their own internal mechanisms.

The `editres` command is an interactive, X-based program and can be started simply by issuing it as a command from an `xterm` window:

```
editres &
```

The `editres` utility doesn't support any program-specific options on the command line, so it's always launched in the same way. After `editres` has started, you'll see a window like the one in Figure 8.1. The best way to understand the nuances of using `editres` is to step through a sample session, following along in the text.

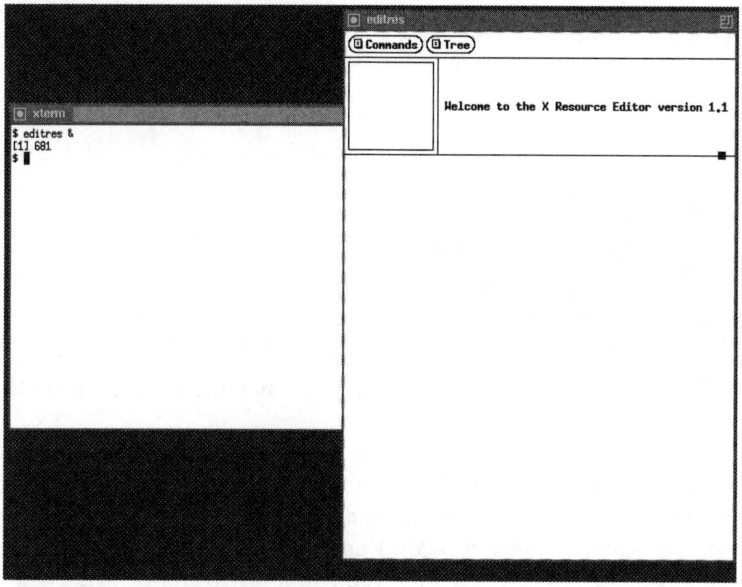

Figure 8.1   The `editres` window as it appears immediately after being launched.

Note that we'll be using color names from the color database and fonts in the form of X Logical Font Descriptors (XLFDs) in the sample session that follows, so if you need to, refer to Chapter 6, "Runtime Session Defaults," for details on the color database. Consult Chapter 4, "Standard XFree86 Programs and Utilities," for information on using the `xfontsel` command to find X Logical Font Descriptors.

A Sample editres Session

At first glance, the editres window is quite boring: an empty canvas with two drop-down menus at the top, Commands and Tree. To begin to illustrate the basic use of editres, let's configure the xterm from which it was just launched. Start by selecting the first entry in the Commands drop-down, Get Tree, and then clicking the active cursor (which appears as a cross) in the xterm window. A small, sideways tree appears in the canvas area, as shown in Figure 8.2.

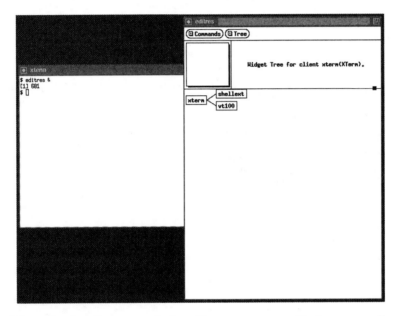

Figure 8.2   After selecting the xterm window, the editres pane displays a small widget tree.

This tree is a list of the three main widgets in the xterm program: xterm, the main widget; vt100, which is responsible for xterm's imitation of a Digital Equipment Corporation VT100 dumb terminal; and shellext, which is responsible for some aspects of xterm's interaction with the outside X world and the window manager. Each of these widgets is likely to support a list of configurable properties, or resources, which you can alter to change the behavior of the widget. Let's start by changing an obvious property of the main widget, xterm. Select the xterm widget by clicking on it. It will be highlighted to indicate that you have selected it. Then, select Show Resource Box from the Commands drop-down menu. A window with several columns of cryptic names will appear, as shown in Figure 8.3.

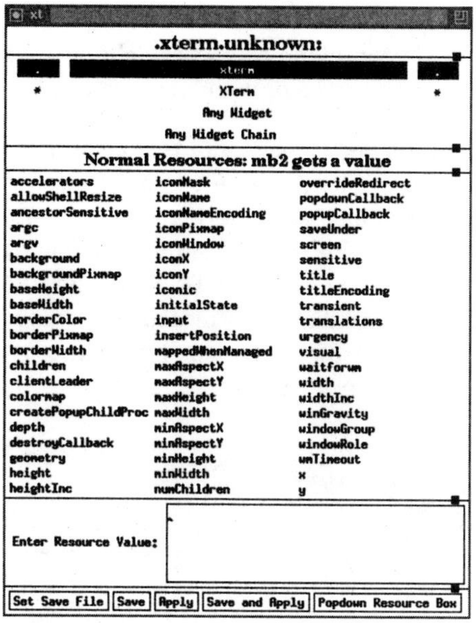

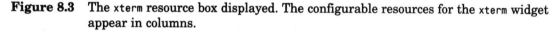

Figure 8.3 The xterm resource box displayed. The configurable resources for the xterm widget appear in columns.

The first thing to notice about the resource box window is that there are several buttons at the top of the window. The most important of these are the buttons in the top row, which construct, using buttons, a resource string of the type described earlier. At the extreme top of the window is a textual representation of the resource currently being worked on. Note that, initially, the string (as it appears in Figure 8.3) ends in unknown because no property has been selected yet.

Before we do anything else, let's prepare to save any changes that we make to object or widget properties. Click the Set Save File button at the bottom of the window, and enter the name new_xterm into the box that appears. Any changes we make to xterm will now be saved to the file called new_xterm in the current directory.

Now that we've selected a place to save our changes, choose the title resource in the columnized list. Note by looking at the top of the window that the resource now being worked on has changed from unknown to

```
xterm.title:
```

Type a replacement title into the entry box labeled Enter Resource Value and click the Apply button. The title of the xterm window instantly changes to reflect the new value. For this example, we'll enter Reversed text xterm into the box and click Save and Apply, causing the new title to be displayed in the title bar and the change to be saved to the file. Note that clicking the Apply button alone causes the change to be made to the window but not saved to the file, while clicking the Save button alone causes the change to be saved to the file but not made active in the window. The Save and Apply button is a combination of the two.

Changing the title is nice, but what about fonts and text colors? Because we see no reference to a foreground or font resource in the list, it is safe to assume that the xterm widget doesn't directly have such properties. Remember that there are two other central widgets in the xterm application, vt100 and shellext. Close the xterm resource window by clicking the Popdown Resource Box button at the bottom of the window. Because a vt100 is a type of dumb terminal display, it is logical to assume that any display-oriented properties belong to the vt100 widget. Deselect the xterm widget in the main editres canvas by clicking it once again, and select the vt100 widget instead, as shown in Figure 8.4.

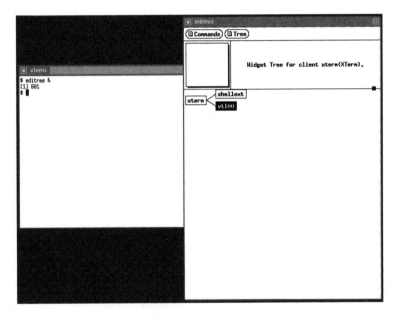

Figure 8.4 The vt100 widget is now selected.

Again choose the Show Resource Box option from the Commands drop-down menu. A window appears that is likely much larger than your display. This is your first experience with what is an unfortunate reality in editres; namely, the very large, unscrollable windows it produces. In most cases, you will have to move editres windows up and down, extending them both off the top and bottom of the display, in order to see the section you're interested in. In twm, such movement can be accomplished using the default root menu's Move option. Many other default window manager configurations include a similar option somewhere in the root menu. If this isn't the case on your desktop, you might find that holding down the Alt key, clicking and holding inside a window, and then dragging the mouse will move the window.

If you are unable to move the `editres` window effectively without the title bar on the screen, you might need to refer to Chapter 9, "Runtime Environment Configuration," for information on adding such capability to your environment before continuing with `editres`.

Back to our sample session. Assuming that you can move the window both up and down effectively, you can see that there are a large number of configurable resources for the `vt100` widget of `xterm`. Among these are the foreground, background, and font resources. Selecting the foreground resource and then checking at the very top of the resource window reveals the following resource string:

```
xterm.vt100.foreground:
```

Move to the bottom of the window and enter a color name from the X color database or the RGB colorspace into the entry box, and then click the Apply button. For this example, enter the word white and click Save and Apply. The text of the `xterm` window immediately changes to the new color you just specified, in this case making the text seem invisible against the default white background. To fix this problem, select the background resource from the list. Checking at the very top of the window, you can see that the resource now reads

```
xterm.vt100.background:
```

Move to the entry box toward the bottom of the window and enter the word black, and then click the Save and Apply button. The background of the window is now black, and the changes have again been saved to our file.

Finally, just for fun, find the font resource in the list and select it. Checking at the top of the window, you can see that the resource string given is

```
xterm.vt100.font:
```

Move to the bottom of the window and enter a valid font in the form of an XLFD of the sort generated by the `xfontsel` command. For this example, we'll use the following XLFD, generated by `xfontsel`:

```
-*-courier-bold-r-normal-*-14-*-*-*-*-*-*-*
```

After entering this font into the box and clicking Save and Apply, the font in the `xterm` window instantly changes to reflect our new preferences, and this latest change is saved to our file as well. The final result of our changes is shown in Figures 8.5 and 8.6.

The most basic use of the `editres` command should now be fairly clear; it's all a matter of selecting the widget you'd like to modify in the main `editres` canvas, and then bringing up the resource window to edit the properties of the widget in question.

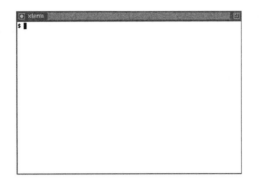

Figure 8.5 The original xterm window: black text on a white background, using a miscellaneous font with a boring title.

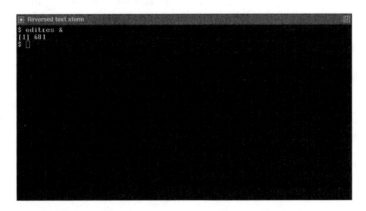

Figure 8.6 The updated xterm window: white text on a black background, using a courier font with an updated title.

Remember that we created a file called new_xterm over the course of this walk-through. You might have noticed that it doesn't seem to have had any effect—that is to say, if you start another xterm, none of the changes made to the first xterm seem to apply to newer instances of the application. Don't throw the file away yet—it's going to be useful in the next section.

Which Widgets Are Which?

The most fundamental question about using editres and changing resources is which resources ought to be changed, or, to put it another way, which widget properties do what. There is no easy answer to this question; many applications don't include widget documentation, and it's really up to you to try to figure out, based on the property and widget names, what does what. Unfortunately, programmers aren't always extremely helpful in choosing clear and explanatory widget or property names.

Most of the standard Xt and Athena widgets and widget classes and their properties are fairly well documented, though such documentation is well beyond the scope of this text (and is really complex enough to warrant an entire text on its own). However, such documentation is often complex and of little use to anyone but the X *programmer*—certainly not to the X *user*. Most of the time, users will want to consult the application's manual page or GNU info page (using the info command) for documentation for an application's resources. For example, xterm's manual page contains a large amount of information documenting the xterm resources. The emacs editor, on the other hand, documents most of its resources in a series of info pages.

If the resources for a given application aren't documented in the application's manual page, in the info page, or in some other included file, it often comes down to simple guessing and experimentation. In our walk-through, the meanings of the resources seemed obvious. On the other hand, there were also resources for several other fonts and several other colors in the vt100 widget. As luck would have it, they all refer to properties of a vt100 terminal, and anyone familiar with such a terminal recognizes them quickly. The point here is that context and intuition should be used when experimenting with resources; if one thing doesn't work, try another. Another trick for helping with resource configuration will be covered a little later in the chapter when we discuss application default files. For now, just remember that it will often come down to experimentation and your own technical street smarts alone.

Resources and Files

Although editres is nice, you might have noticed that the changes it makes don't seem to work on new instances of applications that were launched after the Apply button was clicked, and that the Save button and resultant file haven't yet had any effect. This is because we've taken only the first step toward making changes permanent.

Resource File Formats

Take a look at the file that we created in our sample editres section working on xterm in the previous section. A listing of the file as generated by cat can be found in Listing 8.1.

Listing 8.1   The new_xterm File, Generated by editres

```
.xterm.vt100.title: Reversed text xterm
.xterm.vt100.foreground: white
.xterm.vt100.background: black
.xterm.vt100.font: -*-courier-bold-r-normal-*-14-*-*-*-*-*-*
```

Files that contain X resource information for the X resource database generally contain information formatted this way. That is to say, the format generally follows this pattern:

```
app1.resource.property1: value
app1.resource.property2: value
app2.resource.property1: value
app2.resource.property2: value
```

Any number of X resources can be configured in a single file; some resource files have been known to stretch into the hundreds of kilobytes, configuring many, many properties across a large number of applications. Most users won't need files of this magnitude because the defaults for most applications are acceptable. Usually, the changes the average user makes will be changes to colors or fonts here and there.

Note that, although we haven't discussed it yet, wildcard characters are allowed in the resource strings, often used simply to shorten them, but sometimes also to apply to multiple widgets. For example, the resources from our sample file could appear like this without significantly changing their impact:

```
*xterm*title: Reversed text xterm
*xterm*foreground: white
*xterm*background: black
*xterm*font: -*-courier-bold-r-normal-*-14-*-*-*-*-*-*
```

You might have noticed that some of the buttons at the top of editres windows cause asterisks to appear in the resource string; this wildcard capability is the reason for those buttons, though they aren't normally needed when configuring a single property inside editres.

Any file that follows the basic formats above can be used in configuring X resources. However, not all files will be used as such—at least not automatically.

The xrdb Command

The xrdb command is the command used to merge an X resource configuration file into the running X resource database. After the resources in a file have been merged in, they will remain in effect until the session ends, affecting all future instances of any applications or widgets configured in the file. For example, to make our xterm changes apply to any xterm launched for the remainder of the current XFree86 session, the xrdb command would be used like this:

```
xrdb -merge new_xterm
```

After the file has been merged, try launching a new xterm window again from any existing xterm:

```
xterm &
```

Note when it starts that the changes made during the sample session now appear in the new xterm window. The changes have become permanent, at least for the remainder of the session. The xrdb command accepts several additional arguments, shown in Table 8.1.

Table 8.1   Most Common xrdb Command-Line Arguments

Argument	Description
-n	Display the resource database changes, to standard output, but don't actually make them in the resource database.
-quiet	Don't print warnings about duplicate entries.
-cpp program	The name of an alternative preprocessor program to use. Normally, cpp is used to allow for C-style preprocessing directives to appear in resource files, but an alternative can be used if it supports the -I, -D, and -U options.
-nocpp	Don't run the file through a preprocessor of any kind.
-query	List the current set of properties.
-load	Load the new file instead of the original set of defined resource properties, replacing them completely.
-merge	Load the new file in addition to the original set of defined resource properties, adding to the environment rather than redefining it.
-edit filename	Merge changes in the environment back into a resources file, replacing lines in the file with matching resource lines in the environment. This is one way to save editres-style updates back to a resource file.
-backup suffix	Append the given suffix to the filename given by -edit and use the resultant filename as a backup file.

There are several additional, more specialized xrdb arguments; you can read more about them by studying the xrdb manual page.

The .Xdefaults File

You now know how to use editres to make changes to a running X application that supports X resource database configuration. You also know how to save those changes to a file and use it to make them affect new instances of the applications in question for the remainder of an X session. There is still a gap in your knowledge, however—how to make the changes permanent across multiple X sessions. That is to say, how to have X read your changes from a file each time it starts.

As luck would have it, there is a standard filename that serves just that purpose. The $HOME/.Xdefaults file (note that it begins with a period and is thus hidden under normal conditions) is merged into the resource database each time X is launched by most (including the standard) xinitrc scripts. When you have decided that you want resource changes to become permanent, they should be added to the end of $HOME/.Xdefaults; they will then be merged into the database each time a new X session starts, before any applications are launched.

A similar effect can be achieved by inserting a call to xrdb in your own personal xinit script. For example, if instead of using the $HOME/.Xdefaults file to store your xterm changes, you wanted to leave them in the file as-is, yet you also wanted them to take effect for each X session you start, you could include the following lines in your $HOME/.xinitrc file:

```
if [ -e ~/new_xterm ]; then
    xrdb -merge ~/new_xterm
fi
```

Although this is certainly not the most elegant solution, it is sometimes desirable.

The temptation to save changes from editres directly to .Xdefaults is high, but such activity should be avoided; it can lead to a cluttered, enlarged, and difficult to follow .Xdefaults file. Rather than save changes directly to .Xdefaults, save them to a separate file first to make sure that you like them. Then, after your changes have been finalized and merged from the new file into the resource database, save them to .Xdefaults using xrdb:

```
xrdb -edit ~/.Xdefaults -backup .bak
```

This will save the changes in final, cleaned-up form to the .Xdefaults file, over any previous configuration for the properties in question, and make a backup of the original .Xdefaults file at ~/.Xdefaults.bak.

The Application Defaults File

One final repository for resource changes exists but is more helpful in configuring resources using editres and your own .Xdefaults file than in any other way.

The lib/X11/app-defaults/ directory off the main XFree86 directory tree contains several files that are named after application instances and contain the default configurations for the applications they name. When an application is launched, X checks the app-defaults directory for a file that matches the application's name. If such a file exists, it is merged into the resource database immediately before the application starts. For example, the file /usr/X11R6/lib/X11/app-defaults/XTerm contains a complete resource configuration for the default appearance and behavior of the xterm application. Similar files exist for most of the standard X programs, and many programs will add their own app-defaults file to the directory when they are installed. Older versions of Netscape Navigator are one example of such an application.

Changes to the files in this directory must normally be made when logged in as root because all the files are normally owned by root, but changes in general to any of the files in the directory are strongly discouraged. It is normally much more desirable to have each login account configure applications via the .Xdefaults files in home directories rather than to implement a systemwide application change using the files in /usr/X11R6/lib/X11/app-defaults. Note that any changes you do make will take instant effect on all future instances of the application because X loads the app-defaults files into the resource database each time an application is launched.

These files do serve a very useful purpose, however: Many of them contain invaluable and lengthy examples of resource configuration for the application to which they belong. Using editres is often a tiring job, involving a great deal of guesswork when it comes to determining what a specific resource or property is for and what type of value it is expecting. The task is made much easier when a sample configuration for the property in question already exists, as is often the case with the files in /usr/X11R6/lib/X11/app-defaults.

Note that, in some instances, properties containing color-oriented configuration go in the file with a -color extension, while all other properties reside in the main file. So, for example, the file /usr/X11R6/lib/X11/app-defaults/XFontSel-color contains color defaults for the xfontsel command, whereas the XFontSel file in the same directory contains all the other properties related to the xfontsel command.

Note also that you can create your own app-defaults file, if necessary, for an application that doesn't supply one, simply by creating a file in the app-defaults directory that is named after an application's root widget as given by editres. Capitalization is important; the name should be chosen based on the second row of buttons in the editres resource box window.

Common Resources and Command-Line Options

The management of X resources for applications that support them is definitely an involved topic, and one that most users don't have the time or energy to deal with in any real depth. Luckily, the need for some measure of simplification was anticipated by the X designers and the object-oriented nature of X widgets.

The Core Xt Resources

Many of the most commonly changed basic properties are consistent across most applications and X toolkit and Athena widgets and can thus be used in a very simplified manner. These are shown in Table 8.2; note the use of wildcard characters to make changes in properties apply across the entire widget tree for a given application. The same resources can also be used on specific widgets, instead of wildcarding them across all widgets.

Table 8.2 Most Common Use of the Core X Toolkit Resources

Resource Use	Effect
app*borderColor: *col*	Changes the border color for all widgets to *col*, a color in the X color database or an RGB colorspace string.
app*borderWidth: *n*	Changes the border width for all widgets to *n* pixels.
app*background: *col*	Changes the background color for all widgets to *col*. Can also appear as Background in some cases.

continues

Table 8.2 Continued

Resource Use	Effect
app*foreground: *col*	Changes the foreground color for all widgets to *col*. Can also appear as Foreground in some cases.
app*font: *XLFD*	Changes the font for all widgets to the X logical font description given by *XLFD*.
app.height: *n*	Sets the default height of the application window to *n* pixels. Can also be used to set the height of specific widgets.
app.width: *n*	Sets the default width of the application window to *n* pixels. Can also be used to set the width of specific widgets.
app.x: *n*	Sets the default location of the application window to *n* pixels from the left edge of the screen. Can also be used to set the position of specific widgets within their parents.
app.y: *n*	Sets the default location of the application window to *n* pixels from the top edge of the screen. Can also be used to set the position of specific widgets within their parents.
app.title: *text*	Sets the title of the application window to *text*.

An example using all the resources in Table 8.2 serves to illustrate their uses. To configure a yellow-on-blue xterm window titled My Terminal using a 14-point Courier font and red borders two pixels thick, which by default starts as a 100×50 text window at a location of 1,1 on the display, the following resources would be used:

```
xterm*borderColor: red
xterm*borderWidth: 2
xterm*background: blue
xterm*foreground: yellow
xterm*font: -*-courier-bold-r-normal-*-14-*-*-*-*-*-*
xterm.height: 50
xterm.width: 100
xterm.x: 1
xterm.y: 1
xterm.title: My Terminal
```

These few resources, which affect the basics of appearance and behavior during application launch, cover the majority of user configuration desires quite nicely; most people just want to be able to make X applications suit their tastes in terms of appearance and start at a predefined size and location on the display.

The Standard Xt/Athena Command-Line Arguments

It is sometimes inconvenient to have to specify all forms of configuration as resource strings, especially when changes as simple as foreground and background color are to be made. So, most Xt and Athena applications support a very basic set of command-line arguments that roughly correspond to the core resource set given in Table 8.2. These command-line arguments are described in the sections that follow.

Border Options: `-bd` and `-bw`

The `-bd` and `-bw` options control the border color and border width for the application widgets, respectively. These arguments correspond to the borderColor and borderWidth properties. They are commonly used as follows:

```
xt-app -bd col -bw n
```

In this example, *col* represents either a color from the X color database or a color specification from the RGB colorspace, and *n* represents the width, in pixels, of widget borders.

Text Options: `-fg`, `-bg`, and `-fn`

These three options control the appearance of text in Xt/Athena applications. The `-fg` argument controls the foreground color of affected text. The `-bg` argument controls the background color of affected text. The `-fn` argument controls the font in which text will be drawn. These arguments correspond to the foreground, background, and font properties, and are generally used like this:

```
xt-app -fg col -bg col -fn XLFD
```

In this example, *col* represents either a color from the X color database or a color specification from the RGB colorspace in both cases. The `-fn` argument accepts an X logical font descriptor of the type generated by the xfontsel utility.

The `-geometry` Option

The `-geometry` option is the option related to window size and placement and is really a special case because it is a composite of four of the core resources, x, y, height, and width, and requires a special argument format. The `-geometry` argument should be used in one of the following ways:

```
xt-app -geometry SZXxSZY
xt-app -geometry [+-]n[+-]n
xt-app -geometry SZXxSZY[+-]n[+-]n
```

The first method of using the -geometry argument provides simply a size in pixels in the X direction (horizontally), SZX, and a size in pixels in the Y direction (vertically), SZY. For example, to call an xclock window with a size of 400×300 pixels, use the following command:

```
xclock -geometry 400x300
```

The second method of using the -geometry argument provides only a location for the application on the display, in an offset from either the left or right, and the top or bottom of the screen, in pixels, respectively. Positive numbers represent offsets from the top and left of the screen, whereas negative numbers represent offsets from the bottom and right of the screen. For example, to start an xclock of default size and place the window at 10 pixels from the left of the screen and five pixels from the top, you might use

```
xclock -geometry +10+5
```

On the other hand, if you wanted to start an xclock that is one pixel from both the bottom and right edges of the screen, you would use

```
xclock -geometry -1-1
```

And, as a final illustration, to start an xclock window 10 pixels from the right of the display and two pixels from the top, the following command would work:

```
xclock -geometry -10+2
```

The final method for using the -geometry argument simply combines the other two methods into a single argument string. For example, to start an xclock window that is 150 pixels wide by 200 pixels tall and 10 pixels from the bottom and left edges of the display, you would use

```
xclock -geometry 150x200+10-10
```

Note that in the cases of windows that are fundamentally text-based widgets, the height and width values can be in characters rather than in pixels. Such is the case with primarily text-based applications such as xterm.

Window Title

The window title can even be changed from the command line, using the -title argument, as follows:

```
xterm -title 'XTerm Window Number Four'
```

Note that because this is occurring on the command line, the text string must either be escaped or delimited with single or double quotes; otherwise, each word will be interpreted as a separate command-line argument.

Changing the Resource Name

One argument that is normally not issued as a resource string is the `-name` argument, which allows an application instance to obtain its resources under another name. For example, you could call the `xterm` command and assign it the name `MyTerm` like this:

```
xterm -name MyTerm
```

This command would launch an `xterm` that would obtain its resource configuration from strings that refer to `MyTerm`, such as these:

```
MyTerm*foreground: blue
MyTerm*background: black
MyTerm*title: This is my terminal!
```

This argument can be useful when using the `-e` option of `xterm` to call `xterm` mainly as a container for text-based applications such as `pine`, `lynx`, and `elm`. Using the `-name` argument, resources could be supplied to give each of these applications its own appearance, font, and window size, even though they all run inside an `xterm` window and aren't normally X-based applications.

This argument also has the side effect with certain window managers (Window Maker) of creating a new app-icon separate from the original instance of the application.

The `-xrm` Argument

One final command-line argument deserves mention in our discussion of X application resources and the resource database. Until now, we've set all resources other than the core resources from inside a resource file, which had to be merged into the resource database by hand or read at the start of the X session.

The command-line arguments we learned were suited only to the core set of properties for the Xt and Athena application widgets. It is possible, however, to set any resource on the command line using the `-xrm` argument. It is very simple to use:

```
xt-app -xrm string -xrm string ...
```

In this example, `string` refers to an X resource string of the type we've been using all along. Thus, the following three methods for altering the foreground color of an application's text all have an identical effect:

```
xterm*foreground: black
xterm -fg black
xterm -xrm 'xterm*foreground: black'
```

Note that the first item is meant to be included in a resource file that is then merged into the resource database, whereas the other two items are ways of launching xterm with those changes already in place. Note also that strings supplied to the -xrm argument should always be escaped to avoid confusion resulting from wildcard characters and unescaped spaces in the resource string.

The xrm command doesn't find a great deal of real-world use, being superseded most of the time by editres, xrdb, the $HOME/.Xdefaults file, and the command-line arguments that correspond to the core properties. On the other hand, it can at times be useful, especially for playing with resources in a quick and dirty way, without having to launch a messy editres window and use a mouse or other pointing device to navigate.

9

Runtime Environment Configuration

The nature of the X Window System and its separation between low-level GUI functions and environment management means that many different environments and window managers are available to the average XFree86 and Linux user. This is fortunate for the user; the wide variety in available choices means that any user can have his or her desktop exactly as he or she wants it.

Unfortunately, it also means that there are as many different ways to configure a desktop as there are users, and such configuration must often be done using *dotfiles*—configuration files written in a specific format that the window manager reads each time it begins, in order to establish its behavior and appearance for the session.

The purpose of this chapter is to introduce you to some basic window manager concepts and to help you configure dotfiles for the three most common window managers installed by Linux distributions—twm, which is installed by all of them, fvwm, which is less used than it once was but is still the default window manager for some distributions, and fvwm2, which picks up where fvwm left off and is also used by some Linux distributions as the default window manager.

There are, of course, other window managers, some of them much more popular or pretty than twm, fvwm, or fvwm2. However, because so many window managers are available, it is impractical to cover all of them or to cover any of them in any great detail in a text like this one. In fact, even twm, fvwm, and fvwm2 aren't completely documented here. For detailed configuration information or for information on advanced options, please consult the manual pages for each window manager and its components, as well as the documentation included with the window manager and the source code of the window manager, in that order.

The Basics

Although each window manager is a beast all its own, with a specific look and feel and unique configuration options, twm, fvwm, and fvwm2 all share a few common elements. Before attempting to configure a dotfile for any of these window managers, it is important to understand what these elements are and how they behave.

Window Appearance

Every window manager covered in this chapter adds decorations to the X client windows it manages. Such decorations are used to show a window's edges, indicate where the current keyboard focus currently resides, and provide a mechanism by which the user can interact with the window manager in the context of a specific window. The common decorations added by window managers can be found in Table 9.1.

Table 9.1   Common Window Decorations

Decoration	Description
Title Bar	Most commonly seen as a horizontal rectangle sitting on top of a window, though vertical title bars do exist, as in the case of the wm2 manager. Usually imprinted with text representing the title of the window. Also usually indicates whether a window is in a focused or an unfocused state, often through a change of color.
Border	In addition to the default border drawn by many X applications that might be only a single pixel wide (or might not be present at all), most window managers draw a border of their own, often with a three-dimensional appearance, to make it easier to see the edges of a window. Sometimes the borders even have some sort of user function, such as resizing the window.
Buttons	Usually located somewhere inside or next to the window's title bar, window buttons are usually small rectangles (though they can be other shapes or even images) that perform specific functions when clicked. Common buttons include a minimize button, also known as an iconify button in some cases, a close or kill button, and, in some cases (like twm), a resize button. Some window managers enable the user to define an arbitrary set of buttons and bind functions to them at will.

Decoration	Description
Handles	Several window managers draw what are known as handles on windows they decorate. Handles are specially marked sections of the window border that behave differently from the rest of the border, usually enabling the user to resize the window when they are clicked.

In addition to this basic set of decorations, others can be added by some window managers, including menus and images, but such decorations are rarely as useful as the basic set discussed here and their configuration is beyond the scope of this text.

Menus

Many window managers provide some method by which applications can be launched without having to start them from an xterm window or other command line in X. Many window managers also provide a list of internal window management functions such as resizing, moving, or minimizing a window. The most common places to catalog such functions and to provide ways for applications to be launched are one or a series of menus that appear when the mouse or pointer is clicked either on the root window or on window decorations.

The root window menu as such is unique to X users for the most part. A few other operating systems like Windows provide a context-sensitive menu on the root window that provides some measure of functionality, but only in X and when using X window managers are large, user-definable root menus traditional, from which applications can be launched and window management functions can be carried out.

Some window managers even allow for *pinnable* root menus (menus that can be made to stay on the display indefinitely), submenus within the root menu, and images and icons inside the root menu. Most window managers' menus are user-definable, and it is thus common for users to put their most-launched applications into window manager menus for easy launching, without the need for a command prompt.

The Pager

Another feature common among users of the X window system but not common outside this community is the use of virtual desktops, a way of maintaining multiple active desktops or a large virtual desktop area inside the computer, though only one desktop or area of the desktop can display at a time. Using a tool usually referred to as a *pager*, users can cause any one of these desktops or any section of a large virtual desktop to appear on the physical screen. The user can then interact with the visible desktop until he or she needs to work on another section of the virtual desktop, at which time he or she will again use the pager to make the desired desktop area visible.

Most window managers that can use multiple virtual desktops or large virtual desktop areas are known as *virtual window managers*, though this terminology is becoming less well-known as time goes by and the feature becomes more and more ubiquitous. The pager used by these window managers is usually represented as a small panel that appears on all active desktops and is split into several sections, each of which represents one virtual area. Using this pager, the user can drag windows back and forth between desktop areas and can switch to the desired desktop area simply by clicking its representation in the pager.

The Icon or Application Manager

The final element common to the three window managers we'll cover here is the presence of some form of icon or application manager that enables the user to minimize and restore windows or obtain a listing of the X clients currently running in some graphical way. The icon or application manager sometimes also provides a mechanism for giving a window focus by clicking on the window's entry in the manager.

In some cases, this functionality exists as an icon manager or icon box of some sort, a place where an icon or minimized representation of a window will always appear when the window is minimized. Clicking one of the icons in the icon box or icon manager results in the window becoming un-minimized and reappearing on the desktop, often on top of all other windows, with focus.

In other configurations, this functionality is provided via a window list that looks rather like a menu, but is updated dynamically to reflect the list of currently active X clients. Selecting any of the windows in the menu then causes that window to come to the forefront of the desktop and to take focus.

Some window managers provide both types of functionality, either alone or simultaneously, providing a powerful method for desktop window management.

Bitmaps and Pixmaps

Before we begin discussing window managers on a program-by-program basis, it is important to mention two image formats native to the X window system with which not all users might be familiar.

When X was developed, only a tiny subset of the graphics formats available today existed, and many of them were protected by closely held copyrights and patents. X programmers therefore have developed two image formats that are native to the X Window System: X bitmaps and X pixmaps.

X Bitmaps

X bitmap files, which end with the .xbm extension, are two-color (black-and-white) images that are stored in a plain-text format which many C programmers will be able to decode instantly. The format is simple: A matrix is defined by specifying a height and width for the image. A series of bits are then specified representing either an on pixel or an off pixel, respectively.

X Pixmaps

X pixmap files, which end with the .xpm extension, are colorized images that are stored in a similar plain-text format readable by C programmers. In X pixmap files, however, the pixels are specified with color values rather than with simple on and off values.

Icons and Window Managers

Many X window managers enable the user to use either X bitmaps or X pixmaps or both to decorate various aspects of the window manager's runtime, from window decorations or title bar buttons to window icons. Unfortunately, X does not natively include a large set of icons with which the user can work. Some newer window managers such as Window Maker can use newer image formats found more commonly in icon collections on the Web, but many (including fvwm, fvwm2, and twm) don't understand any formats but .xbm and .xpm.

It is therefore often necessary to convert icons from other bitmap or image formats to the .xbm and .xpm formats. Several common tools exist that can make these conversions for you; the most common are xv and ImageMagick, both of which are often included with Linux distributions. The convert tool from ImageMagick is especially easy to use; all the following statements are valid and produce exactly the expected result:

```
convert myfile.jpg myicon.xpm
convert myimage.gif myimage.xpm
convert mybitmap.mac mybitmap.xbm
```

The tool runs noninteractively and is thus well suited to script use or shell-based use such as when converting entire directories of icons using for loops. The ImageMagick tools can be found at

```
http://www.wizards.dupont.com/cristy/ImageMagick.html
```

Other tools also exist for converting graphic images—even high-end tools such as GIMP can be used for this purpose—but few are as convenient as ImageMagick.

The fvwm Window Manager

The fvwm family of window managers is one of the oldest and most mature available to Linux users. Although not included with XFree86 or the X Window System, fvwm is traditionally the stock window manager on most Linux distributions, though recent distributions have finally begun to move to KDE or GNOME desktops for their default installation.

Several other window managers have been created as extensions to or *hacks* of the fvwm window managers and share, for the most part, the configuration format of the fvwm dotfiles. The fvwm window managers are best split into two families, the fvwm 1.x managers—which use the configuration file format used by all fvwm version 1 releases (see Figure 9.1)—and the fvwm 2.x managers—which use the configuration file format that is used by all fvwm version 2 releases and that is significantly different from the 1.x configuration file format (see Figure 9.2).

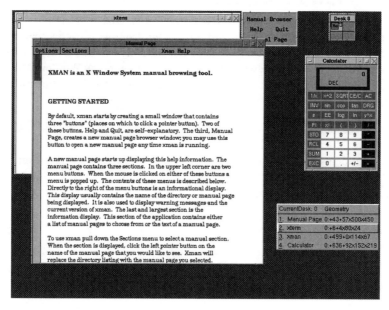

Figure 9.1   The fvwm window manager.

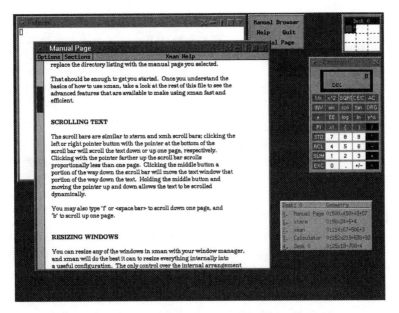

Figure 9.2 The fvwm 2 window manager.

In general, the fvwm managers can be started by calling either the fvwm (for fvwm version 1) or fvwm2 (for fvwm version 2) binaries at the end of your $HOME/.xinitrc file in place of any other window manager (such as twm) or desktop manager (such as gnome-session).

fvwm Configuration File Basics

Regardless of the version of fvwm you're using, all configuration information for fvwm is typically provided in a single dotfile, located at $HOME/.fvwmrc in the case of fvwm 1.x or $HOME/.fvwm2rc in the case of fvwm 2.x. If the related file isn't found in the user's home directory, the files fvwm/system.fvwmrc or fvwm2/system.fvwm2rc off the /usr/X11R6/lib/X11 directory will be used instead.

The fvwm configuration files are largely unstructured and order-unimportant (though there are one or two exceptions to this rule) and are usually simple lists of internal fvwm keywords or functions. Many of the keywords in the file act as flags—that is, when they are present, they alter some aspect of fvwm behavior. To remove the behavior, simply remove the keyword. The rest of the keywords or functions in the file are generally followed by one or more values that can be altered to alter some behavior of fvwm.

Convention dictates that file paths, appearances, and decoration and button configuration keywords go at the top of the file, root menu configuration comes next, followed by module configuration on a per-module basis, and finally, keyboard and mouse bindings at the end of the configuration file. Comments in the fvwm configuration files are indicated by lines that begin with the hash mark (#) and are ignored by fvwm. There is no hard limit to the length of the configuration file, and when a single keyword or function is specified multiple times with a different value each time, only the last occurrence of the keyword or function in the file will be used.

Learning about dotfile configuration can be a confusing process, especially when configuring window managers. It might therefore be helpful to refer to Appendix A, "Sample Window Manager Configurations," and to follow along in the samples as you read.

fvwm 1 Appearance Configuration

Several configuration keywords are related to window decorations, colors, and fonts in the fvwm 1.x series window managers. These are the most commonly modified configuration keywords in the fvwm configuration file. Appearance and decoration-oriented options are shown in Table 9.2.

Note that several additional appearance-related keywords aren't listed here. In large part, they are superseded by window styles and the `Style` keyword, which is discussed in "fvwm 1 Button and Window Styles," several sections ahead.

Table 9.2 Common Appearance Configuration in fvwm 1.x

Keyword	Description
DecorateTransients	If present, instructs fvwm to decorate pop-up dialog windows as if they were normal windows, with a title bar, border, and buttons.
Font *XLFD*	Uses the font referred to by XLFD for titles and entries in the root menu.
HiBackColor *color*	Uses the supplied color as the decoration color for highlighted (focused) windows. The color should be either a name from the X color database or an RGB colorspace specification.
HiForeColor *color*	Uses the supplied color as the window title color for highlighted (focused) windows.
MenuBackColor *color*	Uses the supplied color as the background color for selected fvwm menu entries in menus such as the root menu.
MenuForeColor *color*	Uses the supplied color as the text color for Fselected VWM menu entries.
MWMBorders	Uses the Motif-style border decorations rather than the deeper fvwm-style decorations.

Keyword	Description
MWMMenus	Uses the Motif-style menu appearance rather than the default fvwm style.
WindowFont *XLFD*	Specifies that the named font should be used as the text font in window title bars.
XORValue *n*	Changes the logical exclusive OR value for rubber-band operations. In practice this number should be tweaked until the window outline drawn to represent a window during resize and move operations is easily visible.

Many users spend a great deal of time configuring the colors and fonts fvwm uses. The keywords in Table 9.2 are simple to use—for example, the following options make focused window borders appear with a reddish background and white text:

```
HiForeColor: white
HiBackColor: #ea1600
```

To make the job easier, consider using an application like xcolorsel, which ships as a package with most Linux distributions, and the standard xfontsel utility covered in Chapter 4, "Standard XFree86 Programs and Utilities." Note also that any changes you make won't be reflected in your onscreen display until the fvwm process itself is restarted; the easiest way to do this is to bind the Restart function to a menu entry or keystroke, a process described in the "fvwm 1 Mouse and Keyboard Bindings" section later in this chapter.

fvwm 1 General Behavior Options

Several general behavior-oriented configuration options are available to users of fvwm. Aside from the configuration of colors and fonts, these are the most commonly used configuration options for fvwm users. They enable the user to alter many look-and-feel aspects of fvwm behavior.

The most common general behavior configuration options are shown in Table 9.3.

Table 9.3   Most Common General Behavior Keywords in fvwm

Keyword	Description
AutoRaise *n*	Automatically raises any window that remains focused for *n* milliseconds. If fvwm is in click-to-focus mode and *n* is negative, prevents the initial mouse click from raising the window.
ClickToFocus	Places fvwm into click-to-focus mode. Window focus is changed by clicking inside a new window.
DontMoveOff	Prevents windows from being moved entirely off the accessible desktop.

continues

Table 9.3 Continued

Keyword	Description
NoPPosition	Doesn't allow new windows to place themselves; instead, requires that either fvwm or the user places them.
OpaqueMove *n*	Causes windows smaller than *n* percent of the visible display to remain intact (no rubber-band outline) during moves.
OpaqueResize	Causes windows to remain intact (no rubber-band outline) during resizes.
RandomPlacement	Places new windows randomly. If smart placement is also active, attempts to use it first.
SloppyFocus	Places fvwm into sloppy-focus mode. Window focus goes to whichever window contains the mouse. When the mouse is over root, uses the previous focus.
SmartPlacement	Places new windows intelligently. If no intelligent placement can be found, either uses random placement (if active) or user placement.
StaysOnTop *window*	Causes fvwm to keep the specified window in a permanently raised state. The window is specified using an application name or a window title that can contain wildcard characters.

A common configuration among Linux users includes the following set of behavior-oriented fvwm keywords:

```
SloppyFocus
RandomPlacement
SmartPlacement
NoPPosition
OpaqueMove 100
DontMoveOff
```

These keywords will cause sloppy focus to be used so that whichever window contains the mouse pointer will have focus. fvwm will try to place new windows intelligently, but if it can't figure out how, it will place them randomly rather than allow them to specify their own position. When windows are moved, they will remain visible at all times, regardless of the size of the window, and they will never be allowed to move completely off the usable desktop area.

fvwm 1 Desktop and Client Management

Two main systems exist in fvwm to aid in management of running windows. The first is a system of maintaining a larger desktop area than the monitor can visibly display, known as paging a virtual desktop, and the second is a virtual list of running clients and a set of functions and menus for manipulating and acting on this list.

The Virtual Desktop and the Pager

fvwm enables the user to maintain a set of virtual desktops that are larger than the visible desktop in which to work; in such cases only a fraction of the usable desktop area is visible at any one time. An applet called the Pager enables the user to drag applications between visible and nonvisible areas and to decide which desktop area will be visible at any given moment.

Normally, when virtual desktops are enabled, moving the mouse cursor past the edge of the screen will page over to the next section of the current desktop in that direction. Similarly, dragging a window past the edge of the display will move the window to the next section of the desktop.

fvwm keywords related to virtual desktop and pager functionality and behavior are explained in Table 9.4.

Table 9.4   fvwm Keywords Related to Virtual Desktops

Keyword	Description
DeskTopScale *n*	Uses a virtual desktop of scale *n* with respect to the physical display.
DeskTopSize *n1*x*n2*	Uses a virtual desktop *n1* by *n2* physical screens big.
EdgeResistance *n1 n2*	After the mouse moves past the display's edge, waits *n2* pixels if dragging a window or *n1* milliseconds if not before paging to the next desktop area.
EdgeScroll *n1 n2*	Specifies that each paging action should move the visible area *n1* percent of a screen vertically or *n2* percent of a screen horizontally.
Pager *x y*	Places a desktop pager at *x, y* onscreen when moving across desktops.
PagerForeColor *color*	Uses *color* for the pager's foreground.
PagerBackColor *color*	Uses *color* for the pager's background.
PagerFont *XLFD*	Uses the supplied font in the pager.
PagingDefault *n*	If *n* is 1, enables desktop paging.
StartsOnDesk *window n*	The named window should always be started on virtual desktop page number *n*. The window is specified using an application name or a window title that can contain wildcard characters.
Sticky *window*	The named window should be sticky, staying at the same location on the physical display no matter which area of the desktop is visible.
StickyBackColor *color*	Uses *color* for the background of sticky windows' decorations.
StickyForeColor *color*	Uses *color* for sticky window titles.

It is rather easy to virtual-desktop-enable a desktop that currently isn't configured to contain them; the following is one possible addition to the fvwm configuration file:

```
DesktopScale 4
PagingDefault 1
Pager 1 1
EdgeScroll 100 100
EdgeResistance 333 10
Module FvwmPager
```

These six lines cause fvwm to use a virtual desktop four times the size of the visible desktop with a static pager and a pager at the upper-left corner of the screen when moving across screen boundaries. When the mouse moves past the edge of the screen, it must remain there for a third of a second before the display will page to the next desktop area.

Client Icon and Window Management

In addition to supplying a mechanism for the user to move about inside large virtual desktop space, fvwm also provides the user with mechanisms to manage a list of running X clients. A list of active windows is maintained from which windows can be selected for display or through which the user can cycle. fvwm also provides the capability to minimize a window, removing it from view and replacing it with an icon that represents it. An icon can then be restored later to make a window visible.

In many fvwm configurations, the default behavior is to display a window list when the user middle-clicks on the root window, to minimize a window when the user clicks on a minimize button at the upper-right of the window, and to restore a window when the user clicks on a minimized icon. This behavior can be changed, however, by binding functions such as Iconify and WindowList to other mouse clicks or keystrokes, a process covered in the "fvwm 1 Mouse and Keyboard Bindings" section, later in this chapter.

Keywords that control icon behavior and window list behavior are shown in Tables 9.5 and 9.6. Note that many of the keywords have to do with window circulation, a task performed by several built-in functions that are covered in a moment.

Table 9.5 Keywords Related to Icons and Minimization

Keyword	Description
Icon *window image*	Uses the file *image* as the icon in any minimized representation of *window*. The image file is loaded from one of the image paths, IconPath or PixmapPath, described later in this table. The window is specified using an application name or a window title that can contain wildcard characters.

Keyword	Description
IconBox *x1 y1 x2 y2*	Places minimized windows (icons) in the area of the screen bounded by a rectangle whose upper-left corner lies at x1, y1 and whose lower-right corner lies at x2, y2, counting from the upper-left corner of the screen.
IconFont *XLFD*	Uses the specified font to label icons.
IconPath *path*	Searches the supplied directories for X bitmap (.xbm) files.
PixmapPath *path*	Searches the supplied directories for X pixmap (.xpm) files.
StickyIcons	Icons should be sticky, staying at the same location on the physical display no matter which area of the desktop is visible.
StubbornIcons	Always restores windows to their original location rather than to the currently visible desktop area.
StubbornIconPlacement	Causes fvwm to avoid placing icons under other windows.
SuppressIcons	Eliminates all icons; iconified windows simply disappear. Useful for window-list-only client management.

Table 9.6 Keywords Related to Window List Behavior

Keyword	Description
CenterOnCirculate	When circulating through windows, centers the selected window in the visible area.
CirculateSkip *window*	When circulating through windows, skips over windows specified with this keyword. A window is specified using an application name or a window title that can contain wildcard characters.
CirculateSkipIcons	When circulating through windows, skips over windows that are in a minimized (iconified) state.
WindowListSkip *window*	Doesn't display the window in the window list. The window is specified using an application name or a window title that can contain wildcard characters.

It is common for a fvwm configuration to include an IconBox and a few icon definitions, as well as a list of windows that shouldn't appear in the window list. For example, consider the following:

```
IconPath /usr/include/X11/bitmaps/
PixmapPath /usr/share/pixmaps/
```

```
IconBox 0 500 800 600
StickyIcons
Icon "xterm" xterm.xpm
Icon "xclock" myclock.xpm
WindowListSkip "xclock"
CirculateSkip "xclock"
CirculateSkipIcons
```

This configuration starts by giving directory paths for bitmap and pixmap files. Minimized window icons appear only in the bottom 100 pixels of an 800×600 display, and all icons always appear on the visible display. The xterm and xclock applications use the icons xterm.xpm and myclock.xpm respectively when iconified. The xclock application doesn't appear in the window list or ever get focus when circulating through windows. Iconified windows also don't get focus when circulating through windows.

fvwm 1 Menus and Functions

fvwm menus, including the root menu, are built inside the configuration file and then bound to keyboard or mouse clicks that cause a given menu to be displayed. The format for creating and structuring these is simple; the following is the general format for building menus:

```
Popup "Menu Name"
    Function "Text Item" [additional...]
    Function "Text Item" [additional...]
    ...
EndMenu
```

A menu specification is started with the Popup keyword followed by the internal name of the menu to be created. This name is referred to elsewhere in the fvwm configuration file when binding it to mouse clicks or keystrokes. A menu is terminated by the EndMenu keyword, and in between the Popup and EndMenu keywords, nearly any valid fvwm function can appear. Each line in the menu will appear to the user as the supplied Text Item, and when selected by the user, the corresponding Function will be carried out.

A list of commonly used built-in fvwm functions appears in Table 9.7. Note that there are many more and that user-definable functions can also be called from menus. When fvwm functions are used inside a menu, the Text Item should always come immediately following the function keyword and before any arguments that are to be passed to the function.

Table 9.7   Commonly Used Built-In fvwm Functions

Function	Description
CirculateDown *window*	If no *window* is supplied, raises the next window in the list of active clients and give it focus. If *window* is supplied, causes the same effect for the named window. The window is specified using an application name or a window title that can contain wildcard characters.
CirculateUp *window*	If no *window* is supplied, raises the previous window in the list of active clients and give it focus. If *window* is supplied, causes the same effect for the named window. The window is specified using an application name or a window title that can contain wildcard characters.
Close	Closes the current window. If there is no current window, allows the user to choose a window to close.
Desk *n1 n2*	Pages *n1* desktop units away from the current one if *n1* is nonzero, or if *n1* is zero, switches to desktop area *n2*.
Destroy	Terminates the current window's client. If there is no current window, enables the user to choose a window to destroy.
Exec *command*	Causes fvwm to fork *command*, which can contain arguments, outside the window manager environment. Usually used to launch X clients from a menu.
Iconify *n*	Minimizes or restores the current window or icon. If there is no current window or icon, enables the user to choose a window or icon to minimize or restore. If *n* is supplied, a positive value will minimize only; a negative value will restore only.
Lower	Lowers the current window. If there is no current window, enables the user to choose a window to lower.
Maximize *x y*	Causes the current window to be resized to occupy the entire visible area. If there is no current window, enables the user to choose a window to maximize. When *x* and *y* are supplied, resizes to *x* percent of screen width and *y* percent of screen height. If *x* or *y* is zero, doesn't resize along that axis.
Move *x y*	Causes the current window to be moved to location *x,y* pixels. If there is no current window, enables the user to choose a window to move. When called without *x* and *y*, moves interactively.
Nop *s*	Does nothing. When called inside a menu and *s* is a null string (""), inserts a horizontal line in the menu. When s is a space enclosed in quotes (" "), inserts a space in the menu.
Popup *menu*	Causes the named menu to be displayed. When inside a menu definition, causes the named menu to appear as a submenu to the menu being defined.

continues

Table 9.7 Continued

Function	Description
Quit	Exits the fvwm window manager.
Raise	Causes the current window to be raised. If there is no current window, enables the user to choose a window to raise.
RaiseLower	If the current window is already raised, lowers it. If not, raises it. If there is no current window, enables the user to choose a window upon which this action will be performed.
Refresh	Redraws the screen to fix display bugs.
Resize *x y*	Causes the current window to be resized to *x* by *y* pixels. If there is no current window, enables the user to choose a window to resize. If called without *x* and *y*, resizes interactively.
Restart *command*	Causes fvwm to restart, rereading its configuration file. If *command* is supplied, causes fvwm to exit and starts *command* (usually another window manager) in its place.
Stick	Causes the current window to become sticky. If there is no current window, enables the user to choose a window.
Title	Causes the Text Item supplied after it in a menu definition to be the menu's visible title.
WindowsDesk *n*	Causes the current window to move to desktop area *n*. If there is no current window, enables the user to choose a window to be moved.
WindowList *n1 n2*	Displays the window list, an automatically generated menu that is a list of running clients. By clicking on a client's entry in the menu, the user causes the client to be restored if necessary, raised, and focused. If *n1* is 1, displays all clients on all desktops by name. If *n1* is 2, displays only visible windows and icons by name. If *n1* is 3, displays only visible windows and icons by icon name. If *n1* is 4, displays only windows on desktop area *n2* by name. If *n1* is 5, displays only windows on desktop area *n2* by icon name.

The majority of these functions are most useful when called from inside a menu, allowing the user in many cases to select a specific window for the action to affect. Some can be called meaningfully only from inside a menu, such as Nop and Title. A simple utility menu that would help in editing the fvwm configuration is defined as follows:

```
Popup "EditMenu"
    Title "fvwm Editing"
    Exec "Edit Configuration" emacs .fvwmrc &
    Restart "Restart fvwm"
    Nop ""
    Quit "Give up!"
EndMenu
```

Once bound to a keystroke or a specific mouse click, the menu, whose title will appear as fvwm Editing, will present the user with three choices: further editing of the configuration file (for which an emacs will be launched), restarting the window manager to activate changes, or (underneath a horizontal line) exiting the window manager altogether.

fvwm 1 Mouse and Keyboard Bindings

Now we've seen how to construct a menu, and we've seen a rather sizable list of common functions, but we haven't yet explained how the menu will be displayed or how to call a function outside a menu. Both of these tasks are accomplished by *binding* a function or menu to a particular keystroke or mouse click.

Mouse Bindings

Two keywords in fvwm bind a function or menu as seen in the last section to a particular action by the keyboard or mouse. The first of these keywords, Mouse, binds a specific type and location of mouse click to a function or menu, causing the function to be executed or the menu to display when the given mouse click is registered. The Mouse keyword follows the following basic form:

```
Mouse Button Context Modifiers Function
```

The number given by Button refers to the mouse button to which this binding applies. Valid button numbers are shown in Table 9.8.

Table 9.8 Valid Button Numbers for the Mouse Keyword

Button	Description
0	This binding applies to a click by any mouse button.
1	This binding applies to a click by button 1, normally the left mouse button.
2	This binding applies to a click by button 2, normally the middle mouse button.
3	This binding applies to a click by button 3, normally the right mouse button.
4	This binding applies to a click by button 4, normally owned by the scroll wheel's up direction on scroll-enabled mice.
5	This binding applies to a click by button 5, normally owned by the scroll wheel's down direction on scroll-enabled mice.

Note that these buttons themselves and their physical positions on the mouse can be altered using xmodmap as detailed in Chapter 7, "Runtime Server Configuration."

The Context to which this line will apply refers to the location of the mouse pointer when the button's click is registered. Each context is represented by a single letter, and multiple letters can be strung together to represent multiple contexts to which a binding applies. The valid contexts are shown in Table 9.9.

Table 9.9 Valid Mouse Contexts

Context	Description
R	The pointer is over the root window.
W	The pointer is inside an application window.
T	The pointer is over a window title bar.
S	The pointer is over the window border.
F	The pointer is on the window frame (handles at the corners of a decorated window's border).
I	The pointer is over a minimized application's icon.
0–9	The pointer is over the title bar button represented by the numbers 0–9. Even-numbered buttons are on the right side of the title bar, odd-numbered buttons are on the left side of the title bar. Normally only three buttons (one at the left, 1, and two on the right, 4 and 2) appear in fvwm. However, more will appear if functions are bound to them using the Mouse keyword. More details on buttons can be found in the next section.
A	The pointer is in any one of the listed contexts except the title bar buttons or the inside of the window.

The Modifier specifies that the binding should apply only to mouse clicks that were registered while a specific modifier was active. Modifiers can be strung together to indicate that multiple modifiers are involved in this binding. A list of valid modifiers can be found in Table 9.10.

Table 9.10 Valid Modifiers for the Mouse Keyword

Modifier	Description
N	Click is valid only when no modifiers are active.
C	Click is valid only when the control modifier is active (normally when the Ctrl key is being held down).
S	Click is valid only when the shift modifier is active (normally when the Shift key is being held down).
M	Click is valid only when the meta modifier is active (normally when the Alt key is being held down).
A	Click is active for any modifier or combination of modifiers.

When multiple modifiers are specified, they must all be active for the click to be valid. Note that a numeric digit or digits can also be used to represent the standard X modifier maps from 1–5. For more information on X modifiers, see Chapter 7.

The Function supplied to the mouse keyword can be any valid function, such as those listed earlier, or any function you've defined yourself (as we'll discuss momentarily). For example, if you've built a pop-up menu called RootMenu and would like it to be displayed whenever any mouse button is clicked over any part of the root window, the following binding would be used:

```
Mouse 0 R A Popup "RootMenu"
```

If you've defined a menu called Operations that should appear whenever the window button at the extreme upper-left of a window is right-clicked, you'd use this binding:

```
Mouse 3 1 A Popup "Operations"
```

Some seemingly very complex operations are possible. For example, this pair of lines will cause the mouse's scroll wheel to circulate up or down through the list of active windows, effectively allowing the user to choose an active window by scrolling through available windows:

```
Mouse 4 A A CirculateUp
Mouse 5 A A CirculateDown
```

The following is also valid:

```
Mouse 123 TSF CSM Destroy
```

This line will cause the window in question to be destroyed if any of the first three buttons are clicked on either the title bar or any part of a window border, given that the Ctrl, Shift, and Alt keys are all being held down at the time.

Keyboard Bindings

Keystroke bindings in fvwm look very much like Mouse bindings. The relevant keyword for binding keystrokes is Key, and it should be used as follows:

```
Key Keysym Context Modifiers Function
```

Keysym should be a symbol from the include/X11/keysymdef.h file off the main /usr/X11R6 directory tree. The key symbols that are bound to functions by most users are the symbols F1–F12, which generally represent the keyboard function keys.

The rest of the arguments given to the Key keyword are identical to those given by the Mouse keyword discussed earlier. To illustrate, however, an example is in order. Remember the example in which the scroll wheel on a mouse was bound to the CirculateUp and CirculateDown window selection functions. If no scroll wheel exists, a user can just as easily bind the same functions to the F11 and F12 keys:

```
Key F11 A A CirculateUp
Key F12 A A CirculateDown
```

One important caveat should be understood when creating keyboard bindings: Some applications need certain keystrokes (such as function keys) to operate. If you've bound the F11 key to a window manager function and find yourself using an application that requires that you press the F11 key, the binding makes it impossible to send F11 to the application.

fvwm 1 User-Defined Functions

Although the list of built-in fvwm functions is extensive, it is sometimes helpful to be able to define one's own functions that can then be bound to mouse or keyboard activity. User-defined functions are created using the Function and EndFunction keyword pair, and are defined using the following structure:

```
Function "FunctionName"
   InternalFunc "trigger" arguments
   InternalFunc "trigger" arguments
   ...
EndFunction
```

In the preceding structure, InternalFunc represents any of the internal fvwm functions outlined earlier or an already defined user function. The arguments are those expected by the built-in function, where necessary, and the trigger is one of the events listed in Table 9.11.

Table 9.11   fvwm Function Triggers

Trigger	Description
Immediate	Calls the function without condition.
Motion	Calls the function if pointer motion is detected.
Click	Calls the function if the mouse is clicked but no pointer motion is detected.
DoubleClick	Calls the function if a double-click is detected.

Although at first it is rather obtuse, this method for defining functions creates a powerful tool for fvwm configuration. For example, the following function is an old standby used by many users (consult the list of built-in functions listed in Table 9.7 if necessary):

```
Function "MoveRaiseLowerMaximize"
    Raise "Motion"
    Move "Motion"
    RaiseLower "Click"
    Maximize "DoubleClick" 80 80
EndFunction
```

This user-defined function is then bound to a mouse click on a window title bar, like this:

```
Mouse 0 T A MoveRaiseLowerMaximize
```

After the function has been defined and bound to the mouse click listed above, window title bars behave as follows: If the user clicks on and drags a window's title bar, the window is raised and then moved with the mouse. If the user clicks on the title bar without moving the mouse, the window is lowered below all other windows if it was already raised or is raised if it wasn't. If the user double-clicks on the title bar, the window is maximized to occupy 80 percent of the visible area.

Two special functions, InitFunction and RestartFunction, are called each time fvwm starts and restarts, respectively. The InitFunction is commonly used to start clients in much the same way that they are often started from the $HOME/.xinitrc script:

```
Function "InitFunction"
    Exec "Immediate" xterm -geometry 80x24+1+1 &
    Exec "Immediate" xclock -geometry 50x50-1-1 &
    ...
EndFunction
```

The RestartFunction is rarely used and exists primarily for the purpose of being able to restart fvwm modules, which don't automatically restart when a Restart function call is issued.

fvwm 1 Button and Window Styles

One of the most powerful aspects of fvwm is its capability to configure a window's decorations, behavior, and appearance on a per-window basis, based on either the application name or the title of a window. There are two major areas of window decoration configurability: buttons and styles.

Buttons

The standard fvwm desktop uses three buttons, one menu button at the left of a window's title bar and two buttons at the right of the title bar, one for minimize and one for maximize. fvwm actually has the capability to display and bind functions to up to 10 buttons per window, numbered as followed:

```
1 3 5 7 9        <Window Title>        0 8 6 4 2
```

In default fvwm configurations only buttons 1, 4, and 2 are visible because only buttons 1, 4, and 2 have mouse clicks bound to them. However, other buttons can be made visible and functional simply by binding mouse clicks to them as we've already seen how to do.

Of course, it's also very nice to be able to indicate visually just what a button does, and to that end, fvwm provides a mechanism for altering the appearance of a button via the ButtonStyle keyword, which should be used like this:

```
ButtonStyle : n1 n2 Point Point Point ...
```

This format is slightly confusing at first but is actually quite powerful and simple in its elegance. It is helpful to think of the format as a logical connect-the-dots game. The first value, $n1$, is the number of the button whose appearance is to be modified. The next value, $n2$, is the number of points in the connect-the-dot pattern, plus one to close the pattern. Then, there should be exactly $n2$ points supplied in the following format (but omit the spaces):

```
X x Y @ n
```

The number X is the horizontal position of the point inside the button, as a percent of the whole. The number Y represents the same idea vertically. For example, a location of 50×50 is exactly in the center of the button. If n is 0, the line segment in question will be drawn in shadow; if n is 1, the segment will be drawn in highlight. For example, a downward-pointing triangle with three-dimensional highlight to the northwest in button position 2 is given by

```
ButtonStyle : 2 4 50x80@1 20x20@1 80x20@1 50x80@0
```

A more complex X button pattern on button 0 is given by this rather lengthy definition (note the backslashes that allow the line to be broken across multiple physical lines):

```
ButtonStyle : 0 17 20x20@1 30x20@1 50x40@1 70x20@1 80x20@1 \
              80x30@0 60x50@0 80x70@1 80x80@0 70x80@0 \
              50x60@0 30x80@0 20x80@0 20x70@0 40x50@1 \
              20x30@0 20x20@1
```

Using button styles such as these and binding buttons to mouse clicks, it is possible to create complex, extremely functional title bar decorations for your windows.

Window Styles

In addition to the capability to apply styles to title bar buttons, fvwm also includes the capability to apply styles to specific groups of application windows. The Style keyword is used in the fvwm configuration file like this:

```
Style "window" option, option, ...
```

The *window* is given either as an application name, such as one finds using editres, or by supplying either a complete or partial window title (which may be completed using wildcard characters). After the window to which the style applies is specified, a list of options is specified. Options can be any of those shown in Table 9.12.

Table 9.12 Options Supported by the Style Keyword

Option	Description
BorderWidth *n*	This window's border should be *n* pixels wide.
HandleWidth *n*	This window's border handles should be *n* pixels wide.
Icon *file*	Use this icon for the window when minimized.
NoIcon	Don't use an icon when minimized.
Title/NoTitle	Display or don't display a window title.
Handles/NoHandles	Display or don't display border handles.
WindowListHit	Display this window in window lists.
WindowListSkip	Don't display this window in window lists.
CirculateHit	When circulating through windows, let this window take focus.
CirculateSkip	When circulating through windows, don't let this window take focus.
StaysOnTop	Ensure that this window is always on top.
StaysPut	Other windows can be raised over this one.
Sticky	Keep this window on the current visual display, regardless of paging.
Slippery	This window should not stay visible when paging to another area of the desktop.
StartIconic	Start this window in a minimized state.
StartNormal	Start this window in a restored state.
Color *fore/back*	Use *fore* as the title color and *back* as the decoration color for this window.
StartsOnDesk *n*	Start this window on desktop area *n*.
StartsAnywhere	Start this window on the visible area.
IconTitle	Display an icon and a title when minimized.

continues

Table 9.12 Continued

Option	Description
NoIconTitle	Display only an icon when minimized.
Button *n*	Button number *n* is visible on this window, if a mouse click has been bound to it.
NoButton *n*	This window should not have a button *n*.

Clearly, the Style keyword merely gives a convenient mechanism by which individual windows or classes of windows can be simultaneously configured, and with great flexibility. For example, consider the following segment of a configuration file:

```
Style "*" Icon unknown.xpm, color white/gray, BorderWidth 4
Style "xterm" Icon xterm.xpm, color red/blue, BorderWidth 2
Style "xclock" NoTitle, WindowListSkip, NoHandles, BorderWidth 2
```

The first line dictates that all applications (note the wildcard character) should use the icon file unknown.xpm when minimized. Unfocused title bars and decorations should appear as white text on a gray background, and the border should be four pixels wide. The second line indicates that an exception to this style is the xterm application, which should use the file xterm.xpm as its icon when minimized, should appear as red on blue when not focused, and should have a border width of only two pixels. The third line indicates that the xclock application should not be endowed with a title bar or border handles, should have a border width of two pixels, and should not appear in the window list.

Using styles in this way, it is possible to microconfigure a desktop's appearance and even the function buttons that appear at the tops of individual windows based on a set of rules created by you, the user—a feat not possible in other operating systems, or even using many other window managers.

fvwm 2 Basics

fvwm 1 is so flexible that configuring it can often turn into a full day's work, and yet fvwm 2 is at least four times the window manager that fvwm was, introducing a dizzying new array of functions and keywords, as well as radically revamping the format of the configuration file. Unfortunately, documenting fvwm 2 completely is far beyond the scope of this text; its complexity is unsimplifiable and often more akin to a programming language than to a configuration file; an adequate tutorial would require a small book of its own.

Still, we can discuss a few fvwm 2 basics, especially as they relate to the original fvwm and the user's ability to change basics (like the menu structure). The first and most important change from fvwm to fvwm 2 is that most of the keywords from fvwm related to appearance and behavior are no longer supported by fvwm 2.

The configuration keywords that did make the cut have been promoted to become functions in fvwm 2 rather than mere keywords, allowing them to be used in many more varied circumstances. Functions in fvwm 2 either can be called directly or can be bound to a keyboard or mouse click or a menu entry. Even keyboard and mouse bindings, though they still use a similar format, are now functions, meaning that the following improbable set of lines (recall the key binding process from fvwm) is now possible:

```
Key F11 A S Key F11 Exec xterm &
Key F11 A M Key F11 -
Key F12 A S Key F12 Exec xcalc &
Key F12 A M Key F12 -
```

Note that the dash (-) in place of a function means to remove a key binding. Note also that because Key is now a function, it can call itself as part of a binding. The effect of these four lines isn't obvious, but with a little study, you'll discover an interesting example of fvwm 2's newfound configuration power. The first line dictates that a Shift+F11 keystroke will bind the command xterm to the unmodified F11 key. The second line indicates that when Alt+F11 is pressed, the unmodified F11 key should be unbound, so that applications can once again receive F11 keystrokes. The next two lines do the same for the F12 key and the xcalc command.

fvwm 2 is bursting at the seams with this kind of capability; because every aspect of fvwm 2's configuration is controlled by a function rather than a keyword, nearly every aspect of fvwm 2's configuration suddenly becomes runtime-configurable, through keystrokes, mouse clicks, or menus.

fvwm 2 Menus

Several important changes occurred in the menu-handling capabilities of fvwm during the upgrade to fvwm 2. Both the method for defining menus and the method for controlling their appearance have changed.

Building Menus

In fvwm, menus were defined with the Popup and EndMenu keyword pair. The menus were built statically in the configuration file and loaded by fvwm at runtime. In fvwm 2, menus are created by adding to them with the AddToMenu function, which is used as follows:

```
AddToMenu MenuName "Text Item" Function [argument ...]
+ "Text Item" Function [argument ...]
+ "Text Item" Function [argument ...]
...
```

There is no need for an EndMenu keyword; a blank line terminates the process of adding to the menu. The function supplied can be any of the functions supported by fvwm 2. Many of the functions that were available in fvwm are also present in fvwm 2, though not all of them survived the rewrite from fvwm to fvwm 2 and a truly countless number of new functions have been added.

After a menu has been created, it can be augmented at any time. For example, you might see the following occur in an fvwm 2 configuration file:

```
AddToMenu MyMenu "Main Menu" Title
+ "Start a Terminal" Exec term &
+ "Start a Calculator" Exec xcalc &

AddToMenu OtherMenu "The Other Menu" Title

+ "Leave fvwm2" Quit
AddToMenu MyMenu "Start Netscape" Exec netscape &
```

Notice that the third call to the AddToMenu function adds to MyMenu, which was created earlier. Instead of overwriting the contents of MyMenu, the AddToMenu function appends a third option, Start Netscape, to the end of MyMenu, demonstrating that the AddToMenu function works in a cumulative manner on any given menu.

Images and Hotkeys

fvwm 2 also provides the capability to incorporate images and hotkey shortcuts into menus in much the same way that operating systems such as Windows do. The following example illustrates the three basic methods of adding images and the basic method of adding keyboard shortcuts to menus in fvwm 2:

```
AddToMenu ImageMenu@vertpic.xpm@ "Image Demo Menu" Title
+ "Start a &Calculator*xcalc.xpm*" Exec xcalc &
+ "Start a &Terminal%xterm.xpm%" Exec xterm &
```

When this menu appears, the image vertpic.xpm will be displayed along the left edge of the menu vertically, beginning at the bottom of the menu. The image in xcalc.xpm will be centered over the menu entry text Start a Calculator, and the image in xterm.xpm will be shown to the left of Start a Terminal in the menu. The hotkeys for these two menu entries will be C for xcalc and T for xterm, because they are preceded by an ampersand (&). Note that image files are still loaded from the paths given by PixmapPath and IconPath in the configuration file.

Using this basic image handling capability and a nice set of images, combined with a few keyboard shortcuts, it is possible to create professional-looking, graphics-enabled menus inside fvwm 2.

Menu Styles

The colors in fvwm 2 menus are no longer controlled by simple keyword and color pairs; fvwm 2 implements a much-improved and much more flexible menu styling system of which the MenuStyle function, which defines menu styles by name, is the center.

The MenuStyle function has a very simple syntax:

```
MenuStyle stylename option, [option, ...]
```

The format is simple, but the list of options supported by the MenuStyle function is rather large. The most basic of these options are shown in Table 9.13.

Table 9.13   Basic MenuStyle Options

Option	Description
FVWM	Draws the menus in the traditional fvwm style, with a three-dimensional effect, submenus that can overlap their parents, and delayed pop-ups.
MWM	Draws the menus in the style of the MWM window manager, with a three-dimensional effect, submenus that don't overlap their parents, and instant pop-ups.
WIN	Draws the menus in the style of Windows, with a flat, solid-colored effect, submenus that don't overlap their parents, and instant pop-ups.
Foreground *color*	Uses *color* as the text color in this menu.
Background *color*	Uses *color* as the background color for this menu.
Font *XLFD*	Uses the specified font for the entries in this menu.
MenuFace *style*	Uses fancy background pixmaps or gradients for the background of this menu. The *style* is one of the style options supported by the other style functions later in the section. Two other gradient styles, DGradient and BGradient, both diagonal, can also be used.

For example, consider the following menu style definition:

```
MenuStyle NormalMenus WIN, Foreground white, Background blue
```

This style defines a style called NormalMenus that will produce windows-style menus with white text on a blue background. To use a menu style like NormalMenus, the ChangeMenuStyle function must be used. The syntax for the ChangeMenuStyle function is also simple and looks like this:

```
ChangeMenuStyle style menuname [menuname ...]
```

For example, to assign the menu style we just created to the menus called MainMenu, ExitStuff, and OpsStuff, the following function would be called:

```
ChangeMenuStyle NormalMenus MainMenu ExitStuff OpsStuff
```

Like almost everything else in fvwm 2, because MenuStyle and ChangeMenuStyle are functions, they can be bound to keyboard or mouse clicks or called from within menus to cause changes to menu appearance at runtime.

fvwm 2 Functions

The new mechanism for creating functions in fvwm 2 is similar to the new mechanism for creating menus. The function in question is `AddToFunc` and is used like this:

```
AddToFunc FunctionName "trigger" Function
+ "trigger" Function
+ "trigger" Function
...
```

Again, there is no need for an `EndFunction` keyword; fvwm 2 will stop adding to the named function at the first blank line it encounters.

The event trigger names in fvwm 2 are also different from the trigger names in fvwm. The triggers in fvwm 2 are simply represented by the first letter of the original trigger name from fvwm: Immediate becomes I, Motion becomes M, and so on. The `MoveRaiseLowerMaximize` function used as an example for fvwm looks like this when defined in fvwm 2:

```
AddToFunc MoveRaiseLowerMaximize "M" Raise
+ "M" Move
+ "C" RaiseLower
+ "D" Maximize 80 80
```

`AddToFunc` is also a function in fvwm 2, unlike the `Function` keyword in fvwm. This means that fvwm 2 functions can be built on-the-fly at runtime based on user interaction, a powerful feature that requires some practice to use well.

Note that the two special functions, `InitFunction` and `RestartFunction`, also exist in fvwm 2 and can be used in much the same way, though they must of course be defined using the new `AddToFunc` function rather than the fvwm `Function` keyword.

fvwm 2 Appearance and Style Handling

In addition to a much-updated set of functions and the capability to rebuild or edit menus and functions on-the-fly at runtime, fvwm 2 also provides a new, powerful set of style-handling functions that allow various styles to be applied to various types of window manager objects. Because these are the primary methods for defining window, menu, and decoration appearance in fvwm 2, it is important to understand them at least a little bit. Unfortunately, they are as complex as they are useful; getting them to work often requires practice.

The basic fvwm 2 style paradigm says that each object in the window manager, from buttons to title bars to windows, has properties that can be configured. Configuration is specified with a `Style` function and can be updated any number of times with an `AddStyle` function. Configuration can also be applied between objects with the `UseStyle` option, so that decorations can share appearances with each other. The style functions are outlined in the paragraphs that follow; their basic format is

```
StyleFunction [btn] [state] [style] [-- [!]flag ...]
```

The `Style` function is one of the functions listed in Table 9.14. Functions that begin with `Add` implement new styles on top of existing ones. Functions that don't begin with `Add` replace existing styles. For style functions that affect title bar buttons, a button specification as per Table 9.15 is required; otherwise, no button is specified.

Table 9.14   fvwm 2 Style Functions

Function	Description
ButtonStyle	Implements a new title bar button style.
AddButtonStyle	Adds a new style element to an existing title bar button style.
TitleStyle	Implements a new title bar style.
AddTitleStyle	Adds a new style element to the existing title bar style.
BorderStyle	Implements a new window border style.
AddBorderStyle	Adds a new style element to the existing window border style.

Table 9.15   fvwm 2 Button Specifications for Style Editing

Specifier	Button
0–9	Style function should act on one of the title bar buttons specifically, as laid out in the original fvwm window manager, with buttons 1, 3, 5, 7, and 9 on the left and buttons 0, 8, 6, 4, and 2 on the right, in that order.
All	Style function should act on all title bar buttons equally.
Left	Style function should act only on buttons that are on the left side of the title bar (odd-numbered buttons).
Right	Style function should act only on buttons that are on the right side of the title bar (even-numbered buttons).

The `state` supplied to a style function is one of the words listed in Table 9.16. If no state is supplied, the style will apply to all states. The `style` supplied to a style function is one of the style directives listed in Table 9.17. After the `state` and/or `style` has been specified, the user may add two dashes and follow these with a series of flags, if necessary. A few of these flags are listed in Table 9.18. If a flag is preceded by an exclamation mark (!), its meaning is inverted.

Table 9.16   Valid Style Function States

State	Description
Active	This style applies when the window has focus. This state is for border styles only.
ActiveUp	This style applies when the window has focus (active) and the widget isn't currently in the middle of a click event (up).
ActiveDown	This style applies when the window has focus (active) and the widget is currently in the middle of a click or drag event (down).
Inactive	This style applies when the window does not have focus.

Table 9.17   Common Style Function Styles

Style Directive	Description
Default	Specifies that this decoration should use the default style compiled into fvwm 2.
Pixmap *file*	Uses the named image as a one-stamp pixmap for the decoration in question.
TiledPixmap *file*	Uses the named image as a wallpaper-style pixmap tile for the decoration in question.
Solid *color*	The decoration should be drawn using *color* in a solid fill.
Vector *n pt pt* ...	The equivalent of the old ButtonStyle keyword in fvwm discussed earlier. The number of points is given by *n* and each *pt* is a valid point and line color. For button style functions only.
VGradient *n c1 c2*	The decoration should be drawn using an *n* color vertical gradient from color *c1* to color *c2*. Note that a second, more powerful form of the VGradient style isn't covered here.
Hgradient *n c1 c2*	The decoration should be drawn using an *n* color horizontal gradient from color *c1* to color *c2*. Note that a second, more powerful form of the HGradient style isn't covered here.
MiniIcon	Draws the application's MiniIcon in the specified button. The MiniIcon concept is discussed in the next section, "fvwm 2 Decors and Window Styles." For button style functions only.

Table 9.18 Common Style Function Flags

Flag	Description
UseTitleStyle	Attempts to take the style for buttons from the current title style.
UseBorderStyle	Attempts to take the style for buttons from the current border style.
Raised	Causes the decoration to appear raised in a three-dimensional way.
Sunk	Causes the decoration to appear sunken in a three-dimensional way.
Flat	Causes the decoration to appear without any three-dimensional edges.
HiddenHandles	Doesn't draw resize handles on the corners of the border. For border style functions only.
NoInset	Doesn't draw an inner bevel around the border but, instead, keeps the border flush with the window. For border style functions only.
Left	Begins tiling or displaying pixmaps on the left side of the decoration.
Right	Begins tiling or displaying pixmaps on the right side of the decoration.
Top	Begins tiling or displaying pixmaps at the top of the decoration.
Bottom	Begins tiling or displaying pixmaps at the bottom of the decoration.

Although the new style interface is consistent, it is certainly more complex than the simple keyword/value lines in the original fvwm. The flexibility gained, however, is considerable. Consider the following example:

```
TitleStyle Inactive HGradient Red Blue -- Flat
TitleStyle ActiveUp TiledPixmap focused.xpm -- Top Left
TitleStyle ActiveDown Solid Red
BorderStyle All -- NoInset HiddenHandles
ButtonStyle All -- UseTitleStyle
AddButtonStyle 1 Vector 4 50x80@1 20x20@1 80x20@1 50x80@0
AddButtonStyle 2 Pixmap button-2.xpm
```

The first three lines give window titles that aren't focused a horizontal gradient from red to blue as a background color. When not focused, titles will be drawn flatly, without three-dimensional effects. When the window is focused, a pixmap called focus.xpm that begins tiling from the upper-left corner of the title bar will be used as the background. When the title bar is clicked or dragged, it will turn a solid red color.

The fourth line dictates that window borders should appear without a three-dimensional bevel around the inside edge or resize handles at the corners.

The last three lines specify that all buttons should take their initial style hints from the current title bar style. Then, button 1 (the left-most button) is updated with a new vector pattern and button 2 (the right-most button) is updated with a new pixmap.

fvwm 2 Decors and Window Styles

The style-handling functions included with fvwm 2 are clearly powerful and flexible, yet the best is still to come. In addition to the style functions just discussed, fvwm 2 provides the capability to create decors, which are collections of styles that can be applied on a window-by-window basis. Decors are built using the AddToDecor function, as follows:

```
AddToDecor decorname
+ StyleFunction [btn] [state] [style] [-- [!]flag ...]
+ StyleFunction [btn] [state] [style] [-- [!]flag ...]
...
```

Again, a decor can be added to at any time, dynamically, and adding is finished when a blank line is encountered in the file. A sample decor using our styles from the last section might look like this:

```
AddToDecor StdDecor
+ TitleStyle Inactive HGradient Red Blue -- Flat
+ TitleStyle ActiveUp TiledPixmap focused.xpm -- Top Left
+ TitleStyle ActiveDown Solid Red
+ BorderStyle All -- NoInset HiddenHandles
+ ButtonStyle All -- UseTitleStyle
+ AddButtonStyle 1 Vector 4 50x80@1 20x20@1 80x20@1 50x80@0
+ AddButtonStyle 2 Pixmap button-2.xpm
```

After the decor known as StdDecor has been defined, the user can decide to assign that decor to specific windows using window styles. The basic Style keyword for use with individual windows is still around for fvwm 2, though in fvwm 2 it is a function. All the options supported by the Style keyword in fvwm 1 still apply, but the new options given in Table 9.19 now apply as well.

Table 9.19 A Few of the New fvwm 2 Window Style Options

Style	Description
UseStyle *style*	Uses a style already defined by another Style function as the basis for this style.
UseDecor *decor*	Uses the named decor when decorating windows named in this style.
MiniIcon *file*	Uses the icon given by *file* as the mini-icon for the window, which can be drawn in title bar buttons when requested.
IconBox *geometry*	Specifies that minimized icons for this window should go into the specified icon box. Similar to the IconBox keyword in fvwm 1, but applies only to the window for which the style applies, and *geometry* is given by an Xt/Athena-style geometry string such as 100×100-1-1'.
IconGrid *x* *y*	Form an imaginary grid in the specified icon box with each cell in the grid *x* pixels wide and *y* pixels high; attempt to place icons only in empty grid cells.

Style	Description
IconFill *pos1* *pos2*	Establish a fill gravity in the icon box. One of the pos arguments must either be top or bottom and the other must be either left or right. For example, a gravity of left as *pos1* and bottom as *pos2* will fill the icon box from left to right and from bottom to top.
MWMBorder/FvwmBorder	Draw window borders in the style of MWM or the style of fvwm, respectively.
SmartPlacement	Place this window intelligently.
DumbPlacement	Don't try to place this window intelligently.
RandomPlacement	Place this window in a random fashion.
ActivePlacement	Allow the user to place this window.
DecorateTransient	Decorate pop-up dialog windows.
NakedTransient	Don't decorate pop-up dialog windows.
SkipMapping	Allow a window to appear and be placed off the visual desktop area.
ShowMapping	Always show a window as it appears and is placed.
ClickToFocus	Require that this window be clicked on to receive focus.
SloppyFocus	Allow this window to accept focus whenever the mouse pointer enters it; if the mouse pointer leaves it again only to enter the root window, keep focus.
MouseFocus	Allow this window to accept focus whenever the mouse pointer enters it; as soon as the mouse pointer leaves, lose focus.

For information on the rest of the new style options, please consult the fvwm2 manual page. Note the existence of both the UseStyle and UseDecor options. With these two style options, it becomes possible to assign all windows a given focus, color, and font style, as well as a decoration and button style, on a window-by-window basis. The following configuration segment illustrates the point:

```
Style "UtlStyle" ClickToFocus, Color white/black, WindowListSkip
Style "AppStyle" SloppyFocus, Color white/blue, Icon "app.xpm"
Style "xclock" UseStyle "UtlStyle" NoTitle
Style "xterm" UseStyle "AppStyle" UseDecor "StdDecor"
Style "xedit" UseStyle "AppStyle" UseDecor "StdDecor" NoButton 1
```

The first two Style lines don't actually apply to any window; they have been named instead to indicate what style they represent, and other applications in subsequent lines are then told to inherit these styles. Both xterm and xedit also use StdDecor, which we defined earlier, though xedit windows won't have a left-most title bar button (button 1).

Note that two more functions, UpdateDecor and Recapture, update windows already on a display to reflect changes in decor and style, respectively. Because all decor and style handling capabilities are implemented in fvwm 2 as functions, they can be bound to menus or keystrokes or even called from other functions, and the subsequent changes can be made to appear with UpdateDecor and Recapture, leading to true runtime visual configuration capabilities when using a properly structured fvwm 2 configuration file.

Finishing Up with fvwm

The fvwm window managers are simply too complex to document easily in a chapter like this one; many important elements have, by necessity, been left out of this text. One of the more important of these elements is the module-handling capability of both versions of fvwm. A list of available modules for your fvwm installation can be found by looking in the lib/X11/fvwm or lib/X11/fvwm2 directory off the main /usr/X11R6 tree. Each module in this directory typically has a manual page of its own that can be consulted for information on how to use the module with fvwm or fvwm 2.

We've only scratched the surface of the capabilities of fvwm and fvwm 2. Hopefully you now know at least enough to copy the system.fvwm2rc file to $HOME/.fvwm2rc and begin to edit menu structure and change some basic aspects of window appearance and desktop behavior. If you plan to use fvwm 2, it is strongly suggested that you take the time to study the fvwm 2 manual page.

The twm Window Manager

The twm window manager is the only window manager included with XFree86. As such, skilled use of the twm window manager is important for users who will be using stock versions of XFree86 for any period of time. Although the twm window manager isn't nearly as complex or as flexible or configurable as the fvwm family of window managers, it remains a favorite standby in the UNIX community thanks to its speed, small memory footprint, and clean appearance (see Figure 9.3).

The systemwide configuration file for twm can usually be found in the lib/X11/twm directory off the /usr/X11R6 tree as system.twmrc. When twm is started, it will first search for $HOME/.twmrc and then fall back on system.twmrc if no user configuration can be found.

You can start twm by placing a call to twm at the end of your $HOME/.xinitrc file after removing calls to any other window managers or session managers.

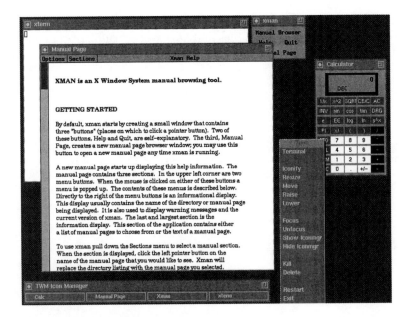

Figure 9.3 The twm window manager.

twm Configuration File Basics

The twm configuration file often appears to be a little more structured than the configuration files of the fvwm window managers. Many aspects of twm configuration are accomplished using lists, structures that sometimes look similar to the structure of C source code, at least superficially. A list can appear in either of the following two formats:

```
function { "item" "item" "item" ... }
```

or

```
function
{
    "item"
    "item"
    "item"
    ...
}
```

The structure of menus in twm follows a similar format, though it is slightly different upon close inspection. For those who have used the MWM window manager from Motif-based systems, twm will seem familiar.

As was the case with fvwm, the dictates of convention keep the twm configuration file from becoming too cluttered and messy. Variables and appearance configuration usually appear first, followed by function definitions, then keyboard and mouse bindings, and, finally, the menu structure.

General Behavior

Several basic behavior-oriented variables can be configured in the twm dotfile. Enough of them exist to give twm basic flexibility comparable in some ways to the basic flexibility of fvwm 1.x window managers. Many of them can be used with lists of affected windows in the following format:

```
Variable
{
   "window-name"
   "window-name"
   ...
}
```

For example, the AutoRaise function should be used to affect specific windows, as follows:

```
AutoRaise
{
   "xterm"
   "xcalc"
   "edit"
}
```

A listing of some commonly used variables and their uses, along with the way in which they must be supplied, can be found in Table 9.20.

Table 9.20 Common twm Behavior Variables and Their Uses

Variable	Description
AutoRaise { *win-list* }	Specifies a list of windows that should be raised automatically whenever focused.
DecorateTransients	Specifies that pop-up dialog windows should be decorated with a title bar and buttons.
DontMoveOff	Doesn't allow windows to be moved off the screen under normal circumstances.
DontSqueezeTitle { *win-list* }	Specifies a list of window titles that should not be squeezed after the SqueezeTitle variable has been used.
MakeTitle { *win-list* }	Specifies that the listed windows should have title bars. Most useful when NoTitle (later in this table) has been globally set.

Variable	Description
MaxWindowSize *geometry*	Supplies a maximum window size in pixels using the -geometry X-by-Y format.
MoveDelta *n*	Specifies that twm should register a mouse click as a click-and-drag if the mouse moves more than *n* pixels while the button is pressed.
NoGrabServer	Instructs twm not to grab the server when displaying pop-up menus or moving windows. Useful for debugging purposes or for getting screen captures.
NoHighlight { *win-list* }	If no list is supplied, disables border highlights to indicate focus. If a list is supplied, disables border highlights for the listed windows.
NoRaiseOnDeiconify	Specifies that windows should not be raised when restored.
NoRaiseOnMove	Specifies that windows should not be raised when moved.
NoRaiseOnResize	Specifies that windows should not be raised when resized.
NoTitle { *win-list* }	If no list is supplied, disables title bars on all windows. If a list is supplied, disables title bars on listed windows.
NoTitleFocus	Doesn't allow mouse activity over the title bar to change focus; only mouse activity inside the client window will dictate focus.
NoTitleHighlight { *win-list* }	If no list is supplied, disables title highlights to indicate focus. If a list is supplied, disables title highlights for the listed windows.
OpaqueMove	Specifies that windows should remain intact when being moved, rather than being moved as a rubber-band outline.
RandomPlacement	Specifies that twm should randomly place new client windows on the display rather than allow the user to place them.
SqueezeTitle { *win-list* }	Specifies that title bars should be squeezed so that they are only large enough to contain window title text. If a list of windows is supplied, changes will apply only to listed windows.
StartIconified { *win-list* }	If no list is supplied, starts all windows in an iconified state. If a list is supplied, starts the listed windows in an iconified state.

continues

Table 9.20   Continued

Variable	Description
UsePPosition on¦off¦non-zero	Specifies that twm should honor the positioning requests of X clients (on), ignore such requests (off), or honor such requests only if they don't place the new window at pixel 0,0 (non-zero).
XorValue n	Changes the logical exclusive OR value for rubber-band operations. In practice, this number should be tweaked until the window outline drawn to represent a window during resize and move operations is easily visible.
Zoom n	Causes twm to display a zoom up or zoom down animation in n steps whenever a window is minimized or restored.

Note that several of these variables, such as NoTitle/MakeTitle and SqueezeTitle/DontSqueezeTitle, are inverse pairs. When using these variables, one of them is generally supplied without a window list to specify the default behavior. The inverse is then used with a window list to create exceptions, when necessary, to the default.

Decoration Colors

One of the first and most important parts of any window manager configuration is, of course, the choice of colors used to draw all the window decorations and to indicate focus. In twm, all the color properties of a running desktop are configured in one list called Color.

The Color list of a twm configuration file follows the following basic structure:

```
Color
{
   SimpleColorVariable "color"
   SimpleColorVariable "color"
   ...
   ComplexColorVariable "color"
   {
      "excepted window"  "color"
      "excepted window"  "color"
      ...
   }
   ComplexColorVariable "color"
   {
      "excepted window"  "color"
      "excepted window"  "color"
      ...
   }
   ...
}
```

Similar configuration can be done using the Monochrome or Grayscale list in place of the Color list, but for most Linux users, Color is the first choice, for obvious reasons.

Simple Color Variables

The simple color variables that can appear inside the Color list are entered one per line, a variable name followed by a color in quotes, either from the color database or specified from the RGB colorspace. The common simple color variables are listed in Table 9.21.

Table 9.21   Simple twm Color List Variables

Variable	Description
DefaultBackground	The background color for twm information windows, such as the pixel size window when resizing.
DefaultForeground	The foreground color for twm information windows.
MenuBackground	The background color for twm menus.
MenuForeground	The foreground color for twm menus.
MenuTitleBackground	The background color used in displaying twm menu titles.
MenuTitleForeground	The foreground color used in displaying twm menu titles.
MenuShadowColor	The color of the shadow that appears under or behind twm menus.

These variables are simple to use. Consider the following example, whose effects should be easy to understand:

```
Color
{
    MenuTitleForeground "white"
    MenuTitleBackground "blue"
    MenuForeground "#FFAD9F"
    MenuBackground "SteelBlue"
}
```

Although defaults do exist for all of these variables, the defaults are all black and white, leaving, in effect, a monochrome display for any user who chooses not to configure these colors explicitly in the $HOME/.twmrc file.

Complex Color Variables

The complex color variables are a little more difficult to work with than the simple ones, in part because each of them can have its own list to contend with that is nested inside the main Color list. Complex color variables can appear inside the main Color list in one of two ways:

```
ComplexColorVariable "color"
    {
```

```
    "excepted window" "color"
    "excepted window" "color"
    ...
}
```

or

```
ComplexColorVariable "color"
```

When a variable is used the first way, the first line of the variable definition provides the default color to be used for the property in question in all windows. The optional list that follows is a series of pairs that are to be considered exceptions to the default color. Each pair consists of a window name and a matching color that will be used for the property in question in that window only.

The complex color variables that use this format in the Color list are shown in Table 9.22.

Table 9.22   Complex twm Color List Variables

Variable	Description
BorderColor	Sets the color for window borders.
IconManagerHighlight	Sets the color to be used when highlighting a focused window in the twm icon manager.
BorderTileBackground	Sets the background color for the stipple pattern used as the border of unfocused windows.
BorderTileForeground	Sets the foreground color for the stipple pattern used as the border of unfocused windows.
TitleBackground	Sets the background color used in window title bars.
TitleForeground	Sets the foreground color used in window title bars.
IconBackground	Sets the background color for the window when in an iconified state.
IconForeground	Sets the foreground color for the window when in an iconified state.
IconBorderColor	Sets the color of the border used to outline iconified windows.
IconManagerBackground	Sets the background color used by the twm icon manager.
IconManagerForeground	Sets the foreground color used by the twm icon manager.

Each of these complex options can be followed by a list of windows and matching colors that relate to those windows; if no list is supplied, the default (supplied) value is used for all windows. Consider the following example, which builds on our earlier Color list example, but now includes both simple and complex variables:

```
Color
{
    MenuTitleForeground "white"
```

```
MenuTitleBackground "blue"
MenuForeground "#FFAD9F"
MenuBackground "SteelBlue"
IconBackground "blue"
{
    "xterm" "black"
    "xephem" "#cd1032"
}
IconForeground "white"
{
    "xterm" "red"
    "xclock" "#ff9f9f"
    "xcalc" "green"
}
IconBordercolor "orange"
}
```

In this example, all windows will have an icon background color of blue, except for xterm, which will be black, and xephem, which will use a color given from the RGB colorspace. Similarly, all windows have white icon text except for xterm, xclock, and xcalc. All windows will have an orange border; though we could have decided to specify that some windows should have borders of another color, we chose not to include a list of exceptions this time.

General Fonts and Appearance

Although decoration colors are an important factor in determining the look and feel of a graphical user interface, fonts and other aspects of the interface's appearance also have some bearing on the user's experience.

Configuring Fonts

twm includes several variables for configuring the fonts that will be used when displaying various window decorations, icons, and other aspects of the twm environment. The common twm font variables are shown in Table 9.23.

Table 9.23   Common twm Font Variables

Variable	Description
IconFont *XLFD*	Specifies the font twm will use when displaying applications that have been minimized and remapped as icons.
MenuFont *XLFD*	Specifies the font twm will use when displaying pop-up menus built by the user.
ResizeFont *XLFD*	Specifies the font twm will use when displaying window size information during interactive resize operations.
TitleFont *XLFD*	Specifies the font twm will use when displaying window title bars.

Each of the font variables accepts X Logical Font Descriptors of the form generated by the xfontsel command.

Configuring Appearance

In addition to font configuration, twm includes several variables dedicated to configuring other aspects of decoration appearance, including pixel widths and relative positions of decorations inside other decorations. The common appearance variables are shown in Table 9.24.

Table 9.24 Common twm Appearance Variables

Variable	Description
BorderWidth *n*	Specifies that twm should draw window borders *n* pixels wide on decorated windows.
ButtonIndent *n*	Specifies that title bar buttons should be at least *n* pixels from the edges of other decorations.
ForceIcons	Specifies that user-supplied icons should override icons supplied by running clients.
FramePadding *n*	Specifies that title bar text and buttons should be at least *n* pixels from the window frame.
IconDirectory *path*	Specifies the directory in which icon files should be found when supplying icons for application windows.
IconRegion *g v h w h*	Creates an icon box in which iconified window icons should be displayed. The geometry, *g*, is a standard Xt-style geometry specification. The vertical gravity, *v*, should be either North (display icons from the top of the box downward) or South (display icons from the bottom of the box upward). The horizontal gravity, *h*, should similarly be either East or West. Icons are displayed in grid cells of *w* pixels wide by *h* pixels high.
Icons { *win-list* }	Specifies a list of icons that should be used for the given applications. The list should be structured as a series of pairs: first a window name, followed by an icon file.
NoMenuShadows	Disables the appearance of shadows behind pop-up menus.
TitleButtonBorderWidth *n*	Specifies that title bar buttons should be drawn with a border *n* pixels wide.
TitlePadding *n*	Specifies that there should be *n* pixels in empty padding space between buttons, text, and highlights in window title bars.
UnknownIcon *file*	Uses the supplied *file* as the icon for any application that doesn't supply an icon of its own.

Note that the options that apply to icons apply only if icons are being displayed, which isn't normally the case when the icon manager has been enabled (see the next section).

Icon Manager

twm includes a built-in icon manager analogous in some ways to the fvwm window list to aid in management of X clients and minimized windows. The icon manager displays a formatted list of all active clients and allows the user to click on a window's representation in the icon manager to minimize, restore, or raise it.

The normal method for using the icon manager is to disable mapping of minimized windows to icons and enable the display of the twm icon manager. Common options related to the twm icon manager are shown in Table 9.25.

Table 9.25   Common twm Icon Manager Variables

Variable	Description
IconifyByUnmapping	Specifies that windows should be unmapped rather than be recapped to icons when minimized. Normally used in conjunction with the icon manager to prevent windows from creating icons outside the icon manager.
IconManagerDontShow { *list* }	Specifies that the listed windows should not appear in the icon manager. When the list is omitted, specifies that windows should not appear in the icon manager by default.
IconManagerGeometry *geom n*	Specifies that the icon manager should appear with the geometry given by *geom*, an Xt-style geometry string. If supplied, *n* represents the number of columns into which the icon manager display should be split.
IconManagerShow { *list* }	Specifies that the listed windows should appear in the icon manager. Normally used to create exceptions when the IconManagerDontShow variable has been supplied as the default behavior.
ShowIconManager	Indicates that icon managers should be visible when twm is first started.
SortIconManager	Indicates that entries in the icon manager should be sorted alphabetically.

Multiple icon managers can be created if desired using the IconManagers variable when a single icon manager is inadequate. The IconManagers variable is used as follows:

```
IconManagers
{
    "window" "icon-name" "geometry" columns
```

```
    "window" "icon-name" "geometry" columns
    ...
}
```

Each line in the list specifies that the icon manager with the name `icon-name` will manage windows with the specified `window` name. The manager will appear at the location and size given by `geometry` and will appear with `columns` columns in its display.

Mouse/Keyboard Bindings and Functions

The method for binding mouse clicks and keyboard events to actions in twm is somewhat different from the method used by fvwm or fvwm 2, though the basic premise is still the same. The list of mouse or keyboard events is bound to one or several functions that are then executed each time the mouse or keyboard event occurs.

Mouse Event Bindings

The general format for binding functions to mouse clicks in twm is as follows:

```
ButtonN = modifiers : contexts : function
ButtonN = modifiers : contexts : function
...
```

The mouse button N is a number from 1 to 5 representing the logical mouse button as is known to the X server. The list of valid `modifiers` is shown in Table 9.26. The list of valid `contexts` is shown in Table 9.27.

Table 9.26   Modifiers for Mouse Bindings

Modifier	Description
shift	Normally indicates that one or both of the Shift keys are being held down.
control	Normally indicates that one or both of the Ctrl keys are being held down.
lock	Normally indicates that the keyboard Caps Lock is activated.
meta	Normally indicates that one or both of the Alt keys are being held down.
mod1-mod5	Indicates that one of the X modifier maps, 1–5, is active.

If the click event to be bound does not involve the use of a modifier, simply omit any modifier from the mouse binding.

Table 9.27   Contexts for Mouse Bindings

Context	Description
window	Indicates that the mouse pointer is inside the bounds of the window.
title	Indicates that the mouse pointer is within the title bar frame.
icon	Indicates that the mouse pointer is over the applications icon (minimized state).
root	Indicates that the mouse pointer is over the root window.
frame	Indicates that the mouse pointer is over some part of the window frame.
iconmgr	Indicates that the mouse pointer is within one of the running icon managers.
all	This binding applies regardless of the current mouse pointer position.

Multiple modifiers or contexts can be used by separating each item with a vertical bar (|). The function that is bound to the mouse click can be one of several twm built-in functions or a user-built function. The most common twm built-in functions are shown in Table 9.28.

Table 9.28   Most Common Built-In twm Functions

Function	Description
! command	Executes the listed command in the Linux environment.
f.autoraise	Toggles the window's autoraise status. When enabled, a window will automatically be raised when it gets focus.
f.beep	Rings the terminal bell.
f.bottomzoom	Resizes the window to fill the entire bottom half of the display.
f.circledown	Moves the top-most window on the desktop to the bottom of the window stack.
f.circleup	Moves the bottom-most window on the desktop to the top of the window stack.
f.deiconify	Deiconifies (restores) the window.
f.delete	Deletes a window from the list of active windows. Normally has the effect of closing a window.
f.destroy	Destroys a window. Kills the client who owns the window; normally only used in emergencies—all data in the running application will most likely be lost.
f.exec command	Same as the ! function; causes the supplied command to be executed.
f.fullzoom	Resizes the window to fill the entire display. If already zoomed, the window is returned to its original size. More commonly known as a maximize type function.
f.function function	Calls the user-defined function function. See the next section for details on creating user-defined functions.

continues

Table 9.28 Continued

Function	Description
f.hideiconmgr	Unmaps the current icon manager (hides it).
f.horizoom	Resizes the window to occupy the full width of the screen; vertical size is left unaffected.
f.iconify	Iconifies (minimizes) a window or, if it is already minimized, de-iconifies (restores) it.
f.leftzoom	Resizes the window to fill the left half of the display.
f.lower	Lowers the window to the bottom of the stack.
f.menu *menu-name*	Displays the menu whose name is given by *menu-name*.
f.move	Allows the user to interactively move the current window.
f.quit	Causes twm to exit.
f.raise	Raises the window to the top of the stack.
f.raiselower	If the current window is on the top of the window stack, lowers it to the bottom of the stack. Otherwise, raises the window to the top of the stack.
f.refresh	Redraws the display to fix garbage or other display errors.
f.resize	Allows the user to interactively resize the current window.
f.restart	Restarts twm and rereads the twm dotfile.
f.rightzoom	Resizes the window to fill the right half of the display.
f.showiconmgr	Remaps (unhides) an icon manager that has been unmapped (hidden).
f.sorticonmgr	Sorts the entries in the current icon manager alphabetically.
f.topzoom	Resizes the window to fill the top of the display.
f.zoom	Resizes the window to occupy to full height of the screen; horizontal size isn't affected.

Only one function can be bound to any mouse event; if more than one action is required for any single mouse-click event, the user should create a user-defined function that combines several functions into a single procedure.

To illustrate the twm method for binding mouse clicks to functions, consider the following example:

```
Button1 = shift : title ¦ window : f.fullzoom
Button1 = meta : title ¦ window : f.topzoom
Button1 = control : title ¦ window : f.bottomzoom
```

These three lines create a series of mouse bindings that will maximize the window fully if the first mouse button is clicked either in the window's title bar or inside the window while the Shift key is being held down. If the click is made with the Alt key held down, the window will maximize to the top half of the display. If the click is made with the Ctrl key held down, the window will maximize to the bottom half of the display.

Keyboard Event Bindings

The method for binding keyboard events to functions in twm is similar to the method for binding mouse events. However, instead of supplying a button in the form of a word such as Button1, the keystroke to be bound is specified with an X key symbol enclosed in quotes. For a list of valid X key symbols, see the include/X11/keysymdef.h file off of the main /usr/X11R6 directory tree. Omit the XK_ prefix in any key symbol used in defining key bindings. The general format for binding keystrokes is as follows:

```
"Key" = modifiers : contexts : function
"Key" = modifiers : contexts : function
...
```

The same modifiers and contexts that were valid for mouse event bindings are also valid for keyboard event bindings, as are the functions. Most users will find themselves wanting to bind at least the keyboard function keys to commonly used operations, as is the case in the following example:

```
"F1" = : all : f.rightzoom
"F2" = : all : f.leftzoom
```

The set of bindings cause the F1 key to maximize the window to the right half of the display for any modifier map and in any context. The F2 key performs the same function to the left half of the display.

User-Defined Functions

Function definitions in twm are carried out using the Function variable in the dotfile. It is normally helpful to define any functions you want to bind to mouse or keystrokes before you carry out any mouse or keyboard bindings. The format for the Function variable is as follows:

```
Function "function-name"
{
    f.twm-function
    f.twm-function
    ...
}
```

The *function-name* can be any string of text the user wants to use to name the function, but names are case-sensitive and must be supplied exactly as they appear here for them to work properly when called from elsewhere in the dotfile. A special function, f.deltastop, can be used inside user-defined functions to order the function to exit if mouse movement is detected. A common function implemented in twm might look like this:

```
Function "move-or-raiselower"
{
    f.move
    f.deltastop
    f.raiselower
}
```

Once defined, user functions can be bound to keyboard or mouse events or included in menus by using the f.function function.

Building Menus

twm menus are built using the Menu variable followed by a list that composes the body of the message and any functions that are called from within the message body. The general format for the Menu variable and associated list is as follows:

```
Menu "menuname" (textcolor:background)
{
    "Menu item" (textcolor:background) f.twm-function
    "Menu item" (textcolor:background) f.twm-function
    ...
}
```

The menu is given the name menuname, as supplied by the user, and default foreground and background colors of textcolor and background, respectively. Each item in the menu displays the text given by Menu item when seen by the user and calls f.twm-function when selected. Individual colors can be given on a per-item basis as well. Note also that all color specifications are optional; if omitted, the defaults from the Color list in the dotfile will be used instead. One special function, f.title, is used to give a title to a twm menu.

The following is a sample set of two menus, one a submenu to the other. The first menu also contains items to launch two X clients. The second menu contains options to restart or exit the twm window manager.

```
Menu "ExitMenu"
{
    "Exit Menu" f.title
    "Restart TWM" f.restart
    "Exit TWM" f.quit
}

Menu "MainMenu"
{
    "Main Menu" f.title
    "Terminal" ! "xterm &"
    "Calculator" ! "xcalc &"
    "Exit Menu" f.menu "ExitMenu"
}
```

Note that the menu definition is order-important. That is, all submenus must be defined before they are called from menus defined later in the file.

Finishing Up with twm

Although there's more to twm than we've shown here, you should now know enough to be able to copy the system.twmrc file to $HOME/.twmrc and edit it to reflect some of your own preferences. Although the twm manager isn't quite as configurable as fvwm or fvwm 2, it's leaner and faster, available on nearly any UNIX or Linux workstation in existence, and has a clean look that many veteran users prefer.

INTEGRATED LINUX ENVIRONMENTS

10

INTEGRATED ENVIRONMENT VERSUS WINDOW MANAGER

Part IV of this book, "Integrated Linux Environments," is designed to familiarize users of KDE and GNOME with those environments. It is intended primarily for those who received KDE or GNOME with their Linux distribution and have been using the environment already. Although not a part of the XFree86 distribution in the strictest sense, it would be a mistake to assume that a discussion of graphical Linux could take place at this point without some coverage of these integrated environments and a discussion of how these environments relate to traditional window managers and the more traditional X desktop.

Window Managers

In the last chapter, we discussed the three most commonly installed window managers for Linux and XFree86 and alluded to the fact that more are out there. In fact, many more window managers are available than we were able to discuss. The following (listed in alphabetical order) are some of them:

- **AfterStep**—A window manager designed to make a Linux+XFree86 desktop look more like a NeXTStep desktop running on NeXT hardware while preserving some UNIX sensibilities.
- **Enlightenment (E)**—A window manager designed to allow for the maximum amount of appearance configurability.

- **IceWM**—A window manager designed to allow Linux+XFree86 desktops to emulate any other environments, including the OS/2 Workplace shell or Windows environments.

- **Window Maker**—A window manager designed not only to make a Linux+XFree86 desktop look more like a NeXTStep desktop, but to make a Linux desktop behave and think more like a NeXTStep desktop as well.

- **wm2/wmx**—A pair of window managers designed to look even more minimal than twm and to provide only the very basic amount of window management functionality needed by the power user.

In addition to these few, many other window managers for Linux and UNIX systems can be found around the Web as well, some more configurable than others, each different both in behavior and appearance. When it comes to window managers, it's a buyer's market: There's more flexibility, configurability, and variety out there than most users will ever know what to do with.

There are also many powerful programming APIs for developing X applications, some of which were discussed briefly in Chapter 5, "Linux/X Toolkit Particulars." Many applications have been written using these APIs. In Linux, an applications programmer has a wide variety of tools and toolkits to choose from, allowing each programmer to be completely comfortable with the code that he or she writes and the API for which it was written.

This kind of flexibility is unique to Linux and UNIX systems; it doesn't exist in other commodity operating systems commonly used either by end users or by businesses.

Problems with the X Window System and Window Managers

Most users are aware of the development of both the KDE (K Desktop Environment) and GNOME (GNU Network Object Model Environment) over the last couple of years, and are vaguely aware that these environments are beginning to replace window managers like fvwm or twm on distribution-installed Linux desktops. If such variety and power were already available in window managers that existed before KDE and GNOME, why did development of these two environments occur, and why are so many users and distributions beginning to use them?

The answer has to do with the structure of X itself. The X Window System has always implemented a "mechanism, not policy" philosophy, meaning that X wanted to provide only a means for displaying graphics primitives and dictating their behavior across a network—nothing more. All further activity, from drawing the widgets to building the applications, was to be the responsibility of the X user or X programmer. X doesn't even implement window or user-client management; this is done by an external window manager such as twm.

This separation between the underlying graphics system, the applications, and application management has led to the large variety of available window managers and APIs. Unfortunately, there is also a downside to this kind of flexibility and configurability. When 10 different applications use 10 different APIs and 10 different sets of widgets and keyboard/mouse bindings, a desktop quickly becomes confusing or even unusable. With the many window managers for X have come many different configuration file formats and many different ways to interact with the desktop. When moving from one Linux machine to another that is running a different window manager, it is easy (especially for novice users) to become completely disoriented. In short, the learning curve has been made high, and it doesn't diminish as long as new applications must be used on any regular basis.

These problems, which can be seen on many X desktops, are often referred to as desktop fragmentation. The results of desktop fragmentation can be seen in Figure 10.1. Note that each application's widgets look different from one another, and that all appear different from the title bars and decorations created by the window manager. Note also that each of these clients, including the window manager, interacts with the user in a different way, with different key bindings, mouse behavior, and widget feedback.

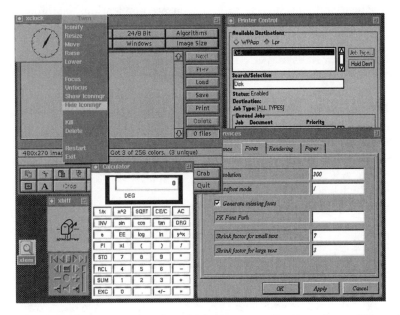

Figure 10.1   Desktop fragmentation, in which many applications have different appearances and behaviors, is common in X.

Even worse, however, is the fact that each of these applications is based on a different API and set of programming libraries, meaning that even though Linux supports sharing of libraries across multiple programs to save memory, each of these programs is actually consuming large amounts of memory on its own because it loads its own library and API code different from the code of the others—in effect, the benefits of shared library or dynamic linking have been partially or completely nullified on many X desktops.

Integrated Environments

Enter KDE and GNOME. Both are more than mere window managers or application toolkits; they are complete integrated environments. Both KDE and GNOME include all the following layers:

- **APIs**—Both KDE and GNOME build their own APIs for programmers to use in creating new applications. These APIs are some of the most powerful available to Linux or UNIX users today.

- **ORBs**—Both KDE and GNOME include some sort of object request broker. An ORB allows an application to use objects from a separate application, meaning better integration, flexibility, and compatibility for the user, as well as faster development for the programmer.

- **Applications**—Both KDE and GNOME come with a base set of applications for general-purpose desktop use: a file manager, a calculator, a mail reader, a text editor, and so on.

- **Window Management**—Both KDE and GNOME include an internal window manager that enjoys good integration with applications created using the window manager's own respective API.

- **Configuration**—Both KDE and GNOME attempt to do away with the necessity of editing dotfiles or the X resource database; both attempt to bring users into the modern age with point-and-click configurability.

- **Session Management**—Both KDE and GNOME implement session management, the capability to save a user's desktop upon logout so that the next time the user logs in, applications and windows will be restarted and restored to their last known positions. X users have always been able to manage sessions with xsm, but KDE and GNOME provide this functionality automatically.

None of these new capabilities or additions is particularly remarkable on its own. We already have numerous window managers and APIs for Linux and X. XFree86 comes with a calculator, a mail reader, a text editor, and so on. Several powerful file managers for X are available for download from the Internet. Several programs already exist to automatically generate configuration dotfiles or edit X resources. Many window managers do session management.

Although none of these things is particularly remarkable on its own, it is the *integration* of the effort that makes both KDE and GNOME so interesting and desirable. In the case of KDE and GNOME, the window manager and applications in the environment are all built with the same API, which consistently behaves in the same way, regardless of which application is in use. The object request broker allows applications to use each other to accomplish tasks, eliminating the reinventing-the-wheel syndrome and accelerating development. The session management capabilities of KDE and GNOME are more powerful than those of window managers because, in KDE and GNOME, the applications are built upon an API that was designed with session management in mind.

The end result of all this detail is the fact that KDE and GNOME are integrated environments, in much the same way that Windows, Mac OS, or the OS/2 Workplace shell are. This desktop unity, shown in Figure 10.2, is really the goal of environments like KDE and GNOME. Users have point-and-click configurability and a consistent look-and-feel, and newly developed applications are guaranteed to behave and appear similarly.

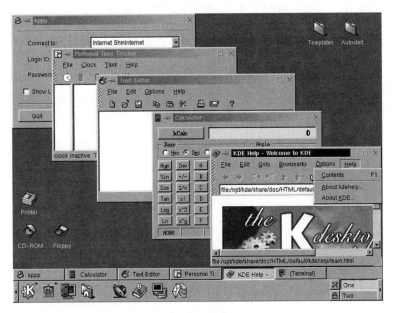

Figure 10.2   Desktop unity, promoted by integrated environments like KDE and GNOME, is generally considered to be good for the user.

Problems with Integrated Environments

Of course, KDE and GNOME have their own problems as well. The largest and most widely understood of these is size. Most users expect operating systems like Windows and OS/2 to have large memory needs for optimal performance. In truth, part of the reason for the Windows resource drain is the fact that Windows maintains a large, flexible API, an object request broker interface, session management, desktop configurability—all powerful ease-of-use features, and all, incidentally, goals shared by both KDE and GNOME.

KDE and GNOME both also occupy many megabytes of hard drive space on the host system. Much of this extra space is the result of duplicate applications—for example, the KDE editor, kedit uses up space on the hard drive and is really xedit's logical twin. The same applies to GNOME's balsa and the XFree86 standard xmh. Having both on the hard drive is, in some sense, a waste of space.

In time, these extra resource requirements will be offset by the fact that more and more desktop applications will switch over to the KDE or GNOME APIs. For the moment, however, the memory and resource requirements of KDE and GNOME plus a desktop full of applications are higher than many Linux users are accustomed to.

In addition to size and performance issues, however, are compatibility issues. Both KDE and GNOME have emerged more or less simultaneously as valid platforms for application development and as useful environments for Linux distribution desktops. Unfortunately, at the moment, KDE and GNOME aren't compatible, nor are they completely interoperable.

They aren't compatible in that application source code written for KDE will not compile using the GNOME API and vice versa. Similarly, compiled KDE binaries must be linked to existing KDE libraries and GNOME binaries to GNOME libraries. When applications from both desktops are used simultaneously, code data from both sets of libraries will be loaded and executed.

KDE and GNOME are also not interoperable. The drag-and-drop desktop and file management from the current KDE system will not accept desktop icons dragged from a GNOME application window. The object request broker interfaces are different; a KDE application cannot embed part of a GNOME application in its window. Even the way in which the user interacts with the two systems is different.

Because of these differences, many users fear that KDE and GNOME will lead to a fragmentation in the Linux market itself, as some distributions adopt KDE as the default desktop and others adopt GNOME instead, leading to the possibility that, in the future, some distributions will not run some applications without lengthy Internet downloads or upgrades. Although these fears are valid to some degree, they aren't likely to be justified in the long term. Efforts are underway to allow KDE and GNOME to interoperate efficiently, and as the number of applications written for KDE and GNOME increases and the use of other APIs decreases, the resource costs of maintaining both types of applications simultaneously will decrease.

Environment or Manager: Which Is Right for Me?

Most distributions currently shipping are using either KDE or GNOME as their default desktop, and this choice reflects the correct one for the average user. Most current Linux users who use X at all will use it as a general-purpose work environment and will benefit greatly from the integration and ease-of-configuration afforded by KDE and GNOME.

Window managers can be difficult to maintain, but they can also provide significant performance increases and resource savings. Window managers are therefore often the choice of power users who don't need the extra configurability or integration offered by KDE and GNOME. For this reason, window managers, especially those with a niche of their own, such as wm2, twm, Window Maker, or Enlightenment, will continue to survive and maintain their popularity.

For those with older, resource-challenged computer systems, KDE and GNOME may be a bad choice. On older systems lacking in memory, hard disk space, colors, or video acceleration, the more traditional set of X applications combined with a small window manager will afford the best levels of performance and usability; environments such as KDE and GNOME will in these cases seem clumsy and slow.

11

THE KDE 1.1.1 ENVIRONMENT

After KDE is installed, navigating the KDE system and getting work done is pretty simple. Even so, most users will want to ensure that they can accomplish the same basic configuration tasks in KDE that they can accomplish with standalone X window managers. Furthermore, if you don't already have KDE installed, a little installation hand-holding can be helpful.

KDE Basics: Getting, Installing, Starting, Configuring

The KDE home page on the World Wide Web is located at
`http://www.kde.org`. Users interested in downloading the KDE should have at least 100 megabytes of free disk space, and really more is required in order for a smooth installation and comfortable use to be possible. The primary location for downloading KDE is at `ftp://ftp.kde.org/pub/kde/stable`. Mirrors are maintained in many countries; to access them, insert the two-letter country code for your country after the ftp. For example, the US mirror is located at `ftp.us.kde.org`. Downloadable packages exist for Debian Linux, S.u.S.E. Linux, Red Hat Linux, Caldera OpenLinux, Slackware Linux, and other Linux and non-Linux operating systems.

KDE from Binary Packages

Most of the platform- or distribution-specific KDE packages include all the components listed in Table 11.1. Packages for some distributions differ; in such cases, README or other text files are generally present in the binary package directory providing specific instructions for installing the KDE on the platform in question.

Table 11.1   Major KDE Packages

Package	Description
kdesupport	Includes all the basic library support that is required for KDE operation but is not actually a part of the KDE, such as graphic image format libraries.
kdelibs	The basic group of KDE libraries, which together support applications written using the KDE API.
kdebase	Basic KDE components such as the window manager, file manager, and icons.
kdegames	Games written for the KDE environment using the KDE API.
kdegraphics	Graphics-oriented applications written for the KDE environment using the KDE API.
kdenetwork	Tools associated with network status and configuration, as well as dial-up tools, mail clients, and so on.
kdetoys	Toys and fun applications that aren't games but aren't otherwise useful.
kdemultimedia	Multimedia applications such as sound players and recorders, movie viewers, and so on.
kdeutils	KDE utilities. These are basic desktop tools like a Notepad, a floppy disk formatter, a desktop calculator, and so on.

Several packages listed in Table 11.1 are order-important and, if installed incorrectly, will cause KDE to fail to function correctly. It is important to install the kdesupport package first, followed by the kdelibs and kdebase packages. After these three packages have been installed in this order, the other packages can generally be installed in any order without any ill effects. After all the packages have been installed, it might be necessary to add the path to the KDE environment to your path before it can be used.

KDE from Source

KDE is also available in source code rather than as a set of binary packages. Compiling from source can give users extra control that isn't present when installing from packages. The source to the current version of KDE is generally located in the same ftp directory tree as the binary versions, on the source subtree. The relevant source packages are the same ones listed in Table 11.1; they can simply be downloaded to the hard drive.

After all the source files have been downloaded, they must be extracted and compiled. The most common way to do this is with the following series of commands:

```
tar -xzvf kde-component-version.tar.gz
cd kde-component-version
./configure
make; make install
```

The output from each of these commands has been included to save space; the basic idea is clear. First extract the archive using the tar utility on the command line. After the package has been extracted, visit the new directory created by the package and run the ./configure program in the directory. After configure has been run, two calls to make will first build the binaries from the source code and then install the binaries into the default install location.

The install location, as well as several other options, can be changed at compile time by passing arguments to the configure script. The arguments available can be listed by passing the help argument to the configure script without other arguments, like this:

```
./configure help
```

When compiling, as was the case when installing from binary packages, it is important to install in the correct order. Again, the order is kdesupport first, followed by kdelibs and then kdebase, with the rest of the source packages being compiled and installed in no particular order.

Starting KDE

Starting KDE, arguably the final step in installing KDE, is generally a fairly simple manner. Ensure that the path to the KDE binary directory is added to your path, either in the /etc/profile file or in your $HOME/.xinitrc script. Then, add a call to the startkde command from the KDE directory tree's binary subdirectory, without arguments, in place of any calls to a window manager. Placing the command at the end of the $HOME/.xinitrc file in place of any window manager should bring the KDE up when you first log in to the X session and allow the session to exit when you exit the KDE.

Configuring KDE

After KDE is installed and running, the first thing most users will want to do is personalize it to suit their own tastes by configuring some of the behavior and appearance options. In KDE, this is all done using point-and-click menus and dialog boxes.

Most objects in KDE generate context-sensitive menus when they are right-clicked, in much the same way that Windows does. On this context-sensitive menu you will often find a Properties item, just as is common in other consumer operating systems. For example, right-clicking on the root window while KDE is running brings up the menu shown in Figure 11.1. Selecting the Properties option brings up a display properties dialog box that will seem familiar to many users, thanks to its similarity to the same dialog in Windows operating systems.

Figure 11.1 You display the properties menu by right-clicking on the root window.

The main method to use when configuring KDE, however, does not rely on context-sensitive menus. The KDE control center is the main avenue for configuring the KDE environment. It collects many dialog boxes from many different context-sensitive windows in a single place, so that the user doesn't have to go hunting through the system for them. To open the KDE control center, click a panel icon like the one shown in Figure 11.2.

Click here

Figure 11.2 An icon on the panel launches the KDE control center.

The KDE control center operates in two halves. On the left is a tree view which has subtrees that can be expanded or collapsed by clicking on the small plus (+) or minus (-) box. Selecting an item from this tree view causes a dialog box to be displayed on the right of the control center window. This dialog box will generally contain several panes with tabs to switch between them, each pane containing a different category of options relating to the KDE aspect selected in the tree on the left side of the window. The KDE control center window is shown in Figure 11.3, later in this chapter.

Thanks to the KDE's goals of being end-user friendly, most of the options that are found in the KDE control center are self-explanatory, and you can generally experiment with those that aren't without fear of causing harm to your desktop. The presence of an Apply button allows changes to be tried without the need to restart one or all components of the desktop. Because configuration is so self-explanatory, a detailed exploration of most parts of the KDE control center is beyond the scope of this text.

Three Major KDE Components

The KDE is not a single entity, though it is designed to look like one. When you look closely, it is actually possible to see several major components that the user interacts with on a regular basis while using the KDE. Each of these components has a special role within the KDE. These components rarely need to be started by hand, so to speak. They should normally be started using the startkde script, included as part of the standard KDE distribution.

Three fundamental components of the KDE really cannot be removed without removing a sizable percentage of KDE's functionality. These three components are the window manager, kwm or krootwm (depending on your KDE version); the panel and icon manager, kpanel; and the file and desktop manager, kfm. Although there are many smaller KDE components and applications, these three components form the bulk of the KDE's functionality.

kwm/krootwm

The kwm binary is a part of the kdebase package and actually performs many of the same tasks normally performed by a window manager not written for the KDE: kwm draws decorations like title bars and buttons around the borders of windows and facilitates their movement and size management. The kwm also provides focus policy and some form of minimization, in cooperation with other KDE components.

The typical window decorations drawn by kwm are shown in Figure 11.3. Note that this appearance reflects only the default KDE behavior; the appearance can easily change based on user preferences.

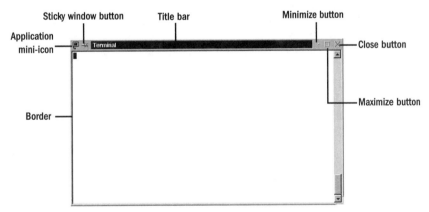

Figure 11.3   Decorations drawn by krootwm.

Most of the tricks relating to the KDE window manager that users will find useful are configuration options that live in a series of panels in the control center dialogs tree. The Windows branch of this tree contains five dialogs related to the nuts-and-bolts of the window managers operation.

Changing the Title Bar Buttons

The Buttons pane in the Windows branch of the control center tree enables the user to select which title bar buttons should and should not appear on decorated applications. The user can also select the position of buttons that should appear.

For each button KDE is capable of displaying, there is a set of three radio buttons: left, right, and off. Choosing left for a particular button will cause the button to be active by default and to appear on the left side of the title bar at the top of an application window. Choosing right for a particular button will cause the button to be active by default and to appear on the right side of the title bar at the top of an application window. Choosing off for a particular button will cause the button not to appear anywhere on the window title bar.

The sample title bar at the top of the pane changes as the button configuration is altered by the user; it is to demonstrate what the resultant window title bar would look like were the user to save the changes.

Changing the Focus Policy

The Properties pane in the Windows branch of the control center contains a section titled Focus Policy toward the bottom of the window that enables the user to edit the focus and general raise policy for windows in the KDE.

In the drop-down list, the user can choose among several classic X window system focus policies. Click to Focus is the Windows-like focus policy in which the mouse must be clicked inside a window for the window to take focus. The Focus Follows Mouse and Classic Sloppy Focus both function as what most users would recognize to be a sloppy focus mechanism. Focus resides with whichever window contains the mouse pointer, or, if no window currently contains the mouse pointer, with the last window to have focus. The classic Focus Follows Mouse Option allows the user to select the traditional focus follows mouse mode, in which the focus goes to whichever window contains the mouse pointer. If no window contains the pointer, no window has focus.

The Auto Raise check box specifies that windows with focus should automatically be raised when they get focus after the delay in milliseconds set by the Delay slider bar next to the Auto Raise check box.

The Click Raise check box specifies that any time the mouse pointer is clicked anywhere inside a window, the window should be raised. This is the default behavior in the Click to Focus focus mode, but in the other focus modes, the default behavior is to raise a window only when the title bar is clicked.

Turning Off Animation

The same Properties pane that is used in configuring focus is also used in configuring window animation. Only one animation option controls all types of KDE animation.

The Resize Animation slider at the top of the window enables the user to select a speed of resize animation. Setting the slider all the way to the left switches the animation off entirely. Moving the slider toward the right makes window minimize, restore, and resize animation progressively faster.

Changing Mouse Bindings and Decoration Functions

It is possible in KDE to change the mouse's bindings to window decorations and to change the bindings of the decorations to different window manager functions. This type of configuration is done using the Mouse pane in the Windows branch of the control center tree.

The Mouse pane presents the user with a list of button events in various contexts down the left side of the pane, and a series of drop-down menus down the right side of the pane in which the user can select the function that should be bound to the given button in the given context. For title bar contexts, two drop-downs exist, allowing the user to bind separate functions to decorations based on whether the window in question is active or inactive (focused or unfocused).

This method for configuring mouse bindings is actually quite elegant and easy to understand; the best way to get a feel for configuring the bindings in KDE is to experiment with this configuration pane, using the Apply button often to see changes take effect.

Altering Decorations or Behavior for Specific Windows

There is no direct equivalent in the KDE to the `Style` keyword for configuring window styles in the fvwm window manager studied in Chapter 9, "Runtime Environment Configuration." However, KDE does provide a primitive method for configuring windows appearances and behaviors on a per-window basis. The mechanism for implementing such configuration is found on the Advanced pane of the control center's Window branch.

At the bottom of the pane is a section titled Filters that includes two sets of user entry lists and a drop-down list. To use the section, enter either a window title into the Titles list or a client class into the Classes list. Then, select a property from the drop-down list. The Have Tiny Decorations and Gave No Decorations properties will cause a window to have no title bar or both no title bar and no border, respectively. The Never Gain Focus property prevents the window from becoming focused and accepting keystrokes. The Start as Sticky property starts the window with the sticky title bar button clicked. The Exclude from Session Management property prevents the window's status from being saved when KDE exits; the window will therefore not be started again when KDE restarts.

After a title or class has been entered and a property selected, clicking on the plus (+) button will cause the change to be saved (added) to the list. This property will then remain active until it is removed.

The process for removing properties is not obvious. To remove a property, enter the title or class of the property you want to remove in the corresponding text entry box and click the minus (-) button.

kpanel

The second most obvious part of the KDE environment is the kpanel, an application launch bar and icon manager that can be placed at various locations on the display. The kpanel also provides functionality for pop-up menus not unlike the root menus traditional in other window managers, as well as for a tray in the tradition of the Windows system tray that holds iconlets for active applications and which usually displays some sort of status information or activity.

The kpanels icon manager bar works closely with the kwm window manager to provide the sort of seamless integration that is KDE's goal. Any running KDE application normally maintains a button on the kpanel's task manager bar. When a window is minimized by clicking on one of the title bar buttons drawn by kwm, it disappears from the main desktop and the title of its button in the kpanel task management bar appears in parentheses. Clicking on the button in the task manager restores the window.

The typical appearance of the kpanel, including task manager, is shown in Figure 11.4. As was the case with the kwm, the appearance of the kpanel can be changed by the user based on user preferences.

Figure 11.4   The kpanel, at the bottom along with the icon manager (taskbar).

Both the location and the behavior of the kpanel are fairly configurable. The configuration options that use configuration dialogs to control kpanel behavior can be found either in the KDE control center or by right-clicking on the panel and selecting the Configure option.

Adding Icons to kpanel

The process of adding an icon to the kpanel is simple. There are two basic ways to accomplish the task, based on where the icon is coming from.

To add an icon from the desktop or the file manager to the kpanel, simply drag the icon from the desktop or file manager window to the kpanel and then release the mouse. File, device, or application icons will appear as clickable icons on the kpanel, and directories that are added will appear as menus.

To add an icon from the K-Menu or a submenu off of the K-Menu, select the K-Menu, and then select Panel and, within that menu, Add application. The Add Application submenu should bring up a clone of the K-Menu; browse this menu and select the item you'd like to add to the panel, and it will appear as the next icon on the kpanel. This process is shown in Figure 11.5.

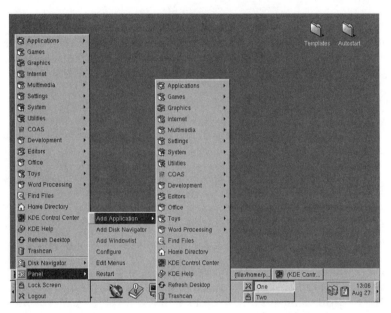

Figure 11.5   Adding an application icon to the kpanel using the K-Menu's Panel, Add Application process.

Changing the Size Position of the Panel and Taskbar

The locations of the panel and taskbar can be configured from inside the control center by expanding the Applications branch and selecting the Panel pane from the list. The panel dialog then appears on the right side of the control panel. Select the Panel tab to see configuration options related to the panel and taskbar position and size.

The upper-left section of the tab pane, Location, controls the location of the panel on the display, which can be one of Top, Left, Bottom, or Right. The upper-right section of the tab pane, Taskbar, selects the position of the taskbar using the same four options.

The size of the panel is controlled by the lower-left section of the tab pane, labeled Style. Selecting Tiny will cause the panel to appear on one mini-icon high or wide on the display. Selecting Normal chooses the default, large-icon size, and selecting Large causes extra pixel space to be inserted between many elements on the panel, further increasing its size.

Managing Virtual Desktops

The number of virtual desktops that will appear on the display and the names of each of the virtual desktops can be configured in the Desktops tab of the Panel entry in the Applications branch of the control center tree.

Two sliders at the bottom of the tab pane, labeled Visible and Width, control the number of accessible virtual desktops and the width of each desktop's button on the kpanel, respectively. The kpanel allows for up to eight desktops total. It is recommended that width not be set too narrow or the labels for each desktop will be truncated on the panel.

Above the two sliders are several text entry boxes, one active box for each of the activated virtual desktops. Clicking in these boxes and entering text will cause the desktop in question to be named with the text entered. This name will appear on the kpanel button for that desktop, provided the button is wide enough to contain the text.

Autohiding the kpanel

Many users moving to KDE+Linux from Windows environments are accustomed to a Windows taskbar that has an autohide mode in which it remains invisible unless the mouse is moved against the edge of the display, in which case the taskbar suddenly becomes visible again.

The kpanel supports similar functionality in the KDE; it can be enabled by expanding the Applications branch of the control center tree, then selecting Panel from the sublist and the Options tab in the resulting dialog. The two options that control the panel's autohide behavior are Auto-hide Panel and Auto-hide Taskbar. These options cause the menu/icon panel and the icon manager taskbar to autohide when checked, respectively.

Two sliders for each option, Delay and Speed, control the aesthetics of the autohide mode. Delay refers to the amount of time that must pass after the mouse has moved away before the item in question will autohide. A longer delay means that the item will stay on the display longer before autohiding. Speed refers to the quickness with which each item reappears when the mouse is moved to the edge of the display.

kfm

The kfm is the KDE file manager. This title is, however, a little misleading because the kfm also provides many other functions, not the least of which is fairly decent Web browsing capability in the tradition of Netscape and other graphical browsers. The kfm is also responsible for much of the desktop drag-and-drop functionality and for creating icons on the desktop in the first place.

The typical appearance of a kfm window, alongside some of the desktop icons that kfm draws, is shown in Figure 11.6.

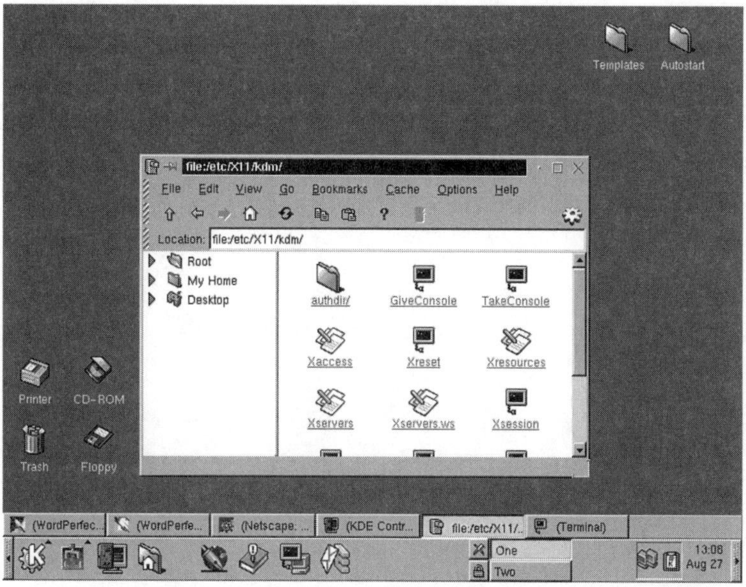

Figure 11.6 A kfm window browsing the local filesystem alongside several desktop kfm icons.

Although some kfm options can be configured from the control panel, most of the interesting kfm configuration and use is done from kfm windows and elsewhere in the Linux system.

Adding Desktop Device Icons

Many kfm icons are really representations of files that end with the .kdelnk extension and describe a device or specific type of file or location. Although the creation of .kdelnk files by hand is beyond the scope of this text, it is actually fairly easy to represent your own devices on your desktop with kfm icons and to have kfm mount and unmount these devices.

Be sure that an entry for such a device, including a valid mount point and filesystem, exists in the /etc/fstab file. All disk devices that are to be represented on the KDE desktop must appear in the /etc/fstab file. In addition, any device that is to be mounted and unmounted by clicking on its icon must have the user flag appear in the fourth column of its entry in the /etc/fstab file. For more information on flags that can be supplied in the fourth column of the /etc/fstab file, please see the mount(8) manual page.

After the /etc/fstab entry for a device has been created, representing the device on the desktop is a multistep process. First, right-click on the desktop and select New, Filesystem Device. In the dialog that pops up, enter a name for the device, ending with the .kdelnk extension. This will cause kfm to create an unconfigured device on your desktop (see Figure 11.7).

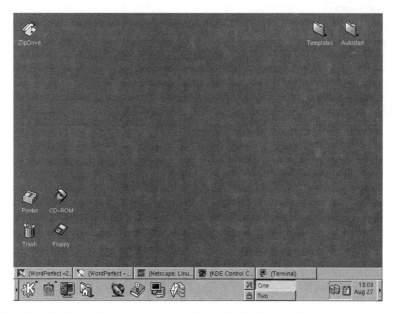

Figure 11.7   The ZipDrive icon is an unconfigured filesystem device icon.

Second, right-click on the unconfigured filesystem device icon and select the Properties item. A dialog appears with three tabs for icon configuration. Only the last tab, Device, interests us here; the rest can be ignored. In the Device tab, enter the device name for your disk, as it appears in the /etc/fstab file, into the text entry box labeled Device.

Finally, click once on Mounted icon and once on Unmounted icon, each time selecting an icon from the dialog full of icons that appears. The mounted icon is the icon that will be used to represent your device on the desktop when it is mounted; the unmounted icon will be used when it is not. Prebuilt icon pairs (one with a simulated LED and one without) exist for several disk types, including floppies, zip drives, and CD-ROM drives.

When you're finished selecting icons, choose OK at the bottom of the dialog. The device icon should now appear with one of the icons you selected, depending on whether in its current state it is mounted or unmounted from the filesystem. To browse (and mount, if necessary) a disk device, simply click on its desktop icon. To unmount an already mounted disk device, right-click on the desktop icon and select Unmount from the context-sensitive menu that appears.

Changing the View

The kfm file manager window provides several different views and properties that cover nearly every possible user-desired contingency when it comes to browsing the filesystem. All these changes are made from the View drop-down menu at the top of a kfm window. The contents of this menu are detailed in Table 11.2.

Table 11.2   Contents of the kfm View Drop-Down Menu

Item	Description
Show Hidden Files	Causes hidden files (those whose names begin with a period) to appear in the kfm window when browsing files.
Show Tree	Causes the window to be split horizontally and a directory tree view to be displayed down the left side of the window to aid in navigation.
Show Thumbnails	Causes files that are of known image formats to appear as thumbnail images in the browser for easier identification.
HTML View	Allows kfm to emulate a Web server locally; when visiting a directory, it will first check to see whether the file index.html exists. If it does, kfm will view the file as a Web page and allow the user to browse it in that capacity.
Icon View	Displays files as icons in the main kfm window, with a text annotation beneath each icon.
Text View	Displays files in a text listing similar (but not identical) to the one generated by the ls -l command.
Long View	Displays files in a text listing similar to the one given by Text View, but with more information about each file.
Short View	Displays files in a text listing one line at a time in the same manner as Text View and Long View, but without all the extra information, just the filename and a mini-icon.

By using some or all of these options in various combinations, the user can browse any given directory in a filesystem in a large variety of ways.

Adding a Background Pixmap to a Window

Any directory that can be browsed by kfm can be displayed with a background image behind the icons or file information. Each window has its own pixmap, and the image will be remembered each time the directory is visited.

To add a background pixmap to the display for a specific directory, right-click in the kfm window (but not on any icon or file) and select Properties from the menu that appears. In the dialog that appears, select the Dir tab. On the resulting pane, there is a drop-down list from which the user can choose a background image for the directory in question. The background image will remain in effect whenever the directory is visited until this configuration dialog is revisited and Default is selected.

Browsing URLs and Linking Them from the Desktop

kfm windows have the capability to act as rather powerful HTML (Web page) browsers on the Internet, thanks to KDE's network-centric design and philosophy. Visiting a URL in an open kfm window is a simple thing to do: Simply enter the URL you want to visit into the Location box and press Enter.

Web pages appear just as they would in Netscape Communicator or another browser, and links can be followed and forms filled out in much the same way. When viewing ftp sites, kfm can even be used to drag-and-drop files from the ftp site to local locations between kfm windows or between a kfm window and the desktop. Bookmarks can be added using the Ctrl+B keystroke in the kfm window or by using the Bookmarks drop-down menu at the top of the window.

Having to always open a window with a local icon and then enter a Web page, however, is slightly inconvenient, so kfm makes it possible to link directly to a URL from an icon. To create a kfm ftp URL icon, right-click on the desktop and chose New, Ftp URL. In the pop-up dialog that appears, enter the (English) name of the ftp site followed by .kdelink as the extension. To create an http URL, follow the same procedure but select New, World Wide Web URL instead from the pop-up menu.

After entering the English name of the .kdelnk file into the dialog box, an icon for either an ftp URL or an http URL appears on the desktop, as shown in Figure 11.8, later in this chapter. It does not yet, however, point to any specific address. To cause the icon to point to a specific address, right-click on the icon and select Properties from the context menu. In the dialog that appears, select the URL tab and enter the full URL into the box provided. When you're finished, click the OK button at the bottom of the dialog.

Clicking on the ftp or WWW icon now opens a new kfm window and loads the specified URL into the window for browsing, or (in the case of ftp) remote file management.

General KDE Tips and Tricks

The KDE is a very large and complex environment; it is impossible to discuss the entire environment in a text like this one. Still, a few tips or tricks that aren't initially obvious might be beneficial to the average power user.

Using a Different Window Manager

Although KDE includes its own window manager, kwm or krootwm depending on your KDE version, which we've already discussed, it is possible to use other window managers with KDE in conjunction with the other KDE components, kfm and kpanel. Although integration isn't always as good as it is with kwm or krootwm, it is improving daily.

The most popular alternative to the default KDE window manager is the Window Maker window manager that can be found at http://www.windowmaker.org. Window Maker's later versions support KDE integration and can thus work well in a KDE environment when started instead of kwm or krootwm.

The next alternative to the default KDE window manager is Blackbox, a light, efficient window manager with a personality all its own. Blackbox can be found on the Internet at http://blackbox.wiw.org. Like Window Maker, Blackbox supports partial KDE integration good enough to replace the kwm or krootwm.

In both of these cases, the window manager in question will almost certainly need to be recompiled with special options in order to integrate properly with the KDE. Thus, see the documentation included with each window manager's source for instructions on compiling for KDE interoperability.

When starting KDE with one of these window managers, call the window manager in the .xinitrc file before the call to startkde; this will cause the kwm or krootwm to abort because a window manager is already running, leaving the replacement window manager running in its place.

Adding Icons, Wallpaper, or Sounds to KDE

There are many dialogs and option boxes in KDE where the user is asked to select an icon or a wallpaper image for the purpose at hand. There is rarely a Browse button to go along with the supplied icons, however, so it is often unclear how new icons should be added.

The KDE maintains its global files in a directory such as /opt/kde, /usr/local/kde, or /usr/kde. To find where your KDE's installation is located, you'll have to check the packages that your distribution installed. After you know the location of your KDE installation's global directories, you can easily globally add icons and wallpaper images as root.

The share/icons directory off the main kde directory contains the icons that will be available to the user when he or she is asked in a dialog to select an icon. KDE icons are normally supplied in X pixmap (.xpm) format. The share/wallpapers directory contains the wallpapers that will be available when configuring desktop properties or setting wallpaper backgrounds for kfm file windows. KDE wallpaper images are normally supplied in JPEG (.jpg) format.

Note that because both of these directories are in the global KDE tree, they are owned by the root user, and additions to these directories will be visible to all KDE users on a multiuser system. To add icons or wallpaper on a user-specific basis, corresponding local KDE directories exist in $HOME/.kde/share/icons and $HOME/.kde/share/wallpapers. These are the directories that should be used for per-user icon and wallpaper installations.

The corresponding directories for adding sounds to KDE are the share/sounds directory off the global KDE tree and the $HOME/.kde/share/sounds directory. Sound files are normally supplied in .wav format.

Editing KDE Menus

The K Menu and its submenus are usually fairly exhaustive and contain all the KDE applications plus (if KDE has been correctly installed) many of the non-KDE X applications present on your system. Still, there are definitely times when it is helpful to be able to edit the K Menu and other menus.

The global K Menu is the same for all users and is stored in the global KDE directory tree; it can thus (naturally) be edited only by the superuser. However, each user also has a personal menu that he or she can edit, and which normally appears as a submenu off the K Menu, though it can be made to appear in place of the K Menu using the control center.

To edit a set of menus, either locally or globally, start the KDE menu editor from the K Menu, Utilities submenu (see Figure 11.8).

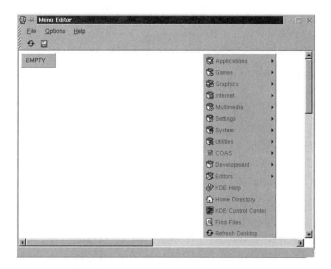

Figure 11.8 The KDE menu editor.

On the left side of the KDE menu editor is the user's local menu, which initially appears only as the word EMPTY. On the right side of the KDE menu editor is the global KDE menu. A personalized menu can be constructed by dragging menus or menu items from the global menu on the right into the personal menu on the left.

In addition, new items can be added to the local menu by right-clicking on the menu and choosing New to generate a new EMPTY entry, then right clicking on that entry and choosing Change to bring up a configuration dialog box for that menu entry. After the local menu structure has been defined to user satisfaction, choosing Save from the File drop-down menu will save the changes to the user's account.

To change the name under which the user's local menu will appear in the K Menu, choose the Change Menuname option from the Options drop-down box at the top of the menu editor window.

Learning More About KDE

There are more tricks to KDE than we could ever possibly cover in a chapter like this, and we haven't even tried to cover the simple configuration and use basics at all. For more tutorial-style information on using KDE, see the KDE help system or, for those who prefer more depth, check out *Sams Teach Yourself KDE in 24 Hours*.

On the left side of the KDE menu editor is the user's local menu, which initially appears only as the word EMPTY. On the right side of the KDE menu editor is the global KDE menu. A personalized menu can be constructed by dragging menus or menu items from the global menu on the right into the personal menu on the left.

In addition, new items can be added to the local menu by right-clicking on the menu and choosing New to generate a new EMPTY entry, then right clicking on that entry and choosing Change to bring up a configuration dialog box for that menu entry. After the local menu structure has been defined to user satisfaction, choosing Save from the File drop-down menu will save the changes to the user's account.

To change the name under which the user's local menu will appear in the K Menu, choose the Change Menuname option from the Options drop-down box at the top of the menu editor window.

Learning More About KDE

There are more tricks to KDE than we could ever possibly cover in a chapter like this, and we haven't even tried to cover the simple configuration and use basics at all. For more tutorial-style information on using KDE, see the KDE help system or, for those who prefer more depth, check out *Sams Teach Yourself KDE in 24 Hours*.

12

The GNOME 1.0 Environment

GNOME, or GNU Network Object Model Environment, was a project started partly in response to the K Desktop Environment (KDE) because several users were worried about KDE's less traditional open-source licensing methods. Over the last couple of years, GNOME has evolved into a complete, usable desktop environment in its own right whose personality is in some ways radically different from the more utilitarian KDE.

This chapter is designed to help you figure out some tips and tricks that might not be immediately obvious and might be helpful while using GNOME. It is written primarily for those who are using GNOME now, most probably having received it as a part of their Linux distribution. For those who don't yet have GNOME but would like to give it a try, we begin with a brief section on getting and installing GNOME.

GNOME Basics: Getting, Installing, Starting, Configuring

The GNOME home page on the World Wide Web can be found at the Web site http://www.gnome.org. Users interested in downloading GNOME should really have at least 200 megabytes of available disk space for installing from packages, or 700–800 megabytes of available disk space if compiling from source. The primary download location for GNOME 1.0 is at the ftp.gnome.org site in the /pub/gnome/gnome-1.0 directory, but this site can often prove extremely busy and difficult to access. It is therefore suggested that users access one of the following mirrors, taken from the rejection notice that ftp.gnome.org sends when it is overloaded.

United States and Canada:

- ftp://ftp.cybertrails.com/pub/gnome/
- ftp://ftp.geo.net/pub/gnome/
- ftp://ftp.net.lut.ac.uk/gnome/
- ftp://ftp.snoopy.net/pub/mirrors/GNOME/
- ftp://gnomeftp.wgn.net/pub/gnome/
- ftp://server.ph.ucla.edu/pub/mirror/ftp.gnome.org/
- ftp://sod.inter mezzo.org/mirror/ftp.gnome.org/

Australia:

- ftp://ftp.tas.gov.au/gnome/
- ftp://mirror.aarnet.edu.au/pub/gnome/

Europe:

- ftp://ceu.fi.udc.es/pub/os/linux/X Window/GNOME/
- ftp://ftp.archive.de.uu.net/pub/X11/GNOME/
- ftp://ftp.dataplus.se/pub/linux/gnome/
- ftp://ftp.dit.upm.es/linux/gnome/
- ftp://ftp.fr.gnome.org/pub/gnome/
- ftp://ftp.gts.cz/pub/gui/gnome/
- ftp://ftp.informatik.uni bonn.de/pub/os/unix/gnome/
- ftp://ftp.linux.hr/pub/gnome/
- ftp://ftp.linux.it/pub/mirrors/gnome/
- ftp://ftp.net.lut.ac.uk/gnome/
- ftp://ftp.sunet.se/pub/X11/GNOME/
- ftp://ftp.task.gda.pl/pub/linux/GNOME/
- ftp://ftp.uni trier.de/pub/unix/X11/toolkits/gnome/
- ftp://ftp.utt.ro/mirrors/ftp.gnome.org/pub/GNOME/
- ftp://ftp3.linux.it/pub/mirrors/gnome/
- ftp://gd.tuwien.ac.at/hci/GNOME/
- http://gd.tuwien.ac.at/hci/GNOME/
- ftp://linux.a2000.nl/gnome/

- `ftp://sunsite.icm.edu.pl/pub/Linux/GNOME/`
- `ftp://sunsite.mff.cuni.cz/X11/Desktops/GNOME/`
- `ftp://unix.hensa.ac.uk/mirrors/ftp.gnome.org/pub/GNOME/`

Asia:

- `ftp://ftp.kddlabs.co.jp:/X11/GNOME`
- `ftp://ftp2.sinica.edu.tw/pub2/gnome`

South America:

- `ftp://ftp.inf.utfsm.cl/pub/Linux/Gnome`
- `ftp://linuxlabs.lci.ufrj.br/pub/gnome`

Downloadable binary packages exist for Debian Linux, Red Hat Linux, Slackware Linux, Stampede Linux, and S.u.S.E. Linux distributions, in some cases across several binary architectures, among them i386, PPC, and Sparc.

GNOME is too large a distribution to fit easily into a specific set of packages; the packages available for a given Linux distribution and the order in which they must be installed aren't consistent across all platforms. Instructions for dealing with packages for a specific Linux distribution exist at

`http://www.gnome.org/gnome 1.0/`

Most binary package sets at least split the packages into two groups, applications packages and development packages. The latter should be installed only if you intend to develop GNOME applications yourself.

GNOME from Source

The process of compiling GNOME from source is a long and harrowing one due to the size and complexity of the GNOME environment, as well as to the variability in installed Linux systems. Compiling GNOME from source is therefore recommended only for those users who have previous experience compiling Linux applications from source. It isn't recommended that any users of libc 5.x distributions compile from source themselves because GNOME was written for libc 6.x distributions. It assumes that the underlying system not only includes the newer version of libc but many other newer, libc 6.x-era components as well. The last libc 5.x releases of several distributions are shown in Table 12.1.

Table 12.1   Final `libc` 5.x Release Before Moving to 6.x

Distribution	Last libc5 Release	First libc6 Release
Red Hat Linux	4.2	5.0
Caldera OpenLinux	1.3	2.2
Slackware Linux	4.0	n/a
Debian GNU/Linux	1.3.1	2.0
S.u.S.E. Linux	5.3	6.0

It is also important to understand that installing GNOME 1.0 even on some `libc` 6.x distributions might require significant amounts of upgrading to other applications that depend on the components that GNOME uses.

To compile GNOME from source, download all the GNOME 1.0 source files from the source subdirectory of the `gnome-1.0/` directory on the GNOME mirror site you chose. You might also need several graphics support libraries listed at the bottom of the left column on the GNOME 1.0 compilation page at

```
http://www.gnome.org/start/gnometar.phtml
```

Note that many of these libraries are later versions of libraries commonly found on Linux systems, so it is a good idea to check before compiling and installing any of these or any of the GNOME 1.0-proper packages against your installed Linux packages to see whether they conflict. If you find conflicts, you'll have to decide how to best cope with them. A discussion of this sort is beyond the scope of this text, and if you find conflicts that you don't know how to resolve, it would probably be best for you to use binary packages or wait to try GNOME.

The majority of the GNOME 1.0 source files can be compiled and installed using the same basic set of commands, which you might recognize from Chapter 11, "The KDE 1.1.1 Environment." These commands, in sequence, are as follows:

```
tar -xzvf gnome-component-version.tar.gz
cd gnome-component-version
./configure
make; make install
```

Note that this sequence of commands will install GNOME 1.0 and its components into the `/usr/local` directory tree. If you want to choose another location for GNOME, it is important that for each package you compile, you issue the following command in place of the `configure` call:

```
./configure --help
```

After issuing this command, you'll be presented with a list of configure options, including the option to specify an installation location and options to specify where previously compiled components have already been installed.

Note that the order in which the packages are compiled is extremely important and compilation won't succeed if they are compiled out of order. For the correct order of compilation, and complete, detailed instructions on compiling and installing GNOME 1.0 from source, consult the GNOME 1.0 compilation page whose URL was supplied earlier. Source packages should be compiled in the order in which they are listed down the left side of the page.

Starting GNOME

Starting GNOME is a fairly simple process after all the wrinkles have been ironed out. It is made slightly more complicated by the fact that Enlightenment, the most commonly used GNOME window manager, installs its binary in a nonstandard location when compiled from source.

If you have installed GNOME from binary packages, it is likely that starting GNOME will be as easy as ensuring that the path to the GNOME binary directory is in your PATH variable and then issuing the gnome-session command. Calling GNOME in your $HOME/.xinitrc file instead of a window manager might therefore look like this:

```
export PATH=$PATH:/opt/gnome/bin
gnome-session
```

Note that the directory /opt/gnome/bin should be replaced with the directory in which your binary packages installed the GNOME binaries. When compiling from source using the default installation paths, the addition to $HOME/.xinitrc would look like this instead, accounting for Enlightenment's slightly different preferences:

```
export PATH=$PATH:/usr/local/bin:/usr/local/enlightenment/bin
gnome-session
```

Be sure to call the gnome-session command at the end of your $HOME/.xinitrc file so that gnome-session is the X session's controlling process and exiting GNOME therefore exits your X session.

Configuring GNOME

Although the default GNOME desktop is attractive and functional, after GNOME is running, the first thing many users want to do is edit the default desktop's appearance because too much has been made of GNOME's configurability.

As was the case with the KDE, nearly every item or applet on a GNOME desktop will present the user with a context-sensitive menu when a right-click event is detected. Often, this context-sensitive menu will contain one or several options related to the configuration of the object in question. For example, right-clicking on the GNOME panel brings up the context-sensitive menu shown in Figure 12.1.

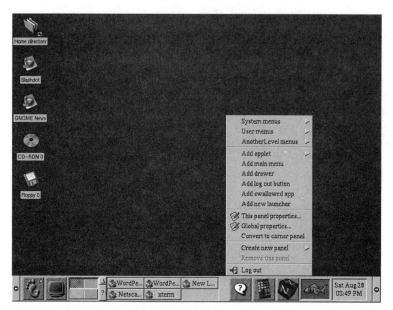

Figure 12.1 The GNOME panel's right-click menu.

In addition to the configuration that is accomplished this way, a great deal of configuration in GNOME (though not all of it, as was the case with KDE) can also be done from the GNOME Control Center, which is located in the Settings submenu of the foot menu.

Much like the KDE Control Center, the GNOME Control Center is split down the middle, with a tree view of option areas on the left and a dialog that presents configuration tabs on the right. Browsing through the tree by selecting either the plus (+) or minus (-) sign and clicking on one configuration area or another will cause a series of related configuration panes with tab tops to appear on the right side of the Control Center window, such as the Sound Events tab (see Figure 12.2).

There are far too many configuration options spread throughout the GNOME environment and even within the GNOME Control Center to document in a chapter like this one. Thanks to the user-friendly nature of the GNOME, however, most users will be able to explore and successfully configure many aspects of GNOME without any kind of formal instruction or reference.

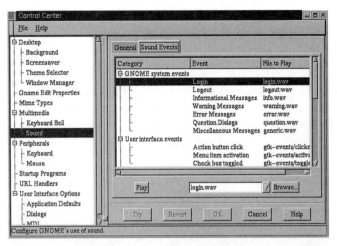

Figure 12.2 Configuring sound events using the GNOME Control Center.

Three Major Visible GNOME Components

GNOME is built from an even larger number of discrete components than is the KDE, and it shows in GNOME's looser integration and more flexible feel. However, there are still a few major components that stand out as important enough in the default visible GNOME composition that, without them, GNOME would be significantly altered in appearance or behavior from the perspective of the average desktop user.

These three components are as follows:

- The GNOME panel application. This is the focus of GNOME desktop activity and really the anchor of GNOME's environment from a user perspective.
- The GNU Midnight Commander, or gmc. The GNOME file manager is responsible for desktop icons, file drag-and-drop capability, and filesystem browsing.
- The Enlightenment window manager. Although hotly contested as a "real part" of GNOME, the Enlightenment window manager has nevertheless come to be associated with GNOME as the window manager of choice for GNOME users.

Enlightenment

The Enlightenment window manager predates GNOME by quite a long time, but it has since been adopted by GNOME in the eyes of many GNOME users and continues to be the window manager most used as a part of the standard GNOME desktop. Even on the GNOME compilation page mentioned earlier in the chapter, the user is directed to the Enlightenment manager as the manager of choice for GNOME.

Enlightenment's role in GNOME is the standard role played by any window manager: to draw decorations on windows and allow the user to interact with them. Enlightenment also features some amount of GNOME integration, of course, so that minimized windows can appear on the panel and then be restored once again by clicking on their panel icon.

One of the primary goals of Enlightenment at its inception and at every step along its development since that time is configurability with respect to appearance: Enlightenment is a chameleon, to say the least. The configuration in question is accomplished by building themes, which are collections of decorations and behaviors that are to be used when managing windows. The Clean theme, one of those included and often used with GNOME, is shown in Figure 12.3. The Brushed Metal theme, also included with Enlightenment, is shown in Figure 12.4 for contrast.

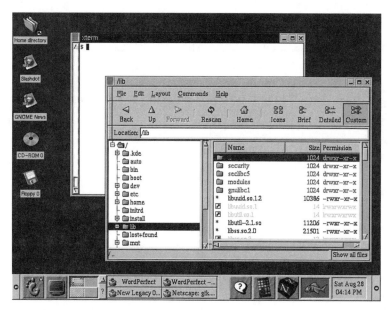

Figure 12.3   The Clean theme is a favorite with many more conservative GNOME users.

Because the function and position of the title bar decorations vary with each different Enlightenment theme, there is no way to document the use of Enlightenment decorations in print; it is simply necessary to try a given theme in order to see how Enlightenment works while the theme is active.

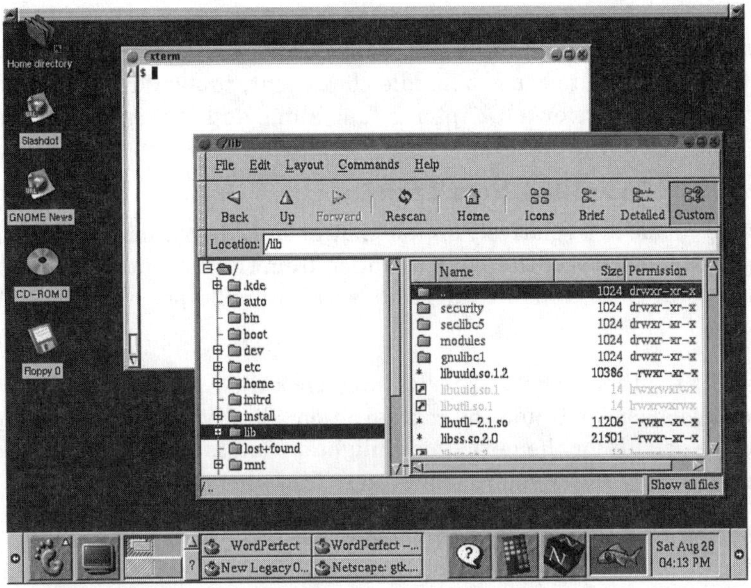

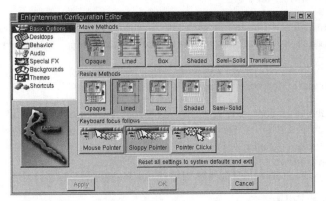

Figure 12.4   The Brushed Metal theme appeals to the more adventurous.

Enlightenment Tips and Tricks

Nearly all the tips we'll discuss are to be found in one way or another at the Enlightenment Configuration dialog, which, in a default GNOME installation, can be found by middle-clicking on the root window and selecting Configuration from the pop-up menu that appears. The Configuration Editor for Enlightenment version 0.15.5 appears (see Figure 12.5).

Figure 12.5   The Enlightenment Configuration Editor from the default GNOME installation.

If your mouse or pointing device doesn't have a middle button, you will normally be able to emulate one by clicking both the left and right mouse buttons simultaneously. If simultaneous left and right clicks don't seem to cause a middle-click event, you will need to edit your X server's configuration; please refer to Chapter 2, "Installing and Configuring XFree86."

Changing Themes or Installing New Themes

Changing the active theme is a relatively simple matter in Enlightenment; after the configuration editor has been started, select the Themes option from the list in the box in the upper-left of the window. A list of themes Enlightenment knows about will appear on the right-hand side of the window.

To try a theme, select the theme you'd like to try and click the Apply button. If you are satisfied with the new theme, click OK and the configuration editor will close, leaving your new theme active and the default for the next time Enlightenment is started. If you aren't satisfied with the new theme, simply select your old one again from the list and reapply it.

Installing new themes for Enlightenment can be a rewarding process because it can reduce eyestrain and improve your work throughput, or simply help you express yourself. Downloading and installing new themes for Enlightenment is thus a common pastime among GNOME-enabled Linux users, and because of this, the Themes.org Web site maintains a subsite just for Enlightenment themes at

```
http://e.themes.org
```

On this Web site, you can browse the list of available themes and download themes that interest you. Themes for current Enlightenment versions are usually just a single file. To install a theme after you've downloaded it, simply copy the theme file to the themes/ directory off the main Enlightenment installation tree.

For example, if you downloaded a theme with the filename eMac.theme and wanted to install it, and your Enlightenment window manager was installed at /opt/gnome/enlightenment, you would use the following command:

```
cp eMac.theme /opt/gnome/enlightenment/themes
```

After the theme file has been copied to the themes directory, restart both Enlightenment and the Enlightenment configuration editor so that the new theme can be selected and made active. Enlightenment can be restarted by middle-clicking on the root window and selecting Restart from the pop-up menu.

Changing the Focus Policy

The Enlightenment focus policy configuration can be found in the Enlightenment Configuration Editor in the first dialog option, Basic Options, on the left side of the window.

The Keyboard Focus Follows section of the Basic Options Configuration dialog determines the focus policy that will be used by Enlightenment in determining when window focus changes. Three focus policies are currently supported. They are shown in Table 12.2.

Table 12.2   Supported Enlightenment Focus Policies

Policy	Description
Mouse Pointer	The equivalent of the classic focus-follows-mouse focus policy from older X window managers. Focus will be given to whichever window currently contains the mouse pointer. If the mouse pointer is over the root window, no window has focus.
Sloppy Pointer	The equivalent of the sloppy-focus mode made popular by the fvwm family of window managers. Focus will be given to the window that currently contains the mouse pointer. If no window contains the mouse pointer, focus will go to the window that was the last to contain the mouse pointer.
Pointer Clicks	The equivalent of the click-to-focus mode that is standard in operating systems like Windows and Mac OS. A window must be explicitly given focus by clicking on its decorations or inside its borders.

More detailed focus options that might appeal to a few users can be found in the Advanced Focus tab of the Behavior Configuration dialog.

Turning Cloud-Shaped Tooltips Off

The large cloud-shaped tooltips that appear when the mouse button is left over an Enlightenment decoration can be switched off by unchecking the Tooltips ON/OFF item in the Miscellaneous tab of the Behavior dialog.

If you prefer to leave the tooltips enabled, but simply make them take longer to appear, leave the item checked and adjust the Delay slider next to the tooltips item.

Managing Virtual Desktops

Unlike in the KDE, where virtual desktop management is performed by the kpanel, in GNOME, responsibility for virtual desktops is left in a more traditional location: at the hands of the window manager. The number of virtual desktops that appear on the display and the number of virtual screens in each of the desktops can be configured in the Desktops dialog of the Enlightenment Configuration Editor.

The right side of the dialog, Separate Desktops, controls the number of complete virtual desktops that Enlightenment will maintain. The slider can be used to create as many as 32 or as few as a single virtual desktop.

The left side of the dialog, Size of Virtual Screen, controls the number of virtual screens that will compose each virtual desktop. The horizontal slider determines the number of virtual screen columns on any one virtual desktop. The vertical slider determines the number of virtual screen rows on any one virtual desktop. Only one virtual screen on one single desktop can be in use and visible on the display at any one time.

For those who prefer that moving the mouse pointer past the edge of the screen should not switch virtual desktops automatically, the Edge Flip Resistance item can be unchecked or the delay adjusted so that screen flips don't occur as readily when the mouse pointer is near the display's edge.

Changing Keyboard Shortcuts

The rather extensive Enlightenment Keyboard Shortcuts configuration system can be found by selecting the Shortcuts option in the Enlightenment Configuration Editor.

To create a new keyboard shortcut to some window manager function, click on the New button and then scroll down to the end of the List of Keyboard Shortcuts where you'll find an entry with the key EDIT ME listed. Select this line and click the Change button. You'll be asked to press a key; this key should be the key to which you want to assign a shortcut—for example, the F1 key. After you've supplied a key, choose a set of modifiers from the Modifier drop-down or NONE if this key is to apply when no modifiers are active. Finally select a window manager function from the Action to Perform list.

To edit an old keyboard shortcut, select the shortcut you'd like to modify. If you want to change the modifiers or the function associated with the shortcut, simply choose them from the Modifier drop-down or Action to Perform list, respectively. If you'd like to change the key assigned to the shortcut, click the Change button and supply a key for the shortcut.

To remove a keyboard shortcut, simply select the shortcut you'd like to remove from the List of Keyboard Shortcuts and then click the Delete button.

After you've finished editing your list of keyboard shortcuts, choose the OK button at the bottom of the configuration editor to activate your changes and make them permanent.

The Panel

The GNOME panel, known simply as panel, is similar in appearance and role to the kpanel used by the KDE desktop. The GNOME panel is used to provide a place for menus of various types to be anchored and for application launch icons to appear. The panel is also used in many cases to maintain a list of currently running tasks and to represent each with a button that can be clicked to bring the task to the top or to restore it if it has been minimized.

The GNOME panel also includes several prebuilt applets that perform various functions, some of them serious, some of them not.

Adding a Task List and Pager to the `Panel`

The default behavior in GNOME is to allow the window manager to handle window minimization separately from the `panel`. In many cases, however, it is desirable to have the `panel` maintain a task list similar to the one maintained by the `kpanel` taskbar. The same goes for virtual desktop management: It is often desirable to have the gnome `panel` maintain a visual pager rather than manage virtual desktops exclusively through the window manager.

Both of these functions are wrapped up into a single function in the case of the GNOME `panel` and are accomplished by adding an applet to the panel called the Gnome Pager.

The Gnome Pager can be added to a panel by right-clicking on the panel in question, and then selecting Add Applet, Utility, Gnome Pager.

When maintaining a large number of virtual screens per desktop or a large number of virtual desktops in total, the applet can sometimes become inconveniently large or misshapen. It can thus be helpful to configure the way in which the pager applet displays virtual desktops.

To configure the pager, right-click on the pager applet and select Properties from the pop-up menu that appears. In the Pager tab of the resulting dialog, you'll be able to configure the number of desktops that appear on each row as well as the width and height of each virtual desktop representation.

Adding Icons to a Panel

There are two ways to add icons to a GNOME panel, both of them equally valid. The first is to right-click on the panel to bring up a panel context menu. The second section from the top on any such menu contains several Add options to add menus or applets to the panel.

The second way to add an icon to the panel is to drag it and drop it onto the panel. Items can be dragged from the desktop, from GNOME menus, from the file manager, or from just about any other area of GNOME and added to the panel.

To remove added items from the panel, right-click the item that is to be removed, and select Remove from Panel on the context-sensitive pop-up menu that appears.

Panel Location and Causing the Panel to Autohide

The GNOME panel is larger than the KDE panel, and it can sometimes be obtrusive, especially when attempting to maximize non-GNOME-compliant applications. It is therefore very important to be able to autohide the GNOME panel.

To cause the panel to autohide, right-click on the panel and select This Panel Properties. In the resulting dialog, the Edge Panel tab will allow you to enable or disable several options, including an Auto Hide option.

This tab will also allow you to configure the location of the panel on the screen, at the left, right, bottom, or top edges.

Adding a Background Image to a Panel

You can apply a background image or color as the background texture for a panel. To select a background image or pixmap for a panel, right-click on the panel and select This Panel Properties. In the dialog that appears, select the second tab, Background.

Three background choices can be made: standard, which lets the background image for the panel be determined by the current appearance of the GNOME widget; pixmap, which will allow you to select an image and will then use it as wallpaper behind the panel; and color, which will allow you to select a color explicitly that will be used to display the background of the panel.

Adding Additional Panels

Unlike KDE, in which there is one kpanel and it alone acts as the user's interface to the desktop, GNOME allows for more than a single panel to appear on the display. To create a new panel, right-click on any panel and choose the Create New Panel submenu from the pop-up menu that appears.

A new Corner Panel will create a panel that resides in a specific corner of the screen and will grow as items are added to it. A new Edge Panel will create a panel like the initial panel that occupies an entire edge of the screen regardless of how many items it contains.

Most of the tips and tricks covered so far with respect to a single panel can be reperformed on a panel-by-panel basis; simply right-click on the panel in question and select options from that panel's context menu. The Global Properties item on any panel's context menu will attempt to apply changes to all panels in the session.

To remove a panel you've created and now don't want any longer, right-click on the panel and select Remove This Panel from the context menu that appears.

GNU Midnight Commander

GNU Midnight Commander, also known by its binary name, gmc, is the file manager used by GNOME to manage the desktop icons and the filesystem while in the GNOME environment. gmc doesn't support some of the more advanced features from the KDE file manager, kfm, such as Web browsing and a local HTML view, but gmc is nevertheless a functional and powerful file manager that is in some ways more user-friendly than kfm.

A typical GNU Midnight Commander window browsing a section of the filesystem is shown in Figure 12.6.

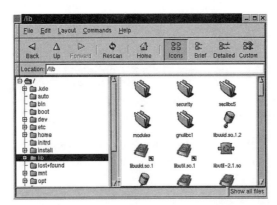

Figure 12.6   The GNU Midnight Commander window browsing a segment of the local filesystem.

The gmc view is split into two halves; on the left is a tree view of the filesystem in question. On the right is the current directory, whose representation is determined by the selected view on the icon bar near the top of the window.

Configuring the View

The views supported by gmc are easily visible in the icon bar near the top of any gmc window. Clicking on any of the listed views selects that view for the current directory shown on the right side of the gmc window. A description of each view can be found in Table 12.3.

Table 12.3   Views Supported by gmc

View	Description
Icons	This is the default view. It shows each file in the current directory using a rather large icon representing the file's type. The name of the file appears below its icon.
Brief	Shows only a mini-icon and a name for each file; the files are shown in a list format rather than on an imaginary grid as is the case for the Icons view.
Detailed	Shows files in a format similar to the format of the Brief view, but also shows a file size and last modification date for each file.
Custom	Shows files in a list format similar to the Detailed and Brief formats, but shows only information dictated by the user.

To configure the types of information that will be listed in a Custom view, select Preferences from the Edit menu at the top of the gmc window, and then select the Custom View tab in the dialog that appears. The list box on the right contains types of data that gmc is capable of displaying for each file. The list box on the left lists the data that actually will be displayed in the custom view. To add data to the custom view, select an item from the list on the left and click the Add button in the middle of the window. To remove data from the custom view, select an item from the list on the right and click the Remove button in the middle of the window.

When you're finished editing the files that are to appear in the custom view, click the OK button at the bottom of the window and the active custom view will be updated to reflect your changes.

Showing Only Certain Files

Using gmc, it is possible to show only certain types of files in any directory that is being browsed. This is called *filtering* the current view.

To filter a viewed directory, select Filter View from the Layout menu at the top of the window. In the dialog box that appears, enter a regular expression that matches the names of the files you'd like to appear in the gmc window.

Adding URL Links to the Desktop

Even though gmc doesn't internally support HTML browsing capability, it is still rather easy to cause gmc to launch a Netscape browser to view URLs you supply when clicking an icon.

To create a new desktop URL icon and assign it a URL, follow these steps. First, right-click on the desktop and select New, URL Link. In the dialog box that appears, enter the URL you'd like to be linked to the icon you're about to create. A new icon will appear that, when double-clicked, will lead you to the URL you entered.

The initial caption of the icon will be the URL you entered, but you can change the caption by clicking on the icon, waiting for several seconds, and then clicking on the caption and entering the new text.

General GNOME Tips and Tricks

GNOME is a large environment without clear beginning or ending points; it would probably be impossible to write a comprehensive GNOME manual at all. Understanding that the only way to really learn about using GNOME is to try it, here are a few more general hints and tips to help you along your way.

Changing Gtk+ Themes

Along with the capability to choose themes for the Enlightenment window manager, GNOME also provides the capability to choose themes for its core widget set, thanks to the theme engine built into the Gtk+ API upon which the GNOME API is layered. When an alternate Gtk+ theme is selected, all gnome widgets will change in appearance, from scrollbars to buttons to text entry boxes.

Several Gtk+ themes are included in the default GNOME desktop; they can be found in the GNOME Control Center in the Desktop subtree, under the Theme Selector option. The theme selector is shown in Figure 12.7.

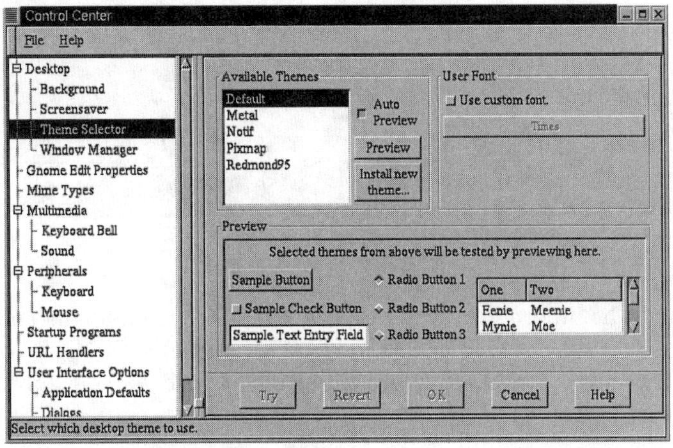

Figure 12.7   The GNOME Gtk+ theme selector in the GNOME Control Center.

Selecting an alternative theme and applying it causes the appearance of all widgets to change. This can be seen in Figure 12.8, in which the Metal theme has been selected and applied.

The included list of themes is minimal and most users will probably want more, especially when so many themes are available for the Enlightenment window manager. Luckily, the Themes.org Web site also maintains a site dedicated to themes for Gtk+ at

```
http://gtk.themes.org
```

To install a Gtk+ theme you've downloaded, you'll usually need to extract it using the tar command:

```
tar -xzvf gtk-theme.tar.gz
```

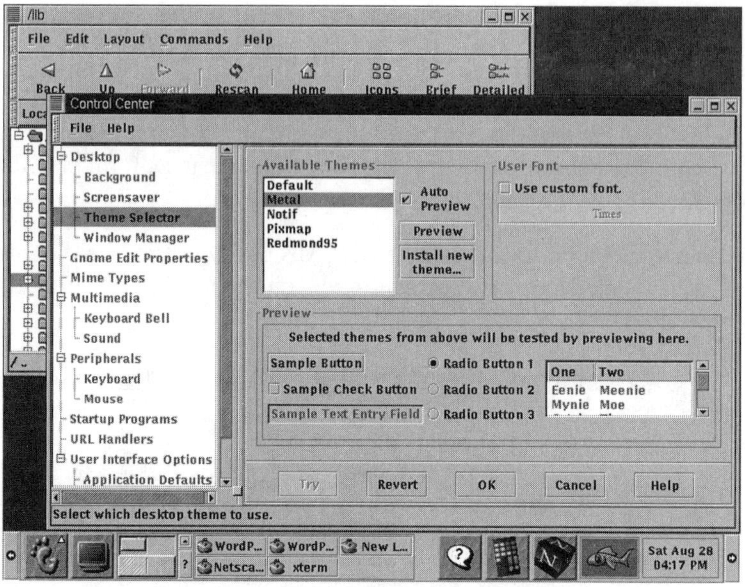

Figure 12.8 The default Gtk+ theme replaced by the Metal theme.

Extracting the archive should produce two files, one ending in `.la` and one ending in `.so`. Copy them both to the `lib/gtk/themes/engines/` directory off the global GNOME directory tree. Restart the GNOME Control Center, and you will be able to use your new theme to radically alter the appearance of GNOME's widgets.

Using a Different Window Manager

As was the case with KDE, several different window managers have now begun to implement some measure of GNOME awareness, enough to be used in conjunction with the GNOME desktop at some level of comfort. Enlightenment is one such manager—perhaps the most popular among GNOME users—but there are others.

IceWM is a window manager whose original goals were to emulate several different alternative computing environments very closely. For example, IceWM includes modes for the OS/2 Workplace Shell and the Windows 95 Explorer. IceWM is probably the second most popular window manager among GNOME users. IceWM can be found on the Internet at

```
http://www.kiss.uni lj.si/~k4fr0235/icewm/
```

The Fvwm2GNOME project at `http://fvwm2gnome.fluid.cx/` maintains a version of the fvwm2 window manager discussed in Chapter 9, "Runtime Environment Configuration," which is GNOME-aware and can be used seamlessly in the GNOME environment. Users who are very familiar with or accustomed to the fvwm2 window manager might prefer to use Fvwm2GNOME rather than Enlightenment as their default window manager.

After an alternative window manager has been installed that is GNOME-compliant, it can be activated in the GNOME Control Center by selecting Settings, GNOME Control Center from the foot menu on the main panel. In the dialog that appears, expand the Desktop tree if necessary and then click on the Window Manager option. A list of GNOME-aware window managers will appear; choose a manager from the list, click OK, and restart GNOME for the new manager to take effect.

Managing Desktop Backgrounds in GNOME+Enlightenment

Many GNOME users have probably noticed that the desktop background options in the GNOME Control Center don't always work, or don't even seem to work at all. Just why this is so isn't immediately clear.

The reason for this behavior is that the Enlightenment window manager also maintains a background image of its own, one that takes precedence over the GNOME background image. That is to say that if you have selected a background image in the Enlightenment Configuration Editor, any background selections you make in the GNOME Control Center won't have any effect while Enlightenment is still running.

To fix this problem, start the Enlightenment Configuration Editor by middle-clicking on the root window and selecting Configuration from the pop-up menu that appears. At the left side of the Enlightenment Configuration Editor, select the Backgrounds option from the column on the left, and then click the No Background button for the desktop in question in the dialog on the right. The representation of the desktop will turn black—meaning that any backgrounds you now specify in the GNOME Control Center will actually appear.

Adding Icons, Wallpaper, or Sounds to GNOME

In several dialogs and option boxes in GNOME, the user is asked to select an icon or a wallpaper image for the purpose at hand. Although a Browse button exists for finding such files around the local filesystem, it is sometimes more convenient to simply add them to the default list of files.

GNOME maintains its global files in a single directory tree. The default source installation places GNOME files in `/usr/local`, but you should check your GNOME binary packages to find the location of your GNOME tree. After you know where your GNOME tree is located, you can globally add icons and wallpaper images as root.

The share/pixmaps directory off the main GNOME directory contains icons that will be available to the user when he or she is asked in a dialog to select an icon. The GNOME icons can be supplied in any format supported by the Imlib library installed on the local machine, which usually means at least support for .xpm, .gif, .jpg, .tiff, and .png files, though this might not always be the case. To add wallpaper images for the desktop background to the GNOME Control Center, simply browse to their location on the local disk and choose them. Afterward, they will appear in the drop-down list of available wallpaper images whenever the dialog is presented.

Sound files in the .wav format can be added to the GNOME global environment as well by copying such files to the share/sounds directory tree off the main GNOME installation directory tree.

Editing GNOME Menus

The foot menu and its submenus are generally well-built and contain all the GNOME applications that have been installed on the system, as well as some of the more common X applications GNOME was able to find when it was installed. Still, there are definitely times when it is helpful to be able to insert items into the menu structure for your own use.

The global foot menu is the same for all users and is stored in the GNOME installation directory tree; it can thus be edited only when the desktop session is owned by the superuser. However, the section of the default foot menu that reads user menus can be edited by each user to suit his or her own needs.

To edit any part of the menu structure, global or in a single-user context, start the GNOME menu editor by selecting Settings, Menu Editor from the foot menu (see Figure 12.9).

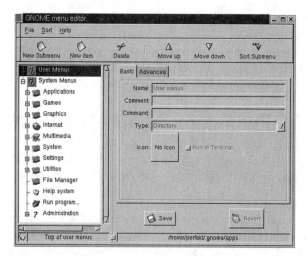

Figure 12.9   The GNOME menu editor.

On the left side of the GNOME menu editor is a tree view of the menu structure, listing user menus first and global menus next. If the active desktop session isn't a root login, the global tree will be browsable, and you'll be able to drag applications from it to the user menus, but you won't be able to edit the global part of the tree.

On the other hand, the local user menu part of the tree is always editable and you are free to insert any commands or menu entries you like into them. To add items from the global menus to the user menus, dragging sometimes works, but unfortunately, it sometimes doesn't, depending on whether or not a buggy version of the menu editor is in use.

In any case, new menus in the User Menus section can always be added by selecting New Submenu from the File menu at the top of the menu editor window and entering the relevant data into the dialog on the right. Similarly, new items can always be added to user submenus by selecting New Item from the File menu at the top of the menu editor window and entering the relevant command and label into the dialog on the right.

When you're ready to save the changes you've made to the GNOME menu structure, simply click the Save button at the bottom of the menu editor dialog.

Learning More About GNOME

There are more clever tricks and undocumented hooks to GNOME than anyone could ever document in a chapter like this, and we haven't even covered basic operation and gnome applications at all. For more manual-style information on using and configuring GNOME, see the GNOME Users Guide Project on the World Wide Web at

```
http://www.gnome.org/users guide/project.shtml
```

The GNOME Users Guide Project makes most existing GNOME documentation available online in several different languages and electronic formats.

## 13

KDE/GNOME/X Issues and Other Linux Environments

It isn't always easy to understand the way in which GNOME and KDE fit in with the rest of the X Window System and the more traditional components of XFree86. It is important to be able to use existing X applications with GNOME and KDE without having to modify or recompile them. Furthermore, GNOME and KDE might not be for everybody—they both have serious resource use issues for some users, and they simply won't run on older distributions.

It is important for users in this situation to have alternatives to the GNOME and KDE desktops.

KDE/GNOME, XFree86, and Other X Software

Using KDE or GNOME with XFree86 is, generally speaking, a smooth sailing sort of a proposition. Most users will have few problems integrating KDE or GNOME in with their normal X use patterns, especially if their Linux distribution shipped with KDE or GNOME as the default desktop. However, there are some caveats of which users must be aware in order to maximize their Linux and XFree86 experiences.

Resource Availability

It is widely known that both KDE and GNOME consume large amounts of system resources, from hard disk storage space to memory and swap space. What isn't widely understood, however, is that many of these resource requirements stem from using KDE and GNOME in addition to other X applications.

Recompiling to Update Shared Library Dependencies

The common by-hand installation of KDE or GNOME, especially when compiled from source, tends to lead to a system with many duplicate libraries. For example, GNOME 1.0 requires late versions of the Gtk+ library, whereas many earlier Linux distributions shipped with a GIMP 1.0 application that requires the much earlier Gtk 1.0 library. In such installations, running GIMP inside GNOME means loading two separate versions of the Gtk library and two separate versions of the Glib library, in addition to the environment itself and the program binary.

The solution to this problem is to attempt to make library dependencies match whenever possible. If you were skilled enough to compile GNOME on your own, consider uninstalling your older GIMP installation and recompiling it to use the newer Gtk+ and Glib libraries installed by GNOME, especially if you find yourself short on resources or wanting maximum speed and efficiency from the resources you install. A quick search through the /usr/X11R6/bin directory tree with the ldd command usually reveals several applications that depend on older versions of Gtk, Glib, Qt, or graphics libraries that have been updated by KDE or GNOME. Recompiling these applications from source to use the newer libraries can mean megabytes of savings at runtime.

Choosing Applications from the Environment

Even without recompiling, it is possible to realize some efficiency gains just by observing which shared libraries are in use and attempting to choose applications that don't load additional shared libraries or library code.

For example, the Netscape browser remains a perennial favorite among Linux users but is rather large and cumbersome in terms of memory requirements. In most cases, the kfm file manager will render Web pages correctly and more than adequately for general-purpose use. Using kfm from within the KDE desktop to browse Web pages incurs minimal memory penalties, whereas loading Netscape incurs substantial penalties of this kind. Similarly, GNOME's own spreadsheet, gnumeric, uses the shared GNOME libraries, avoiding the need to load lots of additional library code when compared to spreadsheets that are based on other APIs, such as Wingz.

Even smaller applications can have significant resource impacts when several of them are considered together. Instead of using XFMail, consider using Balsa if you are a GNOME user or KMail if you are a KDE user. Instead of Emacs, try to get by with kedit or gedit for simple editing tasks. The goal is to use tools from the environment whenever possible, avoiding the need to fill system memory with code from other shared libraries just to run a single application.

GNOME and KDE Applications Outside GNOME or KDE

There exists a common misconception among Linux users that after an application is written using the KDE or GNOME APIs, the users of the application are locked in to the environment in question if the application is needed.

This isn't actually the case; it isn't necessary to actually use the entire GNOME environment if you only want to use the gnumeric spreadsheet—it is merely necessary that the necessary GNOME shared libraries be available to the dynamic linker and that the gnumeric binary be installed somewhere in your binary search path. In short, it is only necessary that certain parts of GNOME be installed in order for you to use GNOME. Once installed, it is perfectly legal to call an application from GNOME or KDE from within a normal X session managed by a simple window manager of one kind or another.

That said, there are some things to understand. First, applications that require a high degree of integration with the environment might not function correctly. For example, items that dock into the KDE's kpanel will have nowhere to dock when the kpanel is absent and will thus simply show up as windows on the display. In rare cases, an application might not work if it requires significant amounts of interaction with its own environment. In most cases, however, applications from GNOME or KDE will run without serious problems on desktops where the entire environment isn't running.

The next thing to understand about running KDE and GNOME environments outside KDE or GNOME is that many of the same resource and performance penalties will still apply even if you are running only a single application from the environment in question. This is because many of the resource requirements of these environments are due to large numbers of shared libraries that must be loaded at runtime. Whether you are running the entire environment or just one application from a larger environment, the libraries must still be loaded. In a sense, even if, for example, you are running only a single KDE application, a large part of the entire KDE environment will still be used in memory while the application executes.

Appearance and X Resources

Those who do choose to run non-KDE or non-GNOME applications while in the KDE or GNOME environment will soon discover that the KDE or GNOME appearance, behavior, and style hints won't normally affect non-KDE or non-GNOME applications. That is to say that when you change the current Theme in the GNOME Control Center, you will find that while all of your running GNOME applications update themselves to reflect the new appearance you've selected, non-GNOME applications like Netscape will remain unchanged in their appearance.

Thus, running nonenvironment applications while in an integrated environment can have the effect of nullifying one of the benefits of the integrated environment: the unification (defragmentation) of the desktop and its appearance and use.

That said, it should be noted that the KDE 1.1 and later releases have the capability to make certain applications (those based on the Xt intrinsics, Athena widgets, or Motif API) appear to obey KDE style and appearance hints. Such changes are superficial, however, and are accomplished by setting X resources in much the same way that we were able to do using the `editres` command in Chapter 8, "Runtime Application Configuration." The widgets in such applications will still not behave as the KDE widgets do, and some changes to KDE styles, such as selecting whether applications emulate the Windows appearance or the Motif appearance, will have no effect on non-KDE applications at all. Furthermore, KDE won't always get the resource settings right, leaving some applications with strange, even broken appearances.

The only way to truly unify a desktop in Linux is to choose an integrated environment and then try whenever possible to use the applications that are based on the chosen environment's API.

KDE and GNOME Together

Because KDE and GNOME are two separate environments with separate APIs and separate applications, it is common to wonder whether KDE and GNOME can be integrated together with each other with any degree of sincerity. This is an important question because it speaks to the heart of future Linux growth prospects, as more and more applications will be written for one or the other environment.

The bad news is that, at this point, no real interoperability of any kind exists between KDE and GNOME; drag-and-drop operations between `gmc` and `kfm`, for example, won't work. Objects from KDE applications cannot be embedded into GNOME windows and vice versa. At the moment, it is generally necessary to choose one or the other for a fully integrated desktop.

The good news is that projects are underway as this text is being written to allow KDE and GNOME to cooperate better. A common drag-and-drop protocol is a major goal, and there is a great deal of talk about making the KDE and GNOME object request models compatible so that application integration between the two environments will be complete.

For the moment, as the preceding paragraphs intimated, it is possible to install both sets of libraries and both environments on the same system but in different directory trees, should the user find it necessary to run specific applications from both environments. Understand, however, that only one environment can be running at a time (though applications from both environments can run simultaneously), and that applications from disparate environments will at this point enjoy little integration with each other. Understand also that running both KDE and GNOME applications simultaneously is really the same as begging your computer to grind to a screeching halt—definitely consider installing at least 128 megabytes of memory if you plan to run one or the other environment and to use applications from both.

Environments for Special Situations

Although KDE and GNOME are the most popular integrated environments for Linux today and are generally considered to be the wave of the future as far as Linux and the growth of Linux are concerned, KDE and GNOME don't always fit the requirements of every situation or need. In such cases, two other integrated environments are currently available to Linux users that might better fulfill certain criteria.

OpenWindows (XView)

The Sun Microsystems OpenWindows environment was one of the first integrated environments available for the X Window System. Though no longer maintained or installed with most new systems today, OpenWindows retains a large amount of utility and requires significantly fewer resources to operate than do large, modern environments like KDE and GNOME. OpenWindows has an appealing, three-dimensional appearance in full color and a large number of older applications are available to those wanting to use OpenWindows on a regular basis. A typical OpenWindows desktop is shown in Figure 13.1.

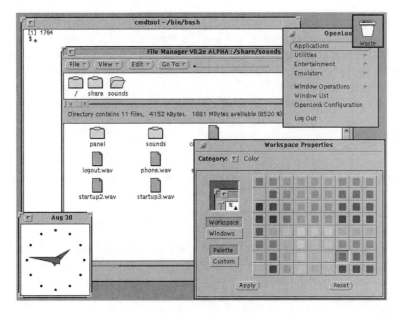

Figure 13.1   The OpenWindows desktop, known as XView in the Linux world, is resource-friendly, has many applications, and sports a pleasing three-dimensional appearance.

Getting XView

Luckily, Sun Microsystems released the OpenWindows code toward the end of its life cycle as a free software, source-code-available product called XView, which was actually included with many early Linux distributions as an integrated environment option. Many Linux users will find that they already have some or all components of the OpenWindows/XView desktop installed at the /usr/openwin tree. Others will find packages on their CD-ROM by searching the package directory like this:

```
ls *view*
```

For those without an existing /usr/openwin tree or any XView packages on their Linux CD-ROM, the XView environment and several related applications can be downloaded from the following sites:

- http://metalab.unc.edu/pub/Linux/X11/libs/xview/
- http://metalab.unc.edu/pub/X11/Openlook/
- http://step.polymtl.ca/~coyote/xview_main.html

All the files provided at these sites are provided as source code only, with the exception of one or two application binaries. In general, if you want a complete XView environment for your Linux box these days, you must compile it yourself. Beware: These sources predate the existence of GNU tools that made compilations easy; compiling XView from source is a job best tackled by those who have previous UNIX programming or compiling experience. Always take time to read any README or similar files included with each source distribution.

Starting XView

The easiest way to launch the OpenWindows/XView environment is to run the following command from a console login, taking care to ensure that the /usr/openwin/bin directory is in your path:

```
openwin
```

This command, which is similar in concept to the startx command discussed in earlier chapters, starts the X server at the default color depth and resolution. The command then starts several XView clients, including one of the XView window managers, olwm (for a standard desktop) or olvwm (for virtual desktop capability).

Those who don't want to use the openwin command to launch XView can generally get by using the traditional startx command in conjunction with the $HOME/.xinitrc script—simply insert a call to either olwm or olvwm at the end of your script so that the XView window manager is the controlling process for the session.

Once inside XView, the best way to maintain desktop integration is simply to use XView binaries in place of X binaries—cmdtool instead of xterm, textedit instead of xedit, and so on. A list of available binaries can be found by browsing the /usr/openwin/bin directory, which by convention contains all the binaries for the XView environment.

Configuring XView

A complete detail on configuring the XView environment is beyond the scope of this text and has a lot to do with configuring the related window manager. For details, see the manual pages for olwm or olvwm. To configure the appearance of the XView desktop along with one or two aspects of keyboard, mouse, and widget behavior, however, another tool applies.

The configuration tool, known as props, is usually called from the root menu (which can be displayed by right-clicking over the root window). An option labeled Configure or Properties is generally present in the default configuration and launches the configuration application. In the absence of such an option, however, props can be called by hand:

```
/usr/openwin/bin/props
```

Note that the absolute path can be omitted if the /usr/openwin/bin directory is in your binary search path.

More Information About XView

Unfortunately, precious little printed information is available for the XView environment anymore, largely because most XView texts went out of print shortly after Sun Microsystems decided to halt development on the XView environment. There might still be one or two XView use and programming texts out there, however, especially at college and university libraries where UNIX workstations have been used over the years.

The best approximation of online XView documentation is the OpenLook FAQ, available at either of the following links:

```
ftp://ftp.math.psu.edu/pub/FAQ/
```

```
http://step.polymtl.ca/~coyote/open-look/index.html
```

Regrettably, the XView source code is becoming outdated, and the amount of available documentation is becoming smaller and smaller. XView is thus best used only by those who need a small, memory-friendly integrated environment with very basic development capability, who don't have any need for access to current software or newer software development technologies.

The Common Desktop Environment (CDE)

The Common Desktop Environment, which is based on the Motif API used by popular Linux applications such as Netscape and WordPerfect, is the only commercial offering for those seeking an integrated Linux environment. Maintained by The Open Group at http://www.opengroup.org, the CDE is a specification originally designed and adopted cooperatively by several major UNIX vendors including Digital, Hewlett-Packard, and Sun Microsystems. Because of this, many commercial UNIX workstations use the CDE as their standard desktop environment.

Unfortunately for Linux users, no free version of the CDE exists; those wanting to use the Common Desktop Environment will have to purchase it. To make matters worse, there is currently only one vendor producing a CDE for Linux, though in the past as many as three separate vendors produced CDE versions for Linux. As a result, pricing has become significantly higher and is out of reach for many Linux users.

The MaXimum/CDE from Xi Graphics is currently the only version of CDE available for Linux and is sold directly by Xi Graphics, whose Web site can be found at

    http://www.xig.com

The CDE is available as a standalone product or as a product integrated with a complete Linux operating system called MaXimum CDE/OS, and ships with the commercial Accelerated-X server, also by Xi Graphics, which replaces XFree86. Laptop versions are also available.

The CDE is a large environment, and a great deal of documentation is available to help those wanting to use the CDE or to develop for it. Because most XFree86 users won't be using the CDE, any discussion of use or configuration is beyond the scope of this text; users interested in the CDE should contact Xi Graphics directly at its Web site.

MULTIUSER AND NETWORKED X

14

DISPLAY MANAGERS

In earlier chapters, the only way to start XFree86 that I've discussed is with the `startx` command from a command shell in a text console. This method for starting XFree86 works fine for a single user to some degree, but there are some deficiencies. Even if a user wants to use only X, he or she must always pass through a character-mode login and issue at least one character-mode command, `startx`. There is no facility for allowing the user or the environment to alter the way in which the session will behave other than to edit the `xinitrc` scripts by hand. Finally, the `startx` command provides no elegant way to start and manage X sessions over a network—only on a local display.

What Is a Display Manager For?

On a practical level, a display manager is a program that is designed to manage authentication and X sessions across several physical displays, as well as over a network if necessary. A display manager is a way to enable users at any X-capable display to log in to a given system on the network with account and password information and start an X session on that system, even if it is displayed remotely. This graphical login replaces a character mode login and eliminates the need to issue a `startx` command on a local display as well. In short, a display manager allows a single-user Linux system to boot into X and a networked Linux system in a multiuser environment to serve X sessions across the network.

On a more technical level, display managers run as a daemon in the background, listening to port 177 for incoming connections, waiting for X Display Manager Control Protocol requests (which you'll cover in Chapter 15, "Working on the Network") that are generated by an X server elsewhere on the network. When such a request is received, indicating that an X server is running on the machine from which the request originated, the display manager presents a graphical login and password prompt and, if a user authenticates him- or herself, starts an X session that displays on the remote machine where the user is, but executes on the local machine where the display manager is running.

The X Display Manager (xdm)

The X Display Manager is a basic solution for users needing display manager functionality. Because it comes as a part of XFree86, no additional software is required to use it. The binary, xdm, should normally be located in your /usr/X11R6/bin binaries directory; if it is absent, you probably need to check your installation to make sure that the xdm package is installed.

Basic Configuration

Before using the display manager, it is necessary to ensure that it is properly configured. The configuration files for the xdm binary included with XFree86 are found in the lib/X11/xdm/ sub-tree off the main /usr/X11R6 installation tree. The following sections detail the files commonly found there and the role of each file in xdm configuration.

For the sake of descriptive clarity, please consult the matching files installed in your xdm/ directory when reading the following sections.

xdm-config

This is the master configuration file for the xdm program; it doesn't usually require user modification, and we will assume for the rest of the chapter that no changes are made to the file, but it might at some point be necessary for you to alter it. The file contains several resources for the display manager that dictate where the display manager will look for further configuration information. Table 14.1 shows the resources and their purposes.

Table 14.1 Resources Listed in xdm-config

Resource	Description
errorLogFile	Specifies the file to which errors will be output as they occur in the xdm runtime.
pidFile	Specifies the name of the file that will contain the process ID of the running xdm daemon.

Resource	Description
servers	The name of the file that will be used to start local X servers at launch time.
accessFile	Specifies the file that will control access to the local system from remote displays requesting XDMCP connections.
authorize	Whether to require authorization for communications to the given host. Should always be set to true, unless authorization isn't supported by the host.
setup	The script to run before displaying the graphical login prompt on the running X server. Often used to display a company logo or pop up a console window.
startup	The script that is run (with root privileges) after a user logs in but before the session is started. Normally used for utilitarian purposes and administration tasks associated with logging in.
reset	The script that is run (with root privileges) after a user logs out and the session ends.
resources	Files where further display manager resources will be configured.
session	Scripts that actually start the user session, run with the user's privileges and group identification.

For any changes made to the xdm-config file to take effect, a running xdm daemon must be killed and a new one started.

Xservers

This is normally the name of the file given by the servers resource in the xdm-config file. Lines that begin with the hash (#) character are comments and are ignored. For most Linux users, this file should contain one noncomment line that starts an X server on the local display when xdm is started. If there is to be no server on the local display, there should be no noncomment lines in the file.

Each noncomment line in the file follows this format:

```
host:display local¦foreign servercmd -args
```

The first column in the line specifies the name of the display that this command will start. The second column can be either local, for a local display, or foreign, for a remote display that doesn't support XDMCP, making explicit instructions to xdm necessary. The remaining data is used as a command to start an X server, if applicable, and any arguments are passed to the command. The default file contains this line, which will be adequate for most users:

```
:0 local /usr/X11R6/bin/X
```

If the local server is to be started in a depth other than the default depth given in the XF86Config file, the -bpp argument can be supplied:

```
:0 local /usr/X11R6/bin/X -bpp 32
```

Entries containing the word foreign in the second column typically are needed only for older X terminal hardware that doesn't support XDMCP.

Note that, because current versions of XFree86 don't support multihead operation, and because most users' networks no longer use XDMCP-incompatible X terminals (or X terminals at all), having more than one noncomment line in this file is rarely necessary.

Xaccess

This file is used to restrict or enable XDMCP requests from remote hosts. In its simplest form, the file is simply a list host or fully qualified domain names, wildcard characters permitted, to which XDMCP service will be denied (if preceded by an exclamation mark) or allowed (if not preceded by an exclamation mark). The NOBROADCAST flag, when listed after a host or set of hosts, specifies that it (they) will be allowed only direct access to XDMCP rather than responding to broadcast queries, which can result in the xdm server appearing on automatically generated session selection menus. For example, consider the following entries:

```
*.starcastle.com NOBROADCAST
*.wavy.hair.net NOBROADCAST
!jackson.wavy.hair.net
!public.wavy.hair.net
x.login.hair.net
```

The preceding lines will allow direct queries from all systems that are in the starcastle.com domain and that match the wavy.hair.net domain, but won't allow broadcast queries from these systems. The systems jackson.wavy.hair.net and public.wavy.hair.net will be denied access altogether, and xdm will respond favorably to both broadcast and direct queries from x.login.hair.net.

For more details on querying xdm sessions directly across the network from one host to another, please see Chapter 15. For details on configuring the chooser in the Xaccess file, which I don't cover in this text, please see the xdm manual page.

Xsetup_0

Although in theory multiple Xsetup files can be present in an XFree86 installation, most users are likely to find or use the Xsetup_0 file only in the xdm/ directory.

This file is a script not unlike the familiar xinitrc scripts; it is run after the server is started and usually contains calls to X Window System binaries and clients that are to be started on the local display after the server is running. There are two important differences between this script and the xinitrc scripts, however: This script is run with root privileges, and it is run before any user logs in. In fact, it is run before the login and password prompts are even displayed.

The file often contains a call to xconsole, causing a console window to be displayed on the xdm login screen, but this line can be removed or the file can be augmented with additional calls to X utilities. One common addition is an xsetroot call to set up the root display before the login prompt is displayed:

```
/usr/X11R6/bin/xsetroot -solid slategrey
```

Perhaps you'd like a clock to be displayed on the authentication screen, in the lower-right corner of the display:

```
/usr/X11R6/bin/xclock -geometry 75x75-1-1 &
```

Note that any clients started in the script will be unmovable and unresizable because no window manager has been started yet in most cases. It is therefore necessary to provide geometry specifications for any clients that are started here. Take care also to avoid security risks and understand what you are doing; remember that any clients started here will be started with root privileges—potentially risky as well as annoying to the user if he or she cannot remove a client after the session has started.

Xresources

This file is used to configure the remaining resources for the display manager and its widgets. Most commonly, the resources in this file are used to configure the behavior and appearance of the xlogin widget, which presents the user with a graphical login and password prompt, as shown in Figure 14.1.

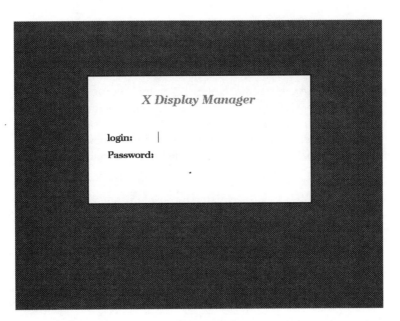

Figure 14.1 The xlogin widget presents the user with a graphical login and password prompt.

The xlogin widget's appearance is fairly configurable, and some of the more common resources associated with xlogin can be found in Table 14.2.

Table 14.2 Common Appearance-Oriented xlogin Resources

Resource	Description
Login.width	The width, in pixels, of the login widget.
Login.height	The height, in pixels, of the login widget.
Login.foreground	The foreground color used to display user-entered text.
Login.font	The font used to display user-entered text.
Login.greeting	The greeting or banner text that appears at the top of the login widget.
Login.greetFont	The font used to display the greeting.
Login.greetColor	The color used to display the greeting.
Login.namePrompt	The text used to prompt for a username (account) for logging in.
Login.passwdPrompt	The text used to prompt for a password.
Login.promptFont	The font used to display the name prompt and password prompt.
Login.promptColor	The color used to display the name prompt and password prompt text.
Login.fail	The text that is displayed when authentication fails.

Resource	Description
Login.failFont	The font used in displaying authentication failure text.
Login.failColor	The color in which authentication failure text will be displayed.
Login.failTimeout	The period of time during which the authentication failure message will appear.

The resources shown in Table 14.2 all have to do with the appearance of the login widget. It is important to discuss one more resource that will affect the behavior of the login widget. The resource in question is Login.translations and is a translation resource, a type of resource I haven't discussed in this text, largely because they apply only to more complex X toolkit applications that Linux users don't often use. In the case of xdm, however, editing translations can be helpful.

Without going into too much detail, the format for modifying or adding to the translation resource is roughly as follows:

```
xlogin*Login.translations: #override \
                    mod<Key>key: action(argument) \n\
                    mod<Key>key: action(argument) \n\
                    mod<Key>key: action(argument)
```

The first line in the resource, #override, causes new key bindings to be added to the existing ones in xdm. The remaining lines each bind a keystroke or set of keystrokes to one of a number of predefined actions. In each line, mod is one of Ctrl, Shift, Meta (for Alt), or is omitted, representing each of the common keyboard modifier states; key is a key symbol, minus the XK_ prefix, from the include/X11/keysymdef.h file off the main X11R6 tree; action is one of a predefined set of actions supported by the xlogin widget; argument is an argument for the action or is omitted if no argumentation is supported. To illustrate, consider the following resource:

```
xlogin*Login.translations: #override \
            Ctrl<Key>BackSpace: erase-line() \n\
            Ctrl<Key>F1: set-session-argument(normal) \n\
            Ctrl<Key>F2: set-session-argument(astep) \n\
            Ctrl<Key>F3: set-session-argument(wmaker) \n\
            Ctrl<Key>F4: set-session-argument(kde) \n\
            Meta<Key>Escape: abort-session
```

In this example, you add a few keystrokes to those that xlogin knows about. First, the Ctrl+Backspace keystroke will now call the erase-line() action, which will delete the entire line of text entered so far. Control+F1, Control+F2, and Control+F3 now all call the set-session-argument() action, which affects the arguments to the Xsession script you'll learn in the next section. Finally, the Alt+Esc keystroke aborts the entire session and restarts the X server.

Some of the commonly modified or added actions supported by the xlogin widget are shown in Table 14.3.

Table 14.3 Actions Supported by the xlogin Widget

Action	Description
move-to-begining()	Move to the beginning of the current text entry box. Note that beginning must be spelled incorrectly.
move-to-end()	Move to the end of the current text entry box.
erase-to-end-of-line()	Erase all text after the cursor.
erase-line()	Erase all text in the entry box.
finish-field()	Move the cursor to the other text entry box.
abort-session()	Kill the X server and restart it.
set-session-argument(arg)	Cause xdm to call the Xsession script (see next session) with arg as an argument.

Most of the time, the default entry-oriented translations are adequate and users won't need to change them. It can, however, be common to use the set-session-argument() action to pass arguments to the Xsession script and thereby allow the user to launch different types of X sessions.

Xsession

This is the script that is called after authentication is complete to start the X session for the user. In a logical sense, the Xsession script replaces the xinitrc script as the primary method for configuring a session and starting clients.

The script typically checks to see whether there is an executable file at $HOME/.xsession and if there is, executes that script instead. If there is no $HOME/.xsession file, the systemwide Xsession script will continue; it is therefore common to see several clients and a window manager started at the end of the Xsession script.

Of particular interest is the fact that the xlogin widget can be made to pass an argument to Xsession when it is called. For example, recall the three translations from the example in the previous section:

```
Ctrl<Key>F1: set-session-argument(normal) \n\
Ctrl<Key>F2: set-session-argument(astep) \n\
Ctrl<Key>F3: set-session-argument(wmaker) \n\
Ctrl<Key>F4: set-session-argument(kde) \n\
```

If, while logging in, the user issues a Control+F1 keystroke and then finishes authenticating, the Xsession script will be called with the word normal as an argument. If the user issues a Control+F2 keystroke and then finishes authenticating, the Xsession script will be called with the word astep as an argument, and so on. Now, consider the simple Xsession script in Listing 14.1.

Listing 14.1   Sample Xsession Script

```
#!/bin/sh

case $1 in
   normal)
      xterm -geometry 80x24+1+1 &
      xclock -geometry 75x75-1-1 &
      exec twm
      ;;
   astep)
      exec afterstep
      ;;
   wmaker)
      exec wmaker
      ;;
   kde)
      exec startkde
esac

if [ -f $HOME/.xsession ]; then
   exec $HOME/.xsession
fi

exec xterm -geometry 80x24+1+1
```

The script in Listing 14.1 is simple, but it serves to illustrate the function of the Xsession script well. The case statement handles the contingencies when the user issues the Control+F1, Control+F2, Control+F3, or Control+F4 keystrokes during authentication, starting twm, afterstep, Window Maker (wmaker), or KDE (startkde), respectively. If none of the keystrokes were issued, then Xsession proceeds to check for a $HOME/.xsession file. If it is found, it is called. If not, the user's session consists only of a controlling xterm client.

authdir

This important directory is mentioned because its absence can often cause the display manager to fail to function. This directory contains automatically generated magic cookies associated with open displays for ongoing authentication purposes. Don't delete or move this directory while xdm is in use.

Starting xdm

With basic configuration out of the way, the only thing left to do is actually start xdm. Before starting xdm, it is important to ensure that the X server starts and runs correctly. This can be done with a simple command as root:

```
X
```

If the server starts and seems to function, you can exit with the Ctrl+Alt+Backspace keystroke (provided you have not disabled it in XF86Config) and continue with xdm.

On the Command Line

The easiest way to start xdm is from a console command line. After taking care to ensure that no X servers are running on the local machine, simply issue the following command:

```
xdm
```

After doing so, you should be presented with the xlogin widget, which displays a login and password prompt, or other text as per your configuration (refer to Figure 14.1). You and other users of the system should be able to start an X session by logging in with username and password.

When the session finishes (usually when the window manager or environment is exited), the display returns to the xlogin widget, waiting for another user to authenticate him- or herself, at which time another X session will be started.

From init

After you've established a working xdm configuration, it is often desirable to cause xdm to launch when the system boots, avoiding text-based logins altogether. This can be accomplished by editing your systemwide init configuration.

The easiest, but least correct way to do this is to add a call to xdm to the end of your rc.local script, usually found in /etc/rc.d, though it can also be found in /etc in some distributions. One such addition might look like this:

```
if [ -x /usr/X11R6/bin/xdm ]; then
    /usr/X11R6/bin/xdm
fi
```

The more correct way to start xdm at boot time is to dedicate a runlevel to a graphical login boot, and then to set that runlevel to be the default. Any running Linux system has a current runlevel, which dictates what sort of functionality will be available to the system and to users. In most current Linux distributions, an xdm runlevel has already been created for you; runlevel 5 is normally configured for booting straight to xdm. In such cases, the only change that must be made to the /etc/inittab file is to change the default runlevel line (normally the first non-comment line) to

```
id:5:initdefault:
```

If you're not sure whether your Linux distribution has been configured in advance for an xdm runlevel, browse the file. Sometimes, you'll see something like this in the comments right at the beginning:

```
# Currently configured runlevels:
#
#   0   halt
#   1   Single user mode
#   2   Multiuser, minimal network
#   3   Multiuser, full network
#   4   unused
#   5   X11
#   6   reboot
```

If a series of comments like this one exists, you should be able to easily see which runlevel has been reconfigured to launch xdm at boot time. If no comments like these exist, check the file for a line that calls xdm at a specific runlevel, like this one:

```
x:4:respawn:/usr/X11R6/bin/xdm
```

This line indicates that setting a default runlevel of 4 will cause xdm to be started when Linux starts. A complete discussion of the /etc/inittab file and the init routine is beyond the scope of this text; if you need further help, please consult the manual pages for init and inittab and edit your /etc/inittab file accordingly.

Troubleshooting

If xdm refuses to start at all, check to make sure that you are attempting to run it with root privileges. Also check all the xdm configuration files to ensure that they are present and well-formed.

The most common problem when dealing with xdm is a faulty X server configuration, which leads to a flashing effect as the server restarts itself over and over again, leaving the console inaccessible and the system, for all intents and purposes, unavailable. This problem is common enough that a quick discussion to get you on the path to a solution is in order. The problem can be exacerbated by an init configuration that starts xdm at boot time, meaning that the system boots straight into this unusable state.

In such cases, the fix is generally to repeatedly press the Ctrl+Alt+Del key sequence until the system reboots. Then, as the system starts again, hold down the Shift key to get the following prompt:

```
LILO boot:
```

At the prompt, most users will be able to type the following text, which will allow Linux to boot into single-user mode:

```
linux single
```

After logging in by issuing the root password, issue the following command to remount the root filesystem as read/write rather than read-only, so that you can alter the offending sections of the init configuration:

```
mount -n -o remount,rw /
```

After this command has been issued and successfully completed, it is necessary to use an editor such as vi to edit either /etc/inittab or /etc/rc.d/rc.local to remove the call to xdm at boot time or switch to a non-xdm runlevel. After xdm has been removed from the boot process, issue a sync command without arguments to ensure that your changes have been saved and then reset, after which you should be able to boot normally to a text console again. Note that these instructions can vary a great deal; adapt them as necessary to fit your configuration.

The root of the problem in cases like this isn't a faulty xdm configuration, but a faulty X server configuration instead. It is important to ensure that the X server runs correctly before enabling an xdm boot.

The KDE Display Manager (kdm)

The KDE display manager provides much of the same functionality provided by the xdm program included with XFree86. Indeed, kdm is based on xdm code to some extent. However, kdm has a much nicer appearance than xdm and contains onscreen tools to help the user choose one from several session types and provide feedback on the currently selected session type. Tools for shutting down or restarting the Linux system graphically are also provided. A typical kdm display can be seen in Figure 14.2.

Basic Configuration

The configuration tree for kdm files is normally located in the share/config/kdm/ subtree off the main KDE directory tree. Some distributions also distribute a modified kdm that will search for kdm configuration files in /etc/X11. The most common locations where the kdm configuration is stored are as follows:

```
/usr/local/share/config/kdm/
/opt/kde/share/config/kdm/
/etc/X11/kdm/
```

If kdm doesn't come preconfigured in your distribution, you will need to configure it yourself. To see if it is configured, check all the directories where kdm configurations might reside and look for a complete complement of files like those that are used to configure xdm. Because kdm is based on xdm, an identical set of files to those in the xdm configuration directory must exist for kdm. If your kdm installation doesn't contain the necessary files, they can generally be copied from an existing xdm installation using the following command:

```
cp -dpR /usr/X11R6/lib/X11/xdm/* /opt/kde/share/config/kdm/
```

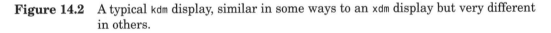

Figure 14.2   A typical kdm display, similar in some ways to an xdm display but very different in others.

Note that the destination directory should be updated to reflect the directory in which your kdm configuration files should reside. The -dpR arguments are used to copy any directories and sub-directories (such as authdir/) in addition to configuration files, and to preserve their permissions. The following sections on configuring kdm assume that you have copied files from an existing xdm configuration.

Reconfiguring xdm-config for kdm

The KDE display manager still uses the xdm-config file in spite of the fact that it isn't called xdm. This file must be edited to reflect a separate path to the new kdm configuration files, rather than pointing to all the files in /usr/X11R6/lib/X11/xdm.

Reconfiguring Xsession for kdm

The Xsession script is also used by kdm, but in kdm, it is important to understand the example in Listing 14.1 of enabling multiple session types by parsing the first argument with a case statement. This is because kdm enables the user to graphically choose a session type, and at least one session type must normally be defined.

Edit the Xsession file to reflect all the session arguments you'd like to support; these will then be added to the kdm login screen when you configure the kdm from inside KDE.

Other Configuration Files

Most of the other files can be left as-is because they have the same meanings for kdm that they had for xdm. Note that the resources configuring the xlogin widget don't apply to kdm and can be ignored completely.

For details on all these files, their contents, and what each file's role is, please refer to the section "The X Display Manager (xdm)," earlier in the chapter.

Configuration Inside KDE

The next step in configuring kdm assumes that you can already start KDE and use the environment. Start KDE with root privileges, usually by logging into a text console as root and typing startkde at the command line. After the desktop has been started, start the KDE Control Center, expand the Applications subtree in the column on the left side of the window, and select Login Manager. The dialog shown in Figure 14.3 appears.

Figure 14.3 kdm configuration in the KDE Control Center.

There are five configuration tabs in the dialog. The first three, Appearance, Fonts, and Background, are self-explanatory to a large degree, and most users will have no trouble navigating them. The last two are a little more involved.

The Users Tab

The KDE display manager has the capability to display icons for a selected set of users on the authentication display and to allow users to log in by clicking on an icon of themselves and then entering only a password. This capability is configured in the Users tab of the kdm configuration dialog.

The middle column of the dialog contains two lists, one containing selected users and the other containing no-show users. The leftmost column of the dialog is a list that contains all users known to the system who aren't assigned to either of the other two lists. On the right side of the dialog are several check boxes.

When the Show Only Selected Users check box is checked, only users in the selected users list will have an icon on the authentication screen. When the Show All Users But No-Show Users check box is checked, all users known to the system who aren't on the no-show list will have an icon on the authentication screen. When the Show Users Box is unchecked, icons for users are disabled altogether.

The icon for each user can vary in appearance as per your preferences; you can configure a user's icon by clicking on the user in one of the three lists and then clicking on the square icon at the upper-right of the dialog. This action will give you the chance to select an icon background image for the user in question. If you choose a new background when no user is selected in any list, the new background will become the default for all user icons.

The Sessions Tab

The Sessions tab configures the sessions that will appear in the kdm session type drop-down list, as well as a few other miscellaneous-type kdm options.

The first section of the tab, Allow to Shutdown, decides whether a Shutdown button will allow the user to shut the system down. The valid choices are Console Only, which will allow any user at the physical console to shut down; Root Only, which will allow shutdowns to occur only after the root password has been entered; All, which will always enable shutdowns; or None.

It should be noted that any shutdown will affect the system running kdm, not the remote system in the case of a remote display.

The second section of the tab, Commands, enables the user to enter the commands that will be run, with root privileges, when a shutdown or reboot is started.

The third section, Session types, enables a list of session arguments to be entered. When at the kdm login screen, it is these arguments that will appear in the Session type drop-down list and that will be passed to the Xsession script, depending on which session type the user chooses at login. Therefore, this list should match the list of sessions you have configured in the Xsession script, usually via a case statement.

Starting kdm

Starting kdm is easy; because kdm is largely a drop-in replacement for xdm, all the same techniques apply. To test a kdm configuration, log in at a text console and simply issue

```
kdm
```

After you are confident that kdm is functioning as you want it to, feel free to add it to the init process and boot straight into X at a kdm login prompt.

For More Information

For more information on configuring and using the KDE display manager, kdm, please use the KDE help browser to visit the Login Manager document tree from the KDE application help index.

The GNOME Display Manager (gdm)

The GNOME display manager, gdm, includes many of the same extra features that are present in kdm but missing in xdm. Among these are the capability to graphically choose among several session types, the capability to shut down or reboot the system, and the capability to log in by clicking on a user's icon. Unlike kdm, however, gdm was written from the ground up, so to speak, and therefore doesn't rely on any of the same configuration files or peculiarities that come from xdm.

Basic Configuration

The basic gdm files are kept in the /etc/gdm directory by default, though some files are kept elsewhere and this path itself varies depending on compilation options. Configuration of gdm is done almost entirely through a single file, gdm.conf. The remainder of configuration is done by placing files into the relevant subdirectories specified in the gdm.conf file.

The gdm.conf File

Before the average user can configure gdm, he or she must first discover where the gdm configuration file resides. Normally gdm looks for its files in the etc/gdm/ directory off the GNOME install tree, but this isn't always the case. Luckily, it is fairly easy to locate your gdm.conf file,

There are five configuration tabs in the dialog. The first three, Appearance, Fonts, and Background, are self-explanatory to a large degree, and most users will have no trouble navigating them. The last two are a little more involved.

The Users Tab

The KDE display manager has the capability to display icons for a selected set of users on the authentication display and to allow users to log in by clicking on an icon of themselves and then entering only a password. This capability is configured in the Users tab of the kdm configuration dialog.

The middle column of the dialog contains two lists, one containing selected users and the other containing no-show users. The leftmost column of the dialog is a list that contains all users known to the system who aren't assigned to either of the other two lists. On the right side of the dialog are several check boxes.

When the Show Only Selected Users check box is checked, only users in the selected users list will have an icon on the authentication screen. When the Show All Users But No-Show Users check box is checked, all users known to the system who aren't on the no-show list will have an icon on the authentication screen. When the Show Users Box is unchecked, icons for users are disabled altogether.

The icon for each user can vary in appearance as per your preferences; you can configure a user's icon by clicking on the user in one of the three lists and then clicking on the square icon at the upper-right of the dialog. This action will give you the chance to select an icon background image for the user in question. If you choose a new background when no user is selected in any list, the new background will become the default for all user icons.

The Sessions Tab

The Sessions tab configures the sessions that will appear in the kdm session type drop-down list, as well as a few other miscellaneous-type kdm options.

The first section of the tab, Allow to Shutdown, decides whether a Shutdown button will allow the user to shut the system down. The valid choices are Console Only, which will allow any user at the physical console to shut down; Root Only, which will allow shutdowns to occur only after the root password has been entered; All, which will always enable shutdowns; or None.

It should be noted that any shutdown will affect the system running kdm, not the remote system in the case of a remote display.

The second section of the tab, Commands, enables the user to enter the commands that will be run, with root privileges, when a shutdown or reboot is started.

The third section, Session types, enables a list of session arguments to be entered. When at the kdm login screen, it is these arguments that will appear in the Session type drop-down list and that will be passed to the Xsession script, depending on which session type the user chooses at login. Therefore, this list should match the list of sessions you have configured in the Xsession script, usually via a case statement.

Starting kdm

Starting kdm is easy; because kdm is largely a drop-in replacement for xdm, all the same techniques apply. To test a kdm configuration, log in at a text console and simply issue

```
kdm
```

After you are confident that kdm is functioning as you want it to, feel free to add it to the init process and boot straight into X at a kdm login prompt.

For More Information

For more information on configuring and using the KDE display manager, kdm, please use the KDE help browser to visit the Login Manager document tree from the KDE application help index.

The GNOME Display Manager (gdm)

The GNOME display manager, gdm, includes many of the same extra features that are present in kdm but missing in xdm. Among these are the capability to graphically choose among several session types, the capability to shut down or reboot the system, and the capability to log in by clicking on a user's icon. Unlike kdm, however, gdm was written from the ground up, so to speak, and therefore doesn't rely on any of the same configuration files or peculiarities that come from xdm.

Basic Configuration

The basic gdm files are kept in the /etc/gdm directory by default, though some files are kept elsewhere and this path itself varies depending on compilation options. Configuration of gdm is done almost entirely through a single file, gdm.conf. The remainder of configuration is done by placing files into the relevant subdirectories specified in the gdm.conf file.

The gdm.conf File

Before the average user can configure gdm, he or she must first discover where the gdm configuration file resides. Normally gdm looks for its files in the etc/gdm/ directory off the GNOME install tree, but this isn't always the case. Luckily, it is fairly easy to locate your gdm.conf file,

There are five configuration tabs in the dialog. The first three, Appearance, Fonts, and Background, are self-explanatory to a large degree, and most users will have no trouble navigating them. The last two are a little more involved.

The Users Tab

The KDE display manager has the capability to display icons for a selected set of users on the authentication display and to allow users to log in by clicking on an icon of themselves and then entering only a password. This capability is configured in the Users tab of the kdm configuration dialog.

The middle column of the dialog contains two lists, one containing selected users and the other containing no-show users. The leftmost column of the dialog is a list that contains all users known to the system who aren't assigned to either of the other two lists. On the right side of the dialog are several check boxes.

When the Show Only Selected Users check box is checked, only users in the selected users list will have an icon on the authentication screen. When the Show All Users But No-Show Users check box is checked, all users known to the system who aren't on the no-show list will have an icon on the authentication screen. When the Show Users Box is unchecked, icons for users are disabled altogether.

The icon for each user can vary in appearance as per your preferences; you can configure a user's icon by clicking on the user in one of the three lists and then clicking on the square icon at the upper-right of the dialog. This action will give you the chance to select an icon background image for the user in question. If you choose a new background when no user is selected in any list, the new background will become the default for all user icons.

The Sessions Tab

The Sessions tab configures the sessions that will appear in the kdm session type drop-down list, as well as a few other miscellaneous-type kdm options.

The first section of the tab, Allow to Shutdown, decides whether a Shutdown button will allow the user to shut the system down. The valid choices are Console Only, which will allow any user at the physical console to shut down; Root Only, which will allow shutdowns to occur only after the root password has been entered; All, which will always enable shutdowns; or None.

It should be noted that any shutdown will affect the system running kdm, not the remote system in the case of a remote display.

The second section of the tab, Commands, enables the user to enter the commands that will be run, with root privileges, when a shutdown or reboot is started.

The third section, Session types, enables a list of session arguments to be entered. When at the kdm login screen, it is these arguments that will appear in the Session type drop-down list and that will be passed to the Xsession script, depending on which session type the user chooses at login. Therefore, this list should match the list of sessions you have configured in the Xsession script, usually via a case statement.

Starting kdm

Starting kdm is easy; because kdm is largely a drop-in replacement for xdm, all the same techniques apply. To test a kdm configuration, log in at a text console and simply issue

```
kdm
```

After you are confident that kdm is functioning as you want it to, feel free to add it to the init process and boot straight into X at a kdm login prompt.

For More Information

For more information on configuring and using the KDE display manager, kdm, please use the KDE help browser to visit the Login Manager document tree from the KDE application help index.

The GNOME Display Manager (gdm)

The GNOME display manager, gdm, includes many of the same extra features that are present in kdm but missing in xdm. Among these are the capability to graphically choose among several session types, the capability to shut down or reboot the system, and the capability to log in by clicking on a user's icon. Unlike kdm, however, gdm was written from the ground up, so to speak, and therefore doesn't rely on any of the same configuration files or peculiarities that come from xdm.

Basic Configuration

The basic gdm files are kept in the /etc/gdm directory by default, though some files are kept elsewhere and this path itself varies depending on compilation options. Configuration of gdm is done almost entirely through a single file, gdm.conf. The remainder of configuration is done by placing files into the relevant subdirectories specified in the gdm.conf file.

The gdm.conf File

Before the average user can configure gdm, he or she must first discover where the gdm configuration file resides. Normally gdm looks for its files in the etc/gdm/ directory off the GNOME install tree, but this isn't always the case. Luckily, it is fairly easy to locate your gdm.conf file,

There are five configuration tabs in the dialog. The first three, Appearance, Fonts, and Background, are self-explanatory to a large degree, and most users will have no trouble navigating them. The last two are a little more involved.

The Users Tab

The KDE display manager has the capability to display icons for a selected set of users on the authentication display and to allow users to log in by clicking on an icon of themselves and then entering only a password. This capability is configured in the Users tab of the kdm configuration dialog.

The middle column of the dialog contains two lists, one containing selected users and the other containing no-show users. The leftmost column of the dialog is a list that contains all users known to the system who aren't assigned to either of the other two lists. On the right side of the dialog are several check boxes.

When the Show Only Selected Users check box is checked, only users in the selected users list will have an icon on the authentication screen. When the Show All Users But No-Show Users check box is checked, all users known to the system who aren't on the no-show list will have an icon on the authentication screen. When the Show Users Box is unchecked, icons for users are disabled altogether.

The icon for each user can vary in appearance as per your preferences; you can configure a user's icon by clicking on the user in one of the three lists and then clicking on the square icon at the upper-right of the dialog. This action will give you the chance to select an icon background image for the user in question. If you choose a new background when no user is selected in any list, the new background will become the default for all user icons.

The Sessions Tab

The Sessions tab configures the sessions that will appear in the kdm session type drop-down list, as well as a few other miscellaneous-type kdm options.

The first section of the tab, Allow to Shutdown, decides whether a Shutdown button will allow the user to shut the system down. The valid choices are Console Only, which will allow any user at the physical console to shut down; Root Only, which will allow shutdowns to occur only after the root password has been entered; All, which will always enable shutdowns; or None.

It should be noted that any shutdown will affect the system running kdm, not the remote system in the case of a remote display.

The second section of the tab, Commands, enables the user to enter the commands that will be run, with root privileges, when a shutdown or reboot is started.

The third section, Session types, enables a list of session arguments to be entered. When at the kdm login screen, it is these arguments that will appear in the Session type drop-down list and that will be passed to the Xsession script, depending on which session type the user chooses at login. Therefore, this list should match the list of sessions you have configured in the Xsession script, usually via a case statement.

Starting kdm

Starting kdm is easy; because kdm is largely a drop-in replacement for xdm, all the same techniques apply. To test a kdm configuration, log in at a text console and simply issue

```
kdm
```

After you are confident that kdm is functioning as you want it to, feel free to add it to the init process and boot straight into X at a kdm login prompt.

For More Information

For more information on configuring and using the KDE display manager, kdm, please use the KDE help browser to visit the Login Manager document tree from the KDE application help index.

The GNOME Display Manager (gdm)

The GNOME display manager, gdm, includes many of the same extra features that are present in kdm but missing in xdm. Among these are the capability to graphically choose among several session types, the capability to shut down or reboot the system, and the capability to log in by clicking on a user's icon. Unlike kdm, however, gdm was written from the ground up, so to speak, and therefore doesn't rely on any of the same configuration files or peculiarities that come from xdm.

Basic Configuration

The basic gdm files are kept in the /etc/gdm directory by default, though some files are kept elsewhere and this path itself varies depending on compilation options. Configuration of gdm is done almost entirely through a single file, gdm.conf. The remainder of configuration is done by placing files into the relevant subdirectories specified in the gdm.conf file.

The gdm.conf File

Before the average user can configure gdm, he or she must first discover where the gdm configuration file resides. Normally gdm looks for its files in the etc/gdm/ directory off the GNOME install tree, but this isn't always the case. Luckily, it is fairly easy to locate your gdm.conf file,

or at least to locate where it should be. First, try using the locate command to try to find an existing gdm.conf file:

```
locate gdm.conf
```

If this command doesn't turn up any useful result, simply try running the gdm binary on the command line with root privileges and make a note of the error message you receive:

```
$ gdm
gdm_config_parse: No configuration file: /etc/gdm/gdm.conf.
Aborting.
```

From this error message, it is clear that the gdm.conf file you create should be placed into the /etc/gdm directory. You are now ready to proceed with configuration.

The gdm configuration file is structured similarly to the Samba configuration files familiar to Linux users; the file is split into several sections that are denoted by a section header in brackets. Following each section header are the options that pertain to the section in question. The seven sections of the file and their options are documented in Tables 14.4 through 14.10.

Table 14.4 Section [appearance]

Option	Description
Browser=*n*	Turns the face browser (user icons) on if *n* is 1 or off if *n* is 0.
Logo=*n*	Turns the logo image on if *n* is 1 or off if *n* is 0.
LogoImage=*path*	Path to the logo that will be displayed if the logo image is enabled. The image must be in a format supported by Imlib.
NoFaceImage=*path*	Path to the default icon for users in the face browser. Normally, gdm checks each user's account for a $HOME/.gnome/photo file that will be the icon for the user in the face browser. If the file isn't found, this file is used instead.
GlobalImageDir=*path*	Path to the directory containing icons for users on a per-user basis. For example, if an image file called jsmith with no extension was present in the global image directory, it would be displayed as the icon for the user smith.
Quiver=*n*	Turns on display shaking when an incorrect password is entered if *n* is 1 or off if *n* is 0.
Iconify=*n*	Allows the greeter window (where login and password are entered) to be iconified if *n* is 1 or doesn't allow this action if *n* is 0.
IconFile=*path*	Path to the image to use for the greeter's icon representation when minimized.
Completion=*n*	Turns on Tab key username completion when *n* is 1 or off when *n* is 0.

Table 14.5 Section [system]

Option	Description
ShutdownMenu=*n*	Turns shutdown/halt functionality on if *n* is 1 or off if *n* is 0.
SuspendCommand=*cmd*	A full command string to use for suspending the system. Usually used with portables and other power management-enabled machines.
UserIconMaxWidth=*n*	Limits user-supplied icons to *n* pixels wide.
UserIconMaxHeight=*n*	Limits user-supplied icons to *n* pixels high.
DefaultPath=*paths*	Specifies the default binary search path that will be set for the $PATH variable in the user's session.

Table 14.6 Section [messages]

Option	Description
Welcome=*text*	Specifies the text that should appear at the top of the greeter. Some special strings apply: %h will expand to the gdm host's name, %d will expand to the display host's name.

Table 14.7 Section [daemon]

Option	Description
SessionDir=*path*	The path to the directory containing session scripts. The default directory is Session/ in /etc/gdm.
PidFile=*path*	The path to the file that will hold the gdm process ID while gdm is running.
Greeter=*path*	The path to the gdm greeter program that normally resides in the GNOME binaries directory.
Chooser=*path*	The path to the gdm chooser program that normally resides in the GNOME binaries directory.
User=*name*	The name of the user under which gdm will run. Default is gdm.
Group=*name*	The name of the group under which gdm will run. Default is gdm.
DisplayInitDir=*path*	The path to the directory containing display initialization scripts. The default directory is Init/ in /etc/gdm.
KillInitClients=*n*	Causes gdm to kill any clients started by the display initialization scripts when a user logs in if *n* is 1, or not if *n* is 0.
PreSessionScriptDir=*path*	The path to the directory containing scripts that will be run at the beginning of the session. The default directory is PreSession/ in /etc/gdm.

Option	Description
PostSessionScriptDir=*path*	The path to the directory containing scripts that will be run at the end of the session. The default directory is PostSession/ in /etc/gdm.
AuthDir=*path*	The path to the directory that will be used to hold magic cookie files. The directory should be owned by the gdm user and group specified using other options in this table and should have permissions 750.
LogDir=*path*	The path to the directory to which display logs are written. The default behavior is to use the AuthDir directory.

Table 14.8   Section [servers]

Option	Description
n=*command*	Specifies that display *n* should be started using the given command. Most often, only one line will exist in this section and will be the line for display 0, calling the X binary to start the X server.

Table 14.9   Section [xdmcp]

Option	Description
Enable=*n*	Enables the management of port 177 and XDMCP request handling by gdm if *n* is 1, or disables such behavior if *n* is 0.
MaxLoadAvg=*n*	The load average, *n*, at which gdm will refuse new XDMCP queries.
MaxPending=*n*	The maximum number of displays, *n*, which can be started at any one time. Doesn't limit final display count, only the number of connections that can be pending at any one time.
MaxSessions=*n*	The maximum number of displays, *n*, that gdm will support in total.
Port=*n*	The port on which gdm is to listen for XDMCP queries. Normally *n* is 177.

Table 14.10   Section [chooser]

Option	Description
ImageDir=*path*	Path to the directory that will contain icons representing other hosts in the chooser. Each icon filename should match the fully qualified domain name of the host exactly.
DefaultImage=*path*	Path to the file representing hosts in the chooser when no host-specific icon can be found.

There are many configuration options, and it is generally necessary to specify them all. The maze of default values for each of the options is confusing, and some of the documentation that comes with gdm is incorrect with regard to the default values. It is thus safer to specify all values explicitly.

The Init/ Directory

The Init/ directory given by the DisplayInitDir option in Table 14.7 contains scripts that will be run after the X server has been started but before the greeter window is displayed; it is similar in purpose to the Xsetup scripts used by xdm.

Each display will try to run a script named after itself in the Init/ directory. For example, the first local display will attempt to run a script with :0 as its filename in the Init/ directory, the second display a script called :1, and so on.

If the KillInitClient=1 option has been specified in the gdm.conf file, any clients started by the scripts in the Init/ directory will be killed when a user actually logs in.

If no script matching the name of the current display can be found, a script called Default in the Init/ directory will be run instead to configure the display.

Note that the Init/ scripts aren't mandatory and can be omitted if such functionality isn't needed or desired.

The PreSession/ and PostSession/ Directories

After a user has authenticated him- or herself, gdm will attempt to start a script named after the current display in the PreSession/ directory given by the PreSessionScriptDir option in Table 14.7. So, for example, a user logging in on the first display would cause gdm to try to execute the file at PreSession/:0. If no script matching the local display name can be found, the script Default will be used instead.

The PreSession/ scripts are used to perform user-oriented tasks such as merging resources with xrdb, starting clients that need to be launched at login, and so on. Note that the controlling process (that is, window manager or environment) should not be started from the PreSession/ scripts, but from the Session/ scripts that are described in the next session.

The PostSession/ scripts, located in the directory given by the PostSessionScriptDir option in Table 14.7, are synonymous with the PreSession/ scripts in that they are named after the display and will be executed when the user logs out. If no script matching the display name can be found in the PostSession/ directory, the script called Default will be started instead.

Note that the PreSession/ and PostSession/ scripts aren't mandatory and that either or both can be omitted if such functionality isn't needed or desired.

The Session/ Directory

After the PreSession/ script has executed, gdm will execute a script from the Session/ directory given by the SessionDir option in Table 14.7. This script should start the controlling process for the session (that is, window manager or environment). The script gdm chooses to execute depends on the session type the user chose at the gdm login. The list of session types available to the user at that point is built by listing all the scripts in the Session/ directory.

If the user doesn't choose a session, but instead leaves the choice blank, the script called Default will be executed. If there is no Default script, the first script found will be executed.

There must be at least one script in the Session/ directory for gdm to be able to start an X session for a user after he or she has authenticated him- or herself.

Starting gdm

As was the case with kdm, gdm is a simple daemon to start. First, to test out the configuration and make sure gdm is functioning properly, call it as root:

```
gdm
```

After you are satisfied with the results and are able to log in and start sessions at will, you might want to add gdm to your init process and use it as your display manager of choice.

Troubleshooting

Unfortunately, gdm, like much of GNOME, is currently a work in progress. Several well-documented bugs often affect gdm, particularly when it is running on Linux distributions other than Red Hat Linux.

If you're having trouble getting gdm to work, verify the ownership (gdm.gdm), access permissions, and locations of all the files listed in the gdm.conf configuration file. Double-check all scripts and check to make sure that the gdm, gdmgreeter, and gdmchooser binaries are intact.

As a last resort, some aspiring gdm users have resorted to using kdm or xdm instead because gdm on some systems simply refuses to work, even though the packages that installed it were built by distribution maintainers. The second version of gdm will fix many of these problems, but unfortunately, it is still under development and isn't ready for widespread use yet.

For More Information

For more information on using and configuring the GNOME display manager, gdm, please visit the doc/ subtree of your GNOME installation directory tree and read the file gdm-manual.txt.

15

WORKING ON THE
NETWORK

You might remember the assertion from Chapter 1, "X11R6 and the XFree86 Project," that X is really, at its heart, a data stream that can be used as a network protocol. This implies that a stream of windows, icons, fonts, and pointer movements can be sent across a network just as easily as text information can be sent, and in today's distributed office environment, this is an important goal. So far, however, with the exception of a few hints in this direction in Chapter 14, "Display Managers," we haven't seen much of the network-readiness of X. How does one take advantage of the basic network-centric nature of X?

Taking Advantage of Network-Centric X

Recall from Chapter 1 that all X programs are really clients that run on a host machine and connect to an X server that can be running on the same host or a second host elsewhere on the network. It is this X server that will draw client windows and graphics and enable the user to interact with them. The default behavior when a client is started is to connect to the X server running on the local machine (the machine on which the client is running). The real goal, then, in network-enabling your X use, is to be able to tell clients to connect to a remote machine's X server instead of trying to connect to the X server on their own machines.

Referring to X Displays on the Network

The first step in fulfilling this goal is being able to describe another machine on the network to X clients. All Linux users should be familiar with Internet-style domain names that are used when browsing the Web using the HTTP protocol, getting files using the FTP protocol, or reading netnews using the NNTP protocol. In all these cases, referring to the machine in question is a simple matter—the fully qualified domain name of the host or server in question is enough to start a connection and transfer data.

Unfortunately, things are a little more complicated with the X Window System. Although XFree86 on Linux machines doesn't yet enjoy such capability, many X Window System machines based on more traditional UNIX hardware can have multiple X displays, and each of those displays can have multiple screens. When connecting to an X server in hopes of displaying an X client, it is therefore necessary to specify not only a machine where the client should display itself, but also a display and, in some cases, a screen within that display. Specifying a display can also be helpful in cases where X servers are running on a single machine on multiple virtual consoles. The basic format for a host, display, and screen specification is as follows:

```
[fqdn.on.the.net]:d[.s]
```

The optional first part of the address before the colon is the fully qualified domain name of the machine in question, or, alternatively, a host name if the machine is on your local network. If no host or domain name is given, the local host is assumed. After the mandatory colon, d indicates the display number on the host, 0 being the first display, 1 being the second, and so on. An optional addition to the address is a period followed by s, the screen number on the specified display, with 0 being the first screen, 1 being the second, and so on. Table 15.1 dissects a few X network addresses.

Table 15.1   Some X Network Addresses

Address	Description
:0	The first screen (assumed) on the first display on the local host. This is the default display to which clients connect unless told to do otherwise. When connecting to the local machine this way, clients will connect to the server using the fastest possible transport method, usually UNIX domain sockets.
:0.0	The first screen on the first display on the local host. Equivalent to :0 and sometimes seen instead.
:1.1	The second screen on the second display on the local host. Never seen on Linux/x86 systems running XFree86, but might be seen on other UNIX machines.

Address	Description
localhost:0	The functional near-equivalent to :0 with the exception that the connection will take place over the loopback (network) interface, regardless of whether faster internal connection methods are available.
jpbigchip:0	The first screen (assumed) on the first display on the host jpbigchip, which is on the local network.
x.conquer.net:0	The first screen (assumed) on the first display on the host x.conquer.net.
x.conquer.net:1.0	The first screen on the second display on the host x.conquer.net.
www.zivver.com:3.1	The second screen on the fourth display on the host www.zivver.com.

Knowing how to properly refer to X displays across the network is only half the battle; the other half is supplying such a reference to a client.

The DISPLAY Environment Variable

The primary method for specifying which display clients should use is through the DISPLAY environment variable, which holds the address to the default display to which clients should connect. For example, consider the following shell session fragment, issued in an xterm on a machine called foobar:

```
ahsiao@foobar$ echo $DISPLAY
:0.0
ahsiao@foobar$
```

The contents of the DISPLAY variable on this system show that the default display to which clients will connect if no other host is specified is the first screen on the first display of the local machine. Most Linux/x86 users working in X on the local machine will find that their DISPLAY environment variable contains the same thing.

Assume for a moment that an open, unsecured system called pokey is on the local area network, and that an active X server is running on pokey's only display. From the xterm window, I issue the following commands:

```
ahsiao@foobar$ export DISPLAY=pokey:0.0
ahsiao@foobar$ xclock -geometry 1024x768+0+0 &
[1] 26414
ahsiao@foobar$
```

The xclock doesn't appear on foobar's display, but it has clearly been started—a process ID has been assigned and returned. Where did it go? A quick check on pokey's display reveals the answer: A giant xclock now appears on pokey, though the xclock program is actually running on foobar. The default display for any clients started from this xterm window is now pokey's display, instead of the foobar's display, even though the xterm is on foobar's display.

It is important to keep shell environment scope in mind when dealing with the DISPLAY variable. Remember that setting the DISPLAY variable from the command line will affect the variable only in the shell from which the assignment was issued. This means that if I start a second xterm on foobar by clicking on an icon or selecting an item from a root menu, the DISPLAY variable in the new xterm will contain :0.0 and any clients started there will thus appear on foobar's display.

The -display Argument

Because working with environment variables for something so fundamental is a little bit clumsy, most X applications also support the -display command-line argument. Although originally an X toolkit (Xt) argument, most application toolkits have adopted it because of its utility.

To explicitly specify a display somewhere on the network when starting an X client, use the -display argument followed by the display on which the client should appear and interact:

```
xterm -display x44.pibber.edu:0
xcalc -display monkeyhost:1.1
netscape -display server.fargus.copale.com:1
```

For the rare application that does not accept the -display argument, the DISPLAY environment variable should be used instead.

Controlling Access, Authenticating Connections

After the examples you've seen so far in this chapter, it should be obvious that it's important to have a mechanism to control access to a running X server—otherwise, the network capabilities of X would create more problems than they solve.

To control access, an X server can be instructed to require authentication of any incoming connections before the connection will be accepted. This authentication can take two separate forms: host-based authentication or token-based authentication.

Host-Based Authentication

The most basic way for controlling access to an X server is based on a list of host names kept internally by the server. Hosts that are on the list are allowed to connect. Hosts that aren't on the list aren't allowed to connect. If no other mechanism for controlling access to the server is in place, the list contains one host: the host on which the server is running.

The /etc/Xn.hosts File

The primary method for editing the list of permitted hosts is to add hosts to or remove hosts from the /etc/Xn.hosts file, where *n* is the number of the display on the local host to which the file will apply. The file should contain simply a list of allowed hosts, one per line:

```
client32.multiply.net
client33.multiply.net
pokey
foobar
thejameshost
```

When the X server is started, the /etc/Xn.hosts file will be read, and the list will be built using its contents. Changing the contents of the file after the X server has started will not change the X server's internal list—the X server must be restarted if an edited file needs to take effect.

The xhost Command

To edit the list after the X server is running, the xhost command can be used. The xhost command must (obviously) be run from a host that already has permission to access the server, and is used in one of two ways:

```
xhost +host.to.add
xhost -host.to.remove
```

The first of the two calls to xhost adds the host to the list hosts that can connect to the server. The second of the two calls to xhost removes the host from the list. An additional, kamikaze method for editing the list is to call xhost like this:

```
xhost +
```

When the plus sign is used as an argument alone, without preceding a host name, the X server is rendered completely insecure: Connections are allowed from any host, anywhere. Needless to say, there are few situations in which such a command would ever make sense. To reverse the decision to disable access control, issue the inverse command:

```
xhost -
```

To display the current host access list, call the xhost command without arguments:

```
$ xhost
INET:client32.multiply.net
INET:client33.multiply.net
INET:pokey
INET:foobar
LOCAL:
```

Host-Based Authentication Issues

Although the host-based method for granting or denying access to the X server is convenient, it is not very secure. The host-based method is thus best used only on smaller networks where the local network in question is behind a firewall if the network is connected to the Internet.

It is also important to understand that although removing a host from the access list will deny new connections from the host in question, it will have no effect on existing connections.

Token-Based Authentication

Token-based authentication decides who connects and who doesn't by checking a token offered by a connecting client against a token maintained locally, usually in a user's $HOME/.Xauthority file. It is more secure than host-based authentication, which attempts to decide who gets access and who doesn't just by looking at the connecting host's name (which can be fudged in any number of ways), and which can't prevent any particular user from connecting to a display.

Token-based authentication comes in several forms, but can be more difficult to administer in general than the rather simple to understand host-based method.

How Token-Based Authentication Works

The basic premise behind token-based authentication is a user-to-user identification check. That is to say that the server is secured for a particular user's use only, and subsequently, only that user is theoretically able to start clients on the server. This task is accomplished by comparing two magic cookies, one supplied by the client and one maintained by the server. If the cookie of a connecting client doesn't match the cookie used by the server, the connection is refused.

The mechanism behind this premise can at first seem complex but is really quite simple. First, a random magic cookie string is generated and saved to a file. Then the X server is started in the following manner:

```
X -auth authfile
```

Of course, it is rare to start an X server alone in this fashion, so if the user starts a session from a console using startx, the argument is passed to the server like this:

```
startx -- -auth authfile
```

The authfile supplied is the file containing the random magic cookie string. It is usually called $HOME/.Xauthority on the machine where the server will run. Assuming that the list of hosts in /etc/Xn.hosts for host-based authentication is empty, the server is now secured and will accept incoming connections only from clients who can authenticate themselves.

When the user tries to connect clients to the X server in question, whether they are local or remote, the server will challenge the connecting clients for the correct magic cookie. The connecting clients supply the magic cookie found on the client machine in the $HOME/.Xauthority file to the server, and if the cookies match, the server allows the connection to proceed. If the cookies don't match, the connection is refused.

If both clients and server are running on the same machine and are started by the same user, the magic cookie will always match because the $HOME/.Xauthority file seen by the server is the same physical file seen by the clients. If the $HOME/.Xauthority files are different physical files, either because the clients and server are running on separate machines or because the clients and server are run by two separate users, the server's magic cookie must be transferred somehow to the client $HOME/.Xauthority file before a client connection can be made.

Note that the token file clients will use can be changed from its default of $HOME/.Xauthority by setting the XAUTHORITY environment variable to the name of the file that contains the magic cookie.

Automatic Token-Based Authentication

The X Display Manager and other display managers covered in Chapter 14 have a special role in the use of token-based authentication. Most display managers for the X Window System automatically enable token-based authentication, eliminating the need to call x or startx with extra arguments.

When a user logs in to an X session using a display manager such as xdm, the display manager automatically generates a random cookie for the server and stores it in a cookie file whose path has already been passed to the X server using the -auth argument at launch. If the xdm login has taken place remotely via an XDMCP-queried session, the magic cookie file is updated on the X client-side system as well, eliminating the need to update magic cookies at all unless client connections from a third system will be required. For more information on starting an xdm login remotely via an XDMCP query, see "Working with Applications and Sessions," later in this chapter.

Because of the automation xdm provides in maintaining the magic cookie control mechanism, it is usually preferable to run and log in via xdm whenever X will be used in a network-oriented environment. The automation of token-oriented tasks on the initiating client machine and the accepting server machine ensures that all users are operating with the more secure access control mechanism while eliminating much of the risk of user error.

Manipulating the Cookie File with xauth

The magic cookie at $HOME/.Xauthority can actually be a little more complex than I've made it appear because it can contain several magic cookies at a time, for example, if the user needs to start clients that will connect to several different X servers, each with its own magic cookie.

The xauth command is designed to enable users to add and remove cookies from their $HOME/.Xauthority file safely, without having to try to edit it by hand. The four xauth operations you're concerned with are the add, remove, merge, and extract operations.

To add a magic cookie to your token file, use xauth with the add command, like this:

```
xauth add host:display . keyvalue
```

The host:display specified should be an address of the type discussed earlier in "Referring to X Displays on the Network." The keyvalue should be a large numeric value with an even number of digits generated by some random means. For example, to set a magic cookie for the first display on the host known as pokey using the current date and time as a keyvalue, you'd use

```
xauth add pokey:0 . `date +%m%d%y%H%M%S`
```

To remove a magic cookie from your token file, use xauth with the remove command, like this:

```
xauth remove host:display
```

In this case, host:display must refer to a host for which a cookie already exists in your token file. For example, to remove the cookie for pokey:0, you'd use

```
xauth remove pokey:0
```

To extract a magic cookie for a given host and write it to a file, xauth is called this way:

```
xauth extract outputfile host:display
```

If the specified outputfile is just a dash (-), the cookie is written to standard output. For example, to display the cookie for pokey:0 to standard output, you'd use

```
xauth extract - pokey:0
```

Finally, to merge a magic cookie for a given host from an existing file into your default token file, xauth is called with the merge command:

```
xauth merge mergefile
```

If the specified mergefile is just a dash (-), the cookie is read from standard input.

Transferring Cookies Between Hosts

It sometimes becomes necessary to transfer a magic cookie from the $HOME/.Xauthority file on one host to your $HOME/.Xauthority file on another host, for example, when you have started an X server by hand with the -auth argument on the host called pokey, but now need to start clients from a separate machine, foobar. Because you didn't start the session with xdm, the magic cookie for the session exists only on pokey; any connections from foobar will be refused until your $HOME/.Xauthority file on foobar contains the same cookie.

To transfer the cookie from pokey:0 to your account at foobar, the `rsh` command can be used in conjunction with the `xauth` command in the following rather convenient way:

```
xauth extract - :0 ¦ rsh foobar xauth merge -
```

Assuming that it is run from pokey's display, this command first extracts the magic cookie for the local display, and then pipes it to foobar, where it is merged into the `$HOME/.Xauthority` file. Of course, you must be able to use `rsh` between pokey and foobar in order for this command to be useful; if you can't, you'll have to use some other method for transferring the cookie, perhaps using `ftp` or some other common method for file exchange.

Token-Based Authentication Issues

The first and most obvious issue with token-based authentication is the fact that if the cookie can be obtained by an untrusted third party, an unwanted connection (a security breach) can occur. To avoid the unauthorized stealing of magic cookies for running servers, two steps must be taken. First, be sure to keep the `$HOME/.Xauthority` file ownership correct (owned by the user who owns `$HOME`) and the permissions limited to read and write for the owner only. Next, avoid sending magic cookies across the network in unencrypted form where they can be stolen by an untrusted third party. An easy-to-use method for encrypting magic cookie exchanges and the entire X protocol is covered in Chapter 16, "Tunneling X Through `ssh` (Secure Shell)," but any method of encryption or compression can be used to make the transfer safer.

Another issue with token-based authentication is the way in which it interacts with host-based authentication. The two methods are not exclusive; that is to say, connections from any hosts in the allowed hosts list will be accepted, even if token-based authentication is also in use. The correct magic cookie will be required only for connections coming from systems not in the permitted hosts list. It is thus a good idea to maintain an empty hosts list if magic cookie authentication is to remain secure.

It should be noted that more than one type of magic cookie can actually be used; the magic cookie type discussed here is the default type, MIT-MAGIC-COOKIE-1. For information on using other cookie types, including DES-encrypted and Kerberos-exchanged cookies, please see the `Xsecurity` and `xauth` manual pages.

Working with Applications and Sessions

You now know how to keep an X server reasonably secure once running. If you are going to be working on the network, it is also important to understand how to perform three basic networked-X tasks: starting a remote client on the local display, starting a local client on a remote display, and using an XDMCP query to start an entire session across the network.

The examples in the following sections assume that X servers are running on machines called foobar and pokey and that you are sitting in front of foobar. These examples also assume that you have taken care of any authentication issues, such as exchanging magic cookies between systems when necessary.

Starting Remote Clients on the Local Display

Perhaps the most common type of network use for X users is the use of clients that are running on remote hosts but which display by connecting to a local X server. Depending on whether you'll be starting multiple clients on the same remote machine or just a single client on each remote machine, you'll probably want to do one of two things.

Starting Multiple Clients

If you plan to start multiple remote clients from the same machine, the easiest thing to do is often to start a shell session on that machine using `rlogin` or `telnet`:

```
rlogin pokey
```

After the session has begun, set the DISPLAY environment variable to point to your local display:

```
you@pokey$ export DISPLAY=foobar:0
```

After you've set the DISPLAY environment variable to point to your local display, simply start clients as you normally would from the shell:

```
you@pokey$ xterm &
[1] 26332
you@pokey$ netscape &
[2] 26335
you@pokey$
```

Notice that any of the clients you start in the shell on pokey display themselves and interact with you on `foobar:0`.

Starting Single Clients

If you only need to start a single remote client, or if you need to start remote clients on several different remote hosts, the `rsh` command is again more helpful. For example, to start an xterm on pokey that will display on `foobar:0`, you'd use

```
rsh pokey xterm -display foobar:0
```

Of course, this will tie up your shell until the client exits, so it might be more helpful to start the `rsh` and client in the background:

```
rsh pokey xterm -display foobar:0 &
```

Unfortunately, this will leave a stopped process after xterm exits on pokey, because rsh will be waiting for a line of input. To solve this problem on Linux machines, you could use either the -n argument to rsh or a redirection from /dev/null:

```
rsh -n pokey xterm -display foobar:0 &
rsh pokey netscape -display foobar:0 </dev/null &
rsh pokey xclock -display foobar:0 </dev/null &
```

These commands will all behave more or less as background processes should behave, and will display on foobar:0 even though they are running on pokey.

Starting Local Clients on Remote Displays

The process of starting local clients and displaying them remotely is somewhat simpler and was discussed in a roundabout way at the beginning of the chapter, but it bears repeating again in a new context.

If you need to start several local clients and display them all on a remote host, it might be helpful to start a shell, set the DISPLAY environment variable to the target system, and then call the clients just as you normally would:

```
$ export DISPLAY=pokey:0
$ xterm &
[4] 17438
$ xclock &
[5] 17439
$ netscape &
[6] 17441
$
```

All the clients started this way are now displaying on pokey:0, even though they are running locally on foobar. If you plan to start only one client, or if you need to display on multiple remote hosts, the -display argument might be more practical:

```
xterm -display pokey:0 &
```

The -display argument won't work on all clients, however, so it can at times be necessary to start certain clients after setting the DISPLAY environment variable.

Querying a Session Across the Network

The preceding two sections have assumed that X servers were already running on both pokey and foobar and that you were logged in on both machines. But what if you simply want to sit at foobar but execute all your clients on pokey? In this case, foobar is really acting merely as a terminal, displaying X primitives and accepting user input. To start an xdm login at foobar that runs on pokey, start the X server with the -query option on foobar, like this:

```
X -query pokey
```

Note that the x command cannot normally be executed by nonroot users, so if you are using foobar from a nonroot account, you should instead use

```
Xwrapper -query pokey
```

Assuming that an XDMCP daemon such as xdm, kdm, or gdm is running on pokey and is set to accept connections from foobar in the Xaccess file (see Chapter 14 for details), the xdm xlogin widget, the kdm login window, or the gdm greeter will appear and allow you to log in to pokey, using foobar as your primary display. In such a case, the display manager will take care of the creation and exchange of magic cookies in order to secure the display, and your local display will act as a graphics terminal connected to the remote machine via the network.

Getting Fonts Across the Network

After you are able to connect clients and servers across the network, it is also helpful to be able to use fonts installed on a remote machine while using the local X server. Such a sharing feat is accomplished by running an X font server on the remote system and adding a reference to this remote system in your local X server's font path using xset.

Installing and Running a Font Server

The X font server, xfs, is quite simple to configure and use. Before the server can be started, a configuration file must be created to supply the location of the fonts to the font server and to specify a number of operational options.

The Font Server Config File

The default path to the font server configuration file is lib/X11/fs/config off the /usr/X11R6 directory tree. The font server config file as supplied by XFree86 is quite sane and should be adequate for most purposes. Most users will not need to edit the file at all; a few who have installed extra fonts might want to edit the comma-separated list of font directories supplied to the catalogue keyword in the file.

A partial list of the other keywords that can appear in the file and the meanings associated with each is shown in Table 15.2.

Table 15.2   Keywords in the Font Server Config File

Keyword	Description
catalogue = *path*, *path*, ...	Specifies a list of directories in which fonts are to be found. XFree86 fonts are normally installed in /usr/X11R6/lib/X11/fonts.
client-limit = *n*	The number of clients, *n*, this server will accept before denying new connections.

Keyword	Description
`clone-self = on¦off`	If on, the server will clone itself to serve connection requests beyond the client limit rather than deny new connections.
`error-file = path`	Specifies the file to which all warnings and errors should be logged.
`port = n`	Causes the server to listen on port *n* rather than the default of 7100.
`use-syslog = on¦off`	If on, the server will log all warnings and errors via the syslog facility.

For a complete list of keywords that can appear in the xfs config file, please see the xfs manual page. Two user-suppliable arguments are also supported by the font server; these are shown in Table 15.3.

Table 15.3 Command-Line Arguments Supported by the Font Server

Argument	Description
`-config path`	Specifies a full path to the config file that should be used instead of `/usr/X11R6/lib/X11/fs/config`.
`-port n`	Specifies that the font server should listen for incoming connections on port *n* rather than the default port 7100 or the port specified in the font server config file.

Running the Font Server

After the configuration file exists and points to a valid set of fonts, the font server can be started simply by launching it in the background:

```
xfs &
```

On systems where the font server is to be continually available, the font server should be launched somewhere in init, so that reboots don't affect font availability.

Using Fonts from a Font Server

After a font server is running on a remote machine, the xset command can be used to add the fonts on the remote font server to the local X server's font path. The syntax is

```
xset fp+ transport/host:port
```

For example, to use the set of fonts being served by the pokey on port 7100, you'd issue the following command:

```
xset fp+ tcp/pokey:7100
```

Normally, only the tcp transport method is of interest to Linux users. The port should be assumed to be port 7100 unless the font server on the remote machine has explicitly been configured to listen on a different port.

After the xset command has been used to add remote fonts to the font path, the new fonts will show up when xlsfonts is called to list the fonts in the current font path. To remove a font server from your font path, use the following format:

```
xset fp- tcp/pokey:7100
```

For more information on using the xset command, please refer to Chapter 7. For more information on using xlsfonts, please see Chapter 4, "Standard XFree86 Programs and Utilities."

## 16

Tunneling X Through ssh (Secure Shell)

Chapter 15, "Working on the Network," discussed token-based authentication, which is theoretically the most secure way to run an X server, and mentioned that one of the flaws in token-based security is that anyone who gets hold of a magic cookie sent across the network can breach that security. The obvious answer is never to send the cookie across the network at all, but it is sometimes necessary in order to work efficiently on the network.

And there are other issues with the X network capability. What about the X protocol itself? If the X Window System is to be a viable network solution for multiple purposes, it is important that an X data stream not be easily interceptable by some undesired third party with malicious or thieving intent. Is there any way to ensure that the X data stream isn't stolen right out from under you as you work?

The best way to keep tokens from being stolen and the X data stream from being intercepted is to install and use ssh, the secure shell, on your network for all X transactions.

What Happens When I Use ssh?

It's unquestionably true that the use of ssh adds an additional layer of complexity to an X network management scheme that can already seem complex to some users. It's also true that ssh requires the download of software over the Internet and its subsequent installation and configuration. Because of these hindrances, many users are reluctant to download and use ssh, preferring instead to take the risk, especially when it isn't clear just what exactly ssh does.

Security Is Improved

The ssh command works like the rsh command in that it enables the user to execute commands on a remote machine. Unlike rsh, however, ssh encrypts data passing between the systems so that it cannot easily be intercepted and used by malicious third parties. In fact, ssh virtually eliminates several types of attacks and misbehavior, including IP spoofing, intercepting of plain text data (like magic cookies or password), and attacks built using IP source routing.

The ssh system additionally can tunnel several types of binary data streams through its encrypted connection, among them the X data stream, so that applications run remotely by tunneling them through ssh have secure, encrypted X data streams. The secure shell accomplishes this feat by setting up a proxy X server that is actually the sshd daemon; the remote system connects to the local system via the encrypted proxy X connection, and the sshd daemon in turn connects locally to the X server and sends the data in unencrypted form that the X server can use. In this way, unencrypted data is prevented from being sent over the network without any changes having to be made to existing X servers.

A good, human-readable discussion of ssh, its function, and its benefits can be found in SunWorld Online at the URL

```
http://www.sunworld.com/sunworldonline/swol 02 1998/swol 02 security.html
```

Because of these benefits, ssh should be used in almost any case where X data streams or X authentication cookies will be sent over the network. After using ssh becomes second nature (and it will), the effort involved in using it certainly is smaller than the risk you will be taking by not using it.

Speed Is Improved

Because ssh includes the option to compress data streams on-the-fly, ssh can actually improve network performance when used on machines whose processors can handle the encryption/decryption tasks adequately. This can be extremely useful on congested networks or on slower links when every last bit of bandwidth must be exploited.

The method of compression used by ssh is the same method of compression used by the fast and ubiquitous gzip command, and as is the case with gzip, the compression efficiency can be adjusted from level 1 (fastest) to level 9 (most compression). This added benefit of compressibility alone is enough to cause many users to use ssh to tunnel X connections.

Getting and Installing ssh

Because of the maze of export and patent restrictions on encryption code in the United States, you might not find a working ssh distribution or packages in your Linux installation or on your Linux distribution's CD-ROM.

The home site and primary distribution node for ssh software is the ssh homepage in Finland, which can be found at http://www.ssh.fi, but ssh can also be downloaded from several mirror sites, the addresses of which can be found at the ssh home page.

I'm going to discuss the older 1.2.x version of ssh in this chapter rather than the recent 2.x versions for several reasons. First, multiplatform compatibility is important in a distributed X environment, and ssh 1.x is more likely to be compatible with existing ssh installations or installations on non-UNIX platforms. Next, most of the tutorial information and documentation existing on the Web refers to ssh 1.x rather than the newer releases. Finally, the 1.x versions of ssh are under the GNU General Public License (GPL) as is Linux, although the 2.x versions are not.

Compiling ssh

After you've downloaded the ssh tarball from the primary distribution site or one of the mirrors, the first thing to do is extract the source:

```
$ tar -xzf ssh-1.2.nn.tar.gz
$
```

After the source has been extracted, use cd to visit the directory containing the ssh source, and use the configure command there to configure the source for compilation on your machine:

```
$ ./configure
$
```

A list of options to configure can be found by supplying the −help option to configure. Usually, however, no options are needed. After configure has run its course, you should be able to compile the source by issuing the make command and install it afterward with a make install as root:

```
$ make
...[ make output ]...
$ su root
Password:
# make install
...[ install output ]...
```

When installing, the default ssh configuration files and a public and private key for the machine in question will also be built. It is recommended that ssh be compiled and installed on each machine separately so that the public and private keys for each machine on your network will automatically be built without need for your intervention, greatly simplifying the process.

The default location for the ssh daemon binary is in /usr/local/sbin, and the default location for the other ssh binaries is /usr/local/bin. The manual pages will be installed in /usr/local/man, and the configuration files and key files that ssh has built for the machine can be seen by typing

```
ls /etc/*ssh*
```

After make install has been run this way, ssh is completely configured for general-purpose use in most cases.

Configuring the Secure Shell

The two most important components of the secure shell package are ssh, the program that will initiate outgoing connections, and sshd, the program that will accept incoming connections requested by an ssh on a remote machine. For our purposes, configuring the secure shell package is really a matter of configuring the ssh and sshd binaries.

Usually, the configuration, as installed by default, will be adequate. In some cases, however, it will be necessary to edit the ssh and sshd configuration files for your local circumstances; for example, if you plan to use ssh for multiple tasks on the system outside tunneling the X protocol, or if you want to restrict access to ssh to a specific group of users.

Configuring sshd

The primary method for altering the behavior of the sshd daemon is by editing the configuration file that should normally be located at /etc/sshd_config. The file is formatted simply as a list of keyword and value pairs, one pair per line. Lines that begin with the hash (#) character are assumed to be comments and are ignored. Some of the more common keywords known to sshd 1.2.x are shown in Table 16.1.

Table 16.1   Common Keywords Known to sshd

Keyword	Description
AllowGroups ptn, ptn, ...	Allows only users whose primary group name matches one of the supplied patterns to connect.
AllowHosts ptn, ptn, ...	Allows only hosts whose names match one of the supplied patterns to connect.
AllowUsers ptn, ptn, ...	Allows only users whose names match one of the supplied patterns to connect. Patterns will match either user accounts or user@host format strings.
DenyGroups ptn, ptn, ...	Denies groups whose names match the supplied pattern's connections.
DenyHosts ptn, ptn, ...	Denies hosts whose names match the supplied pattern's connections.

Keyword	Description
DenyUsers ptn, ptn, ...	Denies users whose names match the supplied pattern's connections.
FascistLogging yes¦no	If yes, sshd will perform extreme and copious amounts of logging. If no, sshd will perform normal amounts of logging.
IdleTimeout n[s¦m¦h]	Specifies that a connection should be killed if no data is transferred for a period of n seconds, hours, or minutes, depending on whether n is followed by h, m, or s, respectively.
KeyRegenerationInterval n	Specifies that the server encryption key should be regenerated and updated every n seconds to prevent the ability to decrypt stolen sessions. The default is to update every 3600 seconds.
PermitRootLogin yes¦no	Specifies whether root logins should be allowed. The default is yes, but some users will need to change this.
Port n	Specifies that sshd should listen for incoming connections on port n. The default is port 22.
QuietMode yes¦no	If yes, causes sshd to operate in quiet mode, with minimal amounts of logging. The default is no.
X11Forwarding yes¦no	Specifies whether X11 forwarding is permitted. The default value is yes, and for the purposes of this text should not be changed.
X11DisplayOffset n	Specifies the display number to use for the sshd proxy X11 connection. This display should be set high enough to avoid conflicting with existing displays on the system in question.
XauthLocation path	Specifies the default path to the xauth program binary.

For information on additional keywords that can be supplied in the /etc/sshd_config file, such as those pertaining to authentication via .rhosts and /etc/hosts.equiv files, please see the sshd manual page. Note that the default /etc/sshd_config is fairly sane, so users should edit it if possible rather than starting from scratch.

Configuring ssh

The ssh configuration is normally stored in the /etc/ssh_config file. The /etc/ssh_config file is broken into sections, each section beginning with a Host keyword followed by a pattern that matches hosts to which the section applies. Within each section are several keyword and value pairs, each on a separate line. Some common keywords that can appear in /etc/ssh_config are shown in Table 16.2.

Table 16.2 Common Keywords Known to ssh

Keyword	Description
Cipher type	Specifies the type of cipher to use for encrypting data over the connection. Valid methods are idea, des, 3des, blowfish, arcfour, or none for no encryption by default. The default is to use idea, and it should be noted that not all methods are available on all systems.
Compression yes¦no	Specifies whether compression should be used by default.
CompressionLevel n	Specifies that ssh should use gzip compression level n to compress the data stream. Compression level 1 is the least processor-intensive method but results in the lowest compressibility. Compression level 9 results in better compression but is more host-intensive.
ConnectionAttempts n	Specifies the maximum level of connection attempts, n, before ssh will either fall back to rsh (see next keyword) or give up.
FallBackToRsh yes¦no	Specifies that if ssh is unable to connect to the remote host after the number of attempts specified by ConnectionAttempts, rsh will be used as a fallback mechanism.
ForwardX11 yes¦no	When yes, specifies that X11 connections will automatically be redirected over the encrypted link using sshd's proxy X server capability.
NumberOfPasswordPrompts n	Specifies that ssh should try to authenticate the user up to n (not more than 5) times before giving up.
PasswordPromptHost yes¦no	Specifies whether to display the remote host name when prompting for a password.
PasswordPromptLogin yes¦no	Specifies whether to display the username when prompting for a password.
Port n	Specifies that ssh should attempt to connect to port n on the remote machine by default. The default value is port 22.
XauthLocation path	Specifies the path to the xauth program binary.

Note that although the global ssh configuration is stored on each system at /etc/ssh_config, each user can have a personalized ssh configuration file of the same format that will override any global settings. This file is found at $HOME/.ssh_config. For complete details on the keywords supported by ssh, please refer to the ssh manual page.

Using ssh with X

Two primary types of data should be encrypted when working with X on the network. The first is the transmission of magic cookies for token-based authentication; the second is the X data stream itself. Note that ssh will automatically exchange encrypted magic cookies for you when tunneling an X data stream, so in reality, after ssh is installed, you'll rarely need to exchange cookies manually.

Before either form of secure transfer can be accomplished, the sshd daemon must be running on the machines that will need to accept ssh connections.

Starting the sshd Daemon

The sshd daemon is easy to start from the command line. Simply become root and issue the following command:

```
/usr/local/sbin/sshd
```

Because sshd considers itself to be a daemon, it kindly places itself in the background automatically. For systems that will be used on an X network on a continuous basis, it is more helpful to insert a call to sshd from within the init process. This can be in the /etc/rc.d/rc.local file or sooner in the process. One possible addition to /etc/rc.d/rc.local would be

```
/bin/echo -n 'Starting sshd: '
if [ -x /usr/local/sbin/sshd ]; then
    /usr/local/sbin/sshd
    /bin/echo done
else
    /bin/echo not found
fi
```

Some users might object to the idea of having an sshd daemon hanging around all the time and might want to have inetd start sshd each time a connection is requested. The sshd daemon allows this kind of functionality as long as the -i option is supplied on the command line. To have inetd start sshd each time an incoming connection must be started, edit the /etc/services file to contain the following line:

```
ssh        22/tcp       # secure shell
```

Then, edit the /etc/inetd.conf file to contain the following line:

```
ssh stream tcp nowait root   /usr/sbin/tcpd /opt/bin/sshd -i
```

After the changes have been made, restart the inetd server using the hangup signal to have it reread its configuration files:

```
killall -HUP inetd
```

The sshd server should now start by itself whenever an incoming ssh connection is requested. Note that starting sshd on-the-fly will work only on faster systems; the time it takes to generate the server key each time it starts may cause connections to time out on slower systems.

For more information on the formats of the /etc/services and /etc/inetd.conf files, please see the manual pages for services and for inetd, respectively.

Using ssh to Transfer Magic Cookies

Recall that in Chapter 15, the following command was introduced to facilitate the transfer of a magic cookie from one host to another:

```
xauth extract - :0 ¦ rsh foobar xauth merge -
```

This command had the effect of transferring the magic cookie for the local display to the host foobar so that clients from foobar could connect to the local X server. The only problem with this technique was that the magic cookie was sent via rsh in plain-text form over the network, and the entire process was therefore susceptible to breach by unscrupulous third parties.

With the ssh command substituted instead of rsh, the process repairs itself because the data stream is now encrypted:

```
xauth extract - :0 ¦ ssh foobar xauth merge -
```

If you are running the ssh command for the first time, you might have to wait a moment as a random seed file is generated, and you might be presented with a few bits of status text. You will also be prompted for your password on the remote system; enter it at the prompt and the cookie is transferred over the encrypted channel and merged into the $HOME/.Xauthority file securely on the remote system, foobar.

Using ssh to Tunnel X Sessions

Because ssh employs a mechanism to tunnel X sessions automatically, the process of launching remote clients over the encrypted channel is remarkably simple. In most cases, you can simply issue a command like the following one:

```
ssh foobar /usr/X11R6/bin/xterm
```

After asking you for your password, a new xterm window will appear on the host foobar's display. To see evidence of the encrypted connections, try using the netstat command in the new xterm window, or alternatively, check the DISPLAY variable in the new xterm window:

```
user@foobar$ echo $DISPLAY
foobar:10.0
User@foobar$
```

Notice that the display number is not 0 or another existing display, but is a number higher than the number of any existing display (usually 10). This is evidence of the sshd X protocol proxy at work; the X data stream is moving over the encrypted channel. It is good policy to use ssh at all times when connecting clients to X servers using network interfaces, and to instruct users to do the same.

Any X client that can be started over the network by other means can also be connected over the network across a secure ssh channel. When combined with token-based authentication, ssh provides one of the best methods for securing X services available, and it is much easier to manage than alternative services such as Kerberos.

Accepting Incoming Encrypted X Connections

After the sshd server is either running or configured to run on the local display, there is really little more that needs to be done to safely accept and administer incoming X client requests.

The sshd daemon works with existing access control mechanisms, both host-based and token-based, and in addition implements several access control mechanisms of its own in the /etc/sshd_config file.

More on ssh

This chapter has hinted at the ssh's capability to tunnel other types of network protocols across the encrypted channel. There are other ways of using ssh as well, for example, with $HOME/.rhosts-like access, avoiding the need for the user to supply a password for each connection.

A complete discussion of ssh configuration in multihost environments or the many uses of ssh is beyond the scope of this text. However, there are many good resources on the Internet designed to help system administrations install and use ssh to its fullest. Some information that might help you to familiarize yourself with ssh can be found at the following links:

http://www.ssh.org/

http://www.tac.nyc.ny.us/~kim/ssh/

http://www.csua.berkeley.edu/ssh howto.html

http://www.employees.org/~satch/ssh/faq/

More information on using ssh, sshd, slogin, and the other tools that come with ssh, especially with regard to command-line arguments and configuration file formats, can be found by consulting each of their respective system manual pages.

17

HETEROGENEOUS NETWORKS

X on Networks

It's clear that XFree86 is a powerful implementation of the network-centric X window system, and that X was designed from the ground up to work well on a network. In spite of this fact, managing X effectively on the network is not always as easy as it would seem.

On many networks, it is essential to allow users to log in at any one of several graphics consoles in physically different locations. In such cases the user's account, X resources, window manager, and other X runtime elements must function well on each console, accounting for varying resolutions, color depths, and capabilities. Often, X-enabled networks contain a variety of UNIX-style hardware from different vendors, meaning that different versions of X will often be in use and must be able to communicate effectively with one another.

Most important, modern networks are rarely composed of a single type of hardware platform; it is important to understand how X functions on networks that include not only Linux or UNIX machines, but MacOS, Windows, and other operating systems as well.

Multiple Login Points

One common method for dealing with user accounts that have multiple physical login points with varying capabilities is through judicious use of the xinitrc script, both systemwide as well as user-specific.

When editing the xinitrc scripts, it is important to understand something about shell programming. It is also extremely important to know something about the capabilities of the various machines and X consoles on your network and to have a fundamental understanding of the software that is installed on the network.

A complete discussion of shell programming or the fundamentals of UNIX-style networking is beyond the scope of this text. There are, however, a few places that can be good starting points for X-enabling a network.

The DISPLAY Variable

The DISPLAY environment variable is an important hint when managing the X login and initialization process. By keeping track of the capabilities of various X displays (servers) around the network and accounting for the differences in display depth, resolution, and server versions, the first battle will have been won.

Recall that the display variable when a display is used across a network generally contains a value in the following format:

```
host:d.s
```

The host is either a host name or a fully qualified domain name for the display machine in question; d represents the display and s represents the screen. Checking for the host, display, or screen in a script can allow the script to start different clients or to start clients with different arguments based on the known capabilities of the host, display, or screen in question. Table 17.1 lists possible methods for extracting the host name, display, or screen from the DISPLAY environment variable into the X_HOST, X_DISPLAY, or X_SCREEN variables, respectively.

Table 17.1 Extracting Host, Display, and Screen

Value	Sample Command
Host	X_HOST=`cat $DISPLAY¦cut -d: -f1`
Display	X_DISPLAY=`cat $DISPLAY¦cut -d: -f2¦cut -d. -f1`
Screen	X_SCREEN=`cat $DISPLAY¦cut -d: -f2¦cut -d. -f2`

The DISPLAY variable is useful for finding information about the machine running the X server and making decisions based on such information.

The uname Command

The uname command is one of the network administrator's best friends when it comes to managing multiple login hosts for user accounts. By supplying various arguments to the uname command and applying the information returned, decisions can be made based on the system on which the xinitrc scripts are actually running. Table 17.2 shows the most common arguments to the uname command and their meanings.

Table 17.2 Common uname Arguments and Meanings

Argument	Description
-s	Displays the operating system in use, for example, Linux.
-m	Displays the type of hardware in use, for example, m68k or i386.
-r	Displays the operating system release, for example, 2.2.5ac6.
-n	Displays the machine's full host name.

The uname command is useful for finding information about the machine that will be running the X clients and making decisions based on such information.

Root Window Color Depth

It is also sometimes helpful to know the depth of the root window or the type of visual used by the root window, especially on Linux-based XFree86 installations that will be started at any of several color depths.

In such cases, the xdpyinfo command, covered in complete detail in Chapter 4, "Standard XFree86 Programs and Utilities," is the command of choice. Through judicious use of commands like grep and awk, it is possible to extract the relevant information from xdpyinfo and store it in a variable. For example, the following command gets the depth of the root window and stores it in a shell variable:

```
X_DEPTH=`xdpyinfo¦grep depth.*r.*:¦cut -d: -f2¦awk '{print $1}'`
```

Clearly, some understanding of shell programming basics is required to be able to extract information from xdpyinfo effectively.

Putting It All Together: An Example

In this case, the best way to illustrate one way in which these techniques can all be assembled is with a simple example. Imagine a network in which users with valid accounts are to have access to their accounts from any number of machines, each of which may be of a different platform. The X displays are also of varied platforms and color depths. What sort of scripting could take place during the startup process to compensate for this variability? Listing 17.1 shows one possible small script fragment from such an environment.

Listing 17.1 Script Fragment, Varied Network Environment

```
X_HOST=`cat $DISPLAY|cut -d: -f1`
X_DEPTH=`xdpyinfo|grep depth.*r.*:|cut -d: -f2|awk '{print $1}'`
X_CLIENT=`uname -n|cut -d. -f1`
X_CLARC=`uname -m`
#
# X resolution first assumed to be 1152x900
#
X_RES=1152x900
#
# See if resolution adjustment is necessary
#
[ X_HOST = pokey ] && X_RES=1024x768
[ X_HOST = foobar ] && X_RES=800x600
#
# Adjust FVWM config based on depth and resolution
#
[ X_DEPTH = 8 ] && FVWM_CONFIG=$HOME/.fvwmrc-8bit-$X_RES
[ X_DEPTH != 8 ] && FVWM_CONFIG=$HOME/.fvwmrc-16.24.32bit-$X_RES
[ ! -e $FVWM_CONFIG ] && FVWM_CONFIG=$HOME/.fvwmrc-default
#
# Mount local X binaries directory based on platform
#
if [ X_CLARC = m68k ]|'|[ X_CLARC = sparc]; then
    mount /usr/X11R6/local/$X_CLARC/bin
    export PATH=$PATH:/usr/X11R6/local/$X_CLARC/bin
    rm $HOME/xbin; ln -s /usr/X11R6/local/$X_CLARC/bin $HOME/xbin
else
    mount /usr/X11R6/local/ix86/bin
    export PATH=$PATH:/usr/X11R6/local/ix86/bin
    rm $HOME/xbin; ln -s /usr/X11R6/local/ix86/bin $HOME/xbin
fi
#
# Launch window manager
#
fvwm -f $FVWM_CONFIG
```

This script fragment isn't intended for production use, but rather as an illustration of some of the ways in which information about the current X runtime, client machine, and server host can be used.

Command-Line Arguments

Several commonly used X binaries accept command-line arguments that can be useful when trying to adapt XFree86 to a multiplatform or multihost network. Most of these arguments allow an alternate configuration file to be specified, in cases where a single default file is inadequate. A list of some of these command-line arguments can be found in Table 17.3.

Table 17.3 Helpful Command-Line Arguments

Command	Description
fvwm -f *file*	Launch the fvwm window manager using *file* as the window manager configuration file.
fvwm2 -f *file*	Launch the fvwm2 window manager using *file* as the window manager configuration file.
twm -f *file*	Launch the twm window manager using *file* as the window manager configuration file.
xdm -session *script*	Use *script* as the session management script in place of the default Xsession script.
xdm -config *file*	Use *file* as the xdm configuration file rather than the default xdm-config file in /usr/X11R6/lib/X11/xdm.
X -audit *level*	Set the connection audit level. If *level* is 1, rejected connections are reported. If *level* is 2, all connection openings or closings are reported. If *level* is 4, all security information is also logged. If *level* is 0, auditing is turned off.
X -auth *file*	Use *file* as the magic cookie file for authorizing users using token-based authentication.
X -query *host*	Query an XDMCP session (login manager) from the given *host*.

Note that the x binary is not normally called directly, but is more often called via either Xwrapper or startx. For more information on using startx, please refer to Chapter 3, "Launching XFree86."

Mixing Client and Server Versions

As is the case with any type of software interoperability, the closer together two software items are in terms of release versions, the more likely they are to work together happily. The same wisdom applies to the world of networked X, where many different versions of X remain in widespread use.

X11R6 Releases

Most X installations based on one of the X11R6 releases, including the great majority of existing Linux installations, will safely interoperate with each other with a minimum of compatibility problems.

Subreleases of X11R6 include X11R6.2, X11R6.3, and X11R6.4. Specific extensions unique to XFree86 releases are less likely to work than standard X protocols when used in multiple version environments, and local extensions like DGA will not display across the network at all.

X11R6 servers work well with clients from X11R5 and X11R4 machines, though some modifications to source code might be necessary when applications are recompiled. X11R6 servers are less friendly to pre-X11R4 clients, many of which won't operate at all, and users should make every attempt to use at least X11R4 clients when later clients are available.

X11R5 Releases

The X11R5 release was close enough in substance to the X11R6 releases that the great majority of X11R5 software is interoperable with X11R6 installations.

X11R5 servers will run a surprisingly complete number of X11R6 clients without modification, and adapting client source code between X11R5 and X11R6 is generally very easy to accomplish. Most X11R4 clients will function on X11R5 servers without modification, though again some source code must often be modified if applications are to be recompiled.

X11R4 Releases

The X11R4 release is two versions distant from X11R6 installations, and it shows; X11R4 clients are less likely to operate correctly with X11R6 servers than are X11R5 clients, and many small bugs and peculiarities begin to appear in program function when attempting to use X11R4 clients with X11R6 servers.

X11R4 servers will have trouble with a large segment of X11R5 and X11R6 clients due to fundamental differences such as the lack of scalable font capability. X11R4 clients should be used with X11R4 servers whenever possible.

Pre-X11R4 Releases

Pre-X11R4 clients and servers should be regarded as completely depreciated and should be avoided whenever possible. Compatibility with later X releases is minimal at best in most cases, and source code is different enough to make porting to R5 or R6 systems a major job.

Most pre-X11R4 machines are old enough to have lost much of their utility anyway and should be retired for X use unless a suitable distribution of XFree86 or some other X11R6-based X installation can be found.

X Servers for Non-UNIX Operating Systems

Although it is certainly possible to restrict remote X access to UNIX and Linux machines only on a given network, it is often inconvenient to do so. In many cases, the preferred solution is a network on which every host is X server–enabled and remote X clients can thus be displayed anywhere, not just on UNIX or Linux hosts.

Many X servers are available for several different common hardware and operating system platforms. After an X server is installed, most such platforms can act as more than adequate X login, session, or client display points.

X Servers for Windows

Quite a few X servers are available for Windows machines, ranging in functionality from basic X11R5-style servers to X functionality integrated into a large connectivity suite. The servers listed in this section are predominantly that: standalone X servers or X distributions in the traditional sense. Prices and specifications vary widely; if in doubt, it is best to contact the vendor and inquire about pricing and specific capabilities or components.

X-WinPro from Labtam Finland Ltd.

The X-WinPro suite from Labtam Finland Ltd. is an X11R5-based X distribution that runs on all versions of Windows from Windows 3.1 to Windows 95/98 and Windows NT. Several X clients and Motif-based clients are included in the standard packages, which retail for $99.00 for a single user or as little as $60.00 per user for a 100+ user license purchase.

The X-WinPro Web site can be found at `http://www.labf.com/xwpweb/`.

KEA!X from Attachmate

The KEA!X server from Attachmate is an X11R6.3-based X server that supports low-bandwidth X protocol mode in addition to the standard X protocol. The server runs on all versions of Windows from Windows 3.1 to Windows 95/98 and Windows NT. It includes NFS client support on Windows 95/98 and NT-based systems.

For pricing and availability, please contact Attachmate at 1-800-933-6751 or visit the KEA!X Web site at `http://www.attachmate.com/OSG/KEA!X/`.

Exceed from Hummingbird

The Exceed X server from Hummingbird remains one of the most popular X servers among Windows users. Versions are available supporting all Windows releases from 3.1 to 95/98 and NT. The latest Exceed server is X11R6.4-based. The Exceed server supports several advanced features including multidisplay support and Kerberos authentication.

For pricing and availability, please visit the Exceed Web site at
`http://www.hummingbird.com/products/nc/exceed/`.

MI/X from Microimages

The MI/X server from Microimages held the distinction for quite some time of being the only freely available X server for Windows-based computing environments. With the 2.0 release of MI/X for Windows, this is no longer the case, with pricing at $25.00 per user for a single user or as little as $17.50 per user for 500+ users. The MI/X server is based on X11R5 and does not support xdm query type functionality.

For availability and purchase information, please see the MI/X for Windows home page at http://www.microimages.com/mix/.

PC-Xware from NCD

The PC-Xware server from classic X-terminal manufacturer Network Computing Devices, Inc. (NCD) is based on the X11R6 release and runs on all versions of Windows from 3.1 to Windows 95/98 and Windows NT. The package includes an NFS client as well as a TCP/IP stack for Windows 3.x machines.

For pricing and availability, please see the PC-Xware home page at http://www.ncd.com/ppcx/ or visit the order page at https://www.ncd.com/ppcx/pcxorder.html.

X-Deep/32 from Pexus Systems

The X-Deep/32 distribution from Pexus Systems is a complete X11R6.1 distribution, including server, clients, twm window manager, and other standard X11R6.1 components. The distribution is compatible with Windows 95/98 and NT machines and is available on CD for $49.95 per user.

For more information, please see the Pexus Systems home page at http://www.pexus.com/. For order information, please visit the X-Deep/32 order page at http://www.pexus.com/Sales/sales.html.

XVision Eclipse from SCO

The XVision Eclipse server from Santa Cruz Operation, Inc. (SCO) is a complete, plug-and-play X11R6.3 server for Windows 95/98 and NT machines. Pricing begins at $429.00 for a single-user license.

For complete information, as well as pricing and availability, please visit the XVision Eclipse Web site at http://www.sco.com/vision/products/eclipse/info.html.

Interix X Products from Softway Systems, Inc.

Softway Systems, Inc. sells a complete line of X servers and X-based products for Windows PCs under the Interix name. For complete information on Interix products, including X11R5

and X11R6 servers and development environments, please visit the Interix home page at
http://www.interix.com.

X-Win32 from StarNet Communications Corporation

The X-Win32 product from StarNet Communications Corporation is an X server for Windows
3.1, 95/98, and NT-based systems. The X-Win32 product supports some Xsecurity extensions
and low-bandwidth X protocol extensions. Pricing is $200.00 per user with volume discounts
available for 10+ license purchases.

For complete information, pricing, and availability please visit the X-Win32 home page at
http://www.starnet.com/product.htm.

Omni-X from XLink

The Omni-X server from XLink is an X11R5/6 server for computers running Windows 95/98 or
Windows NT operating systems. Omni-X supports XFree86-style virtual panning and full
XDMCP connectivity. Pricing begins at $69.00 for an academic single-user license or $135.00
for a single-user license.

For additional information and availability, please visit the Omni-X home page at
http://www.xlink.com/nfs_products/Omni X_Server/Omni X_Server.htm or see the XLink home
page at http://www.xlink.com.

X Server for Macintosh

The majority of non-UNIX and non-Linux X servers are available for the Windows+x86 platform only. Macintosh users aren't completely left out, however. The current server of choice for
many users, in part because of its price (free) is the MI/X server for Macintosh, an X11R5-
based server similar to the MI/X server for Windows.

The MI/X server for Macintosh requires a Power Macintosh machine and can be downloaded
from the MI/X for Macintosh home page at http://www.microimages.com/freestuf/mix/
macindex.htm.

X11R6.4 Distribution, with Server, for OS/2

The XFree86 Project maintains a complete XFree86 distribution for OS/2 machines similar to
the distribution for Linux machines. The XFree86 3.3.5 release supports OS/2 Warp 3 (all versions), Warp Connect, Warp Server, and Warp 4. The binaries directory for XFree86 3.3.5 for
OS/2 can be found at ftp://ftp.xfree86.org/pub/XFree86/3.3.5/binaries/OS2/.

XFree86 3.3.5 for OS/2 supports the same set of graphics hardware supported by XFree86
3.3.5 for Linux and can be compiled from source by OS/2 users if desired.

Virtual Network Computing

An interesting method for achieving XDMCP-like network transparency across multiple platforms can be found at the Virtual Network Computing home page at `http://www.uk.research.att.com/vnc/`.

Virtual Network Computing is a freely available system that provides functionality similar to the functionality provided by an X server, in that a running graphical desktop can be displayed remotely from the machine on which the applications are actually executing. Virtual Network Computing is not, however, an X server in its own right.

Downloads are free for several UNIX platforms: Linux, Macintosh, Windows, and Java. A complete discussion of Virtual Network Computing is beyond the scope of this text; if you think that Virtual Network Computing might work for you, please visit the home page listed previously.

PART VI

APPENDIXES

Sample Window Manager Configurations

These sample window manager configurations each present a simple yet functional basis upon which more personalized configurations can be built. Of course, they can also be used as-is if desired. They are commented for clarity, but for a complete understanding of each file, please consult the manual page for the window manager in question.

These configurations assume a screen geometry of 800×600 and a video accelerator fast enough to allow opaque moves.

Sample $HOME/.twmrc Without Icons

```
#
# Sample twm configuration with icon manager
#
# Based on the distributed system.twmrc originally by the X
# Consortium, included with XFree86 3.3.5
#
# This sample configuration is extremely basic, but should form
# the basis for a very workable desktop for most users using the
# TWM window manager. Study the comments throughout the file for
# details.
#

TitleFont "-adobe-helvetica-bold-r-normal--*-120-*-*-*-*-*-*"
ResizeFont "-adobe-helvetica-bold-r-normal--*-120-*-*-*-*-*-*"
MenuFont "-adobe-helvetica-bold-r-normal--*-120-*-*-*-*-*-*"
```

```
IconFont "-adobe-helvetica-bold-r-normal--*-100-*-*-*-*-*-*"
IconManagerFont "-adobe-helvetica-bold-r-normal--*-100-*-*-*"

#
# Previous section: font configuration
# Next section: color configuration
#

Color
{
    BorderColor "slategrey"
    DefaultBackground "steelblue4"
    DefaultForeground "white"
    TitleBackground "steelblue4"
    TitleForeground "white"
    MenuBackground "steelblue4"
    MenuForeground "white"
    MenuTitleBackground "slategrey"
    MenuTitleForeground "white"
    IconManagerBackground "steelblue4"
    IconManagerForeground "white"
    IconManagerHighlight "red"
}

#
# A few behavioral changes: move windows opaquely, don't
# grab the X server during pop-ups, and attempt to restart in
# a sane state.
#
OpaqueMove
NoGrabServer
RestartPreviousState

#
# Set up icon manager and cause windows to minimize to it, rather
# than minimizing to icons outside the manager. Eliminate the
# manager title bar. Set the size to be as large as needed
# (manager will expand as windows are started) and five columns
# wide.
#

ShowIconManager
IconifyByUnmapping
SortIconManager
IconManagerGeometry "800x600+0+0" 5
NoTitle { "TWM Icon Manager" }

#
# Define some useful functions for motion or click actions, which
# will be bound to mouse clicks in just a moment.
#
```

```
Function "move-or-raiselower" { f.move f.deltastop f.raiselower }
Function "move-or-maximize" { f.move f.deltastop f.fullzoom }
Function "move-or-identify" { f.move f.deltastop f.identify }

#
# Bind root-window clicks. Left-click displays the main menu,
# middle-click displays a window operations menu, right-click
# displays an applications menu. Menus are defined after bindings
# are complete.
#

Button1 = : root : f.menu "main-menu"
Button2 = : root : f.menu "window-ops"
Button3 = : root : f.menu "applications"

#
# Bind -titlebar clicks. When any button is used to drag the
# title bar, the window is moved. When the left button is
# clicked, the window will be raised, or, if it is already
# raised, it will be lowered. When the middle button is clicked,
# the window is maximized or unmaximized. When the right button
# is clicked, the window will be identified.
#

Button1 = : title : f.function "move-or-raiselower"
Button2 = : title : f.function "move-or-maximize"
Button3 = : title : f.function "move-or-identify"

#
# Bind icon manager clicks. Left-click minimizes or restores a
# window. Middle-click deletes the indicated window, and right-
# click destroys the indicated window.
#

Button1 = : iconmgr : f.iconify
Button2 = : iconmgr : f.delete
Button3 = : iconmgr : f.destroy

#
# Now, we bind all of the functions in the window operations
# menu plus one or two more to the shifted function keys.
#

"F1" = shift : all : f.iconify
"F2" = shift : all : f.resize
"F3" = shift : all : f.move
"F4" = shift : all : f.raise
"F5" = shift : all : f.lower
"F6" = shift : all : f.delete
"F7" = shift : all : f.destroy
"F8" = shift : all : f.refresh
```

```
"F9"  = shift : all : f.restart
"F10" = shift : all : f.quit

#
# A brief (and therefore easy to maintain) yet complete menu
# system for launching most common applications and performing
# most common window tasks, including hiding or restoring the
# icon manager itself.
#

menu "window-ops"
{
"Management"      f.title
"Iconify"         f.iconify
"Resize"          f.resize
"Move"         f.move
"Raise"         f.raise
"Lower"         f.lower
""              f.nop
"Hide Iconmgr"    f.hideiconmgr
"Show Iconmgr"    f.showiconmgr
""              f.nop
"Kill"         f.destroy
"Delete"         f.delete
""              f.nop
"Refresh"         f.refresh
"Restart"          f.restart
}

menu "exit"
{
"Exit TWM?"    f.title
"Yes, exit."    f.quit
"No, don't."    f.refresh
}

menu "applications"
{
"Applications"    f.title
"Emacs"         f.exec "emacs &"
"WordPerfect"    f.exec "xwp &"
"Wingz"         f.exec "Wingz &"
"Netscape"         f.exec "netscape &"
}

menu "desktop"
{
"Desktop"         f.title
"Clipboard"    f.exec "xclipboard &"
"Editor"         f.exec "xedit &"
"Resources"    f.exec "editres &"
```

```
"Bitmap"        f.exec "bitmap &"
"Fonts"         f.exec "xfontsel &"
"Colors"        f.exec "xcolorsel &"
}

menu "graphics"
{
"Graphics"         f.title
"GIMP"          f.exec "gimp &"
"XV"            f.exec "xv &"
"Paint"         f.exec "xpaint &"
"Scene Editor"    f.exec "sced &"
"Raytracer"     f.exec "xpovray &"
"Blender"          f.exec "blender &"
}


#
# This is the main menu, from which other menus are called.
#

menu "main-menu"
{
"X Session"     f.title
"Terminal"         f.exec "xterm &"
"Calculator"    f.exec "xcalc &"
""              f.nop
"Applications"    f.menu "applications"
"Desktop"          f.menu "desktop"
"Graphics"         f.menu "graphics"
""              f.nop
"Management"     f.menu "window-ops"
"Exit"          f.menu "exit"
}


#
# End sample twm configuration without icons
#
```

Sample $HOME/.twmrc with Icons

```
#
# Sample twm configuration without icon manager
#
# Based on the distributed system.twmrc originally by the X
# Consortium, included with XFree86 3.3.5
#
# This sample configuration is extremely basic, but should form
# the basis for a very workable desktop for most users using the
# TWM window manager. Study the comments throughout the file for
# details.
```

```
#

TitleFont "-adobe-helvetica-bold-r-normal--*-120-*-*-*-*-*-*"
ResizeFont "-adobe-helvetica-bold-r-normal--*-120-*-*-*-*-*-*"
MenuFont "-adobe-helvetica-bold-r-normal--*-120-*-*-*-*-*-*"
IconFont "-adobe-helvetica-bold-r-normal--*-100-*-*-*-*-*-*"
IconManagerFont "-adobe-helvetica-bold-r-normal--*-100-*-*-*"

#
# Previous section: font configuration
# Next section: color configuration
#

Color
{
    BorderColor "slategrey"
    DefaultBackground "steelblue4"
    DefaultForeground "white"
    TitleBackground "steelblue4"
    TitleForeground "white"
    MenuBackground "steelblue4"
    MenuForeground "white"
    MenuTitleBackground "slategrey"
    MenuTitleForeground "white"
    IconBackground "steelblue4"
    IconForeground "white"
    IconBorderColor "slategrey"
}

#
# A few behavioral changes: move windows opaquely, don't
# grab the X server during pop-ups, and attempt to restart in
# a sane state.
#

OpaqueMove
NoGrabServer
RestartPreviousState

#
# Use the X logo for applications that don't supply a minimized
# icon, and cause icons to fill as tightly as possible from the
# lower-right of the display upward and leftward.
#

IconDirectory "/usr/X11R6/include/X11/bitmaps/"
UnknownIcon "xlogo32"
IconRegion "800x600+0+0" South East 0 0

#
# Define some useful functions for motion or click actions, which
```

```
# will be bound to mouse clicks in just a moment.
#

Function "move-or-raiselower" { f.move f.deltastop f.raiselower }
Function "move-or-maximize" { f.move f.deltastop f.fullzoom }
Function "move-or-identify" { f.move f.deltastop f.identify }


#
# Bind root-window clicks. Left-click displays the main menu,
# middle-click displays a window operations menu, right-click
# displays an applications menu. Menus are defined after bindings
# are complete.
#

Button1 = : root : f.menu "main-menu"
Button2 = : root : f.menu "window-ops"
Button3 = : root : f.menu "applications"


#
# Bind -titlebar clicks. When any button is used to drag the
# title bar, the window is moved. When the left button is
# clicked, the window will be raised, or, if it is already
# raised, it will be lowered. When the middle button is clicked,
# the window is maximized or unmaximized. When the right button
# is clicked, the window will be identified.
#

Button1 = : title : f.function "move-or-raiselower"
Button2 = : title : f.function "move-or-maximize"
Button3 = : title : f.function "move-or-identify"


#
# Bind icon manager clicks. Left-click minimizes or restores a
# window. Middle-click deletes the indicated window, and right-
# click destroys the indicated window.
#

Button1 = : iconmgr : f.iconify
Button2 = : iconmgr : f.delete
Button3 = : iconmgr : f.destroy


#
# Now, we bind all of the functions in the window operations
# menu plus one or two more to the shifted function keys.
#

"F1"  = shift : all : f.iconify
"F2"  = shift : all : f.resize
"F3"  = shift : all : f.move
"F4"  = shift : all : f.raise
"F5"  = shift : all : f.lower
```

```
"F6"  = shift : all : f.delete
"F7"  = shift : all : f.destroy
"F8"  = shift : all : f.refresh
"F9"  = shift : all : f.restart
"F10" = shift : all : f.quit

#
# A brief (and therefore easy to maintain) yet complete menu
# system for launching most common applications and performing
# most common window tasks, including hiding or restoring the
# icon manager itself.
#

menu "window-ops"
{
"Management"    f.title
"Iconify"        f.iconify
"Resize"         f.resize
"Move"        f.move
"Raise"          f.raise
"Lower"          f.lower
""            f.nop
"Show Iconmgr"    f.showiconmgr
"Hide Iconmgr"    f.hideiconmgr
""            f.nop
"Kill"        f.destroy
"Delete"          f.delete
""            f.nop
"Refresh"          f.refresh
"Restart"          f.restart
}

menu "exit"
{
"Exit TWM?"     f.title
"Yes, exit."    f.quit
"No, don't."    f.refresh
}

menu "applications"
{
"Applications"    f.title
"Emacs"          f.exec "emacs &"
"WordPerfect"    f.exec "xwp &"
"Wingz"          f.exec "Wingz &"
"Netscape"          f.exec "netscape &"
}

menu "desktop"
{
"Desktop"          f.title
```

```
"Clipboard"    f.exec "xclipboard &"
"Editor"       f.exec "xedit &"
"Resources"    f.exec "editres &"
"Bitmap"       f.exec "bitmap &"
"Fonts"        f.exec "xfontsel &"
"Colors"       f.exec "xcolorsel &"
}

menu "graphics"
{
"Graphics"        f.title
"GIMP"         f.exec "gimp &"
"XV"           f.exec "xv &"
"Paint"        f.exec "xpaint &"
"Scene Editor"    f.exec "sced &"
"Raytracer"    f.exec "xpovray &"
"Blender"         f.exec "blender &"
}


#
# This is the main menu, from which other menus are called.
#

menu "main-menu"
{
"X Session"    f.title
"Terminal"        f.exec "xterm &"
"Calculator"      f.exec "xcalc &"
""          f.nop
"Applications"    f.menu "applications"
"Desktop"         f.menu "desktop"
"Graphics"        f.menu "graphics"
""          f.nop
"Management"      f.menu "window-ops"
"Exit"         f.menu "exit"
}


#
# End sample twm configuration with icons
#
```

Sample $HOME/.fvwmrc Without Icons

```
#
# Sample fvwm configuration without icons
#
# This .fvwmrc file uses the same basic colors, fonts, and
# menu structure used earlier in the twm configurations, but adds
# some fvwm sensibilities. This configuration does not use icons,
# but instead uses the built-in FVWM window list to manage
```

```
# minimized windows.
#

StdForeColor    white
StdBackColor    steelblue4
HiForeColor     white
HiBackColor     steelblue3
MenuForeColor   white
MenuBackColor   steelblue4

#
# Above: color configuration
# Below: font configuration
#

Font    -adobe-helvetica-bold-r-normal--*-120-*-*-*-*-*-*
WindowFont          -adobe-helvetica-bold-r-normal--*-120-*-*-*-*-*-*

#
# Now, some behavioral policy. We want a sloppy focus policy,
# opaque moves, no paging, MWM-style window decorations, and an
# XOR value of 56.
#

SloppyFocus
OpaqueMove 100
PagingDefault 0
MWMBorders
XORValue 56

#
# Configure the window button appearances. The left-side button
# (1) is a small square. The right-side buttons (which are
# even-numbered) are, from left to right, a horizontal bar, a
# vertical bar, a large square, and a downward-pointing triangle.
#

ButtonStyle : 1 5 55x35@0 55x55@0 35x55@0 35x35@1 55x35@1
ButtonStyle : 8 5 70x35@0 70x50@0 20x50@0 20x35@1 70x35@1
ButtonStyle : 6 5 55x25@0 55x70@0 40x70@0 40x25@1 55x25@1
ButtonStyle : 4 5 70x25@1 70x70@0 30x70@0 30x25@1 70x25@1
ButtonStyle : 2 4 30x25@1 50x70@1 70x25@0 30x25@1

#
# Now, we configure some window styles. The basic style for
# all windows says that there will be no icon, since we want
# to use the window list to manage windows instead.
#

Style "*"    NoIcon
```

```
#
# A number of functions are defined here. Each will be commented.
# This function either resizes (when dragged) or raises/lowers
# (when clicked).
#

Function "Resize-or-Raiselower"
RaiseLower       "Click"
Resize           "Motion"
EndFunction


#
# This function either maximizes and raises (when clicked) or
# maximizes and lowers (when double-clicked).
#

Function "Maximize-and-Raise-or-Lower"
Maximize         "Click"
Raise            "Click"
Maximize         "DoubleClick"
Lower            "DoubleClick"
EndFunction


#
# This function either maximizes horizontally and raises (when
# clicked) or maximizes horizontally and lowers (when double-
# clicked).
#

Function "Maximize-Horizontal-and-Raise-or-Lower"
Maximize         "Click" 100 0
Raise            "Click"
Maximize         "DoubleClick" 100 0
Lower            "DoubleClick"
EndFunction


#
# This function performs the same as the previous function, but
# acts vertically instead of horizontally.
#

Function "Maximize-Vertical-and-Raise-or-Lower"
Maximize         "Click" 0 100
Raise            "Click"
Maximize         "DoubleClick" 0 100
Lower            "DoubleClick"
EndFunction


#
# This function moves if dragged, or raises/lowers when clicked,
# or lowers when double clicked.
```

```
#

Function "Move-or-Raiselower"
Move            "Motion"
Raise           "Motion"
RaiseLower       "Click"
Lower           "DoubleClick"
EndFunction


#
# This function minimizes if clicked, or kills if double-clicked.
#

Function "Iconify-or-Kill"
Iconify       "Click"
Close           "DoubleClick"
EndFunction


#
# A brief (and therefore easy to maintain) yet complete menu
# system for launching most common applications and performing
# most common window tasks.
#

Popup "window-ops"
Title         "Management"
Iconify     "Iconify"
Resize      "Resize"
Move        "Move"
Raise       "Raise"
Lower       "Lower"
Nop         " "
Destroy     "Kill"
Close        "Delete"
Nop         " "
Refresh     "Refresh"
Restart     "Restart"
EndPopup
Popup "exit"
Title        "Exit FVWM?"
Quit        "Yes, exit."
Refresh     "No, don't."
EndPopup


Popup "applications"
Title         "Applications"
Exec          "Emacs"         emacs &
Exec          "WordPerfect"    xwp &
Exec          "Wingz"         Wingz &
Exec          "Netscape"        netscape &
EndPopup
```

```
Popup "desktop"
Title       "Desktop"
Exec        "Clipboard"   xclipboard &
Exec        "Editor"       xedit &
Exec        "Resources"   editres &
Exec        "Bitmap"       bitmap &
Exec        "Fonts"       xfontsel &
Exec        "Colors"       xcolorsel &
EndPopup

Popup "graphics"
Title       "Graphics"
Exec        "GIMP"         gimp &
Exec        "XV"           xv &
Exec        "Paint"       xpaint &
Exec        "Scene Editor"   sced &
Exec        "Raytracer"   xpovray &
Exec        "Blender"       blender &
EndPopup


#
# This is the main menu, from which other menus are called.
#

Popup "main-menu"
Title       "X Session"
Exec        "Terminal"       xterm &
Exec        "Calculator"   xcalc &
Nop         " "
Popup       "Applications"   applications
Popup       "Desktop"       desktop
Popup       "Graphics"       graphics
Nop         " "
Popup       "Management"   window-ops
Popup       "Exit"         exit
EndPopup


#
# The special functions that follow call pop-ups. Pop-ups are
# called from functions instead of directly so that either click
# or motion events can activate them.
#

Function "Session-Menu-Function"
Popup       "Click"     main-menu
Popup       "Motion"     main-menu
EndFunction

Function "Window-List-Function"
WindowList   "Click"     0 0
WindowList   "Motion"     0 0
EndFunction
```

```
Function "Window-Operations-Function"
Popup        "Click"   window-ops
Popup        "Motion"  window-ops
EndFunction

Function "Applications-Menu-Function"
Popup        "Click"   applications
Popup        "Motion"  applications
EndFunction

#
# This first set of mouse bindings is for the right-side
# -titlebar buttons. Mouse button 0 (any button) is bound using
# context A (any context) to the listed window button and
# function in each case.
#

Mouse 0 2 A    Function "Iconify-or-Kill"
Mouse 0 4 A    Function "Maximize-and-Raise-or-Lower"
Mouse 0 6 A    Function "Maximize-Vertical-and-Raise-or-Lower"
Mouse 0 8 A    Function "Maximize-Horizontal-and-Raise-or-Lower"

#
# This second set of mouse bindings takes care of the left-side
# -titlebar button. Right or left-clicks on the leftmost title
# bar button will display a window operations menu, but a middle
# click will display the window list.
#

Mouse 1 1 A    Function "Window-Operations-Function"
Mouse 2 1 A    Function "Window-List-Function"
Mouse 3 1 A    Function "Window-Operations-Function"

#
# This third set of bindings binds functions to the window title
# bar itself and to parts of the window frame.
#

Mouse 0 TS A   Function "Move-or-Raiselower"
Mouse 0 F  A   Function "Resize-or-Raiselower"

#
# This final set of mouse bindings binds functions to mouse
# events over the root window. The left button opens the
# main menu. The middle button opens the window list,
# and the right button opens the applications menu.
#

Mouse 1 R A    Function "Session-Menu-Function"
Mouse 2 R A    Function "Window-List-Function"
Mouse 3 R A    Function "Applications-Menu-Function"
```

```
#
# Now, we bind all the functions in the window operations
# menu plus one or two more to the shifted function keys.
#

Key F1  A S    Iconify
Key F2  A S    Resize
Key F3  A S    Move
Key F4  A S    Raise
Key F5  A S    Lower
Key F6  A S    Close
Key F7  A S    Destroy
Key F8  A S    Refresh
Key F9  A S    Restart
Key F10 A S    Quit


#
# End sample fvwm configuration without icons
#
```

Sample $HOME/.fvwmrc with Icons

```
#
# Sample fvwm configuration with icons
#
# This .fvwmrc file uses the same basic colors, fonts, and
# menu structure used earlier in the twm configurations, but adds
# some fvwm sensibilities.
#

StdForeColor    white
StdBackColor    steelblue4
HiForeColor     white
HiBackColor     steelblue3
MenuForeColor   white
MenuBackColor   steelblue4


#
# Above: color configuration
# Below: font configuration
#

Font            -adobe-helvetica-bold-r-normal--*-120-*-*-*-*-*-*
WindowFont      -adobe-helvetica-bold-r-normal--*-120-*-*-*-*-*-*
IconFont        -adobe-helvetica-bold-r-normal--*-100-*-*-*-*-*-*


#
# Now, some behavioral policy. We want a sloppy focus policy,
# opaque moves, no paging, MWM-style window decorations, and an
# XOR value of 56.
#
```

```
SloppyFocus
OpaqueMove 100
PagingDefault 0
MWMBorders
XORValue 56

#
# Specify an icon box along the bottom of the display and
# specify a default icon for applications that don't provide
# their own icons.
#

IconBox 10 550 790 600
IconPath "/usr/X11R6/include/X11/bitmaps/"
Icon "" xlogo32
StubbornIconPlacement

#
# Configure the window button appearances. The left-side button
# (1) is a small square. The right-side buttons (which are
# even-numbered) are, from left to right, a horizontal bar, a
# vertical bar, a large square, and a downward-pointing triangle.
#

ButtonStyle : 1 5 55x35@0 55x55@0 35x55@0 35x35@1 55x35@1
ButtonStyle : 8 5 70x35@0 70x50@0 20x50@0 20x35@1 70x35@1
ButtonStyle : 6 5 55x25@0 55x70@0 40x70@0 40x25@1 55x25@1
ButtonStyle : 4 5 70x25@1 70x70@0 30x70@0 30x25@1 70x25@1
ButtonStyle : 2 4 30x25@1 50x70@1 70x25@0 30x25@1

#
# A number of functions are defined here. Each will be commented.
# This function either resizes (when dragged) or raises/lowers
# (when clicked).
#

Function "Resize-or-Raiselower"
RaiseLower      "Click"
Resize       "Motion"
EndFunction

#
# This function either maximizes and raises (when clicked) or
# maximizes and lowers (when double-clicked).
#

Function "Maximize-and-Raise-or-Lower"
Maximize       "Click"
Raise        "Click"
Maximize       "DoubleClick"
Lower         "DoubleClick"
EndFunction
```

```
#
# This function either maximizes horizontally and raises (when
# clicked) or maximizes horizontally and lowers (when double-
# clicked).
#

Function "Maximize-Horizontal-and-Raise-or-Lower"
Maximize        "Click" 100 0
Raise            "Click"
Maximize        "DoubleClick" 100 0
Lower            "DoubleClick"
EndFunction


#
# This function performs the same as the previous function, but
# acts vertically instead of horizontally.
#

Function "Maximize-Vertical-and-Raise-or-Lower"
Maximize        "Click" 0 100
Raise            "Click"
Maximize        "DoubleClick" 0 100
Lower            "DoubleClick"
EndFunction


#
# This function moves if dragged, or raises/lowers when clicked,
# or lowers when double-clicked.
#

Function "Move-or-Raiselower"
Move            "Motion"
Raise            "Motion"
RaiseLower       "Click"
Lower            "DoubleClick"
EndFunction


#
# This function minimizes if clicked, or kills if double-clicked.
#

Function "Iconify-or-Kill"
Iconify         "Click"
Close            "DoubleClick"
EndFunction


#
# This function moves if dragged, iconifies and raises if clicked, or
# iconifies and lowers if double-clicked.
#

Function "Move-or-Iconify-and-Raise-or-Lower"
Move            "Motion"
```

```
Iconify      "Click"
Raise         "Click"
Iconify      "DoubleClick"
Lower          "DoubleClick"
EndFunction

#
# A brief (and therefore easy to maintain) yet complete menu
# system for launching most common applications and performing
# most common window tasks.
#

Popup "window-ops"
Title        "Management"
Iconify    "Iconify"
Resize     "Resize"
Move        "Move"
Raise       "Raise"
Lower       "Lower"
Nop         " "
Destroy    "Kill"
Close       "Delete"
Nop         " "
Refresh    "Refresh"
Restart    "Restart"
EndPopup

Popup "exit"
Title        "Exit FVWM?"
Quit         "Yes, exit."
Refresh    "No, don't."
EndPopup

Popup "applications"
Title         "Applications"
Exec        "Emacs"         emacs &
Exec        "WordPerfect"   xwp &
Exec        "Wingz"         Wingz &
Exec         "Netscape"       netscape &
EndPopup

Popup "desktop"
Title         "Desktop"
Exec         "Clipboard"    xclipboard &
Exec         "Editor"        xedit &
Exec         "Resources"    editres &
Exec         "Bitmap"        bitmap &
Exec         "Fonts"        xfontsel &
Exec         "Colors"        xcolorsel &
EndPopup
```

```
Popup "graphics"
Title       "Graphics"
Exec        "GIMP"        gimp &
Exec        "XV"           xv &
Exec        "Paint"       xpaint &
Exec        "Scene Editor"   sced &
Exec        "Raytracer"   xpovray &
Exec        "Blender"        blender &
EndPopup

#
# This is the main menu, from which other menus are called.
#

Popup "main-menu"
Title       "X Session"
Exec        "Terminal"        xterm &
Exec        "Calculator"    xcalc &
Nop          " "
Popup        "Applications"    applications
Popup        "Desktop"         desktop
Popup        "Graphics"        graphics
Nop          " "
Popup        "Management"    window-ops
Popup        "Exit"         exit
EndPopup

#
# The special functions that follow call pop-ups. Pop-ups are
# called from functions instead of directly so that either click
# or motion events can activate them.
#

Function "Session-Menu-Function"
Popup        "Click"    main-menu
Popup        "Motion"    main-menu
EndFunction

Function "Window-List-Function"
WindowList    "Click"    0 0
WindowList    "Motion"     0 0
EndFunction

Function "Window-Operations-Function"
Popup        "Click"    window-ops
Popup        "Motion"    window-ops
EndFunction

Function "Applications-Menu-Function"
Popup        "Click"    applications
Popup        "Motion"    applications
EndFunction
```

```
#
# This first set of mouse bindings is for the right-side
# -titlebar buttons. Mouse button 0 (any button) is bound using
# context A (any context) to the listed window button and
# function in each case.
#

Mouse 0 2 A    Function "Iconify-or-Kill"
Mouse 0 4 A    Function "Maximize-and-Raise-or-Lower"
Mouse 0 6 A    Function "Maximize-Vertical-and-Raise-or-Lower"
Mouse 0 8 A    Function "Maximize-Horizontal-and-Raise-or-Lower"

#
# This second set of mouse bindings takes care of the left-side
# -titlebar button. Right or left-clicks on the leftmost
# titlebar button will display a window operations menu, but a middle-
# click will display the window list.
#

Mouse 1 1 A    Function "Window-Operations-Function"
Mouse 2 1 A    Function "Window-List-Function"
Mouse 3 1 A    Function "Window-Operations-Function"

#
# This third set of bindings binds functions to the window
# titlebar itself and to parts of the window frame, as well as to icons.
#

Mouse 0 I  A    Function "Move-or-Iconify-and-Raise-or-Lower"
Mouse 0 TS A    Function "Move-or-Raiselower"
Mouse 0 F  A    Function "Resize-or-Raiselower"

#
# This final set of mouse bindings binds functions to mouse
# events over the root window. The left button opens the
# main menu. The middle button opens the window list,
# and the right button opens the applications menu.
#

Mouse 1 R A    Function "Session-Menu-Function"
Mouse 2 R A    Function "Window-List-Function"
Mouse 3 R A    Function "Applications-Menu-Function"

#
# Now, we bind all the functions in the window operations
# menu plus one or two more to the shifted function keys.
#

Key F1  A S    Iconify
Key F2  A S    Resize
Key F3  A S    Move
```

```
Popup "graphics"
Title        "Graphics"
Exec         "GIMP"          gimp &
Exec         "XV"            xv &
Exec         "Paint"        xpaint &
Exec         "Scene Editor"   sced &
Exec         "Raytracer"    xpovray &
Exec         "Blender"       blender &
EndPopup

#
# This is the main menu, from which other menus are called.
#

Popup "main-menu"
Title        "X Session"
Exec         "Terminal"       xterm &
Exec         "Calculator"    xcalc &
Nop          " "
Popup        "Applications"    applications
Popup        "Desktop"        desktop
Popup        "Graphics"        graphics
Nop          " "
Popup        "Management"     window-ops
Popup        "Exit"          exit
EndPopup

#
# The special functions that follow call pop-ups. Pop-ups are
# called from functions instead of directly so that either click
# or motion events can activate them.
#

Function "Session-Menu-Function"
Popup        "Click"     main-menu
Popup        "Motion"    main-menu
EndFunction

Function "Window-List-Function"
WindowList    "Click"     0 0
WindowList    "Motion"    0 0
EndFunction

Function "Window-Operations-Function"
Popup        "Click"     window-ops
Popup        "Motion"    window-ops
EndFunction

Function "Applications-Menu-Function"
Popup        "Click"     applications
Popup        "Motion"    applications
EndFunction
```

```
#
# This first set of mouse bindings is for the right-side
# -titlebar buttons. Mouse button 0 (any button) is bound using
# context A (any context) to the listed window button and
# function in each case.
#

Mouse 0 2 A     Function "Iconify-or-Kill"
Mouse 0 4 A     Function "Maximize-and-Raise-or-Lower"
Mouse 0 6 A     Function "Maximize-Vertical-and-Raise-or-Lower"
Mouse 0 8 A     Function "Maximize-Horizontal-and-Raise-or-Lower"

#
# This second set of mouse bindings takes care of the left-side
# -titlebar button. Right or left-clicks on the leftmost
# titlebar button will display a window operations menu, but a middle-
# click will display the window list.
#

Mouse 1 1 A     Function "Window-Operations-Function"
Mouse 2 1 A     Function "Window-List-Function"
Mouse 3 1 A     Function "Window-Operations-Function"

#
# This third set of bindings binds functions to the window
# titlebar itself and to parts of the window frame, as well as to icons.
#

Mouse 0 I  A    Function "Move-or-Iconify-and-Raise-or-Lower"
Mouse 0 TS A    Function "Move-or-Raiselower"
Mouse 0 F  A    Function "Resize-or-Raiselower"

#
# This final set of mouse bindings binds functions to mouse
# events over the root window. The left button opens the
# main menu. The middle button opens the window list,
# and the right button opens the applications menu.
#

Mouse 1 R A     Function "Session-Menu-Function"
Mouse 2 R A     Function "Window-List-Function"
Mouse 3 R A     Function "Applications-Menu-Function"

#
# Now, we bind all the functions in the window operations
# menu plus one or two more to the shifted function keys.
#

Key F1  A S     Iconify
Key F2  A S     Resize
Key F3  A S     Move
```

```
Key F4  A S    Raise
Key F5  A S    Lower
Key F6  A S    Close
Key F7  A S    Destroy
Key F8  A S    Refresh
Key F9  A S    Restart
Key F10 A S    Quit

#
# End sample fvwm configuration with icons
#
```

Sample $HOME/.fvwm2rc Without Icons

```
#
# Sample fvwm2 configuration without icons
#
# This .fvwm2rc file uses the same basic colors, fonts, and
# menu structure used earlier in the twm and fvwm configurations, but
# adds a few extra twists. This configuration doesn't use icons,
# instead unmapping minimized windows so that the window list can
# manage them.
#


#
# Use the default title style for the most part, but left-
# justify the title text and draw 'flat' titles on inactive
# windows.
#

TitleStyle LeftJustified
TitleStyle Inactive -- Flat


#
# Use the default border style for the most part, but
# make handles invisible and remove the inset from inactive
# windows.
#

BorderStyle Inactive -- HiddenHandles NoInset
BorderStyle Active -- HiddenHandles


#
# Draw all the buttons using vector specifications and cause
# inactive buttons to be flat.
#

ButtonStyle 1 Vector 5 55x35@0 55x55@0 35x55@0 35x35@1 55x35@1
ButtonStyle 8 Vector 5 70x35@0 70x50@0 20x50@0 20x35@1 70x35@1
ButtonStyle 6 Vector 5 55x25@0 55x70@0 40x70@0 40x25@1 55x25@1
```

```
ButtonStyle 4 Vector 5 70x25@1 70x70@0 30x70@0 30x25@1 70x25@1
ButtonStyle 2 Vector 4 30x25@1 50x70@1 70x25@0 30x25@1
AddButtonStyle All Inactive -- Flat

#
# Draw an FVWM-style menu.
#

MenuStyle    white steelblue4 slategrey \
-adobe-helvetica-bold-r-normal--*-120-*-*-*-*-*-* \
fvwm

#
# Specify the default colors for windows with focus.
#

HilightColor    white steelblue3

#
# Here is the default font for windows.
#

WindowFont          -adobe-helvetica-bold-r-normal--*-120-*-*-*-*-*-*

#
# Here is the default style for all windows: MWM-style borders,
# colors, sloppy focus, and icon box specification.
#

Style "*"    MWMBorder, Color white/steelblue4, SloppyFocus, \
NoIcon

#
# Cause windows to be moved opaquely and turn paging off.
#

OpaqueMoveSize                    100
DeskTopSize                  1x1

#
# A number of functions are defined here. Each will be commented.
# This function either resizes (when dragged) or raises/lowers
# (when clicked).
#

AddToFunc Resize-or-Raiselower
+ "C" RaiseLower
+ "M" Resize

#
# This function either maximizes and raises (when clicked) or
# maximizes and lowers (when double-clicked).
```

```
#

AddToFunc Maximize-and-Raise-or-Lower
+ "C" Maximize
+ "C" Raise
+ "D" Maximize
+ "D" Lower


#
# This function either maximizes horizontally and raises (when
# clicked) or maximizes horizontally and lowers (when double-
# clicked).
#

AddToFunc Maximize-Horizontal-and-Raise-or-Lower
+ "C" Maximize 100 0
+ "C" Raise
+ "D" Maximize 100 0
+ "D" Lower


#
# This function performs the same as the previous function, but
# acts vertically instead of horizontally.
#

AddToFunc Maximize-Vertical-and-Raise-or-Lower
+ "C" Maximize 0 100
+ "C" Raise
+ "D" Maximize 0 100
+ "D" Lower


#
# This function moves if dragged, or raises/lowers when clicked.
#

AddToFunc Move-or-Raiselower
+ "M" Move
+ "M" Raise
+ "C" RaiseLower
+ "D" Lower


#
# This function minimizes if clicked, or kills if double-clicked.
#

AddToFunc Iconify-or-Kill
+ "C" Iconify
+ "D" Close


#
```

```
# A brief (and therefore easy to maintain) yet complete menu
# system for launching most common applications and performing
# most common window tasks.
#

AddToMenu Window-Ops
+ "Management"       Title
+ "Iconify"          Iconify
+ "Resize"           Resize
+ "Move"             Move
+ "Raise"            Raise
+ "Lower"            Lower
+ " "               Nop
+ "Kill"             Destroy
+ "Delete"           Close
+ " "               Nop
+ "Refresh"          Refresh
+ "Restart"          Restart

AddToMenu Exit
+ "Exit FVWM2?"      Title
+ "Yes, exit."       Quit
+ "No, don't."       Refresh

AddToMenu Applications
+ "Applications"     Title
+ "Emacs"            Exec emacs &
+ "WordPerfect"      Exec xwp &
+ "Wingz"            Exec Wingz &
+ "Netscape"         Exec netscape &

AddToMenu Desktop
+ "Desktop"          Title
+ "Clipboard"        Exec xclipboard &
+ "Editor"           Exec xedit &
+ "Resources"        Exec editres &
+ "Bitmap"           Exec bitmap &
+ "Fonts"            Exec xfontsel &
+ "Colors"           Exec xcolorsel &

AddToMenu Graphics
+ "Graphics"         Title
+ "GIMP"             Exec gimp &
+ "XV"               Exec xv &
+ "Paint"            Exec xpaint &
+ "Scene Editor"     Exec sced &
+ "Raytracer"        Exec xpovray &
+ "Blender"          Exec blender &

#
# This is the main menu, from which other menus are called.
```

```
#

AddToMenu Session-Menu
+ "X Session"        Title
+ "Terminal"         Exec xterm &
+ "Calculator"        Exec xcalc &
+ " "               Nop
+ "Applications"       Popup Applications
+ "Desktop"         Popup Desktop
+ "Graphics"        Popup Graphics
+ " "               Nop
+ "Management"       Popup Window-Ops
+ "Exit"            Popup Exit


#
# This first set of mouse bindings is for the right-side
# -titlebar buttons. Mouse button 0 (any button) is bound using
# context A (any context) to the listed window button and
# function in each case.
#

Mouse 0 2 A    Iconify-or-Kill
Mouse 0 4 A    Maximize-and-Raise-or-Lower
Mouse 0 6 A    Maximize-Vertical-and-Raise-or-Lower
Mouse 0 8 A    Maximize-Horizontal-and-Raise-or-Lower

#
# This second set of mouse bindings takes care of the left-side
# -titlebar button. Right or left-clicks on the leftmost
# titlebar button will display a window operations menu, but a middle
# click will display the window list.
#

Mouse 1 1 A    Menu Window-Ops
Mouse 2 1 A    WindowList
Mouse 3 1 A    Menu Window-Ops

#
# This third set of bindings binds functions to the window
# title bar itself and to parts of the window frame.
#

Mouse 0 TS A    Move-or-Raiselower
Mouse 0 F  A    Resize-or-Raiselower

#
# This final set of mouse bindings binds functions to mouse
# events over the root window. The left button opens the
# main menu. The middle button opens the window list,
# and the right button opens the applications menu.
#
```

```
Mouse 1 R A    Menu Session-Menu
Mouse 2 R A    WindowList
Mouse 3 R A    Menu Applications

#
# Now, we bind all of the functions in the window operations
# menu plus one or two more to the shifted function keys.
#

Key F1  A S    Iconify
Key F2  A S    Resize
Key F3  A S    Move
Key F4  A S    Raise
Key F5  A S    Lower
Key F6  A S    Close
Key F7  A S    Destroy
Key F8  A S    Refresh
Key F9  A S    Restart
Key F10 A S    Quit


#
# End sample fvwm2 configuration without icons
#
```

Sample $HOME/.fvwm2rc with Icons

```
#
# Sample fvwm2 configuration with icons
#
# This .fvwm2rc file uses the same basic colors, fonts, and
# menu structure used earlier in the twm and fvwm configurations, but
# adds a few extra twists.
#


#
# Use the default title style for the most part, but left-
# justify the title text and draw 'flat' titles on inactive
# windows.
#

TitleStyle LeftJustified
TitleStyle Inactive -- Flat


#
# Use the default border style for the most part, but
# make handles invisible and remove the inset from inactive
# windows.
#

BorderStyle Inactive -- HiddenHandles NoInset
BorderStyle Active -- HiddenHandles
```

```
#
# Draw all the buttons using vector specifications and cause
# inactive buttons to be flat.
#

ButtonStyle 1 Vector 5 55x35@0 55x55@0 35x55@0 35x35@1 55x35@1
ButtonStyle 8 Vector 5 70x35@0 70x50@0 20x50@0 20x35@1 70x35@1
ButtonStyle 6 Vector 5 55x25@0 55x70@0 40x70@0 40x25@1 55x25@1
ButtonStyle 4 Vector 5 70x25@1 70x70@0 30x70@0 30x25@1 70x25@1
ButtonStyle 2 Vector 4 30x25@1 50x70@1 70x25@0 30x25@1
AddButtonStyle All Inactive -- Flat


#
# Draw an FVWM-style menu.
#

MenuStyle    white steelblue4 slategrey \
-adobe-helvetica-bold-r-normal--*-120-*-*-*-*-*-* \
fvwm


#
# Specify the default colors for windows with focus.
#

HilightColor    white steelblue3


#
# Here are the default fonts for windows and icons.
#

WindowFont         -adobe-helvetica-bold-r-normal--*-120-*-*-*-*-*-*
IconFont           -adobe-helvetica-bold-r-normal--*-100-*-*-*-*-*-*


#
# Here is the default style for all windows: MWM-style borders,
# colors, sloppy focus, and icon box specification.
#

Style "*"    MWMBorder, Color white/steelblue4, SloppyFocus, \
IconBox 10 550 790 600


#
# Cause windows to be moved opaquely and turn paging off.
#

OpaqueMoveSize              100
DeskTopSize             1x1


#
# A number of functions are defined here. Each will be commented.
# This function either resizes (when dragged) or raises/lowers
# (when clicked).
```

```
#

AddToFunc Resize-or-Raiselower
+ "C" RaiseLower
+ "M" Resize

#
# This function either maximizes and raises (when clicked) or
# maximizes and lowers (when double-clicked).
#

AddToFunc Maximize-and-Raise-or-Lower
+ "C" Maximize
+ "C" Raise
+ "D" Maximize
+ "D" Lower

#
# This function either maximizes horizontally and raises (when
# clicked) or maximizes horizontally and lowers (when double-
# clicked).
#

AddToFunc Maximize-Horizontal-and-Raise-or-Lower
+ "C" Maximize 100 0
+ "C" Raise
+ "D" Maximize 100 0
+ "D" Lower

#
# This function performs the same as the previous function, but
# acts vertically instead of horizontally.
#

AddToFunc Maximize-Vertical-and-Raise-or-Lower
+ "C" Maximize 0 100
+ "C" Raise
+ "D" Maximize 0 100
+ "D" Lower

#
# This function moves if dragged, or raises/lowers when clicked.
#

AddToFunc Move-or-Raiselower
+ "M" Move
+ "M" Raise
+ "C" RaiseLower
+ "D" Lower

#
# This function minimizes if clicked, or kills if double-clicked.
```

```
#

AddToFunc Iconify-or-Kill
+ "C" Iconify
+ "D" Close

#
# This function moves if dragged, iconifies and raises if
# clicked, or iconifies and lowers if double-clicked.
#

AddToFunc Move-or-Iconify-and-Raise-or-Lower
+ "M" Move
+ "C" Iconify
+ "C" Raise
+ "D" Iconify
+ "D" Lower

#
# A brief (and therefore easy to maintain) yet complete menu
# system for launching most common applications and performing
# most common window tasks.
#

AddToMenu Window-Ops
+ "Management"       Title
+ "Iconify"         Iconify
+ "Resize"            Resize
+ "Move"         Move
+ "Raise"        Raise
+ "Lower"        Lower
+ " "                Nop
+ "Kill"         Destroy
+ "Delete"           Close
+ " "                Nop
+ "Refresh"      Refresh
+ "Restart"      Restart

AddToMenu Exit
+ "Exit FVWM2?"      Title
+ "Yes, exit."       Quit
+ "No, don't."       Refresh

AddToMenu Applications
+ "Applications"     Title
+ "Emacs"        Exec emacs &
+ "WordPerfect"      Exec xwp &
+ "Wingz"        Exec Wingz &
+ "Netscape"         Exec netscape &

AddToMenu Desktop
+ "Desktop"      Title
```

```
+ "Clipboard"        Exec xclipboard &
+ "Editor"            Exec xedit &
+ "Resources"        Exec editres &
+ "Bitmap"            Exec bitmap &
+ "Fonts"     Exec xfontsel &
+ "Colors"             Exec xcolorsel &

AddToMenu Graphics
+ "Graphics"         Title
+ "GIMP"      Exec gimp &
+ "XV"                Exec xv &
+ "Paint"          Exec xpaint &
+ "Scene Editor"       Exec sced &
+ "Raytracer"        Exec xpovray &
+ "Blender"          Exec blender &

#
# This is the main menu, from which other menus are called.
#

AddToMenu Session-Menu
+ "X Session"        Title
+ "Terminal"         Exec xterm &
+ "Calculator"        Exec xcalc &
+ " "                 Nop
+ "Applications"        Popup Applications
+ "Desktop"          Popup Desktop
+ "Graphics"          Popup Graphics
+ " "                 Nop
+ "Management"         Popup Window-Ops
+ "Exit"      Popup Exit

#
# This first set of mouse bindings is for the right-side
# -titlebar buttons. Mouse button 0 (any button) is bound using
# context A (any context) to the listed window button and
# function in each case.
#

Mouse 0 2 A    Iconify-or-Kill
Mouse 0 4 A     Maximize-and-Raise-or-Lower
Mouse 0 6 A     Maximize-Vertical-and-Raise-or-Lower
Mouse 0 8 A     Maximize-Horizontal-and-Raise-or-Lower

#
# This second set of mouse bindings takes care of the left-side
# -titlebar button. Right- or left-clicks on the leftmost
# titlebar button will display a window operations menu, but a middle-
# click will display the window list.
#
```

```
Mouse 1 1 A    Menu Window-Ops
Mouse 2 1 A    WindowList
Mouse 3 1 A    Menu Window-Ops

#
# This third set of bindings binds functions to the window
# titlebar itself and to parts of the window frame, as well as to
# icons.
#

Mouse 0 I  A    Move-or-Iconify-and-Raise-or-Lower
Mouse 0 TS A    Move-or-Raiselower
Mouse 0 F  A    Resize-or-Raiselower

#
# This final set of mouse bindings binds functions to mouse
# events over the root window. The left button opens the
# main menu. The middle button opens the window list,
# and the right button opens the applications menu.
#

Mouse 1 R A    Menu Session-Menu
Mouse 2 R A    WindowList
Mouse 3 R A    Menu Applications

#
# Now, we bind all the functions in the window operations
# menu plus one or two more to the shifted function keys.
#

Key F1  A S    Iconify
Key F2  A S    Resize
Key F3  A S    Move
Key F4  A S    Raise
Key F5  A S    Lower
Key F6  A S    Close
Key F7  A S    Destroy
Key F8  A S    Refresh
Key F9  A S    Restart
Key F10 A S    Quit

#
# End sample fvwm2 configuration with icons.
#
```

B

XFREE86 3.3.5 DETAILS

Supported Graphics Hardware in XFree86 3.3.5

The list of graphics hardware contains two kinds of entries: video cards and video chipsets. If your specific make and model of card are not listed, please check to see if your card's chipset is listed instead. In certain cases, chipsets may be listed alphabetically by their own name rather than by their manufacturer (for example, Riva 128 rather than nVidia Riva 128).

All hardware is listed by server. Some graphics hardware can be found listed under more than one server. Such graphics hardware is supported by both servers:

Server	Graphics Card/Chipset
XF86_3DLabs	3DLabs Oxygen GMX
XF86_3DLabs	AccelStar Permedia II AGP
XF86_3DLabs	Creative Blaster Exxtreme
XF86_3DLabs	Diamond Fire GL 1000
XF86_3DLabs	Diamond Fire GL 1000 PRO
XF86_3DLabs	Diamond Fire GL 3000
XF86_3DLabs	ELSA GLoria Synergy
XF86_3DLabs	ELSA GLoria-L

continues

Server	Graphics Card/Chipset
XF86_3DLabs	ELSA GLoria-L/MX
XF86_3DLabs	ELSA GLoria-S
XF86_3DLabs	ELSA GLoria-XL
XF86_3DLabs	ELSA Winner 2000/Office
XF86_3DLabs	Leadtek WinFast 2300
XF86_AGX	AGX (generic)
XF86_AGX	Boca Vortex (Sierra RAMDAC)
XF86_AGX	EIZO (VRAM)
XF86_AGX	Hercules Graphite HG210
XF86_AGX	Hercules Graphite Power
XF86_AGX	Hercules Graphite Pro
XF86_AGX	Orchid Celsius (AT&T RAMDAC)
XF86_AGX	Orchid Celsius (Sierra RAMDAC)
XF86_AGX	Spider Black Widow
XF86_AGX	Spider Black Widow Plus
XF86_AGX	XGA-1 (ISA bus)
XF86_AGX	XGA-2 (ISA bus)
XF86_I128	Number Nine Imagine I-128 (2–8MB)
XF86_I128	Number Nine Imagine I-128 Series 2 (2–4MB)
XF86_I128	Number Nine Imagine-128-T2R
XF86_I128	Number Nine Revolution 3D AGP (4–8MB SGRAM)
XF86_I128	Revolution 3D (T2R)
XF86_Mach32	ATI Graphics Ultra Pro
XF86_Mach32	ATI Mach32
XF86_Mach32	ATI Ultra Plus
XF86_Mach64	ASUS PCI-AV264CT
XF86_Mach64	ASUS PCI-V264CT
XF86_Mach64	ATI 3D Pro Turbo
XF86_Mach64	ATI 3D Pro Turbo PC2TV
XF86_Mach64	ATI 3D Xpression
XF86_Mach64	ATI 3D Xpression+
XF86_Mach64	ATI 3D Xpression+ PC2TV
XF86_Mach64	ATI All-in-Wonder
XF86_Mach64	ATI All-in-Wonder Pro
XF86_Mach64	ATI Graphics Pro Turbo

Server	Graphics Card/Chipset
XF86_Mach64	ATI Graphics Pro Turbo 1600
XF86_Mach64	ATI Graphics Pro Turbo with AT&T 20C408 RAMDAC
XF86_Mach64	ATI Graphics Pro Turbo with ATI68860 RAMDAC
XF86_Mach64	ATI Graphics Pro Turbo with ATI68860B RAMDAC
XF86_Mach64	ATI Graphics Pro Turbo with ATI68860C RAMDAC
XF86_Mach64	ATI Graphics Pro Turbo with ATI68875 RAMDAC
XF86_Mach64	ATI Graphics Pro Turbo with CH8398 RAMDAC
XF86_Mach64	ATI Graphics Pro Turbo with STG1702 RAMDAC
XF86_Mach64	ATI Graphics Pro Turbo with STG1703 RAMDAC
XF86_Mach64	ATI Graphics Pro Turbo with TLC34075 RAMDAC
XF86_Mach64	ATI Graphics Xpression
XF86_Mach64	ATI Graphics Xpression with AT&T 20C408 RAMDAC
XF86_Mach64	ATI Graphics Xpression with ATI68860 RAMDAC
XF86_Mach64	ATI Graphics Xpression with ATI68860B RAMDAC
XF86_Mach64	ATI Graphics Xpression with ATI68860C RAMDAC
XF86_Mach64	ATI Graphics Xpression with ATI68875 RAMDAC
XF86_Mach64	ATI Graphics Xpression with CH8398 RAMDAC
XF86_Mach64	ATI Graphics Xpression with Mach64 CT (264CT)
XF86_Mach64	ATI Graphics Xpression with STG1702 RAMDAC
XF86_Mach64	ATI Graphics Xpression with STG1703 RAMDAC
XF86_Mach64	ATI Graphics Xpression with TLC34075 RAMDAC
XF86_Mach64	ATI Mach64
XF86_Mach64	ATI Mach64 3D RAGE II
XF86_Mach64	ATI Mach64 3D RAGE II+DVD
XF86_Mach64	ATI Mach64 3D Rage IIC
XF86_Mach64	ATI Mach64 3D Rage Pro
XF86_Mach64	ATI Mach64 CT (264CT), Internal RAMDAC
XF86_Mach64	ATI Mach64 GT (264GT), aka 3D RAGE, Int. RAMDAC
XF86_Mach64	ATI Mach64 VT (264VT), Internal RAMDAC
XF86_Mach64	ATI Mach64 with AT&T 20C408 RAMDAC
XF86_Mach64	ATI Mach64 with ATI68860 RAMDAC
XF86_Mach64	ATI Mach64 with ATI68860B RAMDAC
XF86_Mach64	ATI Mach64 with ATI68860C RAMDAC
XF86_Mach64	ATI Mach64 with ATI68875 RAMDAC

continues

Server	Graphics Card/Chipset
XF86_Mach64	ATI Mach64 with CH8398 RAMDAC
XF86_Mach64	ATI Mach64 with IBM RGB514 RAMDAC
XF86_Mach64	ATI Mach64 with Internal RAMDAC
XF86_Mach64	ATI Mach64 with STG1702 RAMDAC
XF86_Mach64	ATI Mach64 with STG1703 RAMDAC
XF86_Mach64	ATI Mach64 with TLC34075 RAMDAC
XF86_Mach64	ATI Pro Turbo+PC2TV, 3D Rage II+DVD
XF86_Mach64	ATI Video Xpression
XF86_Mach64	ATI Video Xpression+
XF86_Mach64	ATI Win Boost with AT&T 20C408 RAMDAC
XF86_Mach64	ATI Win Turbo
XF86_Mach64	ATI WinBoost
XF86_Mach64	ATI WinBoost with ATI68860 RAMDAC
XF86_Mach64	ATI WinBoost with ATI68860B RAMDAC
XF86_Mach64	ATI WinBoost with ATI68860C RAMDAC
XF86_Mach64	ATI WinBoost with ATI68875 RAMDAC
XF86_Mach64	ATI WinBoost with CH8398 RAMDAC
XF86_Mach64	ATI WinBoost with Mach64 CT (264CT)
XF86_Mach64	ATI WinBoost with STG1702 RAMDAC
XF86_Mach64	ATI WinBoost with STG1703 RAMDAC
XF86_Mach64	ATI WinBoost with TLC34075 RAMDAC
XF86_Mach64	ATI WinCharger
XF86_Mach64	ATI WinCharger with AT&T 20C408 RAMDAC
XF86_Mach64	ATI WinCharger with ATI68860 RAMDAC
XF86_Mach64	ATI WinCharger with ATI68860B RAMDAC
XF86_Mach64	ATI WinCharger with ATI68860C RAMDAC
XF86_Mach64	ATI WinCharger with ATI68875 RAMDAC
XF86_Mach64	ATI WinCharger with CH8398 RAMDAC
XF86_Mach64	ATI WinCharger with Mach64 CT (264CT)
XF86_Mach64	ATI WinCharger with STG1702 RAMDAC
XF86_Mach64	ATI WinCharger with STG1703 RAMDAC
XF86_Mach64	ATI WinCharger with TLC34075 RAMDAC
XF86_Mach64	ATI WinTurbo with AT&T 20C408 RAMDAC
XF86_Mach64	ATI WinTurbo with ATI68860 RAMDAC
XF86_Mach64	ATI WinTurbo with ATI68860B RAMDAC

Server	Graphics Card/Chipset
XF86_Mach64	ATI WinTurbo with ATI68860C RAMDAC
XF86_Mach64	ATI WinTurbo with ATI68875 RAMDAC
XF86_Mach64	ATI WinTurbo with CH8398 RAMDAC
XF86_Mach64	ATI WinTurbo with Mach64 CT (264CT)
XF86_Mach64	ATI WinTurbo with STG1702 RAMDAC
XF86_Mach64	ATI WinTurbo with STG1703 RAMDAC
XF86_Mach64	ATI WinTurbo with TLC34075 RAMDAC
XF86_Mach64	ATI Xpert 98
XF86_Mach64	ATI Xpert XL
XF86_Mach64	ATI Xpert@Play 98
XF86_Mach64	ATI Xpert@Play PCI and AGP, 3D Rage Pro
XF86_Mach64	ATI Xpert@Work, 3D Rage Pro
XF86_Mach64	ATI integrated on Intel Maui MU440EX board
XF86_Mach8	ATI 8514 Ultra (no VGA)
XF86_Mach8	ATI Graphics Ultra
XF86_P9000	Diamond Viper PCI 2MB
XF86_P9000	Diamond Viper VLB 2MB
XF86_P9000	Orchid P9000 VLB
XF86_S3	2 the Max MAXColor S3 Trio64V+
XF86_S3	928Movie
XF86_S3	ASUS Video Magic PCI V864
XF86_S3	ASUS Video Magic PCI VT64
XF86_S3	Actix GE32+ 2MB
XF86_S3	Actix GE32i
XF86_S3	Actix GE64
XF86_S3	Actix Ultra
XF86_S3	Cardex Trio64
XF86_S3	COMPAQ Armada 7380DMT
XF86_S3	COMPAQ Armada 7730MT
XF86_S3	Dell S3 805
XF86_S3	Diamond Stealth 24
XF86_S3	Diamond Stealth 64 DRAM with S3 SDAC
XF86_S3	Diamond Stealth 64 VRAM
XF86_S3	Diamond Stealth 64 Video VRAM (TI RAMDAC)

continues

Server	Graphics Card/Chipset
XF86_S3	Diamond Stealth Pro
XF86_S3	Diamond Stealth VRAM
XF86_S3	Diamond Stealth Video DRAM
XF86_S3	Diamond Stealth64 Graphics 2xx0 series
XF86_S3	Diamond Stealth64 Video 2120/2200
XF86_S3	Diamond Stealth64 Video 3200
XF86_S3	Diamond Stealth64 Video 3240/3400 (IBM RAMDAC)
XF86_S3	Diamond Stealth64 Video 3240/3400 (TI RAMDAC)
XF86_S3	ELSA Gloria-4
XF86_S3	ELSA Gloria-8
XF86_S3	ELSA WINNER 1000/T2D
XF86_S3	ELSA Winner 1000AVI (AT&T 20C409 version)
XF86_S3	ELSA Winner 1000AVI (SDAC version)
XF86_S3	ELSA Winner 1000ISA
XF86_S3	ELSA Winner 1000PRO with S3 SDAC
XF86_S3	ELSA Winner 1000PRO with STG1700 or AT&T RAMDAC
XF86_S3	ELSA Winner 1000PRO/X
XF86_S3	ELSA Winner 1000TwinBus
XF86_S3	ELSA Winner 1000VL
XF86_S3	ELSA Winner 2000
XF86_S3	ELSA Winner 2000AVI
XF86_S3	ELSA Winner 2000PRO-2
XF86_S3	ELSA Winner 2000PRO-4
XF86_S3	ELSA Winner 2000PRO/X-2
XF86_S3	ELSA Winner 2000PRO/X-4
XF86_S3	ELSA Winner 2000PRO/X-8
XF86_S3	Genoa Phantom 64i with S3 SDAC
XF86_S3	Genoa VideoBlitz III AV
XF86_S3	Hercules Graphite Terminator 64
XF86_S3	Hercules Graphite Terminator Pro 64
XF86_S3	JAX 8241
XF86_S3	LeadTek WinFast S430
XF86_S3	LeadTek WinFast S510
XF86_S3	Miro Crystal 10SD with GenDAC
XF86_S3	Miro Crystal 16S

Server	Graphics Card/Chipset
XF86_S3	Miro Crystal 20SD PCI with S3 SDAC
XF86_S3	Miro Crystal 20SD VLB with S3 SDAC (BIOS 3.xx)
XF86_S3	Miro Crystal 20SD with ICD2061A (BIOS 2.xx)
XF86_S3	Miro Crystal 20SD with ICS2494 (BIOS 1.xx)
XF86_S3	Miro Crystal 20SV
XF86_S3	Miro Crystal 40SV
XF86_S3	Miro Crystal 80SV
XF86_S3	Miro Crystal 8S
XF86_S3	Miro Video 20SV
XF86_S3	Number Nine FX Motion 531
XF86_S3	Number Nine FX Motion 771
XF86_S3	Number Nine GXE Level 10/11/12
XF86_S3	Number Nine GXE Level 14/16
XF86_S3	Number Nine GXE64
XF86_S3	Number Nine GXE64 Pro
XF86_S3	Orchid Fahrenheit 1280
XF86_S3	Orchid Fahrenheit VA
XF86_S3	Orchid Fahrenheit-1280+
XF86_S3	S3 801/805 (generic)
XF86_S3	S3 801/805 with ATT20c490 RAMDAC
XF86_S3	S3 801/805 with ATT20c490 RAMDAC and ICD2061A
XF86_S3	S3 801/805 with Chrontel 8391
XF86_S3	S3 801/805 with S3 GenDAC
XF86_S3	S3 801/805 with SC1148{2,3,4} RAMDAC
XF86_S3	S3 801/805 with SC1148{5,7,9} RAMDAC
XF86_S3	S3 864 (generic)
XF86_S3	S3 864 with ATT 20C498 or 21C498
XF86_S3	S3 864 with SDAC (86C716)
XF86_S3	S3 864 with STG1703
XF86_S3	S3 868 (generic)
XF86_S3	S3 868 with ATT 20C409
XF86_S3	S3 868 with ATT 20C498 or 21C498
XF86_S3	S3 868 with SDAC (86C716)
XF86_S3	S3 86C801 (generic)

continues

Server	Graphics Card/Chipset
XF86_S3	S3 86C805 (generic)
XF86_S3	S3 86C864 (generic)
XF86_S3	S3 86C868 (generic)
XF86_S3	S3 86C911 (generic)
XF86_S3	S3 86C924 (generic)
XF86_S3	S3 86C928 (generic)
XF86_S3	S3 86C964 (generic)
XF86_S3	S3 86C968 (generic)
XF86_S3	S3 86CM65
XF86_S3	S3 911/924 (generic)
XF86_S3	S3 924 with SC1148 DAC
XF86_S3	S3 928 (generic)
XF86_S3	S3 964 (generic)
XF86_S3	S3 968 (generic)
XF86_S3	S3 Aurora64V+ (generic)
XF86_S3	S3 Vision864 (generic)
XF86_S3	S3 Vision868 (generic)
XF86_S3	S3 Vision964 (generic)
XF86_S3	S3 Vision968 (generic)
XF86_S3	SHARP 9080
XF86_S3	SHARP 9090
XF86_S3	SPEA Mercury 64
XF86_S3	SPEA Mirage
XF86_S3	SPEA/V7 Mercury
XF86_S3	SPEA/V7 Mirage P64
XF86_S3	SPEA/V7 Mirage P64 with S3 Trio64
XF86_S3	STB Pegasus
XF86_S3	STB Powergraph X-24
XF86_S3	STB Velocity 64 Video
XF86_S3	Spider Tarantula 64
XF86_S3	VL-41
XF86_S3	VidTech FastMax P20
XF86_S3	VideoLogic GrafixStar 500
XF86_S3	VideoLogic GrafixStar 700
XF86_S3	WinFast S430

Server	Graphics Card/Chipset
XF86_S3	WinFast S510
XF86_S3	Cardex Trio64Pro
XF86_S3	DSV3326
XF86_S3	DataExpert DSV3365
XF86_S3	Diamond Stealth 64 DRAM SE
XF86_S3	Diamond Stealth 64 DRAM with S3 Trio64
XF86_S3	Diamond Stealth64 Graphics 2xx0 series (Trio64)
XF86_S3	Diamond Stealth64 Video 2001 series (2121/2201)
XF86_S3	ELSA Winner 1000TRIO
XF86_S3	ELSA Winner 1000TRIO/V
XF86_S3	ExpertColor DSV3365
XF86_S3	Hercules Graphite Terminator 64/DRAM
XF86_S3	Hercules Terminator 64/Video
XF86_S3	Miro Crystal 12SD
XF86_S3	Miro Crystal 22SD
XF86_S3	Number Nine FX Motion 331
XF86_S3	Number Nine FX Vision 330
XF86_S3	Number Nine GXE64 with S3 Trio64
XF86_S3	S3 86C764 (generic)
XF86_S3	S3 86C765 (generic)
XF86_S3	S3 86C775 (generic)
XF86_S3	S3 86C785 (generic)
XF86_S3	S3 Trio32 (generic)
XF86_S3	S3 Trio64 (generic)
XF86_S3	S3 Trio64V+ (generic)
XF86_S3	S3 Trio64V2 (generic)
XF86_S3	S3 Trio64V2/DX (generic)
XF86_S3	S3 Trio64V2/GX (generic)
XF86_S3	STB Powergraph 64
XF86_S3	STB Powergraph 64 Video
XF86_S3	VideoLogic GrafixStar 300
XF86_S3	VideoLogic GrafixStar 400
XF86_SVGA	3dfx Voodoo Banshee
XF86_SVGA	3dfx Voodoo3

continues

Server	Graphics Card/Chipset
XF86_SVGA	3dfx Voodoo3 2000
XF86_SVGA	3dfx Voodoo3 3000
XF86_SVGA	3dfx Voodoo3 3500
XF86_SVGA	ALG-5434(E)
XF86_SVGA	ASUS 3Dexplorer
XF86_SVGA	AT25
XF86_SVGA	AT3D
XF86_SVGA	ATI Wonder SVGA
XF86_SVGA	ATrend ATC-2165A
XF86_SVGA	Actix ProStar
XF86_SVGA	Actix ProStar 64
XF86_SVGA	Acumos AVGA3
XF86_SVGA	Alliance ProMotion 6422
XF86_SVGA	Ark Logic ARK1000PV (generic)
XF86_SVGA	Ark Logic ARK1000VL (generic)
XF86_SVGA	Ark Logic ARK2000MT (generic)
XF86_SVGA	Ark Logic ARK2000PV (generic)
XF86_SVGA	Avance Logic 2101
XF86_SVGA	Avance Logic 2228
XF86_SVGA	Avance Logic 2301
XF86_SVGA	Avance Logic 2302
XF86_SVGA	Avance Logic 2308
XF86_SVGA	Avance Logic 2401
XF86_SVGA	Binar Graphics AnyView
XF86_SVGA	California Graphics SunTracer 6000
XF86_SVGA	Canopus Co. Power Window 3DV
XF86_SVGA	Canopus Total-3D
XF86_SVGA	Cardex Challenger (Pro)
XF86_SVGA	Cardex Cobra
XF86_SVGA	Chips & Technologies CT64200
XF86_SVGA	Chips & Technologies CT64300
XF86_SVGA	Chips & Technologies CT65520
XF86_SVGA	Chips & Technologies CT65525
XF86_SVGA	Chips & Technologies CT65530
XF86_SVGA	Chips & Technologies CT65535

Server	Graphics Card/Chipset
XF86_SVGA	Chips & Technologies CT65540
XF86_SVGA	Chips & Technologies CT65545
XF86_SVGA	Chips & Technologies CT65546
XF86_SVGA	Chips & Technologies CT65548
XF86_SVGA	Chips & Technologies CT65550
XF86_SVGA	Chips & Technologies CT65554
XF86_SVGA	Chips & Technologies CT65555
XF86_SVGA	Chips & Technologies CT68554
XF86_SVGA	Chips & Technologies CT69000
XF86_SVGA	Cirrus Logic GD542x
XF86_SVGA	Cirrus Logic GD543x
XF86_SVGA	Cirrus Logic GD5446
XF86_SVGA	Cirrus Logic GD544x
XF86_SVGA	Cirrus Logic GD5462
XF86_SVGA	Cirrus Logic GD5464
XF86_SVGA	Cirrus Logic GD5465
XF86_SVGA	Cirrus Logic GD5480
XF86_SVGA	Cirrus Logic GD62xx (laptop)
XF86_SVGA	Cirrus Logic GD64xx (laptop)
XF86_SVGA	Cirrus Logic GD754x (laptop)
XF86_SVGA	Colorgraphic Dual Lightning
XF86_SVGA	Creative Labs 3D Blaster PCI (Verite 1000)
XF86_SVGA	Creative Labs Graphics Blaster 3D
XF86_SVGA	Creative Labs Graphics Blaster MA201
XF86_SVGA	Creative Labs Graphics Blaster MA202
XF86_SVGA	Creative Labs Graphics Blaster MA302
XF86_SVGA	Creative Labs Graphics Blaster MA334
XF86_SVGA	DFI-WG1000
XF86_SVGA	DFI-WG5000
XF86_SVGA	DFI-WG6000
XF86_SVGA	DSV3325
XF86_SVGA	DataExpert DSV3325
XF86_SVGA	Dell onboard ET4000
XF86_SVGA	Diamond Edge 3D

continues

Server	Graphics Card/Chipset
XF86_SVGA	Diamond Multimedia Stealth 3D 2000
XF86_SVGA	Diamond Multimedia Stealth 3D 2000 PRO
XF86_SVGA	Diamond SpeedStar (Plus)
XF86_SVGA	Diamond SpeedStar 24
XF86_SVGA	Diamond SpeedStar 24X (not fully supported)
XF86_SVGA	Diamond SpeedStar 64
XF86_SVGA	Diamond SpeedStar A50
XF86_SVGA	Diamond SpeedStar HiColor
XF86_SVGA	Diamond SpeedStar Pro (not SE)
XF86_SVGA	Diamond SpeedStar Pro 1100
XF86_SVGA	Diamond SpeedStar Pro SE (CL-GD5430/5434)
XF86_SVGA	Diamond SpeedStar64 Graphics 2000/2200
XF86_SVGA	Diamond Stealth 32
XF86_SVGA	Diamond Stealth 3D 2000
XF86_SVGA	Diamond Stealth 3D 2000 PRO
XF86_SVGA	Diamond Stealth 3D 3000
XF86_SVGA	Diamond Stealth 3D 4000
XF86_SVGA	Diamond Stealth II S220
XF86_SVGA	Diamond Stealth Video 2500
XF86_SVGA	Diamond Stealth64 Graphics 2001 series
XF86_SVGA	Diamond Viper 330
XF86_SVGA	Diamond Viper 550
XF86_SVGA	Diamond Viper Pro Video
XF86_SVGA	ELSA ERAZOR II
XF86_SVGA	ELSA VICTORY ERAZOR
XF86_SVGA	ELSA Victory 3D
XF86_SVGA	ELSA Victory 3DX
XF86_SVGA	ELSA Winner 1000 R3D
XF86_SVGA	ELSA Winner 2000AVI/3D
XF86_SVGA	ELSA Winner 3000
XF86_SVGA	ELSA Winner 3000-L-42
XF86_SVGA	ELSA Winner 3000-M-22
XF86_SVGA	ELSA Winner 3000-S
XF86_SVGA	EPSON CardPC (onboard)
XF86_SVGA	ET3000 (generic)

Server	Graphics Card/Chipset
XF86_SVGA	ET4000 (generic)
XF86_SVGA	ET4000 W32i, W32p (generic)
XF86_SVGA	ET4000/W32 (generic)
XF86_SVGA	ET6000 (generic)
XF86_SVGA	ET6100 (generic)
XF86_SVGA	ExpertColor DSV3325
XF86_SVGA	Genoa 5400
XF86_SVGA	Genoa 8500VL(-28)
XF86_SVGA	Genoa 8900 Phantom 32i
XF86_SVGA	Hercules Dynamite
XF86_SVGA	Hercules Dynamite 128/Video
XF86_SVGA	Hercules Dynamite Power
XF86_SVGA	Hercules Dynamite Pro
XF86_SVGA	Hercules Stingray
XF86_SVGA	Hercules Stingray 128 3D
XF86_SVGA	Hercules Stingray 64/V with ICS5342
XF86_SVGA	Hercules Stingray 64/V with ZoomDAC
XF86_SVGA	Hercules Stingray Pro
XF86_SVGA	Hercules Stingray Pro/V
XF86_SVGA	Hercules Terminator 3D/DX
XF86_SVGA	Hercules Terminator 64/3D
XF86_SVGA	Hercules Thriller3D
XF86_SVGA	Integral FlashPoint
XF86_SVGA	Intel 5430
XF86_SVGA	Intel i740
XF86_SVGA	Interay PMC Viper
XF86_SVGA	Jaton Video-58P
XF86_SVGA	Jaton Video-70P
XF86_SVGA	Jazz Multimedia G-Force 128
XF86_SVGA	LeadTek WinFast 3D S600
XF86_SVGA	LeadTek WinFast 3D S680
XF86_SVGA	LeadTek WinFast S200
XF86_SVGA	MELCO WGP-VG4S
XF86_SVGA	MELCO WGP-VX8

continues

Server	Graphics Card/Chipset
XF86_SVGA	MSI MS-4417
XF86_SVGA	Matrox Comet
XF86_SVGA	Matrox G400
XF86_SVGA	Matrox Marvel II
XF86_SVGA	Matrox Millennium 2/4/8MB
XF86_SVGA	Matrox Millennium G200 4/8/16MB
XF86_SVGA	Matrox Millennium G200 SD 4/8/16MB
XF86_SVGA	Matrox Mystique
XF86_SVGA	Matrox Mystique G200 4/8/16MB
XF86_SVGA	Matrox Productiva G100 4/8MB
XF86_SVGA	MediaGX
XF86_SVGA	MediaVision Proaxcel 128
XF86_SVGA	Mirage Z-128
XF86_SVGA	Miro Crystal DVD
XF86_SVGA	Miro miroCRYSTAL VRX
XF86_SVGA	Miro miroMedia 3D
XF86_SVGA	Miro MiroVideo 20TD
XF86_SVGA	Neomagic
XF86_SVGA	Number Nine FX Motion 332
XF86_SVGA	Number Nine Visual 9FX Reality 332
XF86_SVGA	Oak 87 ISA (generic)
XF86_SVGA	Oak 87 VLB (generic)
XF86_SVGA	Oak ISA Card (generic)
XF86_SVGA	Ocean (octek) VL-VGA-1000
XF86_SVGA	Octek AVGA-20
XF86_SVGA	Octek Combo-26
XF86_SVGA	Octek Combo-28
XF86_SVGA	Octek VL-VGA-26
XF86_SVGA	Octek VL-VGA-28
XF86_SVGA	Orchid Kelvin 64
XF86_SVGA	Orchid Kelvin 64 VLB Rev A
XF86_SVGA	Orchid Kelvin 64 VLB Rev B
XF86_SVGA	Orchid Technology Fahrenheit Video 3D
XF86_SVGA	PC-Chips M567 Mainboard
XF86_SVGA	Paradise Accelerator Value

Server	Graphics Card/Chipset
XF86_SVGA	Paradise/WD 90CXX
XF86_SVGA	PixelView Combo TV 3D AGP (Prolink)
XF86_SVGA	PixelView Combo TV Pro (Prolink)
XF86_SVGA	RIVA 128
XF86_SVGA	RIVA TNT
XF86_SVGA	RIVA TNT2
XF86_SVGA	Rendition Verite 1000
XF86_SVGA	Rendition Verite 2x00
XF86_SVGA	S3 86C260 (generic)
XF86_SVGA	S3 86C280 (generic)
XF86_SVGA	S3 86C325 (generic)
XF86_SVGA	S3 86C357 (generic)
XF86_SVGA	S3 86C375 (generic)
XF86_SVGA	S3 86C385 (generic)
XF86_SVGA	S3 86C988 (generic)
XF86_SVGA	S3 Savage3D (generic)
XF86_SVGA	S3 Savage4 (generic)
XF86_SVGA	S3 Trio3D (generic)
XF86_SVGA	S3 Trio3D/2X (generic)
XF86_SVGA	S3 ViRGE (generic)
XF86_SVGA	S3 ViRGE (old S3V server)
XF86_SVGA	S3 ViRGE/DX (generic)
XF86_SVGA	S3 ViRGE/GX (generic)
XF86_SVGA	S3 ViRGE/GX2 (generic)
XF86_SVGA	S3 ViRGE/MX (generic)
XF86_SVGA	S3 ViRGE/MX+ (generic)
XF86_SVGA	S3 ViRGE/VX (generic)
XF86_SVGA	SNI PC5H W32
XF86_SVGA	SNI Scenic W32
XF86_SVGA	SPEA/V7 Mirage VEGA Plus
XF86_SVGA	SPEA/V7 ShowTime Plus
XF86_SVGA	STB Horizon
XF86_SVGA	STB Horizon Video
XF86_SVGA	STB LightSpeed

continues

Server	Graphics Card/Chipset
XF86_SVGA	STB LightSpeed 128
XF86_SVGA	STB MVP-2
XF86_SVGA	STB MVP-2 PCI
XF86_SVGA	STB MVP-2X
XF86_SVGA	STB MVP-4 PCI
XF86_SVGA	STB MVP-4X
XF86_SVGA	STB Nitro (64)
XF86_SVGA	STB Nitro 3D
XF86_SVGA	STB Nitro 64 Video
XF86_SVGA	STB Systems Powergraph 3D
XF86_SVGA	STB Systems Velocity 3D
XF86_SVGA	STB Velocity 128
XF86_SVGA	STB nvidia 128
XF86_SVGA	SiS 3D PRO AGP
XF86_SVGA	SiS 530
XF86_SVGA	SiS 5597
XF86_SVGA	SiS 5598
XF86_SVGA	SiS 620
XF86_SVGA	SiS 6326
XF86_SVGA	SiS SG86C201
XF86_SVGA	SiS SG86C205
XF86_SVGA	SiS SG86C215
XF86_SVGA	SiS SG86C225
XF86_SVGA	Sierra Screaming 3D
XF86_SVGA	Sigma Concorde
XF86_SVGA	Sigma Legend
XF86_SVGA	Spider VLB Plus
XF86_SVGA	TechWorks Thunderbolt
XF86_SVGA	Techworks Ultimate 3D
XF86_SVGA	Toshiba Tecra 540CDT
XF86_SVGA	Toshiba Tecra 550CDT
XF86_SVGA	Toshiba Tecra 750CDT
XF86_SVGA	Toshiba Tecra 750DVD
XF86_SVGA	Trident 3DImage975 (generic)
XF86_SVGA	Trident 3DImage975 AGP (generic)

Server	Graphics Card/Chipset
XF86_SVGA	Trident 3DImage985 (generic)
XF86_SVGA	Trident 8900/9000 (generic)
XF86_SVGA	Trident 8900D (generic)
XF86_SVGA	Trident Blade3D (generic)
XF86_SVGA	Trident Cyber 9382 (generic)
XF86_SVGA	Trident Cyber 9385 (generic)
XF86_SVGA	Trident Cyber 9388 (generic)
XF86_SVGA	Trident Cyber 9397 (generic)
XF86_SVGA	Trident Cyber 9525 (generic)
XF86_SVGA	Trident CyberBlade (generic)
XF86_SVGA	Trident TGUI9400CXi (generic)
XF86_SVGA	Trident TGUI9420DGi (generic)
XF86_SVGA	Trident TGUI9430DGi (generic)
XF86_SVGA	Trident TGUI9440 (generic)
XF86_SVGA	Trident TGUI9660 (generic)
XF86_SVGA	Trident TGUI9680 (generic)
XF86_SVGA	Trident TGUI9682 (generic)
XF86_SVGA	Trident TGUI9685 (generic)
XF86_SVGA	Trident TVGA9200CXr (generic)
XF86_SVGA	VI720
XF86_SVGA	VideoLogic GrafixStar 550
XF86_SVGA	VideoLogic GrafixStar 560 (PCI/AGP)
XF86_SVGA	VideoLogic GrafixStar 600
XF86_SVGA	ViewTop PCI
XF86_SVGA	WD 90C24 (laptop)
XF86_SVGA	WD 90C24A or 90C24A2 (laptop)
XF86_SVGA	Weitek P9100 (generic)
XF86_SVGA	WinFast 3D S600
XF86_SVGA	WinFast 3D S600
XF86_SVGA	WinFast S200
XF86_SVGA	Matrox Millennium (MGA)
XF86_SVGA	Matrox Millennium II 4/8/16MB
XF86_SVGA	Matrox Millennium II AGP
XF86_TGA	Digital 24-plane TGA (ZLXp-E2)

continues

Server	Graphics Card/Chipset
XF86_TGA	Digital 24-plane+3D TGA (ZLXp-E3)
XF86_TGA	Digital 8-plane TGA (UDB/Multia)
XF86_TGA	Digital 8-plane TGA (ZLXp-E1)
XF86_VGA16	Generic VGA compatible
XF86_VGA16	S3 86C365 (Trio3D)
XF86_VGA16	S3 86C391 (Savage3D)
XF86_VGA16	S3 Savage3D
XF86_VGA16	S3 Trio3D
XF86_VGA16	Trident TVGA 8800BR
XF86_VGA16	Trident TVGA 8800CS
XF86_VGA16	Unsupported VGA compatible

Basic Fonts Included with XFree86 3.3.5

This section lists the X Logical Font descriptions for the explicitly bitmapped fonts in the 75dpi/ directory and the XLFDs for the scaled fonts in the Type1/ and Speedo/ directories. 100dpi/ and nonwestern fonts are not shown here.

Font XLFDs in 75dpi/

The fonts in the 75dpi/ directory are bitmapped fonts, meaning that they come in a predefined set of sizes and that any scaling that takes place will likely result in fonts that are imperfect in appearance. The following X Logical Font descriptions are the complete list of explicitly bitmapped font faces and sizes included in XFree86 3.3.5. Sizes not listed here will be scaled or displayed incorrectly if displaying on a remote or local server that either does not permit or does not support font scaling.

```
-adobe-courier-bold-o-normal--10-100-75-75-m-60-iso8859-1
-adobe-courier-bold-o-normal--12-120-75-75-m-70-iso8859-1
-adobe-courier-bold-o-normal--14-140-75-75-m-90-iso8859-1
-adobe-courier-bold-o-normal--18-180-75-75-m-110-iso8859-1
-adobe-courier-bold-o-normal--24-240-75-75-m-150-iso8859-1
-adobe-courier-bold-o-normal--8-80-75-75-m-50-iso8859-1
-adobe-courier-bold-r-normal--10-100-75-75-m-60-iso8859-1
-adobe-courier-bold-r-normal--12-120-75-75-m-70-iso8859-1
-adobe-courier-bold-r-normal--14-140-75-75-m-90-iso8859-1
-adobe-courier-bold-r-normal--18-180-75-75-m-110-iso8859-1
-adobe-courier-bold-r-normal--24-240-75-75-m-150-iso8859-1
-adobe-courier-bold-r-normal--8-80-75-75-m-50-iso8859-1
-adobe-courier-medium-o-normal--10-100-75-75-m-60-iso8859-1
-adobe-courier-medium-o-normal--12-120-75-75-m-70-iso8859-1
-adobe-courier-medium-o-normal--14-140-75-75-m-90-iso8859-1
```

```
-adobe-courier-medium-o-normal--18-180-75-75-m-110-iso8859-1
-adobe-courier-medium-o-normal--24-240-75-75-m-150-iso8859-1
-adobe-courier-medium-o-normal--8-80-75-75-m-50-iso8859-1
-adobe-courier-medium-r-normal--10-100-75-75-m-60-iso8859-1
-adobe-courier-medium-r-normal--12-120-75-75-m-70-iso8859-1
-adobe-courier-medium-r-normal--14-140-75-75-m-90-iso8859-1
-adobe-courier-medium-r-normal--18-180-75-75-m-110-iso8859-1
-adobe-courier-medium-r-normal--24-240-75-75-m-150-iso8859-1
-adobe-courier-medium-r-normal--8-80-75-75-m-50-iso8859-1
-adobe-helvetica-bold-o-normal--10-100-75-75-p-60-iso8859-1
-adobe-helvetica-bold-o-normal--12-120-75-75-p-69-iso8859-1
-adobe-helvetica-bold-o-normal--14-140-75-75-p-82-iso8859-1
-adobe-helvetica-bold-o-normal--18-180-75-75-p-104-iso8859-1
-adobe-helvetica-bold-o-normal--24-240-75-75-p-138-iso8859-1
-adobe-helvetica-bold-o-normal--8-80-75-75-p-50-iso8859-1
-adobe-helvetica-bold-r-normal--10-100-75-75-p-60-iso8859-1
-adobe-helvetica-bold-r-normal--12-120-75-75-p-70-iso8859-1
-adobe-helvetica-bold-r-normal--14-140-75-75-p-82-iso8859-1
-adobe-helvetica-bold-r-normal--18-180-75-75-p-103-iso8859-1
-adobe-helvetica-bold-r-normal--24-240-75-75-p-138-iso8859-1
-adobe-helvetica-bold-r-normal--8-80-75-75-p-50-iso8859-1
-adobe-helvetica-medium-o-normal--10-100-75-75-p-57-iso8859-1
-adobe-helvetica-medium-o-normal--12-120-75-75-p-67-iso8859-1
-adobe-helvetica-medium-o-normal--14-140-75-75-p-78-iso8859-1
-adobe-helvetica-medium-o-normal--18-180-75-75-p-98-iso8859-1
-adobe-helvetica-medium-o-normal--24-240-75-75-p-130-iso8859-1
-adobe-helvetica-medium-o-normal--8-80-75-75-p-47-iso8859-1
-adobe-helvetica-medium-r-normal--10-100-75-75-p-56-iso8859-1
-adobe-helvetica-medium-r-normal--12-120-75-75-p-67-iso8859-1
-adobe-helvetica-medium-r-normal--14-140-75-75-p-77-iso8859-1
-adobe-helvetica-medium-r-normal--18-180-75-75-p-98-iso8859-1
-adobe-helvetica-medium-r-normal--24-240-75-75-p-130-iso8859-1
-adobe-helvetica-medium-r-normal--8-80-75-75-p-46-iso8859-1
-adobe-new century schoolbook-bold-i-normal--10-100-75-75-p-66-iso8859-1
-adobe-new century schoolbook-bold-i-normal--12-120-75-75-p-76-iso8859-1
-adobe-new century schoolbook-bold-i-normal--14-140-75-75-p-88-iso8859-1
-adobe-new century schoolbook-bold-i-normal--18-180-75-75-p-111-iso8859-1
-adobe-new century schoolbook-bold-i-normal--24-240-75-75-p-148-iso8859-1
-adobe-new century schoolbook-bold-i-normal--8-80-75-75-p-56-iso8859-1
-adobe-new century schoolbook-bold-r-normal--10-100-75-75-p-66-iso8859-1
-adobe-new century schoolbook-bold-r-normal--12-120-75-75-p-77-iso8859-1
-adobe-new century schoolbook-bold-r-normal--14-140-75-75-p-87-iso8859-1
-adobe-new century schoolbook-bold-r-normal--18-180-75-75-p-113-iso8859-1
-adobe-new century schoolbook-bold-r-normal--24-240-75-75-p-149-iso8859-1
-adobe-new century schoolbook-bold-r-normal--8-80-75-75-p-56-iso8859-1
-adobe-new century schoolbook-medium-i-normal--10-100-75-75-p-60-iso8859-1
-adobe-new century schoolbook-medium-i-normal--12-120-75-75-p-70-iso8859-1
-adobe-new century schoolbook-medium-i-normal--14-140-75-75-p-81-iso8859-1
-adobe-new century schoolbook-medium-i-normal--18-180-75-75-p-104-iso8859-1
-adobe-new century schoolbook-medium-i-normal--24-240-75-75-p-136-iso8859-1
-adobe-new century schoolbook-medium-i-normal--8-80-75-75-p-50-iso8859-1
-adobe-new century schoolbook-medium-r-normal--10-100-75-75-p-60-iso8859-1
```

```
-adobe-new century schoolbook-medium-r-normal--12-120-75-75-p-70-iso8859-1
-adobe-new century schoolbook-medium-r-normal--14-140-75-75-p-82-iso8859-1
-adobe-new century schoolbook-medium-r-normal--18-180-75-75-p-103-iso8859-1
-adobe-new century schoolbook-medium-r-normal--24-240-75-75-p-137-iso8859-1
-adobe-new century schoolbook-medium-r-normal--8-80-75-75-p-50-iso8859-1
-adobe-symbol-medium-r-normal--10-100-75-75-p-61-adobe-fontspecific
-adobe-symbol-medium-r-normal--12-120-75-75-p-74-adobe-fontspecific
-adobe-symbol-medium-r-normal--14-140-75-75-p-85-adobe-fontspecific
-adobe-symbol-medium-r-normal--18-180-75-75-p-107-adobe-fontspecific
-adobe-symbol-medium-r-normal--24-240-75-75-p-142-adobe-fontspecific
-adobe-symbol-medium-r-normal--8-80-75-75-p-51-adobe-fontspecific
-adobe-times-bold-i-normal--10-100-75-75-p-57-iso8859-1
-adobe-times-bold-i-normal--12-120-75-75-p-68-iso8859-1
-adobe-times-bold-i-normal--14-140-75-75-p-77-iso8859-1
-adobe-times-bold-i-normal--18-180-75-75-p-98-iso8859-1
-adobe-times-bold-i-normal--24-240-75-75-p-128-iso8859-1
-adobe-times-bold-i-normal--8-80-75-75-p-47-iso8859-1
-adobe-times-bold-r-normal--10-100-75-75-p-57-iso8859-1
-adobe-times-bold-r-normal--12-120-75-75-p-67-iso8859-1
-adobe-times-bold-r-normal--14-140-75-75-p-77-iso8859-1
-adobe-times-bold-r-normal--18-180-75-75-p-99-iso8859-1
-adobe-times-bold-r-normal--24-240-75-75-p-132-iso8859-1
-adobe-times-bold-r-normal--8-80-75-75-p-47-iso8859-1
-adobe-times-medium-i-normal--10-100-75-75-p-52-iso8859-1
-adobe-times-medium-i-normal--12-120-75-75-p-63-iso8859-1
-adobe-times-medium-i-normal--14-140-75-75-p-73-iso8859-1
-adobe-times-medium-i-normal--18-180-75-75-p-94-iso8859-1
-adobe-times-medium-i-normal--24-240-75-75-p-125-iso8859-1
-adobe-times-medium-i-normal--8-80-75-75-p-42-iso8859-1
-adobe-times-medium-r-normal--10-100-75-75-p-54-iso8859-1
-adobe-times-medium-r-normal--12-120-75-75-p-64-iso8859-1
-adobe-times-medium-r-normal--14-140-75-75-p-74-iso8859-1
-adobe-times-medium-r-normal--18-180-75-75-p-94-iso8859-1
-adobe-times-medium-r-normal--24-240-75-75-p-124-iso8859-1
-adobe-times-medium-r-normal--8-80-75-75-p-44-iso8859-1
-adobe-utopia-regular-i-normal--10-100-75-75-p-55-iso8859-1
-adobe-utopia-regular-i-normal--12-120-75-75-p-67-iso8859-1
-adobe-utopia-regular-i-normal--15-140-75-75-p-79-iso8859-1
-adobe-utopia-regular-i-normal--19-180-75-75-p-100-iso8859-1
-adobe-utopia-regular-i-normal--25-240-75-75-p-133-iso8859-1
-adobe-utopia-regular-r-normal--10-100-75-75-p-56-iso8859-1
-adobe-utopia-regular-r-normal--12-120-75-75-p-67-iso8859-1
-adobe-utopia-regular-r-normal--15-140-75-75-p-79-iso8859-1
-adobe-utopia-regular-r-normal--19-180-75-75-p-101-iso8859-1
-adobe-utopia-regular-r-normal--25-240-75-75-p-135-iso8859-1
-b&h-lucida-bold-i-normal-sans-10-100-75-75-p-67-iso8859-1
-b&h-lucida-bold-i-normal-sans-12-120-75-75-p-79-iso8859-1
-b&h-lucida-bold-i-normal-sans-14-140-75-75-p-92-iso8859-1
-b&h-lucida-bold-i-normal-sans-18-180-75-75-p-119-iso8859-1
-b&h-lucida-bold-i-normal-sans-19-190-75-75-p-122-iso8859-1
-b&h-lucida-bold-i-normal-sans-24-240-75-75-p-151-iso8859-1
-b&h-lucida-bold-i-normal-sans-8-80-75-75-p-49-iso8859-1
```

```
-b&h-lucida-bold-r-normal-sans-10-100-75-75-p-66-iso8859-1
-b&h-lucida-bold-r-normal-sans-12-120-75-75-p-79-iso8859-1
-b&h-lucida-bold-r-normal-sans-14-140-75-75-p-92-iso8859-1
-b&h-lucida-bold-r-normal-sans-18-180-75-75-p-120-iso8859-1
-b&h-lucida-bold-r-normal-sans-19-190-75-75-p-122-iso8859-1
-b&h-lucida-bold-r-normal-sans-24-240-75-75-p-152-iso8859-1
-b&h-lucida-bold-r-normal-sans-8-80-75-75-p-50-iso8859-1
-b&h-lucida-medium-i-normal-sans-10-100-75-75-p-59-iso8859-1
-b&h-lucida-medium-i-normal-sans-12-120-75-75-p-71-iso8859-1
-b&h-lucida-medium-i-normal-sans-14-140-75-75-p-82-iso8859-1
-b&h-lucida-medium-i-normal-sans-18-180-75-75-p-105-iso8859-1
-b&h-lucida-medium-i-normal-sans-19-190-75-75-p-108-iso8859-1
-b&h-lucida-medium-i-normal-sans-24-240-75-75-p-136-iso8859-1
-b&h-lucida-medium-i-normal-sans-8-80-75-75-p-45-iso8859-1
-b&h-lucida-medium-r-normal-sans-10-100-75-75-p-58-iso8859-1
-b&h-lucida-medium-r-normal-sans-12-120-75-75-p-71-iso8859-1
-b&h-lucida-medium-r-normal-sans-14-140-75-75-p-81-iso8859-1
-b&h-lucida-medium-r-normal-sans-18-180-75-75-p-106-iso8859-1
-b&h-lucida-medium-r-normal-sans-19-190-75-75-p-108-iso8859-1
-b&h-lucida-medium-r-normal-sans-24-240-75-75-p-136-iso8859-1
-b&h-lucida-medium-r-normal-sans-8-80-75-75-p-45-iso8859-1
-b&h-lucidabright-demibold-i-normal--10-100-75-75-p-59-iso8859-1
-b&h-lucidabright-demibold-i-normal--12-120-75-75-p-72-iso8859-1
-b&h-lucidabright-demibold-i-normal--14-140-75-75-p-84-iso8859-1
-b&h-lucidabright-demibold-i-normal--18-180-75-75-p-107-iso8859-1
-b&h-lucidabright-demibold-i-normal--19-190-75-75-p-114-iso8859-1
-b&h-lucidabright-demibold-i-normal--24-240-75-75-p-143-iso8859-1
-b&h-lucidabright-demibold-i-normal--8-80-75-75-p-48-iso8859-1
-b&h-lucidabright-demibold-r-normal--10-100-75-75-p-59-iso8859-1
-b&h-lucidabright-demibold-r-normal--12-120-75-75-p-71-iso8859-1
-b&h-lucidabright-demibold-r-normal--14-140-75-75-p-84-iso8859-1
-b&h-lucidabright-demibold-r-normal--18-180-75-75-p-107-iso8859-1
-b&h-lucidabright-demibold-r-normal--19-190-75-75-p-114-iso8859-1
-b&h-lucidabright-demibold-r-normal--24-240-75-75-p-143-iso8859-1
-b&h-lucidabright-demibold-r-normal--8-80-75-75-p-47-iso8859-1
-b&h-lucidabright-medium-i-normal--10-100-75-75-p-57-iso8859-1
-b&h-lucidabright-medium-i-normal--12-120-75-75-p-67-iso8859-1
-b&h-lucidabright-medium-i-normal--14-140-75-75-p-80-iso8859-1
-b&h-lucidabright-medium-i-normal--18-180-75-75-p-102-iso8859-1
-b&h-lucidabright-medium-i-normal--19-190-75-75-p-109-iso8859-1
-b&h-lucidabright-medium-i-normal--24-240-75-75-p-136-iso8859-1
-b&h-lucidabright-medium-i-normal--8-80-75-75-p-45-iso8859-1
-b&h-lucidabright-medium-r-normal--10-100-75-75-p-56-iso8859-1
-b&h-lucidabright-medium-r-normal--12-120-75-75-p-68-iso8859-1
-b&h-lucidabright-medium-r-normal--14-140-75-75-p-80-iso8859-1
-b&h-lucidabright-medium-r-normal--18-180-75-75-p-103-iso8859-1
-b&h-lucidabright-medium-r-normal--19-190-75-75-p-109-iso8859-1
-b&h-lucidabright-medium-r-normal--24-240-75-75-p-137-iso8859-1
-b&h-lucidabright-medium-r-normal--8-80-75-75-p-45-iso8859-1
-b&h-lucidatypewriter-bold-r-normal-sans-10-100-75-75-m-60-iso8859-1
-b&h-lucidatypewriter-bold-r-normal-sans-12-120-75-75-m-70-iso8859-1
-b&h-lucidatypewriter-bold-r-normal-sans-14-140-75-75-m-90-iso8859-1
```

```
-b&h-lucidatypewriter-bold-r-normal-sans-18-180-75-75-m-110-iso8859-1
-b&h-lucidatypewriter-bold-r-normal-sans-19-190-75-75-m-110-iso8859-1
-b&h-lucidatypewriter-bold-r-normal-sans-24-240-75-75-m-140-iso8859-1
-b&h-lucidatypewriter-bold-r-normal-sans-8-80-75-75-m-50-iso8859-1
-b&h-lucidatypewriter-medium-r-normal-sans-10-100-75-75-m-60-iso8859-1
-b&h-lucidatypewriter-medium-r-normal-sans-12-120-75-75-m-70-iso8859-1
-b&h-lucidatypewriter-medium-r-normal-sans-14-140-75-75-m-90-iso8859-1
-b&h-lucidatypewriter-medium-r-normal-sans-18-180-75-75-m-110-iso8859-1
-b&h-lucidatypewriter-medium-r-normal-sans-19-190-75-75-m-110-iso8859-1
-b&h-lucidatypewriter-medium-r-normal-sans-24-240-75-75-m-140-iso8859-1
-b&h-lucidatypewriter-medium-r-normal-sans-8-80-75-75-m-50-iso8859-1
-bitstream-charter-medium-i-normal--10-100-75-75-p-55-iso8859-1
-bitstream-charter-medium-i-normal--12-120-75-75-p-65-iso8859-1
-bitstream-charter-medium-i-normal--15-140-75-75-p-82-iso8859-1
-bitstream-charter-medium-i-normal--19-180-75-75-p-103-iso8859-1
-bitstream-charter-medium-i-normal--25-240-75-75-p-136-iso8859-1
-bitstream-charter-medium-i-normal--8-80-75-75-p-44-iso8859-1
-bitstream-charter-medium-r-normal--10-100-75-75-p-56-iso8859-1
-bitstream-charter-medium-r-normal--12-120-75-75-p-67-iso8859-1
-bitstream-charter-medium-r-normal--15-140-75-75-p-84-iso8859-1
-bitstream-charter-medium-r-normal--19-180-75-75-p-106-iso8859-1
-bitstream-charter-medium-r-normal--25-240-75-75-p-139-iso8859-1
-bitstream-charter-medium-r-normal--8-80-75-75-p-45-iso8859-1
-dec-terminal-bold-r-normal--14-140-75-75-c-80-dec-dectech
-dec-terminal-bold-r-normal--14-140-75-75-c-80-iso8859-1
-dec-terminal-medium-r-normal--14-140-75-75-c-80-dec-dectech
-dec-terminal-medium-r-normal--14-140-75-75-c-80-iso8859-1
```

Font XLFDs in `Type1/`

The fonts in the `Type1/` directory are scaled fonts, meaning that they can be scaled arbitrarily with a minimum of information loss and appearance damage. They cannot be moved to servers that do not support font scaling, however, because they do not come in explicitly bitmapped form.

```
-adobe-courier-bold-i-normal--0-0-0-0-m-0-iso8859-1
-adobe-courier-bold-r-normal--0-0-0-0-m-0-iso8859-1
-adobe-courier-medium-i-normal--0-0-0-0-m-0-iso8859-1
-adobe-courier-medium-r-normal--0-0-0-0-m-0-iso8859-1
-adobe-utopia-bold-i-normal--0-0-0-0-p-0-iso8859-1
-adobe-utopia-bold-r-normal--0-0-0-0-p-0-iso8859-1
-adobe-utopia-medium-i-normal--0-0-0-0-p-0-iso8859-1
-adobe-utopia-medium-r-normal--0-0-0-0-p-0-iso8859-1
-bitstream-charter-bold-i-normal--0-0-0-0-p-0-iso8859-1
-bitstream-charter-bold-r-normal--0-0-0-0-p-0-iso8859-1
-bitstream-charter-medium-i-normal--0-0-0-0-p-0-iso8859-1
-bitstream-charter-medium-r-normal--0-0-0-0-p-0-iso8859-1
-bitstream-courier-bold-i-normal--0-0-0-0-m-0-iso8859-1
-bitstream-courier-bold-r-normal--0-0-0-0-m-0-iso8859-1
-bitstream-courier-medium-i-normal--0-0-0-0-m-0-iso8859-1
-bitstream-courier-medium-r-normal--0-0-0-0-m-0-iso8859-1
```

Font XLFDs in `Speedo/`

The fonts in the `Speedo/` directory are scaled fonts, meaning that they can be scaled arbitrarily with a minimum of information loss and appearance damage. Again, these fonts cannot be moved to servers that do not support scaled-only fonts.

```
-bitstream-charter-black-i-normal--0-0-0-0-p-0-iso8859-1
-bitstream-charter-black-r-normal--0-0-0-0-p-0-iso8859-1
-bitstream-charter-medium-i-normal--0-0-0-0-p-0-iso8859-1
-bitstream-charter-medium-r-normal--0-0-0-0-p-0-iso8859-1
-bitstream-courier-bold-i-normal--0-0-0-0-m-0-iso8859-1
-bitstream-courier-bold-r-normal--0-0-0-0-m-0-iso8859-1
-bitstream-courier-medium-i-normal--0-0-0-0-m-0-iso8859-1
-bitstream-courier-medium-r-normal--0-0-0-0-m-0-iso8859-1
```

Font XLFDs in `misc/`

The fonts in the `misc/` directory are bitmapped fonts, meaning that they come in a predefined set of sizes and that any scaling which takes place will likely result in fonts which are imperfect in appearance. These XLFDs (especially those in the fixed series) should be considered the baseline fonts for network compatibility and multiplatform interoperability because nearly all systems will have the fixed series of fonts and an alias called *fixed* that refers to one always-present font.

```
-misc-fixed-bold-r-normal--13-120-75-75-c-70-iso8859-1
-misc-fixed-bold-r-normal--13-120-75-75-c-70-iso8859-15
-misc-fixed-bold-r-normal--13-120-75-75-c-80-iso8859-1
-misc-fixed-bold-r-normal--14-130-75-75-c-70-iso8859-1
-misc-fixed-bold-r-normal--15-140-75-75-c-90-iso8859-1
-misc-fixed-bold-r-semicondensed--13-120-75-75-c-60-iso8859-1
-misc-fixed-medium-r-normal--10-100-75-75-c-60-iso8859-1
-misc-fixed-medium-r-normal--13-120-75-75-c-70-iso8859-1
-misc-fixed-medium-r-normal--13-120-75-75-c-70-iso8859-15
-misc-fixed-medium-r-normal--13-120-75-75-c-80-iso8859-1
-misc-fixed-medium-r-normal--13-120-75-75-c-80-iso8859-8
-misc-fixed-medium-r-normal--14-130-75-75-c-140-jisx0208.1983-0
-misc-fixed-medium-r-normal--14-130-75-75-c-70-iso8859-1
-misc-fixed-medium-r-normal--14-130-75-75-c-70-jisx0201.1976-0
-misc-fixed-medium-r-normal--15-140-75-75-c-90-iso8859-1
-misc-fixed-medium-r-normal--20-200-75-75-c-100-iso8859-1
-misc-fixed-medium-r-normal--7-70-75-75-c-50-iso8859-1
-misc-fixed-medium-r-normal--8-80-75-75-c-50-iso646.1991-irv
-misc-fixed-medium-r-normal--9-90-75-75-c-60-iso646.1991-irv
-misc-fixed-medium-r-semicondensed--12-110-75-75-c-60-iso646.1991-irv
-misc-fixed-medium-r-semicondensed--13-120-75-75-c-60-iso8859-1
-misc-fixed-medium-r-semicondensed--13-120-75-75-c-60-iso8859-8
-misc-nil-medium-r-normal--2-20-75-75-c-10-misc-fontspecific
-schumacher-clean-bold-r-normal--10-100-75-75-c-60-iso646.1991-irv
-schumacher-clean-bold-r-normal--10-100-75-75-c-80-iso646.1991-irv
-schumacher-clean-bold-r-normal--12-120-75-75-c-60-iso646.1991-irv
```

```
-schumacher-clean-bold-r-normal--12-120-75-75-c-80-iso646.1991-irv
-schumacher-clean-bold-r-normal--13-130-75-75-c-80-iso646.1991-irv
-schumacher-clean-bold-r-normal--14-140-75-75-c-80-iso646.1991-irv
-schumacher-clean-bold-r-normal--15-150-75-75-c-90-iso646.1991-irv
-schumacher-clean-bold-r-normal--16-160-75-75-c-80-iso646.1991-irv
-schumacher-clean-bold-r-normal--8-80-75-75-c-80-iso646.1991-irv
-schumacher-clean-medium-i-normal--12-120-75-75-c-60-iso646.1991-irv
-schumacher-clean-medium-i-normal--8-80-75-75-c-80-iso646.1991-irv
-schumacher-clean-medium-r-normal--10-100-75-75-c-50-iso646.1991-irv
-schumacher-clean-medium-r-normal--10-100-75-75-c-60-iso646.1991-irv
-schumacher-clean-medium-r-normal--10-100-75-75-c-70-iso646.1991-irv
-schumacher-clean-medium-r-normal--10-100-75-75-c-80-iso646.1991-irv
-schumacher-clean-medium-r-normal--12-120-75-75-c-60-iso646.1991-irv
-schumacher-clean-medium-r-normal--12-120-75-75-c-70-iso646.1991-irv
-schumacher-clean-medium-r-normal--12-120-75-75-c-80-iso646.1991-irv
-schumacher-clean-medium-r-normal--13-130-75-75-c-60-iso646.1991-irv
-schumacher-clean-medium-r-normal--13-130-75-75-c-80-iso646.1991-irv
-schumacher-clean-medium-r-normal--14-140-75-75-c-70-iso646.1991-irv
-schumacher-clean-medium-r-normal--14-140-75-75-c-80-iso646.1991-irv
-schumacher-clean-medium-r-normal--15-150-75-75-c-90-iso646.1991-irv
-schumacher-clean-medium-r-normal--16-160-75-75-c-80-iso646.1991-irv
-schumacher-clean-medium-r-normal--6-60-75-75-c-40-iso646.1991-irv
-schumacher-clean-medium-r-normal--6-60-75-75-c-50-iso646.1991-irv
-schumacher-clean-medium-r-normal--6-60-75-75-c-60-iso646.1991-irv
-schumacher-clean-medium-r-normal--8-80-75-75-c-50-iso646.1991-irv
-schumacher-clean-medium-r-normal--8-80-75-75-c-60-iso646.1991-irv
-schumacher-clean-medium-r-normal--8-80-75-75-c-70-iso646.1991-irv
-schumacher-clean-medium-r-normal--8-80-75-75-c-80-iso646.1991-irv
-sony-fixed-medium-r-normal--16-120-100-100-c-80-iso8859-1
-sony-fixed-medium-r-normal--24-170-100-100-c-120-iso8859-1
```

Common XFree86 Video Timings

It is strongly recommended that users have their XF86Config files generated automatically, using the XF86Setup or xf86config commands. For those who must build this file by hand, XFree86 video timings listed in Tables B.1 through B.7 match those generated by xf86config and represent the bulk of existing monitor capabilities. These timings should be used with the ModeLine keyword in the XF86Config file.

The first column in each table represents the refresh and horizontal scan rates in Hertz and Kilohertz, respectively, for the mode. The remainder of each line are the actual values which make the mode. Modes which have a plus sign (+) in the final column should have +hsync +vsync appended to the end of the modeline. Modes which have a minus sign (-) in the final column should have -hsync -vsync appended to the end of the modeline.

Use extreme caution when trying any of these modes: incorrect use of video timings can severely damage otherwise healthy monitors.

Table B.1   640×480 Modes, Ref=Refresh, Scn=Horizontal Scan

Ref/Scn	Clock	H-Timings	V-Timings	Sync
60/31.5	25.175	640 664 760 800	480 491 493 525	
72/36.5	31.5	640 680 720 864	480 488 491 521	-
75/37.5	36	640 656 720 840	480 481 484 500	-
85/43.27	36	640 696 752 832	480 481 484 509	-
100/53.01	45.8	640 672 768 864	480 488 494 530	-

Table B.2   800×600 Modes, Ref=Refresh, Scn=Horizontal Scan

Ref/Scn	Clock	H-Timings	V-Timings	Sync
56/35.15	36	800 824 896 1024	600 601 603 625	
60/37.8	40	800 840 968 1056	600 601 605 628	+
72/48	50	800 856 976 1040	600 637 643 666	+
85/55.84	60.75	800 864 928 1088	600 616 621 657	-
100/64.02	69.65	800 864 928 1088	600 604 610 640	-

Table B.3   1024×768 Modes, Ref=Refresh, Scn=Horizontal Scan

Ref/Scn	Clock	H-Timings	V-Timings	Sync
60/48.4	65	1024 1032 1176 1344	768 771 777 806	-
70/56.5	75	1024 1048 1184 1328	768 771 777 806	-
76/62.5	85	1024 1032 1152 1360	768 784 787 823	
85/70.24	98.9	1024 1056 1216 1408	768 782 788 822	-
100/80.21	115.5	1024 1056 1248 1440	768 771 781 802	-

Table B.4   1152×864 Modes, Ref=Refresh, Scn=Horizontal Scan

Ref/Scn	Clock	H-Timings	V-Timings	Sync
60/53.5	89.9	1152 1216 1472 1680	864 868 876 892	-
70/62.4	92	1152 1208 1368 1474	864 865 875 895	
78/70.8	110	1152 1240 1324 1552	864 864 876 908	
84/76.0	135	1152 1464 1592 1776	864 864 876 908	
100/89.62	137.65	1152 1184 1312 1536	864 866 885 902	-

Table B.5 1280×1024 Modes, Ref=Refresh, Scn=Horizontal Scan

Ref/Scn	Clock	H-Timings	V-Timings	Sync
61/64.2	110	1280 1328 1512 1712	1024 1025 1028 1054	
70/74.59	126.5	1280 1312 1472 1696	1024 1032 1040 1068	-
74/78.85	135	1280 1312 1456 1712	1024 1027 1030 1064	
76/81.13	135	1280 1312 1416 1664	1024 1027 1030 1064	
85/91.15	157.5	1280 1344 1504 1728	1024 1025 1028 1072	+
100/107.2	181.75	1280 1312 1440 1696	1024 1031 1046 1072	-

Table B.6 1600×1200 Modes, Ref=Refresh, Scn=Horizontal Scan

Ref/Scn	Clock	H-Timings	V-Timings	Sync
60/75	162	1600 1664 1856 2160	1200 1201 1204 1250	+
70/87.50	189	1600 1664 1856 2160	1200 1201 1204 1250	-
75/93.75	202.5	1600 1664 1856 2160	1200 1201 1204 1250	+
85/105.77	220	1600 1616 1808 2080	1200 1204 1207 1244	+

Table B.7 1800×1440 Modes, Ref=Refresh, Scn=Horizontal Scan

Ref/Scn	Clock	H-Timings	V-Timings	Sync
64/96.15	230	1800 1896 2088 2392	1440 1441 1444 1490	+
70/104.52	250	1800 1896 2088 2392	1440 1441 1444 1490	+

C

SUPPORTED LINUX 2.2 FRAMEBUFFERS

The framebuffer console support for x86 machines in newer Linux kernels is young but relatively stable. A wide variety of recent video hardware is supported for PowerPC architectures as well. Table C.1 shows chipsets and cards that are specifically supported by the Linux 2.2 kernel and the corresponding configuration variable for each on the x86 platform.

Supported video hardware for other (non-x86) platforms is listed in Table C.2. Note that this is not an exhaustive list; many minor chipset variations are also supported on multiple platforms.

Table C.1 Chipset-Specific Linux 2.2-x86 Framebuffers

Chipset	Variable	Accel?
3D Labs Permedia 2	`CONFIG_FB_PM2`	Yes
Matrox Millenium I/II	`CONFIG_FB_MATROX_MILLENIUM`	Yes
Matrox Mystique	`CONFIG_FB_MATROX_MYSTIQUE`	Yes
Matrox G100/G200	`CONFIG_FB_MATROX_G100`	Yes
ATI Mach64	`CONFIG_FB_ATY`	Yes
ATI 3D RAGE PRO	`CONFIG_FB_ATY`	Yes
ATI 3D RAGE LT/GT	`CONFIG_FB_ATY`	Yes
ATI 3D RAGE II/II+/IIc	`CONFIG_FB_ATY`	Yes
Generic VGA 640x480x16	`CONFIG_FB_VGA16`	No

Table C.2   Linux 2.2-non-x86 Framebuffers

Chipset	Variable	Platform(s)
Apple 'control'	CONFIG_FB_CONTROL	PowerPC
Apple 'platinum'	CONFIG_FB_PLATINUM	PowerPC
Apple 'valkyrie'	CONFIG_FB_VALKYRIE	PowerPC
ATI Mach64	CONFIG_FB_ATY	PowerPC, Sparc64, Atari
ATI 3D RAGE PRO	CONFIG_FB_ATY	PowerPC
ATI 3D RAGE LT/GT	CONFIG_FB_ATY	PowerPC
ATI 3D RAGE II/II+/IIc	CONFIG_FB_ATY	PowerPC
IMS TwinTurbo	CONFIG_FB_IMSTT	PowerPC
C&T 65550	CONFIG_FB_CT65550	PowerPC
S3 Trio/Trio64	CONFIG_FB_S3TRIO	PowerPC
Digital 21030 (TGA)	CONFIG_FB_TGA	Alpha
Visual Workstation	CONFIG_FB_SGIVW	SGI x86
Creator/Creator3D	CONFIG_FB_CREATOR	Sparc64
Sun CGsix GX/TurboGX	CONFIG_FB_CGSIX	Sparc, Sparc64
Sun CGthree	CONFIG_FB_CGTHREE	Sparc, Sparc64
Sun BWtwo	CONFIG_FB_BWTWO	Sparc, Sparc64
Sparc 4/5 TCX	CONFIG_FB_TCX	Sparc
Sun CGfourteen	CONFIG_FB_CGFOURTEEN	Sparc
Leo	CONFIG_FB_LEO	Sparc, Sparc64
IGA 168x	CONFIG_FB_IGA	Sparc
3D Labs Permedia 2	CONFIG_FB_PM2	Amiga
Amiga (native)	CONFIG_FB_AMIGA	Amiga
Amiga OCS	CONFIG_FB_AMIGA_OCS	Amiga
Amiga ECS	CONFIG_FB_AMIGA_ECS	Amiga
Amiga AGA	CONFIG_FB_AMIGA_AGA	Amiga
CyberVision	CONFIG_FB_CYBER	Amiga
CyberVision 3D	CONFIG_FB_VIRGE	Amiga
Retina Z3	CONFIG_FB_RETINAZ3	Amiga
CLgen	CONFIG_FB_CLGEN	Amiga
FrameMaster/Rainbow II	CONFIG_FB_FM2	Amiga
Atari (native)	CONFIG_FB_ATARI	Atari
Intergraphics Cyber2000	CONFIG_FB_CYBER2000	Netwinder
Macintosh (native)	CONFIG_FB_MAC	Mac68k
HP300 (native)	CONFIG_FB_HP300	HP300

Chipset	Variable	Platform(s)
Acorn VIDC video	CONFIG_FB_ACORN	Acorn
Apollo (native)	CONFIG_FB_APOLLO	Apollo
Q40 (native)	CONFIG_FB_Q40	Q40

The VESA VGA Framebuffer

The VESA VGA framebuffer is a special case because it will work with many different video cards and chipsets by using the card's video BIOS during boot to select the chosen video mode.

Most recent video cards that support the VESA 2.0 standard, including currently unsupported or until-recently-unsupported PCI and AGP video cards will work well with the VESA framebuffer driver and the XFree86 framebuffer server. Understand, however, that it is generally preferable to use either an accelerated chipset-specific X server or an accelerated framebuffer over the VESA framebuffer, since the feature set of the VESA framebuffer is somewhat limited.

The VESA VGA framebuffer is compiled in by setting the CONFIG_FB_VESA variable at compile time.

Arguments Accepted by the VESA VGA Framebuffer

Many arguments can be supplied to the VESA VGA framebuffer at boot time by adding a line similar to this one to the Linux command line:

```
video=vesa:arg,arg,arg
```

The easiest way to append arguments to the Linux command line is at the LILO boot prompt that most users see each time they boot their Linux computer.

ypan and ywrap

The ypan and ywrap arguments enable hardware-based scrolling using video memory as a scrollback buffer. This method of scrolling is faster than the default method but won't work with all cards and can create undesirable artifacts at times.

The ywrap variable differs from ypan in that ywrap is faster because it uses video memory as a circular (rather than linear) buffer for video scrollback.

When enabled, video scrollback is achieved using the Shift+PageUp key combination.

redraw

This is the default method for redrawing (scrolling) the display that works by redrawing the affected part of the display each time scrolling occurs. This method isn't as fast as ypan or ywrap and won't allow for scrollback, but it is safer than either of the other two options.

This behavior is the default scroll method for the VESA VGA framebuffer console.

vgapal and pmipal

vgapal and pmipal tell the VESA VGA console either to use the standard VGA palette registers for color palette changes (in the case of vgapal) or to use the faster protected-mode interface for palette changes (in the case of pmipal).

The default behavior is to use the standard VGA palette registers for changes to the color palette.

mtrr

mtrr enables the use of memory type range registers for faster framebuffer memory access on mtrr-enabled CPUs. Note that you must have a CPU that supports an mtrr and have enabled mtrr support elsewhere in the kernel for this option to function properly.

Only the Pentium II core and later processors have supported mtrr registers in current Linux kernels. The 2.3.x development kernels (or the 2.2 Alan Cox series kernels) implement support for mtrr in non-Intel CPUs with related capabilities, such as the AMD K6-2 or K6-3 series of CPUs.

Framebuffer Code and Documentation

For more information on using specific framebuffer hardware with the Linux 2.2 kernels, please visit one of the kernel source tree subdirectories listed in Table C.3.

Table C.3   Directories of Interest to Framebuffer Users

Directory	Description
Documentation/	General Linux 2.2.x kernel documentation in plain-text format
Documentation/fb/	Plain-text documentation files for various types of framebuffer hardware when used with the Linux 2.2.x kernel
drivers/video/	C source and header files for the various framebuffer devices supported by the Linux 2.2 kernel

INDEX

P